Happy Christmas Barry
Much love - Wendy Andy
Sarah + Jack xxxx

CW01655942

CIRENCESTER: TOWN AND LANDSCAPE

AN URBAN ARCHAEOLOGICAL ASSESSMENT

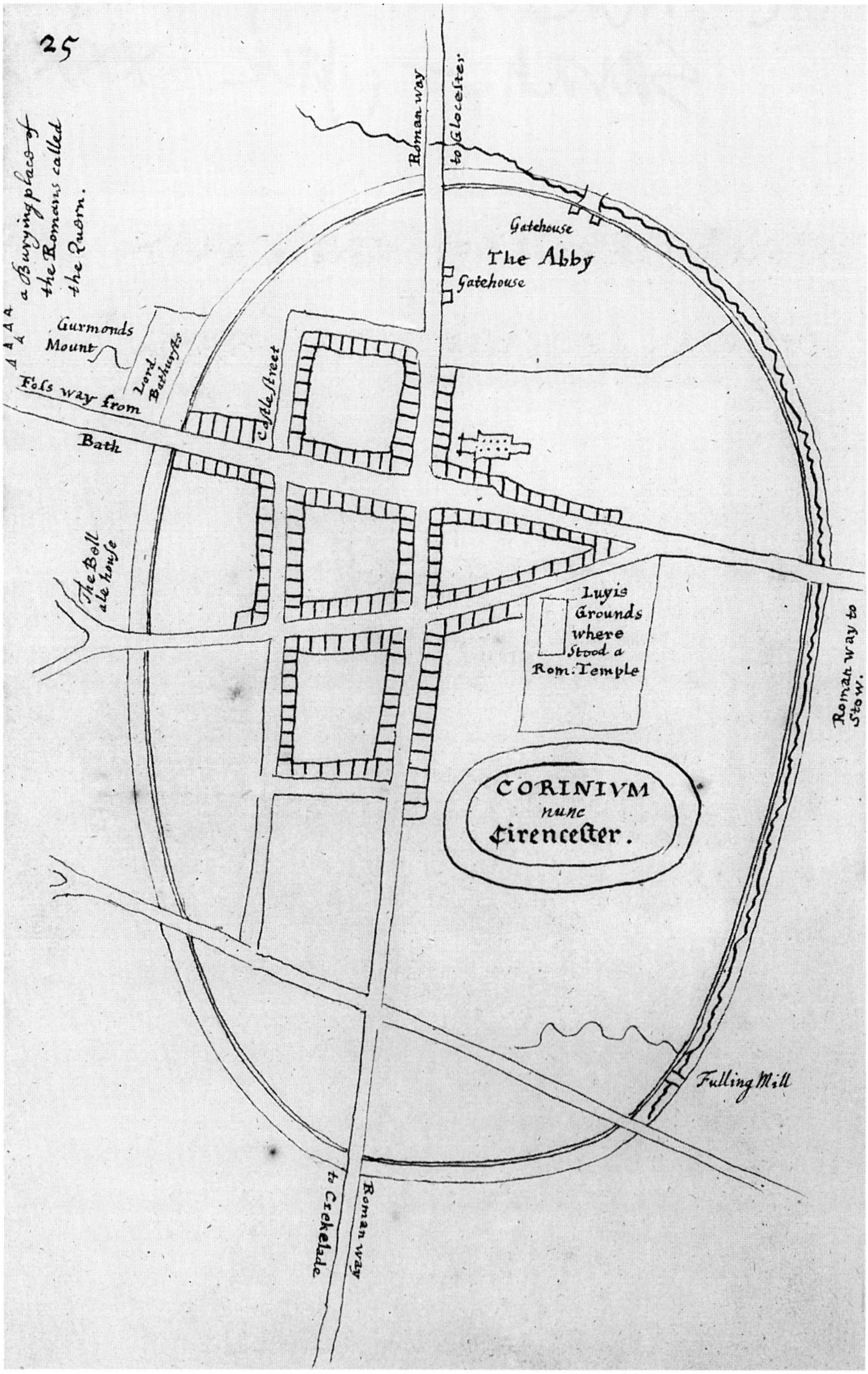

Frontispiece: The earliest known plan of Cirencester drawn by William Stukeley in 1721 (The Bodleian Library, MS Top.Gen.d.13)

CIRENCESTER: TOWN AND LANDSCAPE

AN URBAN ARCHAEOLOGICAL ASSESSMENT

by
Timothy Darvill
and
Christopher Gerrard

with contributions from
Linda Viner and Neil Holbrook

Illustrations by
Alejandra Gutierrez

and reconstruction drawings by
Casper Johnson

Cotswold Archaeological Trust Ltd
Cirencester
1994

Corinium Museum, Park Street, Cirencester, Glos, GL7 2BX, England

ISBN 0 9523196 0 8

The publication of this volume has been supported by English Heritage.

The Cirencester Urban Assessment Project was jointly funded by English Heritage and Cotswold District Council.

Produced by Alan Sutton Publishing Ltd., Stroud, Gloucestershire.
Printed in Britain by
Redwood Books, Trowbridge, Wiltshire.

CONTENTS

List of Figures ix
List of Tables xi
Foreword by Professor Michael Fulford xiii
Authors' Preface and Acknowledgements xv
Summary xvii

Part I Introduction and Methodology

1. **Introduction** 3
   - Background 3
   - The Cirencester Urban Assessment Project 4
   - The Study Area defined 4
   - Records, reports and project archive 4
   - Report structure and content 4

2. **Philosophy and methodology** 7
   - Existing records and system needs 7
   - A theoretical perspective 8
     - Data 8
     - Information 9
     - Knowledge 10
   - An archaeological perspective 10
     - Single monuments 10
     - Urban areas 10
   - Evaluating monuments and accumulated deposits 11
     - Single monuments 11
     - Urban areas 12
   - From sites to knowledge 13
     - Data collection 13
     - Monument definition 13
     - Characterising the urban forms 13
     - Zones of archaeological interest 13
     - Management planning 13

Part II Data Collection

3. **Archaeological endeavour and data sources** by Christopher Gerrard and Linda Viner 17
   - History of endeavour 17
     - The first records 17
     - Travellers, gentlemen and antiquarians 17
     - The Victorian age 18
     - The first professionals 22
   - Source types 24

4. Background data 26

The Study Area 26
Topography 26
Geology and archaeological deposits 26
Building stone and quarries 29
Hydrology and water supply 30
Land classification 30
Land-use 33
Palaeoenvironment 33
Designations 33

5. Archaeological data 34

Site records 34
Site analysis 36
Accumulation and chronological changes 36
Future trends 40

Part III Data Interpretation and Record Development

6. Monuments and deposits 43

Monuments 43
Accumulated deposits 45

7. The Cirencester area in the prehistoric and early Roman periods by Timothy Darvill and Neil Holbrook 47

Palaeolithic and Mesolithic (to 4000 BC) 47
Neolithic (4000–2000 BC) 47
Bronze Age (2000–700 BC) 49
Iron Age (700 BC–AD 50) 49
Pre-urban Roman (*c*AD 50–AD 100) 50
  The road network 50
  The fort and *vicus* 53
Monument discrimination 56

8. *Corinium Dobunnorum*: Roman *Civitas Capital* and Roman Provincial Capital by Neil Holbrook 57

Roman *civitas capital* 57
  The early development of the town 57
  The street pattern 60
  Public buildings 61
  Commerce 62
  Housing 63
  Defences 65
  Little-known, suspected and unlocated monuments 71
Roman provincial capital 74
Accumulated deposits 76
The Roman countryside (*c*AD 80/100 to early fifth century AD) 78
  The urban fringe 78
    i) Civic pride and munificence 78
    ii) Cemeteries 79
    iii) Industry 84
  The countryside 85
Monument discrimination 86

9. ***Cyrnceastre*: a Royal / Ecclesiastical Centre in the early medieval period** by Christopher Gerrard 87

Royal/ecclesiastical centre 90
The streets 91
Housing 91
Religious buildings 92
Accumulated deposits 93
Early medieval countryside 95
Administrative frameworks 95
Settlement, cemeteries, and industry 95
Environment 97
Monument discrimination 97

10. ***Cirencestre*: a Medium-Sized Market Town in the medieval period** by Christopher Gerrard 98

Medium-sized market town (medieval) 98
The streets 98
Public buildings and works 102
Commerce and industry 103
Housing 105
The castle 106
Religious buildings 107
Accumulated deposits 113
Medieval countryside 114
Communications 114
Settlement 115
Religious buildings 115
Economy 117
Industry 118
Monument discrimination 118

11. Cirencester: a Medium-Sized Market Town in the post-medieval period by Christopher Gerrard and Linda Viner 119

Medium-sized market town (post-medieval) 119
Religious and charitable institutions 126
Public buildings and services 129
Hotels, inns and public houses 129
Industry, trade and commerce 130
Battle sites, militia and wartime 131
Accumulated deposits 134
Post-medieval countryside 134
The village communities 134
Roads, canal and railways 134
Agriculture 135
Industry 137
Monument discrimination 137

12. Archaeological sensitivity 138

Survival 138
Potential 139
Group Value (association) 139
Group Value (clustering) 139
Diversity (features) 139
Documentation (archaeological) 140
Documentation (historical) 140

Amenity Value 140
Archaeological interest in the urban area 141
Archaeological interest in the rural area 141

Part IV Archaeology and Development

13. Frameworks for the future 147

Managing change 147
Why is archaeology important? 148
Use value 148
Option value 148
Existence value 148
Existing measures and policies 149
Scheduled Monuments 149
Areas of Archaeological Importance 149
Guardianship Monuments 152
Cotswold Area of Outstanding Natural Beauty 152
Conservation Areas 152
Listed Buildings 152
Burial Grounds 152
Parks and Gardens 153
National Planning Legislation and Policy Guidance 153
Environmental Assessment 154
County Planning Policy 155
Local Planning Policy 155
Other legislation 156
Getting the right information 156
Appraisal 156
Archaeological Assessment 158
Field Evaluation 158
Strategy formulation 159
Strategy implementation 160
Management options 160
Preservation 161
Exploitation 165
Recording 165
Monument and deposit importance in Cirencester 166
Dealing with the unexpected 170
Who does what 170
Standards of archaeological service 172
Conclusion 172

Glossary 174

Appendices

Appendix A Databases and record structure 179
Appendix B List of defined monuments in the study area 185
Appendix C Research objectives 195

Abbreviations 198
Bibliography 199
Cartographic References 217
Index 219

LIST OF FIGURES

Frontispiece: The earliest known plan of Cirencester drawn by William Stukeley in 1721 (The Bodleian Library, MS Top.Gen.d.13)

Figure 1 Location of the Study Area, showing the principal roads and surrounding parishes

Figure 2 A theoretical perspective of urban assessment showing a hierarchy of three levels of perception

Figure 3 The lifting of the Hunting Dogs Mosaic, discovered in Dyer Street in 1849 (*Illustrated London News* 8th September 1849)

Figure 4 The Bathurst Museum, built in Tetbury Road by Earl Bathurst for the display of mosaics discovered in Dyer Street in 1849 (Artist unknown, Corinium Museum)

Figure 5 Open area excavation at The Beeches revealed a bath-suite within the winged-corridor house (Cirencester Excavation Committee)

Figure 6 Topography of the surrounding area, with sections showing the location of Cirencester

Figure 7 Simplified geological map of the surrounding area

Figure 8 Quarry working of Oolitic Limestone at Stratton, pre-1900 (Corinium Museum)

Figure 9 Simplified land classification for 1945 of the surrounding area

Figure 10 Land-use recorded in 1990 within the Study Area

Figure 11 Bar-chart showing the number of sites recorded by type

Figure 12 Graph showing the number of sites recorded by year in the period 1750–1990

Figure 13 Graph showing the number of modern excavations, recorded observations, and watching briefs in the period 1960–1990

Figure 14 The changing morphology of Cirencester from the Roman period to the present day. The 'built-up' areas are shaded

Figure 15 Prehistoric monuments in the Study Area

Figure 16 Pre-urban Roman monuments (*c*AD 50–AD 100)

Figure 17 Early ditches behind the rampart of the pre-urban fort, excavated at Leaholme in 1961 (Cirencester Excavation Committee)

Figure 18 Monuments in the Roman *civitas capital*

Figure 19 Excavations in 1897–8 by Wilfred Cripps exposed the foundations of the *basilica*. This view, looking east, shows the south wall of the aisled hall (Corinium Museum)

Figure 20 Construction of the Bingham Hall in King Street in 1908 revealed foundations of a winged-corridor house (Corinium Museum)

Figure 21 Excavations by St Clair Baddeley in 1922 on the line of the defences in the grounds of the Union Workhouse (Corinium Museum)

Figure 22 The D-shaped drum-tower of the *Verulamium* Gate excavated in 1960, looking south (Cirencester Excavation Committee)

Figure 23 The northern drum-tower of the *Verulamium* Gate, looking north along the line of the town wall (Cirencester Excavation Committee)

Figure 24 Pedestal from the base of a Jupiter column recording the restoration by governor *L Septimius [. . .,* discovered in 1891 (Corinium Museum)

Figure 25 Imaginative reconstruction of the Roman townscape of the provincial capital (From an original drawing by Casper Johnson)

Figure 26 Romano-British monuments in the rural area (see Figure 18 for monuments within the urban form)

Figure 27 Aerial view of The Querns, with the amphitheatre centre left, and the Bath Gate cemetery excavation in the foreground during redevelopment in 1973 (Cirencester Excavation Committee)

Figure 28 Tombstone dedicated to *Genialis*, discovered beside Ermin Street in 1835 (Corinium Museum)

Figure 29 Roman quarrying exposed in 1978 at The Querns (Cirencester Excavation Committee)

Figure 30 Skeleton of an adult male, cut through the Orpheus mosaic at The Barton, discovered in 1909 (Corinium Museum)

Figure 31 Monuments in the early medieval Royal/Ecclesiastical Centre

Figure 32 The south wall of the apse of the Saxon church, with surviving parts of the robbed crypt to the left, and cut by a later tomb (Cirencester Excavation Committee)

Figure 33 Early medieval monuments in the rural area (see Figure 31 for monuments within the urban form)

Figure 34 Monuments in the medieval Medium-Sized Market Town

Figure 35 St Clement's Bridge at the bottom of Cecily Hill, with Monmouth House in the background (Corinium Museum)

Figure 36 The medieval High Cross removed to Cirencester Park (Corinium Museum)

Figure 37 Reconstruction of the medieval townscape of 1400 (From an original drawing by Casper Johnson)

Figure 38 Extensive robbing of the claustral range of the Augustinian abbey in the area of the undercroft, looking south (Cirencester Excavation Committee)

Figure 39 Drawing of the Spitalgate by William Stukeley, 1721 (The Bodleian Library, MS Top.Gen.d.13)

Figure 40 St Thomas's Hospital or Weavers' Hall (centre right), in Thomas Street, endowed by Sir William Nottingham in 1483 (Corinium Museum)

Figure 41 Medieval monuments in the rural area (see Figure 34 for monuments within the urban form)

Figure 42 The spire of Siddington St Peter rising above the medieval barn (Thomas Collection, Bingham Library)

Figure 43 Monuments in the post-medieval Medium-Sized Market Town

Figure 44 32–38 Cricklade Street: plot development (the arrow provides a fixed reference point)

Figure 45 32–38 Cricklade Street on the left, with the 1921 street frontage, looking north (Corinium Museum)

Figure 46 View of Cirencester, engraved by Kip in 1712, showing the seat of Earl Bathurst

Figure 47 The Woodhouse, or Alfred's Hall, in Cirencester Park (Dennis Moss, Corinium Museum)

Figure 48 The Armoury in Cecily Hill, built for the militia in 1856 with mock castellated facade, at the entrance to the Broad Ride of Cirencester Park (Corinium Museum)

Figure 49 Post-medieval monuments in the rural area (see Figure 43 for monuments within the urban form)

Figure 50 Tollhouse at the junction of the Tetbury and Stroud Roads (Corinium Museum)

Figure 51 Zones of archaeological interest in the urban area

Figure 52 Zones of archaeological interest in the rural area

Figure 53 Designations in the urban area (sources: various)

Figure 54 Designations in the rural area (sources: various)

Figure 55 Diagram showing the main stages in integrating archaeological responses with the development process (after Darvill and Gerrard 1990, fig 1)

Figure 56 Common foundation arrangements: A. Strip foundations; B. Pad foundations; C–E. Raft foundations; F. Pile types; G. Pile and slab foundations (sources: various)

Figure 57 Zones of high archaeological interest in the urban area (Reproduced from the Ordnance Survey's 1:10,000 map of 1983 with the permission of the Controller of Her Majesty's Stationery Office, © Crown copyright)

Figure 58 Flow chart to show the archaeological management cycle alongside the planning process

Figure 59 Sites recorded to the south of The Avenue

Figure 60 Defining the monument : the *basilica*

LIST OF TABLES

Table 1 Range of designations within the Study Area

Table 2 Frequency of site types within the Study Area

Table 3 Frequency of monuments in urban and rural situations

Table 4 Frequency of rural monuments by parish

Table 5 Distribution of monuments within the medieval medium-sized market town

Table 6 Comparison of the distribution of medieval monuments in three Gloucestershire towns: Cirencester, Tetbury and Gloucester

Table 7 Minimum site area affected by piles of different diameters (after Ove Arup 1992)

FOREWORD

Back in 1989, when the project reported here was being formulated, assessing the archaeology of urban areas was a relatively undeveloped art. Cirencester, together with four other historic towns in England, was chosen by English Heritage as a test-bed for new approaches to the management of the archaeological resource in urban areas. The pincipal aim of these projects was to build on the foundations laid down by the various historic town studies undertaken in the 1970s and early 1980s by consolidating available data about the archaeological resource and translating that data into the kinds of information and knowledge required for the integration of archaeological resource management with strategic planning and development control. In addition, the urban assessment was seen as a means of synthesising the results of rescue work over the last two decades, and setting out a research framework which could carry forward the next phase of studies.

The publication of this volume, as with the results of pilot studies in other towns, is as much to stimulate and inform debate on the way forward for urban assessments in general as it is to mark the end of a defined stage in one particular project. Accordingly, it is anticipated that this report will be of interest to many organisations and individuals, but principally those with an interest in the management of the urban resource generally, those interested in the assessment of archaeological deposits in towns like Cirencester, those with a direct interest in the archaeology of Cirencester and its environs, and also those seeking to help shape the future growth of Cirencester through development, conservation, or some other form of change.

Urban areas are complicated phenomena not only in their present structure and appearance but also in their archaeological form as well. Continuous sequences of interlocking deposits which may start below the ground in many cases carry through time and space to reveal themselves as above-ground structures or as determinants of the topography and plan of the places in which we now live and work. Documenting, recording, and evaluating this material is complicated too, requiring as it does a certain level of understanding about the easily identificable archaeological remains as well as the less distinctive layers and deposits that surround them.

Sites and Monuments Records have become familiar tools in the process of recording archaeological remains and can easily be accessed for a variety of purposes from planning inquiries to research. They provide the starting point for developing more detailed records of the kind really needed for ever-changing urban areas where development pressures are colossal, the scale of previous archaeological work high, and the complexity of deposits considerable. But while the need for enhanced records for urban areas and their hinterlands was clear, how they should be constructed remained less obvious.

Since the Cirencester Urban Assessment Project was itself essentially an experimental scheme it was felt appropriate that among its aims should be a reappraisal of the nature and structure of archaeological records appropriate to urban areas. Some preliminary work had already been undertaken in connection with small-scale assessments of development sites in the town and this formed the foundation of what has become the 'Cotswold' system. The fundamental difference between this system and other archaeological record systems is the separation of observations or events which generate archaeological data (called sites) and interpretations of that data either in the form of defined and recognisable monuments and urban deposits, or as sets of academic or strategic knowledge.

A full exposition of the system is given in this report, while the assessment itself is an exercise in application both within the urban area itself and in the surrounding countryside. Although not explored in the report, the wider implications of this new pattern of recording are considerable and provide the basis for harnessing the full power of the new technology of Geographical Information Systems. What is set out here is probably the single most radical rethink to date of the way in which SMRs are constructed.

As with all databases, however, the archive created for Cirencester and its hinterland will need constant updating as new data becomes available and new interpretations are made. As development pressures change it may also need expanding to take account of, for example, the archaeology of smaller urban areas represented by the market towns and large villages scattered throughout the Cotswolds. For Cirencester this will be achieved through a partnership between Cotswold Archaeological Trust and Cotswold District Council.

This report, an Urban Archaeological Assessment, attempts to build upon the Cirencester database and synthesise our current understanding of the archaeological resource as a point-in-time statement. Naturally parts of the report will be superceded by changing approaches, fresh legislation, and new data. This is inherent to the dynamic nature of archaeological resource management. Most importantly, however, the present study represents a foundation from which it will be possible to build an urban archaeological strategy which links the aims and objectives of archaeological resource management with planning policies and procedures. The development of this strategy is something for English Heritage, the Cotswold District Council and Cotswold Archaeological Trust to work on together in the coming years. Meanwhile, nationally important monuments will continue to be protected through Scheduling, but English Heritage will, over the next few years, be reviewing the arrangements for Scheduling in Cirencester with a view to rationalising designations in the light of the best and most up to date available information.

Through the combination of the urban database, the present Urban Archaeological Assessment document, and, before long, the Urban Archaeological Strategy, it is to be hoped that the continuing conservation and management of Cirencester's archaeological resource can be achieved in the context of continuing and sustainable economic prosperity for the town.

Professor Michael Fulford
March 1994

AUTHORS' PREFACE AND ACKNOWLEDGEMENTS

This report was first prepared during 1991 as part of the Cirencester Urban Assessment Project funded jointly by English Heritage and Cotswold District Council, and revised in 1994. During the course of the Project many individuals and organisations have given a great deal of valuable help and assistance. From the beginning the staff of the Cotswold District Council assisted greatly by putting at our disposal their map bases, their intimate knowledge of Cirencester and its hinterland, and their technical skills, especially in our work on Geographical Information Systems. In particular we would like to mention Mary Fell and Mike Wier.

The Project was monitored throughout by a team of advisers representing the funding bodies, English Heritage and the Cotswold District Council, together with representatives of the Cotswold Archaeological Trust and Gloucestershire County Council Planning Department. For their advice, support, and constructive discussion we would like to thank: Tony Fleming, Dai Morgan Evans and Roger Thomas (English Heritage); Tony Jones, David Viner and Sheila King (Cotswold District Council); Jan Wills (Gloucestershire County Council); Mick Aston (University of Bristol); Mike Fulford (University of Reading); and Richard Reece (University College London).

In the course of preparing a report of this kind the authors have depended a good deal upon national and local archives. For helping to track down obscure sources while still keeping their patience we would like to thank the staff of the following institutions: the Corinium Museum; the Gloucestershire County Council Sites and Monuments Record; the National Air Photo Library at the Royal Commission on the Historical Monuments of England, Swindon; the Cambridge University Aerial Photographic Collection; the Gloucestershire County Library, Arts and Museums Service; the Bingham Library, Cirencester; the Gloucester City Library Local History Collection; the Bodleian Library; the Royal Commission's National Archive Register; the Ashmolean Museum; and numerous record offices all over Great Britain. In particular we would like to mention Clare King, John Paddock, Danny Darwish, and Jane Isaac who took the time to make searches and assist our work so that nothing was missed and that everything was seen in the least possible time.

For helping us to pick our the vectors from the rasters we would like to say thank you to Adrian Exton and Russell Tinian of Intergraph. For getting on his bike and coming and helping out when the tags got confused a thank you to Steve Stead of English Heritage. Above all though, for their prodigal assistance in times of trouble, we would like to thank Bill Startin and Tony Fleming.

We could go on to record many other acts of kindess but our greatest obligation must be to the people of Cirencester who allowed us into their cellars and gardens and scoured their photograph collections and memories in the name of urban assessment.

The Cirencester Urban Assessment Project was carried out by the Cotswold Archaeological Trust which is based in Cirencester [Job Number 017/Typescript Report 9154]. The day-to-day management was undertaken by Christopher Gerrard and Linda Viner. A number of individuals took part in various phases of the work. They were: Cliff Bateman, Neil Lambert, Anneke de Winter, Sheryle Hobday, Michael Ings, Casper Johnson, Martin Wilson, Anna Cuss, and Alejandra Gutierrez.

Following the completion of the initial project in December 1991, a lengthy period of revision and enchancement occurred to produce this current document. At this later stage Neil Holbrook was commissioned to produce the sections relating to aspects of Roman Cirencester. He would like to thank the following people for their helpful comments and criticisms during this period: Paul Bidwell, Tom Blagg, Alan McWhirr, Richard Reece, and above all John Wacher for generously discussing the text in detail.

The main text of this report was drafted and edited by the principal authors, specific sections being contributed by Linda Viner and Neil Holbrook. Cliff Bateman assisted with the preparation of data for the initial text and drawings. Illustrations were prepared for publication by Alejandra Gutierrez, and Casper Johnson provided reconstruction drawings for the Roman and medieval townscapes. Photography and copying of original prints and drawings was undertaken by Abbey Studios, Cirencester, and Paul Stonell of King Alfred's College, Winchester. Thanks are due to our employing institutions, the University of Bournemouth and King Alfred's College, Winchester, for their help during later revisions of this report. We are grateful to the following people for reading and commenting on the text: Mick Aston, Carolyn Heighway, Alan McWhirr, Richard Reece, Bill Startin, Roger Thomas, Alf Plumb (Bovis Homes Technical Services), Barbara Yorke (King Alfred's College, Winchester), and Tom James (King Alfred's College, Winchester).

This volume is not intended to be a prescription for the study of urban areas. Since 1991, when this work was completed, there have been a number of important new publications which have contributed meaningfully to the debate on how best to investigate our urban areas. Any new study would need to take account of recent discussions held by the Urban Research Committee of the CBA, papers on urbanism circulated at the Conference on Medieval Archaeology in Europe held at York in September 1992, the fruits of new partnerships between the Royal Commission on the Historical Monuments of England and local Sites and Monuments Records (RCHME/EH 1992; RCHME 1993b), developments within the Monuments Protection Programme at English Heritage (English Heritage 1992a, 1992b, 1992c), as well as other published urban assessments (University of Durham 1992; Hereford and Worcestershire County Archaeological Service 1993). This document therefore represents the stage our thinking had reached two years ago and we have not updated the text to incorporate recent advances in thinking. It is clear, however, that few towns or cities would be suited to the approach outlined here, if only because less work has been undertaken there. Towns and cities are very particular phenomena and the urban archaeologist will need to devise various approaches to their analysis and protection.

Timothy Darvill and Christopher Gerrard
The Old Railway Station
Cirencester
1994

SUMMARY

An archaeological assessment of Cirencester and its surrounding countryside was commissioned by English Heritage and the Cotswold District Council in 1990 and undertaken between June 1990 and September 1991. The study area comprises the town of Cirencester and the adjoining civil parishes of Siddington, Baunton and Preston, a total area of 46 square kilometres.

The procedures used for data collection and interpretation are innovative to the assessment of urban areas. Data relating to almost 4000 sites was collected from a variety of sources including aerial photographs, personal recollections, past excavation and fieldwalking programmes, recorded finds, place-names, documents, photographs, illustrations, and maps. A cellar survey, field-checking of monuments, a door-to-door questionnaire, and an archaeological roadshow were undertaken specially for the assessment during the year. These observations have been plotted onto 1:500 scale maps for the town centre and 1:2500 for the rural areas. A series of maps covering the geology, topography, land-use, and land classification within the study area have been prepared to provide essential background data.

On the basis of the archaeological data in the form of identified sites, more than 400 separate single monuments were recognised. These represent all chronological periods from early prehistoric times through to the modern era and reflect the archaeological resource in the rural as well as urban environments. The position and extent of all the identified monuments have been plotted onto map overlays.

Within the urban area of Cirencester, four superimposed urban forms can be recognised: the Roman *Civitas Capital* of *Corinium Dobunnorum*, the Roman Provincial Capital of *Corinium*, the early medieval Royal/Ecclesiastical Centre of *Cyrnceastre*, and the medieval Medium-Sized Market Town of *Cirencestre* (with a sub-division for the post-medieval extent of the Medium-Sized Market Town).

Using the criteria developed for use by the Monuments Protection Programme to appraise monument importance the single monuments of medieval and earlier date within the town and in the surrounding countryside were appraised and important examples identified. The urban deposits within Cirencester were assessed to determine zones of greatest archaeological interest. As a result an approach to the management of the archaeological resource for the town is proposed. Ten areas of high archaeological interest are defined and these are described and mapped. Appropriate responses to development proposals in all areas are considered. To assist in the selection of future projects and the deployment of resources a series of research objectives are set out.

PART I
INTRODUCTION AND METHODOLOGY

1. INTRODUCTION

'It is much to be regretted that the histories of so many of our ancient cities and towns remain unwritten . . . that such delightful and pregnant sources of instruction, and illustration, of general as well as local history, should be neglected; whilst records are continually decaying, and monuments crumbling into dust.'

From an anonymous review of Baily's pamphlet 'Handbook for Cirencester, containing a history of the town and its antiquities . . . with illustrations', printed in the *Gentleman's Magazine* (1842)

'Cirencester very closely resembles some barely recoverable palimpsest, in which a precious underlying original text is seen to have been several times over-scrawled with other writings, penned, or merely scribbled, at far less careful periods.'

Welbore St Clair Baddeley, *A history of Cirencester* (1924)

Background

For over five hundred years the town of Cirencester on the south-eastern edge of the Gloucestershire Cotswolds has been recognised as a place rich in the archaeological remains of its Roman and medieval predecessors.

The archaeology of the town is perhaps best known through the large-scale excavations of the 1960s and 1970s, mainly undertaken by the Cirencester Excavation Committee; but this is only the most recent chapter in a long history of endeavour and research. From the fifteenth to the late twentieth century there has accumulated a mass of unsorted documents, cartographic information, museum archive material, published and unpublished manuscripts, and oral history which has never before been collated into a single comprehensive archaeological survey. Neither have the specific implications of the undoubtedly rich archaeological remains within and around Cirencester been integrated into strategic development plans for the local area or made known to the wider public through archeological publication rather than planning documentation.

Prior to 1990 two main archives of archaeological records existed for the town of Cirencester and its surrounding area. The first comprised a number of gazetteers, lists, and abstracts compiled by the staff of Cirencester Excavation Committee during research for the implementation and subsequent publication of excavations between 1960 and 1980. The second was the Sites and Monuments Record maintained by Gloucestershire County Council and based at Shire Hall in Gloucester. With some additions, this second archive was largely a computerised copy of the first and provides the backbone of national archives for the county such as the National Archaeological Record. Throughout the late 1980s it was recognised that neither record was comprehensive, nor was their structure and content geared to respond to the demands of modern archaeological resource management. In particular, neither record could sensibly be used as a basis to establish priorities for conservation, preservation, display, or research.

The need for an accurate database of recorded sites and monuments for the Cirencester area was stimulated by a number of new initiatives. First, in the local context, the Cotswold District Council was preparing a Cotswold Local Plan which required appropriate policies for planning and archaeology in the Cotswold area. Second, the thrust of national priorities encouraged by English Heritage through the Monuments Protection Programme has widened the focus of interest from the protection of single monuments towards the protection and future management of both the urban archaeological resource and relict cultural landscapes (Darvill *et al* 1987). More than ever before, the careful stewardship of archaeological remains as a finite resource requires a flexible database upon which sound decisions can be based. Third, the tide of local planning applications in the late 1980s, particularly those of large-scale schemes, brought the existing archaeological record under greater scrutiny than ever before and found it lacking in many respects. Fourth, the demise of the university-based, government grant-fed and amateur-supplied Cirencester

Excavation Committee led to the foundation in 1989 of the Cotswold Archaeological Trust, a commercial archaeological unit with charitable objectives which provided, for the first time in the town's history, a permanent and professional archaeological presence in the local area. All the new data generated by the Trust's current work needs to be consolidated and accessed into a suitable database, and a robust framework established for the ongoing assimilation of new data.

The task of the Cirencester Urban Assessment Project was therefore to establish a new and reliable database which would adequately satisfy a range of immediate and future archaeological needs, both strategic and academic.

The Cirencester Urban Assessment Project

The Cirencester Urban Assessment Project was commissioned jointly by English Heritage and the Cotswold District Council in the early summer of 1990, following agreement between interested parties on a detailed Research Design (Darvill 1989). The project was executed by the Cotswold Archaeological Trust between June 1990 and September 1991. There were four main objectives:

a. to create and verify a definitive database of recorded sites and monuments within the Study Area;

b. to survey and assess the survival of archaeological deposits and upstanding remains, providing information on thickness, volume, nature, content, preservation, etc;

c. to develop an archaeological and historical framework for the town and its environs;

d. to formulate policies for the future management of the resource including conservation, preservation, protection, presentation, display, research and contingency options.

The Study Area defined

Figure 1 shows the position and extent of the Study Area in its regional and local setting. The focus is the modern town of Cirencester, but also included are the adjoining civil parishes of Siddington, Baunton, and Preston. The total extent of the Study Area amounts to 46 sq km. Other than Cirencester, the main nucleated settlements are Siddington, Baunton, Preston and Stratton. Outside these built-up areas the countryside lies under arable cultivation, pasture, woodland, and parkland. Summaries of the modern and recent land-use are given in Chapter 4.

Records, reports and project archive

The Cirencester Urban Assessment Project was designed with the aim of creating a number of specific products. First and foremost, was a comprehensive, up-to-date, and easily maintained Archaeological Record for the Study Area: the urban database. This record comprises a series of three interrelated computerised databases and an accompanying set of map overlays. APPENDIX A introduces the records and maps, and summarises the main fields of data used in each record. The original version of the record is housed at the Corinium Museum, Park Street, Cirencester, and is currently maintained and curated by the Cotswold Archaeological Trust as part of its management agreement with Cotswold District Council. Associated with the database is a comprehensive archive containing copies of documents and material assembled and collected during the life of the Project. This has also been deposited at the Corinium Museum.

This report, the urban assessment, is intended as a summary of the Project and its scope, an analysis of the data currently held in the urban database, and a synthesis of the findings and implications. It is anticipated that both the database and this report will together underpin the third product, namely a series of policies relating to the archaeology of the area in the new Local Plan.

Report structure and content

This report is divided into four parts. The first serves as an introduction and includes the present Chapter plus Chapter 2 which sets out the philosophical and methodological basis of the assessment programme and urban database developed for Cirencester. Subsequent Parts unfold the approaches explained in Chapter 2.

Part II is concerned with data collection. Chapter 3 reviews the history of archaeological endeavour in and around Cirencester and considers the principal sources of available data. Chapter 4 summarises background information such as the topographical and physical setting of Cirencester, while Chapter 5 reports upon the strengths and weaknesses of the archaeological record as it has accumulated over the past five hundred years.

Part III develops the data into a series of interpretations, beginning with an introduction to the process in Chapter 6. Each of the following three chapters aims to synthesise and summarise our current knowledge by chronological period. Chapter 7 focuses upon the prehistoric and early Roman archaeology under and around Cirencester. The first town was established at Cirencester in the later first

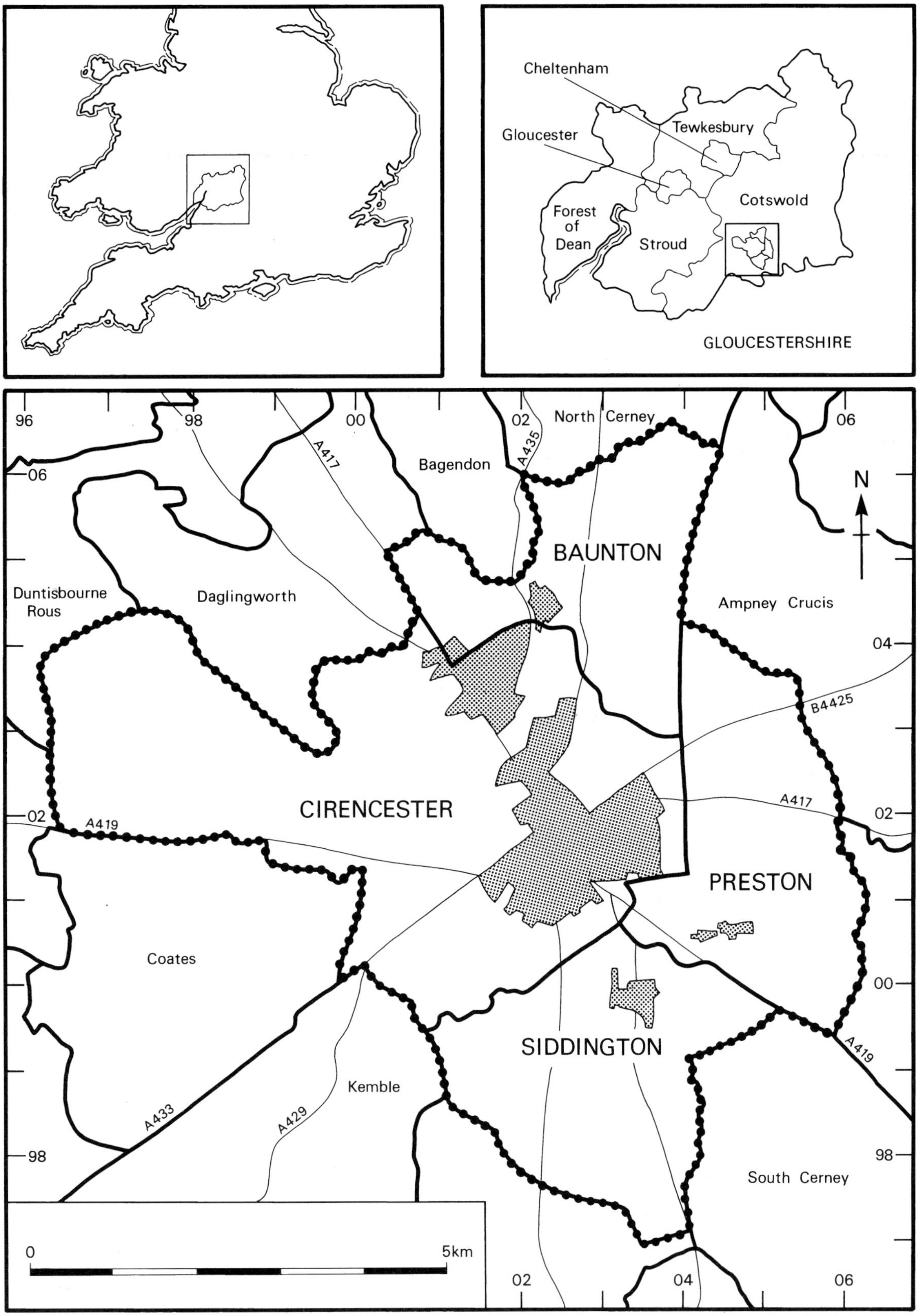

Figure 1
Location of the Study Area, showing the principal roads and surrounding parishes

century AD and this is the subject of Chapter 8 which covers two phases of the Roman town, *Corinium Dobunnorum,* as a *Civitas Capital* and as a Provincial Capital, as well as its extra-mural monuments for both phases. Chapters 9 through to 11 are concerned with successive later forms: *Cyrnceastre* (the early medieval Royal / Ecclesiastical Centre), *Cirencestre* (the medieval Medium-sized Market Town), and Cirencester (the post-medieval phase of the latter form). The name and variations in the spelling of the name reflect the main stages in the evolution of what we now know as Cirencester. Chapter 12 takes a rather different view of the archaeology of the town, one based on the long-term accumulation of monuments and deposits to bring about the characteristics of the place that can be seen and experienced today.

Part IV looks to the future and considers how archaeology and development might be harmonised. Chapter 13 explores the question of how archaeological resource management works in the context of Cirencester and its environs. Consideration is given to existing legislation and policy, available management options, and procedures for balancing the needs of on-going development with archaeological conservation.

Three supporting Appendices are provided. Appendix A lists the data fields used in the compilation of records established in the course of the Project: the Site and Monument Records, Sources, and mapped elements. Appendix B tabulates the monuments defined in the Study Area by period. Appendix C is a statement of future research objectives. Since some of the terms used are given specific and perhaps unfamiliar meanings in this report a Glossary has also been included. The Bibliography incorporates those references having a specific application to this volume with the published and unpublished sources consulted during the course of the Project. A list of Cartographic References completes the volume.

2. PHILOSOPHY AND METHODOLOGY

'I have seen Mr Beecham and from what I can gather his information is quite reliable and at any rate the best available at present. He is not conceited and quite ready to modify his views if any fresh discoveries are made.'
Mrs Helena Cripps in a letter to F W Haverfield, 19th November 1911

Obtaining reliable information is crucial for any study in which justifiable conclusions have to be drawn from base-line data. For archaeological purposes reliable information is often difficult to obtain because of the variable quality of the sources available. The sources themselves are reviewed in a later Chapter, but as a preliminary to this attention is here directed towards the philosophy and methods of the system developed for the recording and analysis of archaeological information in the Cirencester Urban Assessment.

Existing records and system needs

At the start of the project the existing sites and monuments record (SMR) for Cirencester was largely based on the Ordnance Survey's Archaeological Record Cards and a disparate collection of papers, notes, and summaries assembled by the staff working for Cirencester Excavation Committee (CEC). The categorisation, constitution, and classification of the items recorded was inconsistent and insensitive to the nature of the archaeological resource itself, and had been assembled in the first instance as a ready-reference to excavations and observations carried out by CEC. Moreover, it was widely recognised that such a record could not be depended upon to substantiate professional judgements for archaeological resource management because the information it contained was unstructured in terms of the thought processes that produce different levels of interpretation and understanding from otherwise separate items. For example, the database treated investigative procedures such as excavations, and monuments such as the Roman *basilica*, in the same way as negative features such as pit groups. This made sorting and selecting information rather difficult. Recognising the deficiencies of what was already available led to the definition of a series of desirable characteristics which would provide the basis of a structured re-arrangement. It was argued that the new arrangement needed to:

(i) systematically assimilate the many different kinds of data from a wide range of sources, some of uncertain quality, that had accumulated in the course of several centuries of endeavour;

(ii) reflect the essential characteristics of the archaeological resource in and around the urban area, and the ways in which it is recorded and understood;

(iii) provide information that could be used for planning purposes and academic research;

(iv) expound a sufficiently robust structure and logic to the categorisation of the items recorded and the definition of levels of interpretation that it could fully support professional judgements based on it;

(v) assimilate a continuing flow of new data and revised interpretations; and

(vi) be adaptable to changing technologies for the storage, manipulation and analysis of data-sets, especially GIS technology.

Fundamental to the fulfilment of these needs was the construction of a new kind of record system which adequately reflected the complexity of the resource, the integrity of the sources of information about that resource, and the ways in which the resource is perceived and interpreted. The approach adopted drew upon two main sources. First was a methodology used for the characterisation and description of the archaeological resource for a study of a central area of Cirencester which had been identified for redevelopment (EH 1992c). Second was the research and development being undertaken concurrently by English Heritage with specific reference to the needs of the Monuments Protection Programme (Darvill 1991). By bringing together this combination of practical experience and theoretical understanding a methodology for dealing with the complicated archaeological resource of an urban area and its essentially rural environs was developed and tested. In the following sections both the background and the principal features of the 'Cotswold system' are described. Later Chapters document the application of the proposals set out here. Again, it must be emphasised here that this system requires carefully and rigidly defined terminology and application. Many of the distinctions made here cannot profitably be made in smaller or less well-studied urban areas and the methodology proposed here should not be regarded as prescriptive.

A theoretical perspective

At the core of the assessment of the archaeology of Cirencester and its environs is structured thinking which leads from what is actually known about the archaeology of the place (ie the study area) through to an understanding of the archaeological resource as a basis for professional judgements relevant to planning and academic interests. Perception provides a key to this thinking process, and here it is useful to distinguish three perceptual levels within the broad domain of how we might tackle the problem: Data, Information, and Knowledge.

Figure 2 illustrates in diagrammatic form the hierarchical arrangement of these three levels of perception as a system of analysis. The system is a self-organising one in the sense that the patterns which can be seen at any one level are the products or inferences derived from what is perceived rather than what is determined by the system itself. The only fixed links in the arrangement are between levels of perception, the data being the source for any perceptions of information, data and information together being the source for perceptions of knowledge.

Looked at in more detail, each of the three levels of perception can be related directly to the main elements of archaeological resource management, and to the main stages in the construction and analysis of an archaeological database. The following sub-sections describe the levels in more detail.

Data

Data represents the descriptive foundation upon which the evaluation process rests and it is crucially

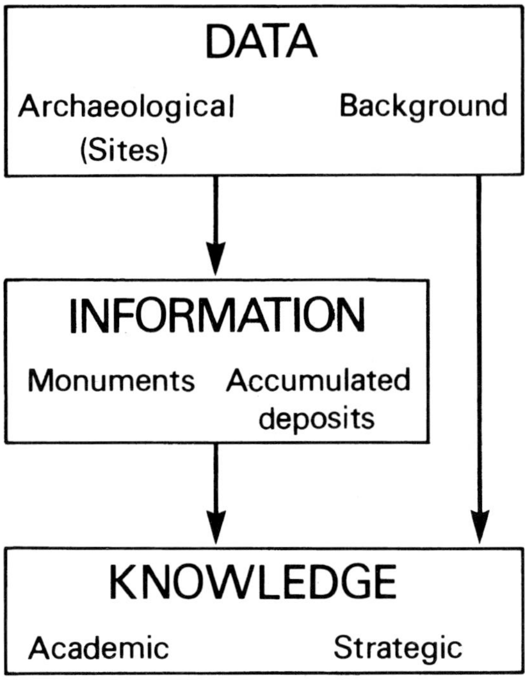

Figure 2
A theoretical perspective of urban assessment showing a hierarchy of three levels of perception

important to understand its constitution as the fundamental facts or things which we use as the basis for inference or reckoning. Two main sets of data can be identified: archaeological data and background data.

Archaeological data units are most usefully perceived as the events or opportunities to observe archaeological remains or deposits. In the Cotswold system the fundamental data units (items) are termed **sites**. These may be regarded as windows or 'sights' onto the archaeological resource; events which represent an engagement between some element of the resource itself and an observer or recorder. The engagement is not neutral, however, because on the one hand the resource may not be fully revealed while, on the other, the actions and perceptions of the observer will be culturally conditioned.

Viewed in this way there are many kinds of site, for example: open area excavations, watching briefs, stray finds, cropmarks on aerial photographs, geophysical surveys, or visual observations of upstanding remains. The quality, nature, scale of application, and reliability of these data units varies considerably; what is important is to recognise this and to appreciate the differences between the main kinds of site.

The units of analysis commonly employed to record archaeological deposits are well understood with reference to excavations: usually a hierarchical system involving **objects** (including artefacts and ecofacts), **contexts**, **features** and **components**, the precise definition of each element being determined through the principles of stratigraphy and association (see Glossary for further definition). The same units of recording can also be applied to archaeological deposits visible in other kinds of site, for example in watching briefs, or as cropmarks. In all cases, the scale of analysis is closely linked to its place within the hierarchy. Thus in excavations the lowest levels of entity commonly encountered are objects and contexts, while in aerial photography, by contrast, the recorded sites are likely to be seen only as features and components.

Background data is also relevant to archaeological inquiries, particularly details relating to topography, situation, geology, hydrology, recent land-use patterns, ancient land-use patterns, and development constraints (eg Scheduled Monuments, Listed Buildings, Conservation Areas etc).

Information

Once a collection of data has been assembled some attempt may be made at comprehending it: giving meaning to the perceived patterns. Archaeological data can be comprehended in two main ways, as monuments and as accumulated deposits. In urban areas the former is especially relevant to the comprehension of individual phases (urban forms – see below) within the development of an urban centre, the latter is germane to the comprehension of superimposition and urban development through time.

The recognition, identification, and definition of monuments or accumulated deposits is based on judgements relating to the intrinsic qualities of the visible or perceived resource. As such any interpretations of data-sets involve an engagement between the record of the archaeological resource (for it may be impossible to see physically all the relevant data at one point in time) and an analyst. In creating a record of the archaeological resource that can be perpetuated and expanded it is therefore appropriate to make explicit the differences between, on the one hand, the data as recorded in the form of observations (ie sites), and, on the other hand, the interpretations which are placed on the information derived from those encounters (ie monuments and accumulated deposits).

Monuments are taken to be regular groupings of associated components which form recognisable and more or less complete entities which often have specific function, use, purpose or symbolic meaning. The idea of a monument is also central to the provisions of the *Ancient Monuments and Archaeological Areas Act 1979* where a monument in the legal sense is defined as:

a. any building, structure or work, whether above or below the surface of the land, and any cave or excavation;

b. any site comprising the remains of any such building, structure or work or of any cave or excavation; and

c. any site comprising, or comprising the remains of, any vehicle, vessel, aircraft or other movable structure or part thereof which neither constitutes nor forms part of any work which is a monument within paragraph a. above; and any machinery attached to a monument shall be regarded as part of the monument if it could not be detached without being dismantled.

The 1979 Act (as amended for England) provides for the protection in law of monuments which are deemed by the Secretary of State for the National Heritage to be of 'National Importance', such monuments being listed on a 'Schedule of Monuments' and hence commonly referred to as Scheduled Monuments. The Schedule has been under review since 1985 through the work of the Monuments Protection Programme which is being carried out by English Heritage (Startin 1988; 1991). This initiative seeks to address the problem of the systematic and consistent evaluation of monuments on a nationwide basis and, in doing so, recommend for Scheduling an appropriate selection of monuments which will create a balanced sample of the national resource.

Accumulated deposits are the sum total of archaeological objects, contexts, features and components present within any defined stratigraphic sequence. Such sequences are likely to vary considerably in depth and complexity. Like single monuments, however, they can be discriminated on the basis of their recorded or predicted nature and quality and the discrimination criteria (see below) provide useful headings under which to explore these matters.

Monuments and accumulated deposits also represent the building-blocks of more complicated entities such as urban areas and relict cultural landscapes (see below).

An important point about this information-based level of perception is that while there is probably a high degree of agreement about data (eg that an excavation took place and that so many contexts, features and components were revealed etc) at this second level there is greater scope for debate and critical analysis. Thus there may be more than one view on the classification of a monument revealed by an excavation or on the quality of the accumulated deposits brought to light during a watching brief. The important point, however, is that the data itself will not change even though revised comprehension (information) may be proposed as new data becomes available or as existing data is reinterpreted.

Knowledge

The final level in this hierarchy relates to knowledge which is here taken to mean a justifiable interpretation based on the sum of available data and information supported with reference to wider and more broadly based frameworks or perspectives. With regard to the kind of archaeology represented at Cirencester there are two main fields of knowledge: academic knowledge and strategic knowledge.

Academic knowledge refers to an understanding of an area and its development in the context of available archaeological models and interpretations pertaining to all related matters in Britain and other countries.

Strategic knowledge refers to an understanding of an area and its archaeological resource in the context of prevailing international, national and local legislation and planning philosophies (eg those relating to conservation, preservation, exploitation etc).

An archaeological perspective

The Cirencester Urban Assessment includes not just the town of Cirencester and its predecessors extending back to the late first century AD but also the surrounding area, represented for convenience by the administrative boundaries of the surrounding parishes. Traditionally this may be seen as a study covering both rural and urban archaeology, yet consideration of the model outlined above causes us to challenge this view in some respects and revise our analysis in others. At the level of 'data', the sorts of events and sources that give rise to what we know are similar throughout the study area, although some site types (eg aerial photography) may be less useful in the built-up areas than in open countryside. The differences become more marked at the first level of interpretation, and here it has become common, for the purposes of archaeological resource management, to recognise three main combinations of monuments and deposits: single monuments, urban areas, and relict cultural landscapes (Darvill 1988a). All three forms are potentially represented in and around Cirencester, although during this urban archaeological assessment programme attention was directed only to single monuments and urban areas.

Single monuments

The archaeological resource is commonly equated with the identification of single monuments. This narrow definition accords well with the main prevailing legislation. Traditionally, monuments have formed the unit of study and analysis in archaeology, not least because they represent a manageable unit in practical terms while having a certain intellectual and visual integrity as well.

Monuments can be hierarchically classified according to how much is known about them. Three main levels are used: **Category** (where only general details are known – eg mill), **Class** (where specific details are known – eg Tower mill); and **Type** (where a great deal of detail is known – eg Smock Mill). Also relevant is a **Descriptor** which can be applied to any of the above-mentioned levels on the basis of recorded tangential detail (eg corn mill). Of these different levels that of Monument Class is the most commonly used, and several hundred such classes have been identified and described to date.

It is sometimes possible to recognise groupings of monuments, for example **clusters** of monuments of the same class, associated **groups** of contemporary monuments of different classes, and **complexes** of functionally related interconnected monuments.

Urban areas

A town or city is a special environment for archaeology. Although urban areas contain many recognisable single monuments, for example motte and bailey castles, churches, monasteries for men, and so on, they also have other characteristics which set them apart from being simple aggregates of single monuments (Carver 1987a; Schofield 1987). There is often continuity between periods of settlement for example, and although development takes place at differing rates within the complex arrangement of land units it is often possible to recognise major occupation horizons. The general urban matrix which results from long periods of intensive occupation and which can best be envisaged as the glue which both engulfs and bonds single monuments together is referred to as **accumulated deposits**. These are the sum total of archaeological objects, contexts, features and components present within any defined stratigraphic sequence. Thus, there are two identifiable but intertwined strands to the archaeology of urban areas: definable single monuments and accumulated deposits. By definition, the latter incorporates the former, but together these two elements provide a reasonably complete picture of a complicated entity. In theory accumulated deposits of the kind described here may also be recognisable outside urban areas. No such deposits have been identified as part of this study but such a dimension may in future hold an important key to the interpretation of non-urban remains of the kind that cannot easily or usefully be classified as single monuments.

Within the sequence of monuments and accumulated deposits in any urban area it is often possible to recognise distinctive horizons. These horizons are referred to as **forms** and on a national basis they can be roughly classified because of traits which they share with one another and because similar patterns have been recognised in several places. A total of 16 main forms have been recognised to date (EH 1992c), four of them being represented at Cirencester. Archaeologically, the key horizons or forms evident in the development of a place are important because it is at these times that it is easiest to reconstruct on paper at least the basic plan and lay-out of the urban area.

Evaluating monuments and accumulated deposits

Not all monuments and sectors of an urban area are of equal importance in archaeological terms and so, as an aid to the development of strategic knowledge, some kind of evaluation must take place to gauge the level of importance. Such analysis is generally called evaluation, but should not be confused with Field Evaluation (see Glossary). In this study the methods of evaluation developed by English Heritage for use within the Monuments Protection Programme (MPP) are followed (Darvill *et al* 1987). The methods themselves are now widely known and have been set out in detail elsewhere for single monuments (Darvill 1988b) and urban areas (EH 1992c). The following notes are intended only as summaries of the main elements.

Single monuments

With reference to single monuments, the overall importance of each identifiable class is assessed through four **characterisation criteria**. These are:

Rarity
Period (currency)
Diversity (form)
Period (representativity)

Together, these provide an overview of the interest in the class as a whole and give a general indication as to what proportion of those known may be regarded as being of national, regional or local importance. English Heritage has undertaken the task of monument characterisation on a national basis in the context of the Monuments Protection Programme and these studies have been drawn upon for the Cirencester Urban Assessment.

Each known example of a monument in each class is then assessed individually so that its archaeological interest (national, regional, or local) can be established. Every monument is assessed with reference to eight **discrimination criteria** so that its qualities can be compared with those of other examples of the same class. The discrimination criteria are:

Survival
Potential
Documentation (archaeological)
Documentation (historical)
Group Value (clustering)
Diversity (features)
Group Value (association)
Amenity Value.

Seven of the criteria can be graded on a tri-partite scale (good–medium–poor), the eighth (Group Value (clustering)) being graded on a bi-partite scale based on presence/absence of clustering. In order to provide a measure of the relative importance of a specific monument a **Monument Interest Value** (MIV) can be calculated through combining the scores assigned through professional judgement to the above-mentioned range of eight criteria. The MIV is calculated in the following way:

$$MIV = \Sigma (CS_1^2 \ldots (CS_n^2)$$

where CS is the Criterion Score assigned during the evaluation of each monument. The maximum score attainable with the criteria used is 58 for monuments where seven criteria are relevant (the field of Documentation (historical) does not apply to early monuments) and 67 for all other monuments. In calculating the MIV scores for this assessment, professional judgements have been made on the basis of the recorded archaeological resource represented in the southern Cotswolds and surrounding areas. In Chapters 7 to 11 the scores obtained by individual monuments are used to identify which monuments are of greatest importance. The MIVs resulting from the work carried out for this assessment project are listed as part of the Project archive but at this stage should only be used as a provisional analysis based on regional and local comparanda; this pending the review of scores as part of the Monuments Protection Programme to be undertaken in due course.

Used mechanistically, any scoring system can be misapplied. The Criterion Score developed in the Monuments Protection Programme should be an 'aid to professional judgement concerning the importance of archaeological sites, *not a replacement* for such judgement'. In particular, the scores given here are allotted on the basis of best available recorded information at a certain moment in time and can be expected to change in the future as new data becomes available.

Urban areas

The main aim of the evaluation here is to identify, in a general way, the most archaeologically important parts of a given urban area, and thus to enable those areas of greatest interest to be distinguished from those of lesser interest as the basis for informing management strategies. The eight discrimination criteria listed above with reference to single monuments can be used as the basis for systematic evaluation at this stage in the process, although as always professional judgement has a role to play too.

There are two ways in which evaluation can be applied. The first is to look at individual forms within the development of a town (ie slices cut horizontally), while the second is to consider the whole sequence as one entity (ie all the slices together). Both approaches were tried in the case of Cirencester and the results are presented in later Chapters. The actual process of evaluation is broadly the same, however, and is carried out as two parallel but separate exercises.

In the first exercise (Chapters 7 to 11) the discrimination criteria are applied to each form in turn, identifying, for example, areas of high archaeological documentation or amenity value in the early medieval urban form. This is particularly helpful later when writing research agendas for each period of the town's history and in reviewing the results of the next stage. Site data which do not fall into the period forms under consideration are omitted from this first exercise.

In the second exercise (Chapter 12) the evaluation of accumulated deposits ignores the classification of data into monument classes and instead uses archaeological and background data from all types of site to produce a general characterisation of the deposits. Emphasis is placed on determining the spatial extent of variations in the categories of interest proposed for each criteria. When considering the factors relevant to each, full account must be taken of the vertical dimension of the recorded archaeological resource represented by the stratigraphic sequence of objects, contexts, features and components. As with the determination of values for the discrimination of single monuments, there is no quick, easy or mechanistic way of judging the factors relevant to each criterion, though results from the first exercise may provide an initial guide. Rather, professional judgement has to be carefully applied to make the best use of all the data contained in the record relating to each site.

All parts of an urban area are considered during the discrimination of accumulated deposits, including those areas which comprise or lie above or below defined monuments. In this way it is possible to gauge any major variations in the factors covered by the criteria within the areal extent of large monuments.

The data which is used to assess each criterion will be contained in the site records. Data from several sites may be needed to produce a single value. When all the criteria, or as many as possible, have been determined for all recorded sites it is possible to produce a zoned map of the urban area for each criterion.

Zoning applied in this sense is a simple contouring process using the values assigned to the discrimination criterion in question for each site as the data-points around which the contours are drawn. The defined zones follow the tri-partite grading of each criterion, thus the defined zones will correspond to the high/medium/low or good/medium/poor judgements made for each site. The number and density of sites with relevant documentation of the criterion in question will determine the resolution of the zoning; at first such zones are likely to be crude and generalised, but as more data accumulates the zones can be depicted in greater detail.

Details of the way that individual criterion are assessed are set out elsewhere together with a summary of the application of a simple scoring system to the process (EH 1992c).

As a result of the evaluation process for urban areas two sets of information are available. First there is information on the nature, extent and importance of defined monuments, and second there is a general plot of the overall archaeological importance of accumulated deposits. As indicated, these should be compiled for each form as well as for the urban area as a whole. The two sets of information overlap only to the extent that the deposit overlay includes coverage of defined monuments as well as the 'grey areas' in between which cannot so easily be defined according to the recognised classification of monuments.

The two analyses are fundamentally different in that the details relating to defined monuments relate to specific and clearly bounded areas whereas the overlay showing the overall importance of accumulated deposits is by its nature generalised and more concerned with broad zones.

From sites to knowledge

In order to fulfil the aims of the Cirencester Urban Assessment Project it is necessary to move through all three levels of the perceptual hierarchy described above and to make full use of the methods of evaluation. In practical terms, attaining the objectives of the project involves five main stages or steps. These may be summarised as follows:

Data collection

The first stage is data collection, during which a wide range of sources are interrogated and documented. The data falls into two broad groups: archaeological data relating directly to the archaeological resource, and relevant background data relating to the context and situation of the archaeological resource. The sources used in compiling the database are considered in detail in Chapter 3.

Archaeological data is recognised to exist at a number of levels. The smallest unit generally appreciated is the 'context', for example the bricks in a wall. These contexts may then build into a 'feature', for example the wall itself, and then, together with other features, into a 'component', such as a gatehouse. Details of the site records which were established are given in APPENDIX A.

Monument definition

The second stage involves the interpretation of the primary data (both archaeological and background). This includes defining and documenting identifiable monuments and characterising the accumulated deposits within the urban area. The documentation developed for monuments and deposits is set out in APPENDIX A.

It is important to note, however, that the interpretation of the data presented here is simply a point-in-time statement based on the best available retrievable information. Accordingly, the list of monuments is neither immutable nor exhaustive. As and when the existing data is supplemented or can be interpreted better an expanded or modified set of monuments may be defined.

Characterising the urban forms

In the third stage the archaeological characteristics of particular **urban forms** become the centre of interest. It is possible, for example, to plot out all the single monuments which pertain to that phase of Cirencester's development which we recognise as the Roman *civitas capital* or the medieval medium-sized market town. Discrimination criteria may be applied to each form in turn so as to identify areas of good survival, poor historical documentation, and so on. Those parts of the town known only as accumulated deposits become more readily appreciated.

Zones of archaeological interest

The fourth stage aims to define zones within the town which are judged to be of differing levels of **archaeological interest**. This is achieved by scoring the discrimination criteria for the urban area as a whole and not by urban form alone as in the third stage. The final maps in this sequence aim to define different zones of archaeological interest for the town and the surrounding rural area by combining the information from the eight mapped discrimination criteria.

Management planning

In the fifth and final stage the information on the individual monuments and the accumulated deposits can be brought together to provide a strategic overview as the basis for management plans and action policies. Two levels or scales of analysis are generally recognised: plot or land-unit specific **management plans**, and strategic overviews of archaeological resource management across the urban area as a whole. Whichever scale is being pursued, many factors will need to be taken into account when formulating appropriate management strategies. Among these, four principal considerations are identified by the management appraisal criteria:

Condition
Fragility
Vulnerability
Conservation Value

The selection of management options requires careful consideration of the alternatives and objectives. This is dealt with in more detail in Chapter 13, but two key options can be recognised, namely: preservation (eg conservation and protection) and exploitation (eg presentation, research priorities etc).

PART II
DATA COLLECTION

3. ARCHAEOLOGICAL ENDEAVOUR AND DATA SOURCES

by Christopher Gerrard and Linda Viner

'The people here had got to depend upon us to keep the record and they may have felt it would be interfering if they took upon themselves to do so. At first I did not know quite how to manage about getting any walls etc planned, until Mr Taylor was suggested to me.'

Mrs Helena Cripps in a letter to F W Haverfield, 15th January 1918

Archaeological data for Cirencester has gradually accumulated over many centuries and as a result of many different kinds of investigation, observation and inquiry. In this Chapter attention is first directed towards the ways in which data has accumulated and then at the kinds of sources that were drawn on for the Project.

History of endeavour

The study of the archaeology and history of Cirencester has moved through four successive phases between 1480 and 1991. Prior to the eighteenth century there were few interested observers, but there then followed a second stage of burgeoning antiquarian activity and artefact study which began with the visit of Stukeley (1721) and lasted until the excavations of Buckman and Newmarch (1850). With Buckman and Newmarch begins a third phase, an era of archaeological endeavour which culminated in 1958 with the setting up of the Cirencester Excavation Committee and the formation of an organised professional body of interested individuals. The history of archaeological endeavour in each of these phases is traced in detail below.

The first records

Before the eighteenth century observations and speculations about Cirencester's past are rare and choked with imaginative historical detail. William of Worcester (alias Botoner, 1415–*c*1485) visited the town, 'anciently called the City of Sparrows', in 1480 and noted in his *Itineraries* the major visible remains such as Grismond's Tower (Grismund's Mount), the Chapel of St Cecilia, the Torre Castle (Tar Barrows), the parish church, and the Augustinian abbey (Harvey 1969). He relates for the first time the local tradition that 'a certain Africanus, who came from Africa, destroyed the city by sending birds over the city with wildfire tied to their tails'. Besides his curiosity with legend and his useful topographical detail, William of Worcester's notes on church architecture formed the basis of later speculation about the layout of the abbey and display a real interest in the material remains of the past.

Seventy-five years later, John Leland (1503–1552), King's Antiquary to Henry VIII, described the walls of Cirencester with its 'towers standing in the wall' (Toulmin Smith 1964). He records the discovery of coins, pavements, and inscriptions, and describes the hills and ditches of what is probably the amphitheatre. Many of Leland's inaccuracies have misled later town historians and his statements on the date of the Abbey Church, the origins of the hospital of St Lawrence and the location of Cirencester Castle should be approached with caution (Fuller 1890–1).

Travellers, gentlemen and antiquarians

The roots of modern archaeological scholarship begin in the later years of the seventeenth century. William Aubrey (1626–1697), the influential antiquarian, mentions in his *Monumenta Britannica* Grismund's Mount, 'a camp called Tarbury', the Roman road system, discusses the derivation of the name *Cyrencester* and relates the discovery of a *'hypocaustum'* (unlocated). But it was in the early years of the next century that the county's first printed history by Sir Robert Atkyns (1647–1711) was printed. This volume, *The ancient and present state of Glocestershire*, was printed in 1712 after the author's death. Atkyns' contribution is largely as a collator of information, an editor rather than a researcher, and his work is perhaps most valuable for the inclusion of two engravings by Kip, one of the Abbey House belonging to the Master family, and one of Earl Bathurst's Cirencester Park. These are the earliest surviving views of the town and show remarkable detail.

The flow of antiquarian research continued with the visit of the antiquarian William Stukeley (1687–1765) on August 23rd 1721, accompanied by Mr Roger Gale. A quarto volume in the Bodleian Library (MS Top.gen.d.13) contains his town plan sketch which is the earliest recorded layout for the streets and tenements (Frontispiece). The street plan is something of a puzzle, in particular the alignment of Lewis Lane and the position of a road cutting through the Watermoor town defences. However, the plan does show accurately the position of the Abbey, the parish church, a fulling mill, the Bell Ale House, Gurmond's Mount (Grismund's Mount) and the Querns cemetery. A number of sketches, of the Hospital gate, a stone sculpture, and the tombstone of Julia Casta, were evidently done on the same visit. The accompanying text, presumably written at the same time, appears in his *Itinerarium curiosum* (1776, first published in 1724). Here he describes the town wall and the 'Lewis Ground' where 'antiquities are dug up every day'. Cirencester reappeared once more towards the end of Stukeley's life under less happy circumstances when, in 1746, he was tricked by the forger Charles Bertram into believing one Richard of Westminster had transcribed a unique itinerary of Roman Britain. In his attempts to authenticate the work Stukeley became convinced that the true identity of the author was one Richard of Cirencester, a monk and known writer with historical interests. Bertram became an Honorary Fellow of the Society of Antiquaries of London for his discoveries and Stukeley died believing the documents to be genuine.

Samuel Rudder (1726–1801) published his *New history of Gloucestershire* in 1779. This history succeeds that of Atkyns and is of greater interest for its references to archaeological finds and Rudder's deeper knowledge of local affairs. Rudder was the first to publish the correct identification of the Roman amphitheatre (McWhirr 1988). In 1800 his compilation for Cirencester was expanded and published separately as *History and antiquities of Cirencester*. The volume went through a number of editions and was the guide to many future visitors to the town, including the Reverend John Skinner in 1824.

Towards the end of the eighteenth century Samuel Lysons (1763–1819), an antiquary of legal training and a draughtsman of great skill, researched and published three volumes of the highest standard: *Etchings of views and antiquities in the county of Gloucester hitherto imperfectly or never engraved* (1791–6), *A collection of Gloucestershire antiquities* (1803–4) and his best known work *Reliquiae Britannico-Romanae* (1801–1817). This last work, itself published in three volumes, has illustrations by Lysons of the 'Marine Scene' mosaic from 60 Dyer Street. It is best not to confuse this Samuel Lysons with his nephew of the same name (1806–1877), the author of several pseudo-historical articles of an idiosyncratic nature, such as *What has Gloucestershire achieved?* (1861).

Also at the end of the eighteenth century, between 1784 and 1789, the Thames and Severn Canal was constructed. This included the digging out of the Sapperton Tunnel which was the longest tunnel attempted at that time. The site was visited by, amongst others, William 'Strata' Smith (1769–1839) who incorporated his observations in his Geological Map of England and Wales in 1815 and his map of Gloucestershire in 1819. Smith promoted the principle that rocks were deposited over long periods of time and so provided the intellectual setting for the later work of Charles Lyell and Charles Darwin.

The Victorian age

In the nineteenth century general antiquarian interest transformed itself into purer archaeological observation. In 1824 the Reverend John Skinner (1772–1839) visited Cirencester writing about the town in his diaries and making sketches. The originals are preserved in the British Museum (BM MS 33679). During his two days in Cirencester he undertook the first recorded excavation in the town which took place in the amphitheatre or Bullring as it was then called. He visited the Querns and noted some 30 skeletons 'interred promiscuously', walked the circuit of the Roman walls just as Stukeley had done one hundred years previously, described finds of tombstones at 'Steep Stairs' and 'Gregory's Nursery', and the finding of the Orpheus pavement at The Barton and coffins in Lord Bathurst's park 'near the House'. He complains with some feeling of the trials of the field archaeologist in the Cotswold winter. 'If I have not gone through fire,' he writes, 'I am sure I did through water, to show what a zealous disciple I am in the School of Antiquities' (11th November 1824).

The Cotteswold Naturalists' Field Club was founded in July 1846. This society provided a forum for all manner of scholarly outpourings ranging over the archaeological and geological debates of the day.

Figure 3
The lifting of the Hunting Dogs Mosaic, discovered in Dyer Street in 1849 (*Illustrated London News* 8th September 1849)

The honorary secretary (1852–1860) and a regular contributor to the Society's Proceedings, was James Buckman (1816–1884), professor of geology and botany at the newly instituted Royal Agricultural College. Through his energies the major challenges of local geology were overcome and the results published (J Buckman 1858).

Buckman's interests did not rest solely with geology. In 1850 he and Charles Newmarch published their *Illustrations of the remains of Roman art in Cirencester*, following the discovery of the Hunting Dogs and Four Seasons mosaics in 1849, during the course of sewer construction in Dyer Street (Figure 3). The Roman building from which these mosaics came also contained another pavement with octagonal designs, the 'Marine Scene' illustrated by Lysons (1801–17), an Orpheus pavement described by Beecham (1887), and another pavement observed during a watching brief in 1972 (McWhirr 1973). Taken together this collection is 'the most remarkable collection of mosaics from any single Roman building in Cirencester, and perhaps even from any town house in Britain' (McWhirr 1976a), and illustrates well how four observations over a 155-year period can help to suggest the identity of a monument. James Buckman went on to publish a series of articles concerning the geological properties of materials found on excavations such as mosaics (1853), quern stones (1866b), and roof tiles (1868).

Following the discovery and lifting of the Four Seasons and Hunting Dogs mosaics in Dyer Street in 1849, archaeological interest in the town mushroomed with many national and county societies from far afield paying visits to the town. The support and benefaction provided by Earl Bathurst was acknowledged in 1868 when he addressed members of the British Archaeological Association as their President (Bathurst 1869, 21–5).

During the second half of the nineteenth century and up to the end of the First World War three events served to encourage interest in archaeology: the coming of the railways, concern for public health, and the founding of two museums in the town. The first, the coming of the railways, focused attention indirectly upon archaeology and new Victorian science through increased interest in the new geological exposures (Taunton 1872). Seemingly every year, there were excursions from societies both local and national to see the latest 'diggings in the town, or the new cuttings for the Sapperton railway tunnel'.

The second was an increasing concern for urban health and standard of living. Improvements to drainage works became more important as Cirencester and the surrounding villages grew in population. Inevitably, with extensive groundworks underway archaeology was uncovered. John Bravender (1830–1923) corresponded with the *Wilts & Gloucestershire Standard* on his observations in Latton and his son Thomas recorded finds from new sewerage works in Cirencester between 1878 and 1880 (T Bravender 1881; 1883–4a). Lindsall Richardson continued the work of J H Taunton and published articles on the boreholes dug in and around the town to investigate water supplies and the underlying geological formations (eg L Richardson 1913, 1924a; Taunton 1868, 1887) culminating in the publication of the Memoir to accompany the Geological Survey (L Richardson 1933).

Perhaps the outstanding achievement of the age was the *History of Cirencester* by Kennett John Beecham (1848–1922) published in 1887. Although from more recent excavation we now know some of the details to be awry, for example his suppositions relating to Cirencester's early church, the book provides a succinct account of the more important late nineteenth-century discoveries in the town, particularly south of Lewis Lane where major construction was underway for the first time since the Roman period. Beecham also included accurate and unique detail about the medieval history and archaeology of Cirencester, full of perceptive criticism (see his comments on Kip's engravings at the beginning of Chapter 12) and descriptions of the late nineteenth-century institutions and public buildings. Addenda to the book were published in the *Wilts & Gloucestershire Standard* and a booklet of additional material came out in 1910 (and was included in the 1978 edition). Information collected between 1910 and 1921 was given to St Clair Baddeley for publication in his own history of the town (1924). It was Rudder who had commented earlier that 'poets are not always good historians' and this was the case with Baddeley.

The third great boost to local archaeology came with the founding of the town's two museums. The credit for this must go to two families, Earl Bathurst who erected a purpose-built museum on the Tetbury Road in 1856 to house the Dyer Street mosaics discovered in 1849 (Figure 4), and Wilfred and Helena Cripps who built an extension onto their private residence at Cripps Mead in Thomas Street to house their collections. The finds collected by John and Thomas Bravender, for example, were catalogued in 1881 and donated to the Bathurst Museum where a museum guide was regularly published to update the collections (Church 1867 to 1922). The building-up of the Cripps collection and the circumstances of archaeological discoveries in the town between 1890 and 1930, including excavations paid for by the Cripps' (the basilica excavations 1897–8, Union Workhouse excavations in 1922 directed by St Clair Baddeley), are faithfully

Figure 4
The Bathurst Museum, built in Tetbury Road by Earl Bathurst for the display of mosaics discovered in Dyer Street in 1849 (Artist unknown, Corinium Museum)

documented in a series of Helena Cripps' personal letters written to Professor F Haverfield at Oxford and now in the Ashmolean Library.

It is notable that both patrons, Cripps and Bathurst, had their loyal disciples, making observations in the town, buying artefacts and reporting back as drainage, gas and electricity were laid in the town for the first time. The most professional of these was F W Taylor, 'the little architect' as Helena Cripps refers to him and also the town surveyor, who assiduously noted his finds and observations and mapped them onto a town plan (see extract at the head of this Chapter) which was later accessioned into the Corinium Museum when the two collections of Bathurst and Cripps were united in 1938. The results from these various sources were gathered together in a series of articles by Haverfield, most notably 'Roman Cirencester' (1920).

His synthesis was far in advance of anything so far written on Roman Cirencester and recognised the importance of the military tombstones, enabling him to predict the later discovery of the fort.

This passion for artefact collecting was parallelled elsewhere in the study and indexing of documents. Roland Austin at the Gloucester Library produced a catalogue of its collections (1928), together with a series of accounts of antiquarian authors such as Atkyns and Rudder. Meanwhile, Frank Hockaday (1855–1924) sorted, numbered and catalogued the books and papers of the Gloucester Diocesan Records. The 'Hockaday Abstracts' as they are called, housed in the Gloucestershire County Library Local History Collection, are an important source in helping to trace original documentation for the Cirencester area.

A number of individuals made contributions towards Cirencester's archaeology between the Wars. Welbore St Clair Baddeley (1856–1946) wrote his *History of Cirencester* in 1924 and a large number of his notebooks are in the Local History Collection in Gloucester. These contain useful bibliographical lists amongst a mass of unreferenced jottings and diary accounts. Baddeley also excavated in Victoria Road and at the Union Workhouse (Baddeley 1922a) under the patronage of the Cripps family and drew attention to the rich medieval heritage of the town (Baddeley 1919b, 1923b). The Reverend E A Fuller published a number of articles concerning aspects of the medieval morphology of the town such as the castle (1890–1), its streets and hundreds (1874), the borough (1884–5) and medieval Cirencester in general (1932), while E C Sewell kept new archaeological discoveries in the public eye through a series of articles he wrote for the *Wilts & Gloucestershire Standard* (1922a and b, 1927) and the *Transactions of the Bristol and Gloucestershire Archaeological Society* (1935).

The first professionals

In 1938 the town's first publicly-owned museum was opened, the Corinium Museum, bringing together the Bathurst and Cripps collections of the previous 80 years under one roof for the first time. Following the end of World War II, Mrs Elsie Clifford, well known for her later work at Bagendon to the north of Cirencester, excavated a mosaic uncovered in Lock's Timber Yard in Victoria Road when a pit was dug to extend the sawmill in 1947 (Clifford 1946–8).

During the 1950s a number of important excavations were carried out in the town at sites such as Watermoor City Bank in 1952 (Rennie 1957), Dyer Court in 1957 (Webster 1959), and Parsonage Field in 1957–8 (Rennie 1971; K M Richardson 1962). These sites were limited in area and hastily executed and the need was keenly felt for a better planned response to the escalating demands from town-centre redevelopment. In this context, following the example set at Verulamium by Sheppard Frere and with the support of the Society of Antiquaries, the Cirencester Excavation Committee (CEC) was formed in 1958 under the guidance of Sir Ian Richmond. Local interest was encouraged, and considerable support was given by members of the Cirencester Archaeological & Historical Society founded in 1955. For the next twenty years excavations were continued annually in the town under the direction of a series of directors – John Wacher, David Brown, and Alan McWhirr. Large scale excavations were undertaken at the Verulamium Gate, Leaholme, Admiral's Walk in St Michael's Field, the Abbey Grounds, the Bath Gate Roman cemetery, the Police Station, the basilica, and the Beeches (Figure 5). During these years Cirencester became a training ground for many archaeologists and, most importantly, the information they retrieved was speedily analysed and published in interim form in the *Antiquaries Journal*, with a planned programme of post-excavation analysis and thematic publication of results in the series of monographs which deal with such topics as early Roman military history, the Roman cemeteries, and the houses of Roman Cirencester (Wacher and McWhirr 1982; McWhirr *et al* 1982; McWhirr 1986 respectively). Future titles in the series will cover the work in the amphitheatre, the town defences and the public and commercial centre of the Roman town around the *basilica* and *forum*, with medieval interest sustained in the publication of major excavations on the site of the Augustinian Abbey of St Mary.

When the larger teams were excavating, Richard Reece directed small-scale excavations at the Grammar School (Reece 1970b), Oakley Cottage in 1960 (Reece 1962b), on the Ashcroft/Mycalex site in 1961 (Reece 1976b), and in the Abbey Grounds (Reece 1962a), amongst others. Individual articles on geology (Torrens 1982), prehistory (Darvill 1978), the Anglo-Saxon legacy (P D C Brown 1976), and Victorian housing (Slater 1976b) reflect the diversity of interests capable of being sustained by the wealth and variety of information available for the town. Archaeological evidence continued to stimulate and inform national academic debate (Reece 1980). During the 1980s CEC excavations became less frequent and more modest in size although groundworks continued to be watched where money could be made available (Zeepvat 1979; Wilkinson 1982, 1984a and b, 1986, 1988a, b and c).

Changes in organisation were clearly required in order to sustain continuity in archaeological monitoring and overcome changes in funding. After

Figure 5
Open area excavation at The Beeches revealed a bath-suite within the winged-corridor house (Cirencester Excavation Committee)

some years preparation the Cotswold Archaeological Trust was formed in March 1989 to take over many of the responsibilities of the Excavation Committee. There are many differences between the two organisations which reflect changing times in urban archaeology. In the first place, the Trust maintains a permanent presence of trained archaeologists in the town throughout the year. Secondly, the Trust is a financially independent company which receives its money for a commercial service as well as through grant-aid. The type of work the Trust undertakes is therefore more varied than that of the Committee, generally smaller in scale, and often keyed-in with the development programmes which continue to pose a potential threat to archaeology in and around the town. Fieldwork, privately-funded desk-top assessments and evaluation excavation of sites in and around Cirencester have succeeded state-funded open-area research excavation in the town centre as archaeology has become more of a constraint in the planning process with legislative teeth to match.

Source types

In the course of the present Project a wide and varied selection of local, regional and national sources were consulted to supply data.

Ordnance Survey maps provided the cartographic foundation for base maps of the urban area at 1:500 scale, and the parishes at 1:2500. For the urban area, maps at 1:500 supplied by the Engineers Department of Cotswold District Council in August 1990 were rectified by copying and enlarging sections of the updated 1:2500 maps held by the Local Plans Section and by field-checking. A scale of 1:2500 was selected for the rural areas and there are 43 of these maps in total, numbered and stored according to Cotswold District Council parish area with an Ordnance Survey map reference concordance available for easy cross-reference.

The Cotswold District Council, as the local planning authority for most matters, provided access to the relevant planning constraints maps covering Conservation Areas, Tree Preservation Orders, footpaths, bridleways, Listed Buildings, Area of Outstanding Natural Beauty (AONB), Gas and Oil pipelines, Electricity lines, Sites of Special Scientific Interest, Cotswold Water Park, Landfill Sites, Mineral Consultation Areas, Nature Reserves, major hazard installations, areas owned by the National Trust, areas subject to Article 4 Directions, Historic Parks etc. All these constraints were transferred to a series of overlays at the standardised 1:500 scale for the urban area and 1:2500 for the rural area.

The Cirencester area was covered by the Geological Survey in 1933 and part of the area was re-surveyed in 1961. These maps have been copied at a scale of 1:25000.

The study area was walked and each field classified according to the land-use classification of the Gloucestershire Sites and Monuments Record, and mapped at 1:2500, 1:10000, and 1:25000. For the urban area, mapped at 1:500, the classes listed in the Schedule to the Town and Country Planning (Use Classes) Order 1987 (Statutory Instrument No. 764) provided a useful glossary, with additions to suit requirements within the study area.

The use of individual properties and fields is subject to change and may become outdated within 10 years but the broader blocks of land-use in the town and countryside are stable and will be useful in determining the survival and potential of known sites. Field-checking also served to determine the topography and aspect of recorded sites and identified monuments.

Within a broader framework, land classification, based on a survey of agricultural land throughout England and Wales (1945) was mapped at 1:25000 to provide an interesting comparison with current land-use.

Cirencester is not designated as an Area of Archaeological Importance (AAI) under the terms of the Ancient Monuments and Archaeological Areas Act 1979 but it does contain one Guardianship monument and a number of Scheduled Monuments. The Cotswold District Council have a map showing the notified and scheduled areas compiled in liaison with English Heritage and these were copied off at the standardised scales.

The Corinium Museum has a number of Accession Registers which date from 1890 onwards. These contain descriptions of the artefacts accessed into the collection with information about the donor, findspot, and date of accession. The registers record objects previously held by the two principal private museums in the town which were amalgamated in 1938 when the then Cirencester Urban District Council assumed responsibility for the care of the collections. The B and C Registers record objects from the Bathurst and Cripps' Museums respectively, with the A Catalogue designation being used for objects donated or acquired by the museum in the period 1938–1971. Since that date all objects have been accessed by year. For a brief period in the 1960s and early 1970s the Non-Roman Museum, administered by the Cirencester Archaeological and Historical Society and housed in a small annexe to the Roman displays in Park Street, adopted the G Catalogue prefix, and in some instances post-Roman objects from the Bathurst and Cripps' collections were given a second number within the G catalogue. More recently the museum has used identification sheets to record material brought into the museum reception for identification where this material remains in the possession of the owner.

In an attempt to record the possible dispersal of material away from the town, museums in the surrounding counties of Wiltshire, Warwickshire, Worcestershire, Oxfordshire, Buckinghamshire, Berkshire, Hampshire, Leicestershire, Devon, Avon and Somerset were contacted. Museums with objects relating to the study area – the Bristol City Museum & Art Gallery, the Ashmolean Museum, and the British Museum – reflect the interests of private collectors at the turn of the century, and the national quality of objects found in Cirencester, for example the Cupid bronze from The Leauses, recorded by Lysons and now in the Ashmolean Museum, and the occulist stamp in the British Museum which was once part of the Purnell Collection.

The Ashmolean Library, with its extensive collection of monographs and complete runs of the major British and European archaeological journals, was the principal source for secondary and published references, augmenting the local access to county and local material held in Cirencester and Gloucester. Included in the unpublished papers are the diaries, letters and private notes of Professor Haverfield. These contain important correspondence with Wilfred and Helena Cripps, Bravender, Baddeley, F W Taylor and Miss Taylor (of the Ashmolean), recording finds and observations made in the town at the turn of the century. The private papers of Sir Ian Richmond and Professor Rolleston were also examined.

Locally, the Bingham Library has extensive collections of local history material with original documents, correspondence, papers and maps. One invaluable source held by the Bingham Library was the corrected and amended map produced by K J Beecham to accompany his *History of Cirencester* (1887) recording archaeological features and sites observed in the course of extensive development of the Ashcroft and Watermoor areas of the town in the period 1870 to 1910.

The parish index held in the Society of Antiquaries' Library provided a useful check against missing sources. Original archive material deposited in the library includes a previously unprovenanced drawing by W H St John Hope 'measured and plotted on the spot 16th November 1897' (which is in fact of the excavations on the site of the *basilica*); drawings by Samuel Lysons of Cirencester and Siddington parish churches; and a collection of sketches of architectural stonework by George Fox, and of the military tombstones from Watermoor by C Lee.

The Bodleian Library as a copyright library holds the published material relevant to the study area. Three sources deposited in the Department of Western Manuscripts were invaluable in providing detail of early observations of the town. The most important of these was a manuscript by William Stukeley compiled during a visit to Cirencester in August 1721 containing drawings of the Norman Arch, known today as Spitalgate, and tombstones found at The Querns with the earliest dated plan of the town in which he pinpoints the site of the Roman temple in the Leauses Grounds, recorded by Atkyns and others as being first excavated in 1683. Two unpublished county histories by Abel Wantner (nd, died 1714) and Richard Parsons (nd, died *c*1711) serve as useful comparisons with Atkyns (1712) and Rudder (1779).

The aerial photographic collections held by the Royal Commission Air Photograph Library in Swindon and the Cambridge University Aerial Photographic Unit, were scanned and features of archaeological interest transcribed onto a 1:2500 scale Ordnance Survey map base. In total 800 photographs were consulted at these two locations, augmented by a small number of photographs from private collections.

The Gloucestershire Record Office houses the bulk of the primary documentation consulted, as well as a range of published literature for the county. The majority of the cartographic evidence for the study area is to be found there and comprises tithe, inclosure, estate and parish surveys.

All the county record offices in the country were contacted. All replied and those that responded with new information were Dorset, Wiltshire, Norfolk, Northamptonshire, Somerset, Northumberland, Oxford, Leicestershire, Hereford & Worcester, Berkshire, Nottinghamshire and Lincolnshire. With the exception of Lincolnshire the documents held in many instances consisted of single references in deeds, wills, or grants of property. Lincolnshire Record Office in contrast contains the Nelthorpe family deposit of papers with numerous references to property in Cirencester, Baunton and Siddington.

The Sites and Monuments Record (SMR) for the county, housed in the Planning Department of the County Council in Gloucester, includes information relating to county property and excavations in the study area. Records of sites within the parish of Cirencester were downloaded using the Superfile package and printouts obtained. For the remaining parishes a manual transcription of specific key fields was made from site files in Gloucester. The SMR provided a cross-check for references within the National Excavation Index, the National Monuments Record, and Ordnance Survey Record Cards.

A cellar survey of all properties in Cirencester was undertaken during May and June 1991. Over 220 cellars were visited and measured by Trust staff, and absence or presence noted for more than 600 properties. Notes were also made on any surviving archaeological or architectural features. The location and extent of cellarage in the town, where it could be established, was then plotted on 1:500 overlays.

At the same time every household in the town centre was leafleted with information about the project, with articles in the local press to enhance and explain the purpose and intent of the project. Trust staff then collected information on a standardised questionnaire form. A great deal of useful information was forthcoming in this way including photographs, plans and personal recollections of archaeological excavations, former buildings, and characters from the town's past.

An Archaeological Roadshow was held in the Corinium Museum in June 1991. It provided a public forum for artefact identification with over 50 people attending between 11am and 4pm, bringing with them artefacts and curiosities for identification and recording. Site record sheets were filled out as new sites were identified.

4. BACKGROUND DATA

'It is noble champaign country, the residence of many of the nobility and gentry, and abounds in verdant plains, downs, corn-fields, parks, woods and little vallies, well supply'd with springs and rivulets, and enjoys a fine healthy air, which . . . has been thought too thin and cold for persons of very tender and delicate constitutions.'

Samuel Rudder, *A new history of Gloucestershire* (1779)

In this Chapter attention is directed towards the physical facets of the landscape and general environment which represent the backdrop against which past human communities lived and worked.

The Study Area

The Study Area is a roughly square-shaped block of land amounting to some 46 square kilometres and incorporating the civil parishes of Cirencester, Baunton, Preston and Siddington. The town of Cirencester lies at its centre and covers some 10% of the area. Smaller nucleated settlements occur at Baunton, Preston, Siddington and Stratton.

Topography

Cirencester, the 'Capital of the Cotswolds', lies in south-east Gloucestershire towards the southern end of the Cotswold Hills on the eastern side of the dip slope. This is an area characterised by wide rolling hills, open country and steep-sided dry valleys (Figure 6).

Earlier this century there was much debate on the definition and extent of the Cotswold Hills (S S Buckman 1895, 1903). The criteria used are not worthy of close scrutiny; it is sufficient to observe that to the south-east of Cirencester is the open, hedge-divided, flat-land of the upper Thames Valley, while to the north and west is the drystone wall country of limestone uplands.

The maximum height OD within the study area is 185m in Oakley Wood, the minimum height OD is 92m at the southern-most tip of Siddington parish. In general, the terrain is gentle, with extensive views from local eminences.

Geology and archaeological deposits

The more important geological formations in the area have been discussed in detail by Torrens (1982). The evidence, much of it antiquarian in style, is drawn from railway cuttings, wells, water boreholes and quarries.

The earliest rocks are those of the Inferior Oolite which outcrop infrequently at the base of valleys such as the Churn (Figure 7). The majority of Inferior Oolite in the study area belongs to the Upper division and is defined by lithological units called the Upper Trigonia Grit overlain by the Clypeus Grit. In hand specimen the Upper Trigonia Grit is a coarse limestone with large broken fossils, typically bivalves, while the Clypeus Grit is more oolitic with marl interleavings and abundant echinoids and brachiopods.

The Inferior Oolite is overlain by a blue clay called Fuller's Earth, used in the past as a cleansing agent. Being impermeable, exposures are usually indicated by the spring line. This clay is capped by a distinctive oyster bed called the *acuminata* beds and a series of coarse shelly limestones (Arkell and Donovan 1952; Channon 1951).

The overlying beds are those of the distinctive White Limestone formation. As with the Fuller's Earth, the railway cuttings between Cirencester and Chedworth provide the standard sequence. Ammonites, gastropods, corals and brachiopods are abundant. Fossil reptilian eggs were recovered from one section in the Hare Bushes Quarry (J Buckman 1860a). The best known unit is 'Dagham Stone', sometimes called Daglingworth Stone, which is a curiously perforated stone riddled with burrow systems and popular in nineteenth-century rustic architecture in Cirencester.

The Forest Marbles lie above the White Limestone formation. Their separation from the Kemble Beds of the Great Oolite beneath is much debated (Harker 1890a). The series varies greatly in lithic structure and comprises sands, clays and limestones. The

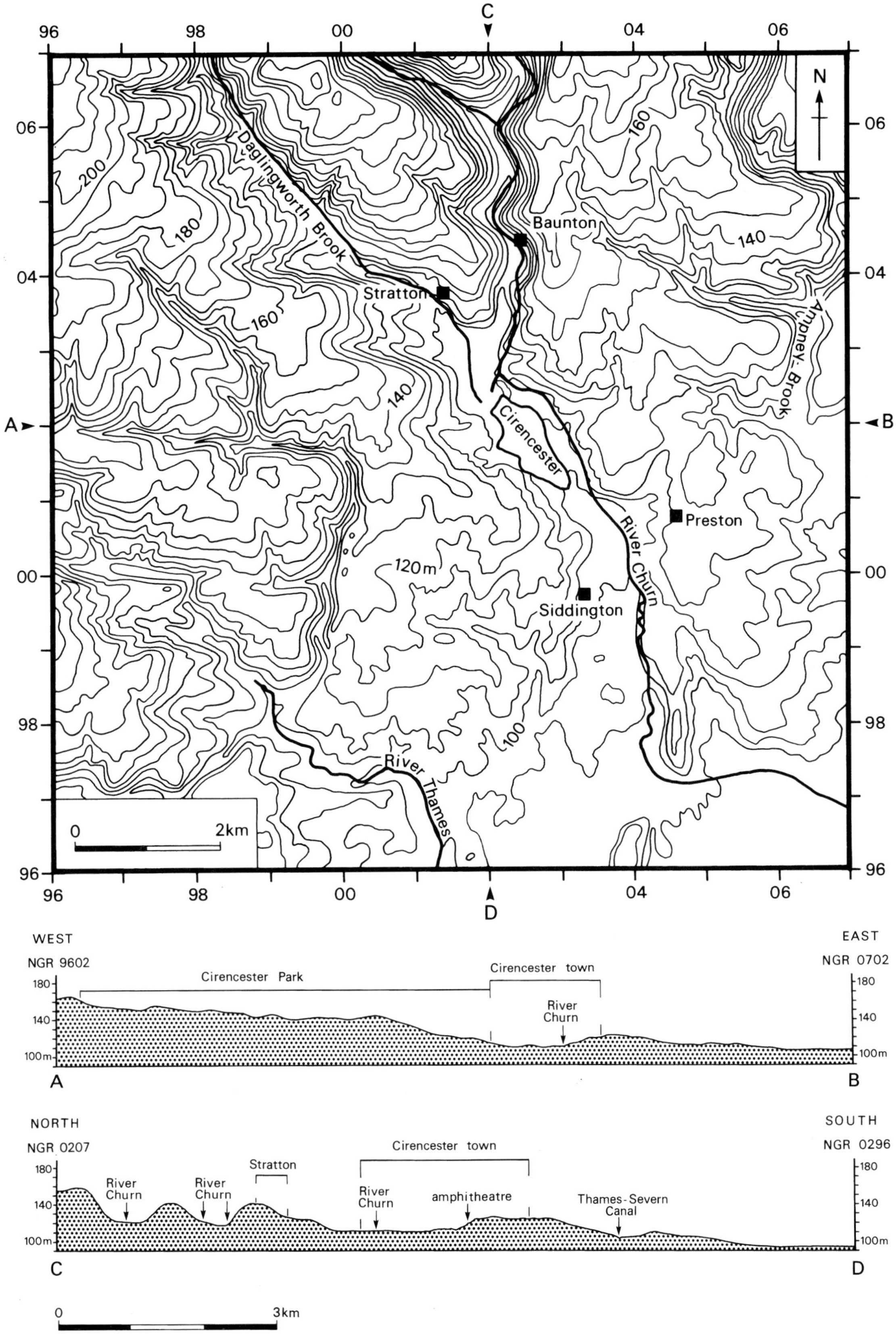

Figure 6
Topography of the surrounding area, with sections showing the location of Cirencester

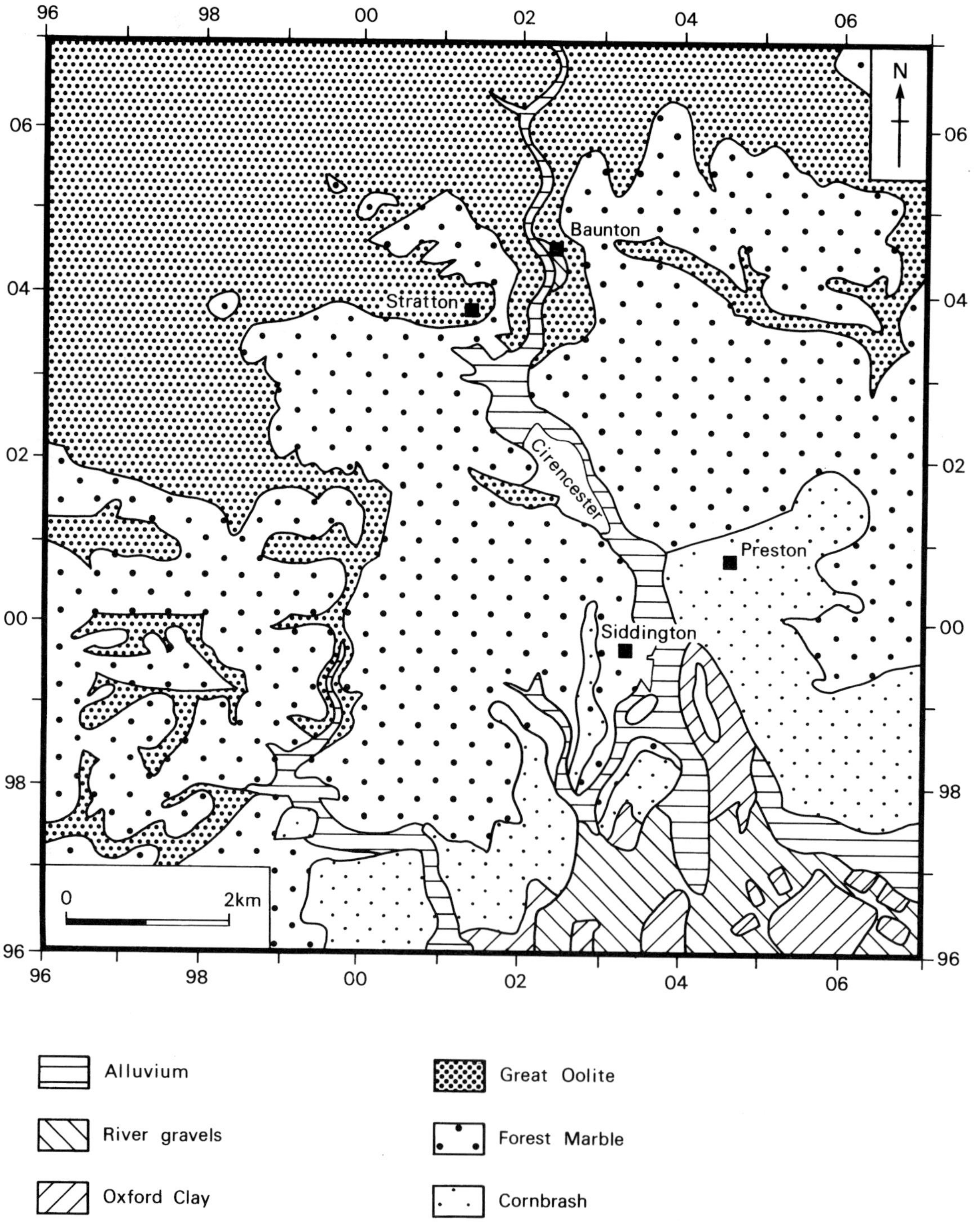

Figure 7
Simplified geological map of the surrounding area

Lewis Lane borehole (L Richardson 1924a) suggested that the formation consists mainly of clay in the immediate vicinity of Cirencester.

Above the Forest Marbles are the ammonite-rich beds of the Cornbrash (Chidlaw and Campbell 1988). The Upper Cornbrash also contains brachiopods including one named after its type locality in Siddington (*Microthyridina Siddingtonesis*). Being a hard limestone this has been quarried for road metalling.

The Kellaways Beds are a sequence of decalcified sands with interbedded sandstones, yielding plant material as well as ammonites. The underlying Kellaways clay and overlying Oxford Clay have been worked for bricks locally (Harker 1886, 184).

The overlying Quaternary gravels are of most interest to the archaeologist. Being well-drained they provide some of the best evidence for aerial photographs and thus a high density of recorded sites. The calcareous gravels of the River Churn are terraces up to 9.14m thick which have been abandoned by the river as it has changed its course and responded to sea-level changes during the Pleistocene period.

Within the town any information on the nature of sub-soils is derived from archaeological excavation, watching briefs, water borings and engineering borehole data. Coverage across the town is patchy and has never been systematically collated but there is sufficient detail to show that archaeological deposits are cut into, or have built up on top of these Quaternary gravels. Except in areas of gravel digging the old turf line of 0.20m of brown clay often survives (R Reece pers comm). Deposits vary in depth depending upon the location of gravel quarries and the height of the former terraces but, generally, since the Roman period the town has risen by up to three metres and infilled the former valley so that the modern town now lies on the flat. This effect has been masked by post-medieval and modern landscape changes just outside the Roman town wall such as earth-moving for the canal, railway and, most recently, the bypass.

Outside the town centre there is almost no information on sub-soil character and depth except where excavation has taken place.

Building stone and quarries

The Cotswolds are well known for the aesthetic and structural qualities of the local Jurassic limestone and

Figure 8
Quarry working of Oolitic Limestone at Stratton, pre-1900 (Corinium Museum)

after the sixteenth century a distinctive style of vernacular architecture developed as timber buildings were refaced or rebuilt. In the villages and towns this gives a misleading though comforting impression of antiquity and stability in the landscape.

There is nothing near Cirencester to match the famous Cotswold quarries of Taynton or Chipping Norton but there are a number of minor post-medieval and modern quarries in the study area (Figure 8). These include the quarry on the Stroud-Cirencester road (from which the Agricultural College was built) and the quarries off the Fosse Way at Hare Bushes and off Chesterton Lane which supplied many buildings, stone walls, and road metallings in the town and countryside throughout the post-medieval period. Not all such quarries provided fine freestone. The composition of the Cotswold limestones varies greatly and some shallow surface quarries produce a fissile limestone which breaks into tabular plates ideal for roofing slates.

Earlier Roman stone quarries are known in The Querns area and excavations have shown that gravel was extracted from areas within the Roman town. More recently gravel was extracted near Cirencester at The Barton.

There was a brickworks taking clays from the Forest Marble at Stratton and Rudder (1779) mentions a quarry for 'plodding coal' at Stratton and the discovery of coal during well digging at Siddington St Peter.

Hydrology and water supply

The study area lies within the hydrological network of the Upper Thames Valley. The source of the river Thames is 5km south-west of Cirencester. The River Churn flows roughly north to south through the study area before joining the Thames at Cricklade. Springs occur locally at outcrops of the Great Oolite/Fuller's Earth clay beds and from wells in the Forest Marble. Particularly deep wells 'in excess of 100ft were sunk at the Royal Agricultural College in 1857' (J Buckman 1858), and at Further Barton and the Bacon Factory, Chesterton Lane (Harker 1891).

Before the turn of the century many houses in Cirencester had their own private wells sunk into the underlying gravel. Rudder (1779) remarks, 'The water is sufficiently pure and pleasant, rising in a fine gravel, about fourteen or fifteen feet below the surface, and almost every house has a pump'. Particularly deep wells are recorded at Oakley Villas and The Beeches (Harker 1891).

Concern over health in the town after 1870 led to much discussion on the possibilities of obtaining a reliable supply of pure water. A borehole was put down at Barton Mill but the site of the former Bowly's Brewery (1832–1882), later for a short time Cripps' Brewery (during 1882), was preferred and acquired by the Cirencester Water Works Company (Taunton 1886). A further borehole was sunk in 1882 and deepened in 1890 (Harker 1891) but proved insufficient to satisfy need and another borehole had to be sunk in 1904 (Hibbert and Richardson 1913).

Between 1900 and 1935 a number of boreholes completed for the Cirencester Urban District Council were observed and published by Lindsall Richardson, who was also responsible for the Geological Survey Memoir on the Cirencester area (L Richardson 1924a for the Lewis Lane borehole; 1925 for additional information on the Lewis Lane borehole; 1933 for Geological Survey Memoir; 1936–8 for Baunton borehole). These boreholes provided much information about the nature and depth of Quaternary gravel deposits directly beneath the town centre as well as successfully providing a new water source for the pumping station on Lewis Lane.

The changing hydrology of the town is poorly understood and much debated. Leland and Rudder, amongst others, believed that the River Churn once flowed through the city and at present it is thought that the river was diverted during the Roman period so that it ran outside the town walls (but see Holbrook Chapter 8, this volume). Since there is some equivocal evidence for flooding in the town at this period this diversion may have been for practical as much as any defensive or status reasons. The situation is confused further by later changes made by the Augustinian Abbey and by landscaping carried out in the Abbey Grounds. No systematic survey of the town's watercourses has so far been undertaken.

Despite the potential for locating waterlogged archaeological deposits in buried valleys there has, until recently, been no evidence for well preserved organic material such as wood or leather in Cirencester. However, recent evaluation work in the City Bank area of the town has demonstrated that such deposits do exist, certainly in the southern half of the town close to the meandering line of the 'inner' River Churn where the water table may be perched (Gerrard 1989c; R King 1990e). Elsewhere it seems that the Quaternary gravels drain the soils quickly and so accelerate decay.

Land classification

Based on the Agricultural Land Classification Map of 1945, and excluding those areas classified as of non-agricultural use (town, village centres and woodland), the study area can be graded as level 3 predominantly, with small areas of grades 1 and 2 to the south and east of the town. The valley of the river Churn provides a corridor of grade 4 land, suitable only for grass or forage crops (Figure 9).

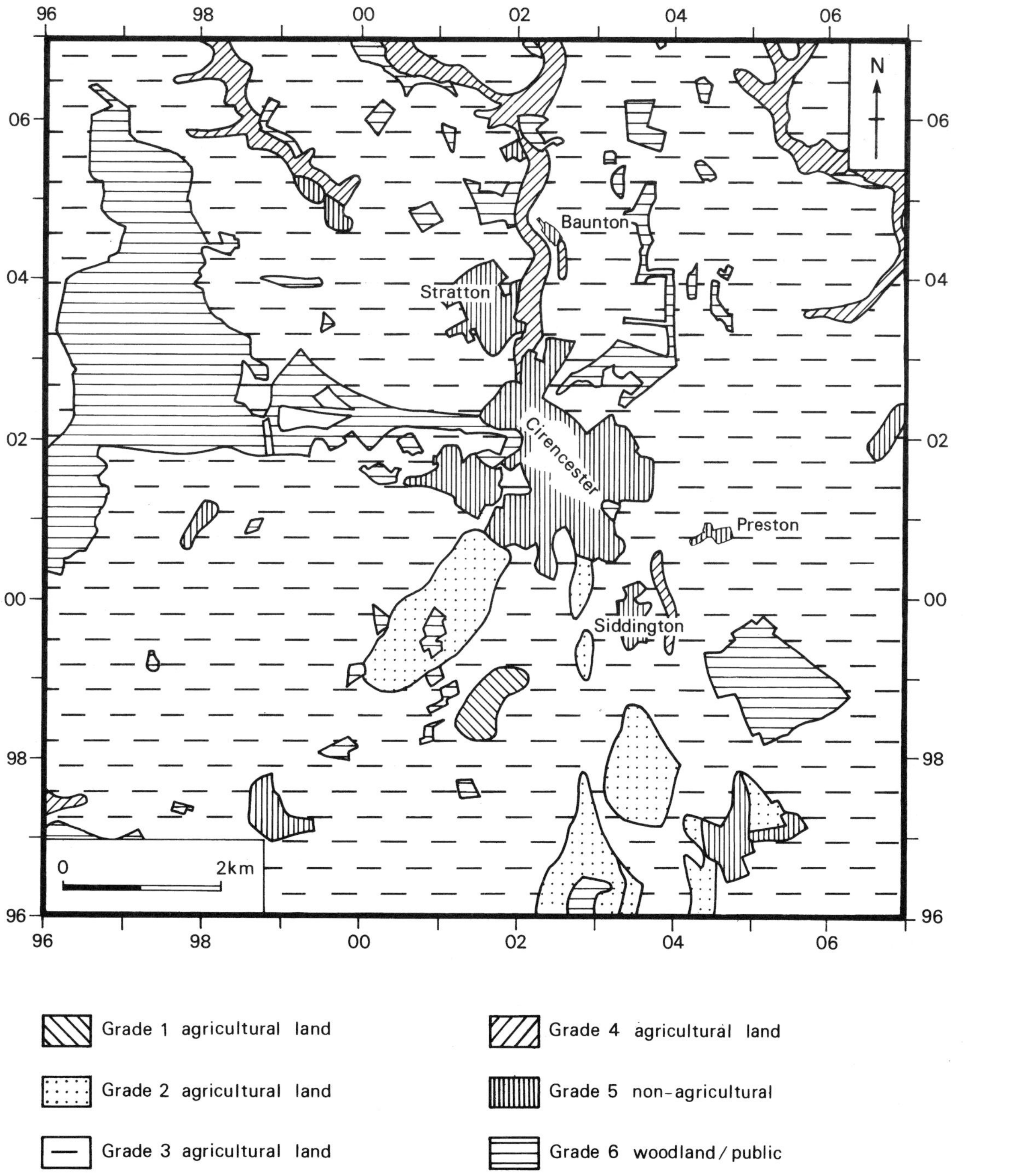

Figure 9
Simplified land classification for 1945 of the surrounding area

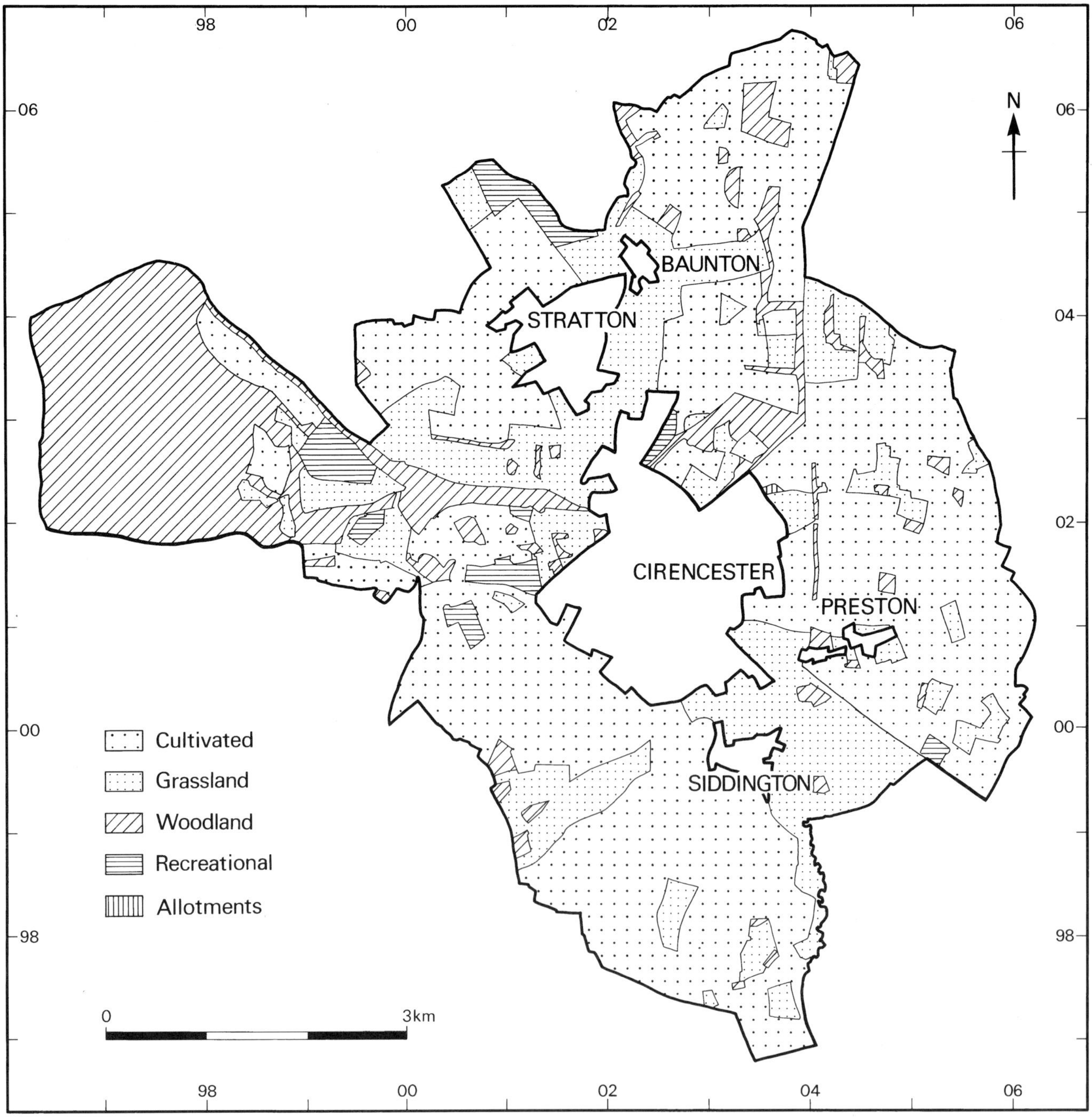

Figure 10
Land-use recorded in 1990 within the Study Area

Land-use

For the rural area field visits in the autumn of 1990 established a record of land-use based on the glossary used by the Gloucestershire Sites and Monuments Record. This information was mapped at 1:2500 and 1:10000. As an interesting comparison with the land classification map these categories were simplified to cultivated land, woodland, and grassland (Figure 10).

The land-use is predominantly arable, partitioned by dry stone walls and populated with dispersed farms and settlements of local stone. To the west of the town areas of wood pasture in Cirencester Park have hampered the recognition of archaeological monuments.

Within the urban area, and mapped at 1:500, a land-use glossary was developed based on the *Town and Country Planning (Use Classes) Order 1987* (Statutory Instrument No 764). Premises, particularly those within the town centre with multi-function, were classified as at ground-floor.

Palaeoenvironment

To date there has been no general palaeo-environmental work undertaken which might give indications of the nature and extent of vegetation cover in the past. It has often been assumed that peat deposits of the kind needed for such work are absent from the area and that buried soils and localised micro-environments provide the best hope for obtaining this kind of data (Bell 1984, 89). Recent finds have challenged this assumption. At Latton, just to the south of the present study area extensive peat deposits have been located adjacent to what appears to be a broadly contemporary area of Iron Age and Romano-British settlement (Johnson 1990a). Within the present Study Area peat deposits tentatively assigned to the 1st millennium AD have been identified in the valley of the River Churn near Baunton (CAT 1990). Locating and investigating peat deposits as an adjunct to work on archaeological sites and documentary accounts must now be a research priority in order to test this outline (see APPENDIX C).

Traditional models suggest that the Cotswolds were more wooded before the eleventh century, certainly in the north of the county (Grundy 1936). The uplands around Cirencester may have been open and largely treeless since the Roman period at least, and this was to the benefit of medieval wool merchants after the fourteenth century. With the exception of parks of wood-pasture, like that created to the west of Cirencester, landscape changes began again after the eighteenth century when the Cotswolds, already the home of gentry, were 'improved' by planting in landscape parks and tree belts (Bravender 1850).

Designations

Parts of the Study Area as well as a number of individual buildings and monuments within it are subject to a range of designations as Table 1 shows. Details of the effect of each designation and the implications for management are dealt with in Part IV.

Designation	Cirencester	Baunton	Preston	Siddington
Area-based				
AONB	P	P		
Conservation Areas	P	P	P	
[where P = present/in part]				
Site-based				
Grade 1 Listed Building	3			
Grade 2* Listed Buildings	33	1	1	2
Grade 2 Listed Buildings	330	16	17	15
Scheduled Monuments	6			2
Guardianship Monuments	1			
Registered Parks and Gardens	1			

TABLE 1 Range of designations within the Study Area

5. ARCHAEOLOGICAL DATA

'The electric light has been laid in Gloucester Street and rather faint traces of the Roman road have been found, but I do not think any fresh light has been thrown on the direction.'

Mrs Helena Cripps in a letter to F W Haverfield, 17th September 1912

'. . . the historical study of single sites has been undertaken by scholars in no country . . . in England, at least, this generally means a long search. . . In short, he must make himself a thorough nuisance to the townspeople, before he attains real results.'

F W Haverfield (1920)

Site records

As described in Chapter 2, the basic units developed for the classification and recording of archaeological data are termed 'sites'. Such sites are defined here as events or actions by which data is recognised, observed or transmitted. No assumptions are made about the validity or accuracy of the data recorded. Cripps' observations on Gloucester Street above would qualify as a site in just the same way as a modern open area excavation of the kind represented on Figure 5. It is, however, fair to say that some site-types are inherently likely to yield more reliable data than others, although, ultimately, the validity of a site can only be judged by reference to related data. Although a piece of data is never intrinsically wrong, its integrity and reliability may thus be called into question. In practice, however, careful examination of the sources suggest that it is often the interpretations associated with data in a given source that are questionable, the basic data is usually sound and can make a significant contribution to the database as constructed here.

APPENDIX A provides a listing of the main fields used in compiling site records. It includes a number of fields which are compatible with the Gloucestershire County SMR. Full details of the controlling glossaries (county and local) are available in the Project Archive and in the operational manuals used for the maintenance of the record. Slightly amended versions of the site record have been adopted by RCHME in connection with the definition of a national standard for urban databases (RCHME 1993b).

In compiling the Site Records a wide range of sources were consulted, as documented in Chapter 3. Data obtained from those sources was then classified according to a suite of site types, the main features of which are described below. It should be emphasised, however, that source may not correspond exactly with site. In some cases a single source may give rise to the definition of a whole series of sites of different types, while in other cases a single site may be reflected in a number of sources, as for example an excavation which is reported in the local paper, in summary form in the archaeological literature, as an interim report, as a final published report, and as an entry in the museum accession register when the finds and archive are deposited for long-term curation.

ANTIQUARIAN EXCAVATION (AE): All excavations before 1940 fall into this site type. With exceptions, the standard of recording is less objective and consistent than might be expected for a modern excavation. Absolute dating techniques and environmental sampling are generally absent whilst artefact collection policies may be idiosyncratic. The 1940 cut-off point is arbitrary. The area mapped will correspond to the trenches dug and therefore several small areas adjacent to each other will typically receive the same site number.

MODERN EXCAVATION (ME): All rescue or research excavations carried out after 1940 fall into this site type. There will be a huge range in the scale of work involved for different projects and in the quality of results achieved. Specifically excluded from this type are evaluation excavations which are intended for assessment purposes only. The area mapped will correspond to the trenches dug and therefore several small areas adjacent to each other will typically receive the same site number.

EVALUATION EXCAVATION (EE): Evaluation (field evaluation in the terminology of PPG16) is defined as one of the five stages in the archaeological management cycle as it can be applied in urban areas (Darvill and Gerrard 1990). The purpose of this exercise is to determine the thickness, depth and depositional history of archaeological deposits, characterise the main stratigraphic phases present and assess the survival of evidence. The factual report provides support for a full planning application, a Scheduled Monument Consent application, or an Environmental Statement. Generally, the volume of deposits excavated is less than 5% of the total and contexts present are sampled rather than fully excavated. It is a matter for professional judgement as to whether or not each individual evaluation hole receives a separate site number or whether (as more usually) the whole evaluation event is seen as a single site.

WATCHING BRIEF (WB): An archaeological watching brief involves the presence of a qualified archaeologist whilst groundworks are taking place. Observations are made on any archaeological deposits uncovered by construction workers on the site, where safety restrictions permit. The area covered by the watching brief will receive a single number rather than separate numbers for each observation within the groundworks.

RECORDED OBSERVATION (RO): This type of observation, usually made by a professional archaeologist or a well-informed amateur, occurs under a wide variety of circumstances. For example, archaeological deposits may be recorded when unmonitored groundworks are underway (eg when drain or telephone cables are being laid) or occur when archaeologists are asked to advise after archaeological remains have already come to light. Usually visible remains of obvious archaeological significance such as a skeleton or walling alert the observer initially and more detailed observation may follow (eg a watching brief). Each observation will be separately numbered.

INTERPRETATION AND MAPPING UNIT (IMU): These are the areas covered by an aerial photograph containing archaeological information (see Whimster 1989). The units will vary in size but their borders will generally correspond to features which are readily appreciable on the ground, for example roads, tracks, and field boundaries. The archaeological interpretation which can be made from information within the IMU will be written onto the site record form. This in turn may lead to the identification of separately numbered monuments and components. Each collection of aerial photographs is a single source and the photographs within it, either singly or in combination, or even in combination with photos from other collections, go to make up the IMU. A good analogy is that the aerial photographic collection is a book (both are defined as sources) with many pages represented by the individual photographs.

SYSTEMATIC SURFACE COLLECTION UNIT (SSCU): These are the areas covered by either line-walking or timed grid-walking, or both when the exercise is nested. Findspots can generally be plotted to within 50 metres and comparisons made between recovery rates within each standardised sample unit. Artefacts of all periods are generally collected unless the project has specialised research aims. The units mapped will vary in size but the edges of the units will correspond generally to visible features or to the Ordnance Survey national grid. Where several discontinuous areas are walked during a large-scale project (eg a bypass corridor) thought must be given to numbering each area walked separately.

UNSYSTEMATIC SURFACE COLLECTION UNIT (USCU): These are the areas covered by teams or individuals collecting artefacts on the ploughsoil surface. Findspots are not so rigorously recorded during collection (typically to the nearest field) and not all artefacts will be recovered. Finds recognition may be variable. The non-systematic nature of the work means that comparisons cannot easily be made between sample units. Some metal-detecting runs will fit into this site type.

RECORDED STRAY FIND (RSF): These are finds made by individuals where the circumstances of discovery are known and the findspot can be pinpointed to within 100 square metres or better. Recorded stray finds might be made when digging the garden or walking the dog and usually by persons with some archaeological awareness. Finds and findspots are generally made known to a local unit or museum.

UNRECORDED STRAY FIND (USF): These are finds made by individuals where the findspot and usually also the circumstances of recovery are unknown. Many antiquarian finds from the nineteenth century are unrecorded stray finds.

GEOPHYSICAL SURVEY UNIT (GSU): The unit refers to the area covered by the survey and should be taken to include all forms of remote sensing. As with the Interpretation and Mapping Units mentioned above the important area to be mapped is that covered by the survey and not the interpreted features within the wider survey area. The area chosen for survey may lie away from visible features but will usually be orientated along the Ordnance Survey National Grid lines.

TOPOGRAPHICAL SURVEY UNIT (TSU): Topographical survey includes all levels of survey from basic sketch plotting through to full interpretative EDM plots. As with Geophysical Survey Units the area chosen for survey may lie away from visible features but will usually be keyed in with the Ordnance Survey National Grid lines.

PLACE-NAME EVIDENCE (PN): Both place-names and street names can help to provide archaeological data. This site type was not fully explored during the Project.

VISIBLE FEATURE (VF): Visible features include all features, components and monuments which exist in such a form as to be apparent to the naked eye in the field. The following visible forms are recognised: buildings, standing structures, earthworks, subterranean and submerged sites. A visible site can be the subject of a Topographical Survey or Standing Structure Record.

CARTOGRAPHIC DEPICTION (CD): All information which can be transcribed from pre-existing maps fits into this type. This will include street-names, place-names, field-names, archaeological finds, earthwork depictions, land-use, geological maps and buildings of historical importance, amongst others. The mapping of cartographic depictions can be best understood by example. In the case of a town map of Cirencester, this is a single source which can be broken down into units of varying size ranging from the area of a former building outline to a single archaeological findspot. The elected size of the units mapped is not important and units can overlap.

INDIRECT RECORD (IR): These are reported secondary accounts, either oral or written. For example, many popular accounts of Cirencester's archaeology are derived from pre-existing archaeological literature. If there is nothing original in the account and it consists only of re-ordered data it must be categorised as an indirect record. Likewise, some diaries and letters recount the actions and words of others without confirmation. These too are indirect records.

DOCUMENTARY RECORD UNIT (DRU): Primary historical documents can contain useful archaeological information either concerning a general area or a particular findspot. The unit size to be mapped remains flexible and can produce several overlapping DRUs. In Cirencester, the number of DRUs for any one monument is surprisingly limited and this reflects the lack of historical analysis of documentary records in recent years. As this bias is corrected more rigorous criteria for inclusion may be considered for this site type.

PICTORIAL UNIT (PU): This is a general term for all works of art or pictorial recording, such as photography, drawing, etc. Architects' elevations fit into this site type.

STANDING STRUCTURE RECORD (SSR): Archaeological principles can be applied to the study of standing buildings when the fabric of a structure comes under critical and/or interpretative analysis.

Site analysis

Site recognition can vary from an antiquarian excavation in the eighteenth century to the interpretation and mapping units of twentieth century aerial photographs. Up to August 1991 there were 3473 sites recorded for the four parishes in the study area (including the urban area of Cirencester). These derive from 1210 different sources. The most numerous single source was fieldwork in connection with the Cirencester Urban Assessment Project which provided a total of 1150 additional sites, followed by the 1875 Ordnance Survey mapping of the town with 167 sites. Of the total number of sites, 3335 are in Cirencester parish, 34 in Baunton, 55 in Siddington, and 49 in Preston.

Accumulation and chronological changes

Table 2 shows the frequency and percentages of different types of site recognition. Indirect records make up 38% of all the site types represented in the study area. A total of 1002 new indirect records (IR, 75%) were collected during the course of the CUA project. Pictorial units (PU) such as photographs and illustrations make up 12%, and cartographic depictions (CD) 10%. In purely statistical terms only a small proportion of the archaeological observations were made during archaeological intervention. There are only 93 modern excavations (ME) which is less than 3% of the total number of sites. These figures are reflected in the bar-chart in Figure 11.

Figure 12 shows the total number of sites made by

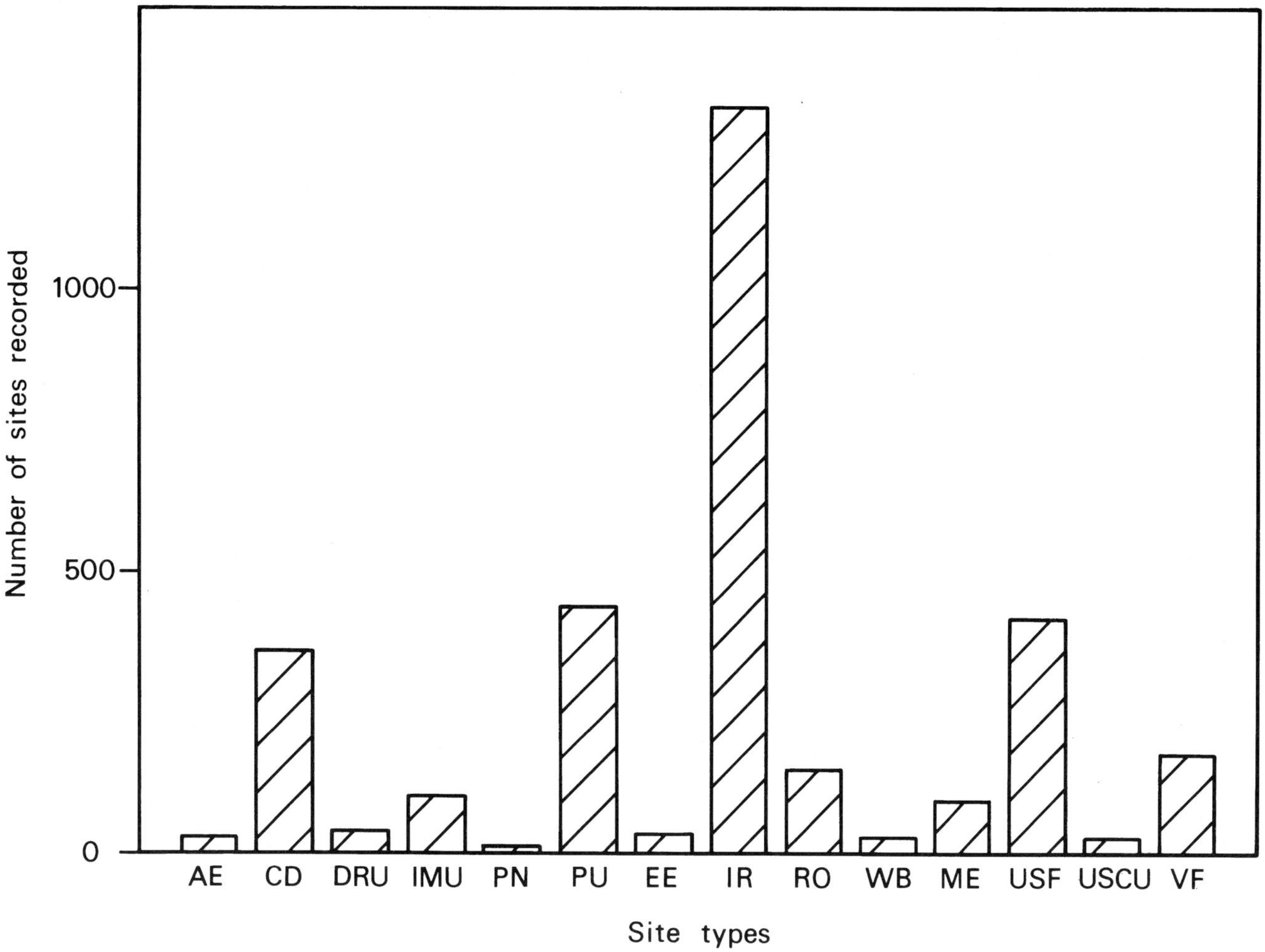

Figure 11
Bar-chart showing the number of sites recorded by type

SITE TYPE	Number	Percentage
Antiquarian excavations	29	00.83
Cartographic depictions	363	10.67
Documentary units	40	01.15
Evaluation excavations	34	00.97
Interpretation and mapping units	102	02.93
Indirect records	1326	38.18
Modern excavations	93	02.67
Place-names	11	00.31
Pictorial units	441	12.69
Recorded stray finds	236	06.79
Recorded observations	147	04.23
Unrecorded stray finds	418	12.03
Unsystematic surface collections	27	00.77
Visible features	177	05.09
Watching briefs	29	00.83
TOTALS	3473	100.00

TABLE 2 Frequency of site types within the Study Area

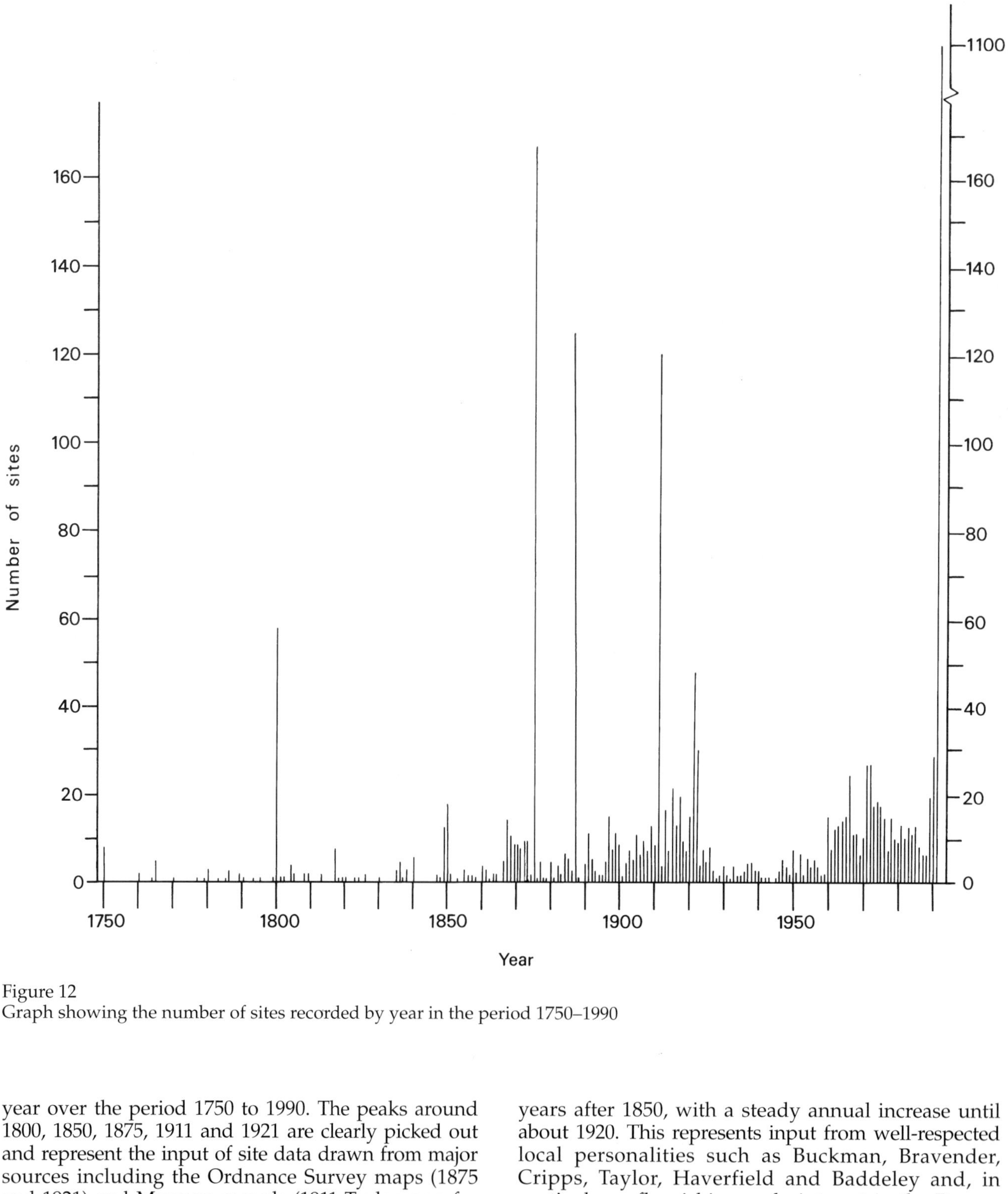

Figure 12
Graph showing the number of sites recorded by year in the period 1750–1990

year over the period 1750 to 1990. The peaks around 1800, 1850, 1875, 1911 and 1921 are clearly picked out and represent the input of site data drawn from major sources including the Ordnance Survey maps (1875 and 1921) and Museum records (1911 Taylor map for the Cripps Museum). Much of the early data is derived from the work of Rudder in 1800 and Beecham in 1887. Aside from these very obvious peaks there is a notable increase in the number of observations made in the years after 1850, with a steady annual increase until about 1920. This represents input from well-respected local personalities such as Buckman, Bravender, Cripps, Taylor, Haverfield and Baddeley and, in particular, a flourishing early interest in the Roman archaeology in Cirencester which was being exposed during the laying of sewers and water pipes and in the Victorian building developments in the southern half of the town.

Between 1920 and 1960 the number of observations dropped away dramatically, most notably between the First and Second World Wars. Following the formation of the Cirencester Excavation Committee in 1958 the number of sites recorded each year begins to rise again and this continues into the 1990s under the auspices of the Cotswold Archaeological Trust.

Individual types of site show patterns of incidence which differ slightly from the general trends. Pictorial units, for example, show a steady stream of examples from 1779 onwards, increasing in the early part of this century as photography begins to make a contribution. Excavations, both AE and ME, show a steady gradient of increasing numbers from about 1875 until a peak in the mid-1960s when the work of the Cirencester Excavation Committee was at its height. Since 1980 there has been a drop in the level of government funding for this kind of archaeology and the inclination has been towards small-scale evaluations as a part of the planning process coupled with the preservation of archaeological sites *in situ* rather than through excavation. The number of excavations fell as the number of recorded observations (RO) increased (Figure 13). Between 1974 and 1988 there were more watching briefs (WB).

Recorded stray finds (RSF) from the study area occur with increasing frequency after 1850. By 1875, 45 recorded observations (RO) were being made a year, whereas 100 years previously the average was only two observations a year. Some 100 years later, in 1975, there were over 90 a year. This reflects increasing antiquarian interest in the late nineteenth century and the influence of professional archaeological interest in the town since about 1960. Different patterning is clear from documentary record units (DRU) which also peak in the late nineteenth century but remain low throughout the twentieth century, reflecting a lack of modern detailed documentary research for the town.

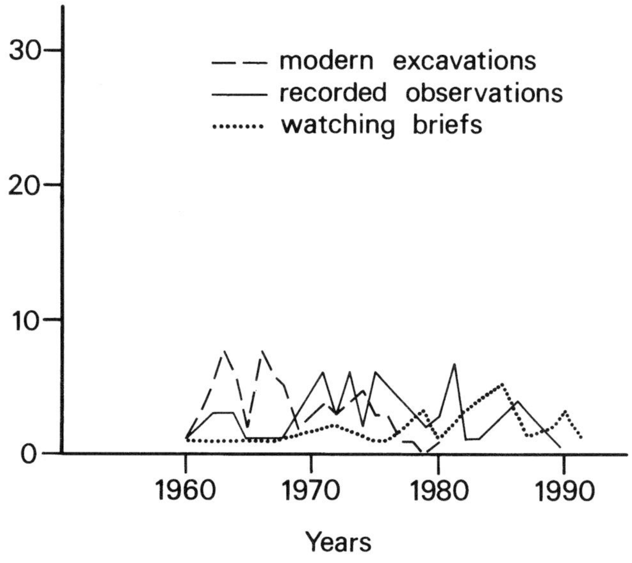

Figure 13
Graph showing the number of modern excavations, recorded observations, and watching briefs in the period 1960–1990

Unrecorded stray finds (USF) have remained roughly constant in number since the mid eighteenth century. Surprisingly, increased agricultural production and urban development since the Second World War has only led to a negligible increase in the number of finds, or perhaps more accurately, the number of known but imprecisely recorded stray finds.

Taking all these patterns into account the most important overall trend is in the quality of the data. Set-piece open-area excavations and evaluations inevitably yield higher quality data (whether positive or negative) than watching briefs and the recovery of unrecorded stray finds. Thus although the number of sites relating to some site-types is small their implications are considerable. Between 1958 and 1976, there were some 37 major open-area excavations (Wacher and McWhirr 1982, fig 2). These ranged from the extensive work at Beeches Road (*c*2900 sq m), the Bath Gate Cemetery (*c*7500 sq m), and Admiral's Walk (*c*4000 sq m) down to cuttings through the defences and the recording of land in advance of small-scale development. Overall, the total area examined by excavation within the Roman town of Cirencester is estimated at *c*64000 sq m, which amounts to approximately 6.6% of the walled town.

This is not to say that stray finds are unimportant, they are not. For example, the inscribed plinth from a Jupiter column, found in 1892 in the garden of a house known as The Firs in Victoria Road, provides important information about the status of the town in the fourth century. Smaller finds such as coins, burials, and even pottery and tile are important indicators of the nature and extent of different kinds of activities within and around the town for all periods.

One other factor which can be discerned from the trends in the accumulation of site records is the lamentable lack of a full-time professional archaeological presence in the town during periods of rapid growth and expansion such as during the early 1960s and 1970s, and to a lesser extent during the early 1980s. Opportunities for boosting site numbers were undeniably lost during this period.

Future trends

In future the number of evaluations looks likely to increase and the number of large-scale urban excavations will remain low. Stray finds will continue to be found while the numbers of pictorial units will rise. It is to be hoped that the lack of documentary research, particularly for the medieval and early post-medieval periods in Cirencester, is soon corrected. It is recognised that site-types such as those derived from place-name evidence, cartographic depictions and documentary records have not yet been fully exploited.

PART III
DATA INTERPRETATION AND RECORD DEVELOPMENT

6. MONUMENTS AND DEPOSITS

'Grismond's Tower by the Chapel of St Cecilia, where King Arthur was crowned, lies west of Cirencester Town, which anciently was called the City of Sparrows.'

William of Worcester, *Itinerarium*, *c*1479, translated from the Latin

'It is certain, therefore, that the Romans, the Saxons, and the Normans, all of them in turn, had respected this barrow; though quite probably the last-mentioned people may have used it as a commanding salient, or barbican, in relation to the neighbouring castle.'

Welbore St Clair Baddeley, *History of Cirencester* (1924)

With the full range of archaeological data to hand the process of recognising individual monuments and deposits can be undertaken. This is the first main level of interpretation and demands just as much if not more skill and professional judgement as the definition of sites; wide experience with the recognition of field monuments and the excavation of archaeological deposits is the best training for this aspect of the work. Fanciful interpretation of the kind reflected in the first citation at the head of the Chapter is all too easy and whilst obvious when taken to extremes it is much more difficult to spot interpretations based on wishful thinking rather than solid data as the second citation shows.

This short Chapter looks briefly at the processes of data interpretation and then considers the scale of the interpreted resource in the Study Area.

Monuments

In practice, the recognition of monuments involves carefully trawling through the available data looking for links and connections that allow examples of defined monument classes to be picked out, or at least the constitution of sets of data which may be classifiable as a monument of some kind. In some cases a single site record will be enough to define a monument, or at least provide the basis of recognition which can be supported by the inclusion of data from other sites deemed to be relevant. Equally, a distinctive monument may be visible through recognition of some small element of it (eg a bath-house); the recognition of such a monument carries with it the implication that the aerial extent of the monument conforms more or less to that of other examples of the class. In this way it may be possible to develop predictions about adjacent areas.

The whole process of recognising monuments is one of interpretation and should be seen not simply as a point-in-time operation but a continuing activity involving different areas of specialism. Things which may not initially seem relevant may be seen to connect together when looked at another way. Familiarity with the data is important here. APPENDIX A provides a listing of the main fields used on the monuments record. There is also a worked example of how a range of site records from the central area of Cirencester come together to allow the recognition of the *basilica*. In viewing the example it is relevant to note that while some of the sites can be seen to relate only to what is here interpreted as the *basilica* (eg 53622 which is itself an interpretative statement) there are others (eg 50022) which also yield data relevant to other monuments with precede or succeed the *basilica* (eg the first-century fort).

A total of 538 single monuments have been identified to date within the Study Area. Of the total, some 111 monuments of medieval and earlier date (pre-1540) are in rural areas and 151 are within the urban area. This bias towards monument recognition in the urban area should be expected (Table 3) and reflects the higher density of Roman and medieval monuments in the town as well as the intensity of construction work and ground investigation in Cirencester itself.

Considering only rural monuments within the four parishes it is clear that Cirencester outweighs the contribution of the other three parishes, containing 54% (105 monuments) of all rural monuments (Table 4). If the urban area is included

Date	Rural	Urban	Total
undated	3		3
prehistoric	37		37
pre-urban	3	3	
Roman	39	82	121
early medieval	12	3	15
medieval	20	63	83
	111	151	262
post-medieval	81	195	276
TOTALS	192	346	538

TABLE 3 Frequency of monuments in urban and rural situations

then the parish of Cirencester contains over 83% of all the monuments recognised within the Study Area. This demonstrates the exceptional pulling power of an urban area like Cirencester and the large number of functionally related monuments which lie all around the town such as cemeteries, quarries, and roads. In fact, the rural parish of Cirencester contains 60 recognised monuments (pre-1540) whereas the rural parish of Siddington contains only 25, Preston 15, and Baunton 11.

If the post-medieval monuments are also taken into account then a further 45 monuments could be added to the rural total for Cirencester and 195 monuments to the total for the urban area. This shows clearly a bias towards the recognition of monuments from the later periods and highlights the fact that there are noticeably fewer single monuments for the earlier periods. This may be because urban functions have become increasingly more specialised in the post-medieval and modern periods with fine functional differences shown between structurally similar monuments (eg between 'public house' and 'inn', or 'post office' and 'exchange'). It must also be due to the greater appreciation of monument differentiation in the documented periods and for times closer to our own experience. In addition, the later monuments will tend to conceal the early urban deposits so that their detection and interpretation will inevitably be made more difficult.

The present list of single monuments in the Study Area will undoubtedly change as new monuments are recognised and the interpretation of site data improves. The presence of some monuments has been predicted from the best available data and it is anticipated that further work, particularly within the urban area, will clarify the identity and extent of some possible monuments. Inevitably there are a number of substantial components of what could be recognised as major monuments if only some more distinctive elements were present. Examples include the recorded existence of rooms and even parts of buildings with mosaic floors and upstanding walls which could be components of anything from the Roman baths to a small private dwelling. Only further data, or perhaps in a few cases some additional analysis of existing data, will resolve such questions.

The monuments already recorded do allow some insights into the distribution and extent of activities at various times in the past. Figure 15 shows the distribution of prehistoric monuments (BC to AD 43) within the Study Area as a whole, including that area later covered by the urban area of Cirencester (Figure 16). Figures 18, 26, 31, 33, 34, 41, 43 and 49 show the distribution of monuments of Roman (AD 43 to AD 450), early medieval (AD 450 to AD 1066), medieval (AD 1066 to AD 1540), and post-medieval (AD 1540 to the present day) date in the Study Area. The date ranges reflect the main phases of the prehistoric and historic calendar in use by the Department of the Environment (1983) and English Heritage (Darvill 1988a).

	Cirencester	Baunton	Preston	Siddington
undated	3			
prehistoric	8	6	9	14
Roman	32	4	1	2
early medieval	7		1	4
medieval	10	1	4	5
	60	11	15	25
post-medieval	45	7	11	18
TOTALS	105	18	26	43
PERCENTAGE	54	11	13	22%

TABLE 4 Frequency of rural monuments by parish

Accumulated deposits

In the case of accumulated deposits the key to recognition involves the identification of interconnecting stratigraphy which is archaeological in origin and which reflects the successive execution of a series of activities in the past. This is necessary to distinguish such deposits from naturally forming sediments and layers such as may occur through geological or geomorphological processes. Also, the process of monument identification can be criticised for being overly mechanistic and can lead to an unwelcome over-emphasis on static historic episodes (eg the Roman period), failing to address the dynamics of change. Consideration of accumulated deposits can be helpful here.

No separate record was made for accumulated deposits as they cannot easily be described in the way that monuments can. The way forward in terms of their future recording is seen in terms of three-dimensional computer generated deposit models (see Carver 1987a for methods of determining deposit quality, and Ove Arup 1991 for York application). These would be based on the data obtained from relevant sites, especially spatial data from excavations and related events. In Cirencester, in spite of a long history of archaeological investigation, there is insufficient available data to provide a reliable model. As indicated in Chapter 2, accumulated deposits can, however, be evaluated in another way in terms of their importance by reference to the non-statutory criteria. This is explored further with reference to specific forms in Chapters 8–11 and with reference to the whole town in Chapter 12.

Before we begin with more detailed discussion of archaeological monuments it is of some interest to consider the changing urban form of Cirencester more generally.

Figure 14 contrasts the formal regularity of a large Roman town against the smaller amorphous medieval town crowded towards the northern half of the former Roman wall circuit. A massive Roman stone form replaced with a more dispersed organic landscape.

During the medieval period attenuated suburbs developed to the north astride the road to Gloucester. Elsewhere, the former Roman town wall has always been substantial enough to impede development across it. The gateways have continued to funnel traffic into the town and clues to the line of walls are still to be seen in the modern ring road system and the web of cul-de-sacs which end at the bank and ditches.

The medieval pattern of land ownership has also had an important impact on modern land-use and the shift of balance from religious to secular authority following the Dissolution is still legible in the urban form. The area of the medieval Abbey precinct which shows clearly as a tongue of empty space to the north of the market place remained as private land until quite recently when it was turned into a public park. Likewise the probable site of the medieval motte and bailey on the western side of the town later became the private estate of Cirencester Park. The ditch or moat for the castle was filled in and turned into a thoroughfare. This gives the modern plan of Cirencester the odd appearance of an apple with two chunks taken out of the western and eastern sides. A process of leapfrogging has taken place here in which the built-up area has expanded leaving gaps and zones of varied land-use behind it.

After relatively slow urban growth in the post-Conquest period, at least in terms of built-up space, in the nineteenth century there came huge leaps in area and scale. Urban infill and the endless subdivision of properties and houses suddenly ended as Cirencester's population was released into the southern part of the town. The full extent of the Roman town was finally reached again after 1875 with planned suburbs and working class housing drawn towards new industries and lines of communication such as the canal and railways on the peripheries of the town. The extra-mural zone also attracted urban uses in need of plenty of space such as cattle markets, garden allotments and water reservoirs and those activities particularly deemed hazardous to health like hospitals and planned urban cemeteries. Infilling continues today with the trend towards large-scale, low density buildings such as supermarkets at the edge of the historic core.

In 1990 nothing much of the Roman town is visible but the urban area remains where it began and in its present form is just the most recent in many phases of major and minor adjustment. Proof of that continuity is in the interlocking of different periods of our past within the same urban context. The site of the Roman *basilica* marked out in the street alongside nineteenth-century residential housing and public parks, looks northwards through the barren townscape of the mis-named Forum car-park to the medieval tower of the parish church of St John the Baptist.

For the archaeologist, all these expansions and contractions in the urban area have had a clear influence on the distribution of accumulated deposits and siting of monuments. As we shall see in more detail in subsequent Chapters, thicker deposits tend to be concentrated where several urban areas are superimposed, whereas single phases of post-medieval accumulation lie on the outskirts of the modern town.

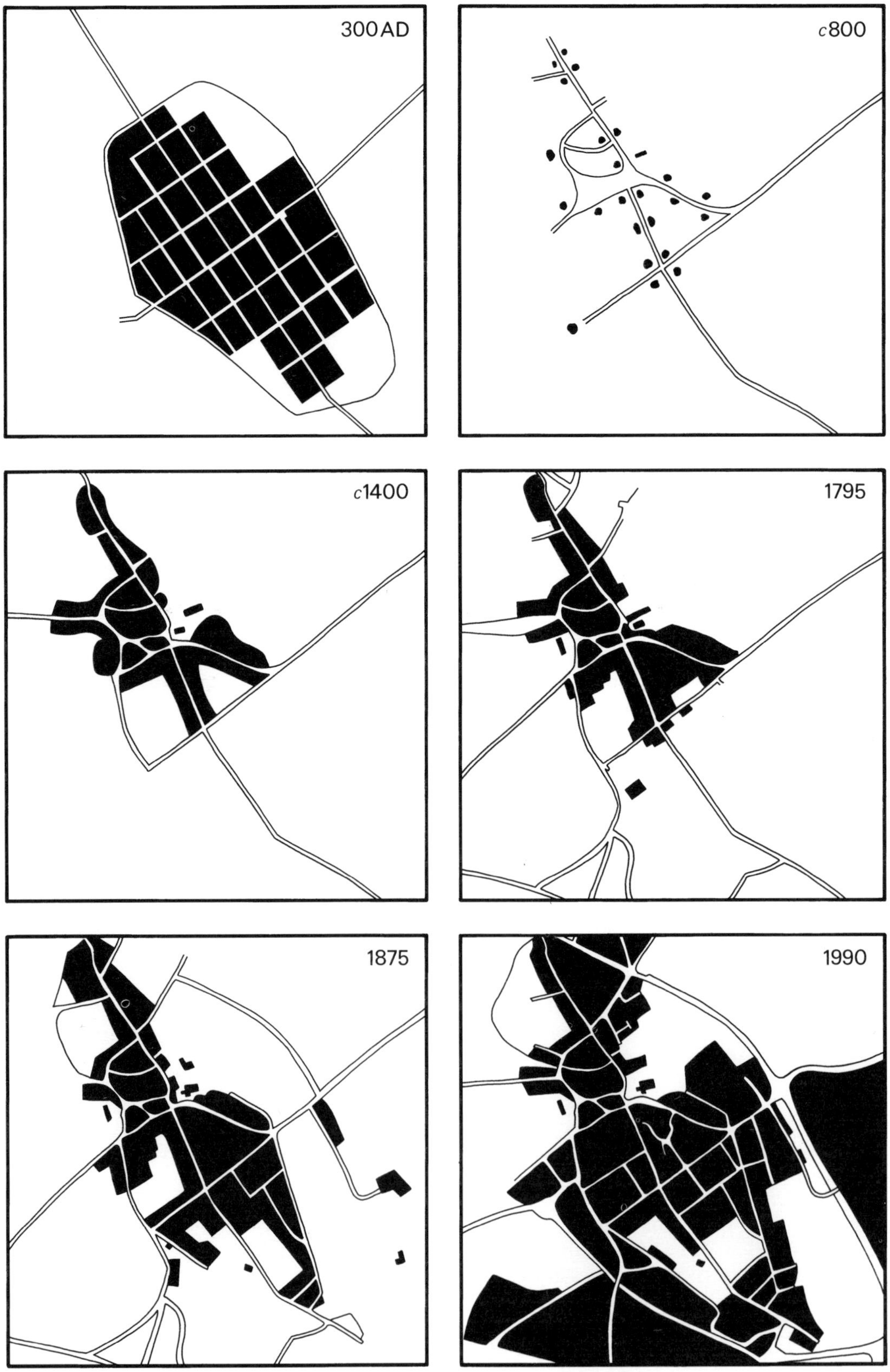

Figure 14
The changing morphology of Cirencester from the Roman period to the present day. The 'built-up' areas are shaded

7. THE CIRENCESTER AREA IN THE PREHISTORIC AND EARLY ROMAN PERIODS

by Timothy Darvill and Neil Holbrook

'Maybe the 'Ala Indiana' occupied for a while some smallish fort. But its ramparts, like those of most early forts, would perhaps have been of earth not stone; its internal structures, too, may well have been wooden, not stone built: but whatever there was has now been built over and effaced in many centuries. If the whole area could be minutely excavated, a skilful excavator might, no doubt, detect the fort by its ditch, or even by the post-holes of its wooden buildings.'

Francis Haverfield writing prophetically in 1920

This Chapter considers both monuments and deposits relating to the prehistoric and early Roman periods, a wide span of time from about 10,000 BC down to the end of the first century AD (Figure 15). During this time there was no urban area where Cirencester now stands and the whole Study Area was essentially rural in its character. The approach adopted is largely chronological, starting with the earliest periods. For many antiquarians and archaeologists concerned with the Roman and later remains of Cirencester the prehistoric period in the area was of no interest. The data which relate to this period are often difficult to handle, and when work is undertaken in a non-scientific manner it is often incapable of all but the most rudimentary reinterpretation.

Palaeolithic and Mesolithic (to 4000 BC)

There is no Palaeolithic material recorded from the Study Area, although abundant stray finds of flint tools have been recorded from gravel terrace deposits in the upper Thames Valley to the south-east of the present area of interest (Saville 1984, 59–79; Darvill 1987a, 20).

The earliest monument known in the study area dates from the Mesolithic period, about 7000 BC, and may tentatively be interpreted as the campsite of a hunter-gatherer community. Such monuments are notoriously difficult to define as they are recognised almost exclusively from worked flint preserved in the topsoil. The example in the study area (54032) is from Preston parish and is defined on the basis of data from a systematic surface collection programme carried out as part of the assessment of the possible route of the Cirencester Bypass (CAT 1991). Over 40 Mesolithic sites are known in Gloucestershire, although relatively few are known on the Cotswold dip-slope. The nearest comparable example is at Bagendon in the Churn Valley (Clifford 1961).

Neolithic (4000–2000 BC)

The Cotswolds are famous for their well-preserved Neolithic funerary monuments, mainly long barrows (Crawford 1925; Darvill 1982a), although contemporary settlements are less well represented.

A long barrow at the Querns on the south-western fringe of Cirencester has variously been claimed as authentic, seemingly on very little firm data (54079; see O'Neil and Grinsell 1960, 75). As a visible feature there is an earthwork 54.8m long by 15.2m wide and up to 0.9m high. Viewed from the north-east in particular this earthwork looks very like a small Cotswold-type long barrow. An antiquarian excavation in *c*1820 brought to light human remains. 'I remember opening it by making transverse cuts through it: but I have no recollection of finding any skeletons in condition capable of measurement' (see Buckman and Newmarch 1850, 12). Data from other sites in the vicinity reveals that the mound lies within an area of Roman quarrying, adjacent to a Roman road, and on the edge of a known Roman cemetery. There is nothing in the data available which substantiates the view that there is a long barrow at the Querns. The earthwork is a Scheduled Ancient Monument, and in the absence of further substantiating evidence it is probably advisable to question its authenticity as a distinct prehistoric monument.

Possible settlements of Neolithic and early Bronze Age date are represented in the Study Area by flint scatters. One of the most marked is north of Hare Bushes where data from a series of sites combine to allow some insights into the possible monument. A concentration of flintwork was noted by Sydney Coombes in 1972 (Coombes Archive, deposited in Corinium Museum). Subsequently, systematic surface collection in 1991 on an adjacent field brought to light further flintwork including a leaf-shaped arrowhead (CAT 1991). It seems likely that the two scatters are contiguous and represent a single monument. Evaluation excavations within the corridor for the proposed Cirencester Bypass failed to reveal sub-surface features; the focus of the monument presumably therefore lies outside the area sampled or has been ploughed away. A second flint scatter was located by systematic surface collection south of Exhibition Barn, Baunton. Subsequent evaluation excavation revealed sub-surface features including pits, but no firm dating evidence was found.

Away from the proposed bypass line, unsystematic surface collection by Coombes in the early 1970s located a number of activity areas, some of which are possibly settlements and trackways (54017, 54023, 54029, 54031). The nature and extent of these possible monuments requires critical review and should be seen more as a prompt for further research rather than definitively-recognised monuments.

That other Neolithic monuments await definition is supported by the number of stray finds of Neolithic material from the Study Area. One such find, a stone adze of Group VI (Great Langdale) rock was found during an excavation at The Beeches in a Roman context. This implement may have been found locally or imported from elsewhere (McWhirr 1986, 124–6), although the former is more likely. Part of a second axe of Cornish Greenstone (Group I) was found during fieldwalking for the proposed Bypass in Preston.

Bronze Age (2000–700 BC)

Evidence of Bronze Age activity within the study area is largely confined to funerary monuments. There is an upstanding mound (54003) to the south of Wellhill Plantation, possibly a bowl barrow, with a diameter of 30m and standing 1.5m high. Beecham (1887, 256) mentions a 'bell-shaped' tumulus (54437) in Stratton Field, 'penetrated in 1868 and found to contain a skeleton'. This monument is unlocated and there are no other known records of the excavation. It is possible, but incapable of proof, that this may refer to the Wellhill barrow. The three other upstanding barrows (Tar Barrows and Grismond's Mount) have traditionally been considered to be Roman, although an earlier date cannot be entirely excluded (see below). Two round barrows previously marked by the OS in the area of the Querns have been considered as doubtful by O'Neil and Grinsell (1960, Cirencester 4, 5); they are most probably mounds of quarry waste or perhaps related to the medieval gallows. In addition to the upstanding barrows a number of ring-ditches, one of the most distinctive components of a number of classes of round barrow but also components of other classes of quite different monuments, have been recorded by aerial photography (Darvill and Grinsell 1989). Ring ditches occur both singly (54137) or in larger groups (54153, 54541 and 54542).

A concentration of ring ditches and other cropmarks is known to the east of Preston village covering an area of approximately 20ha. Five ring ditches are recorded (54133–6, 54040) one of double penannular form. Evaluation trenching of the latter found an internal pit but unfortunately no dating evidence. Adjacent to the ring ditches is a ditched enclosure of probable sub-rectangular form which was evaluated as part of the Bypass project; the upper fill of the ditch yielded sherds of mid-late Bronze Age pottery. Although further work is required to adequately define the plan of the monument, one possible interpretation is as a Neolithic long mortuary enclosure which preceded the construction of the barrow cemetery.

Less than 1km to the south-east of this barrow cemetery further ring ditches are known (54137 and others outside the Study Area), with a flint scatter of probable Neolithic/Bronze Age date in close proximity. One of the ring ditches (which lies immediately outside the Study Area) produced a sherd of an early Bronze Age collared urn.

The complex to the east of Preston is of some interest as it occupies a characteristic barrow setting (an area of locally high ground) at a location close to the interface between the Cotswold dip-slope and the Upper Thames valley. Of the 300 or so barrows and ring ditches recorded from Gloucestershire there is a bias in distribution towards the north Cotswolds and the gravel terraces of the Thames valley. The Preston cemetery is therefore of interest as it lies at the interface of two environmental zones, one of which, the South Cotswolds, is an area where such complexes are rarely encountered (CAT 1991, 121–7).

On the gravel terraces of Siddington a number of ring ditches are known (seven are listed by Darvill and Grinsell 1989, 94–5) and these form part of a much wider distribution of Bronze Age monuments in the Upper Thames valley in Wiltshire and Gloucestershire. Although none of the ring ditches in Siddington have been excavated, work in neighbouring parishes in advance of gravel extraction points to the complexity we might expect. Such work has also brought to light evidence of contemporary settlement. The recent work at Shorncote quarry (5 km south of Cirencester) serves as a suitable example: a late Neolithic/early Bronze Age U-shaped enclosure was found in proximity to several beaker graves and a small Deverel-Rimbury cremation cemetery. On an adjacent site a late Bronze Age settlement comprising round-houses and large pits has been excavated (Glass 1991; Gardiner 1993, 15–16).

Iron Age (700 BC–AD 50)

There is currently comparatively little evidence of early–middle Iron Age activity within the Cirencester area. Sample excavation of a series of enclosures on the higher ground to the east of the Roman town took place in 1974–6. The sites were known from cropmarks (RCHME 1976, 30(5)); the excavations found a ditched enclosure with an exterior pit which showed a sequence of at least three phases at the entrance. The pit produced a sherd of hand-made Iron Age pottery which probably predates the late Iron Age wheel-thrown wares found at Bagendon (Reece 1990, 9–25). There are a number of similar cropmark features visible on aerial photographs which might merit classification as later prehistoric monuments in the future as more information about them becomes available. For example immediately south of the Study Area on the gravel terraces of the Upper Thames a middle Iron Age site spreading over 2ha has recently been evaluated at Spratsgate Lane, Somerford Keynes (Wills 1990, 197; Parry 1991, 235).

In the late Iron Age period any discussion of the Cirencester region would be deficient without some reference to the complex at Bagendon which lies immediately north of the Study Area. A series of discontinuous banks and ditches (dykes) define an area of approximately 200ha which includes valley bottom and adjacent hillsides. Excavations in 1954–6 and 1980–1 have elucidated some details, although much remains to be learnt about the function and chronology of the site. The excavations produced evidence for a number of phases of industrial activity, including the manufacture of Dobunnic coinage. The latter, combined with the presence of imported ceramics and glass (and by inference therefore foodstuffs) mark Bagendon as a site of high status and it has commonly been included within the category of *oppida* (Trow 1990, 108–10).

The chronology of Bagendon remains an outstanding problem. Finds of Arretine and early Gaulish samian pottery (Dannell 1977) suggest occupation a decade or so before the Roman conquest. How long the site was occupied after the invasion is more difficult to determine, especially as only a minute portion of the interior has been investigated. Swan (1975) has attempted to push most of the excavated evidence into the post-conquest period, although further revision may be required in the light of recent research. The general dissimilarity between the coarse pottery from Bagendon and Cirencester suggests that occupation had largely ceased prior to the military occupation at Cirencester. Regarding the function of Bagendon there seems no doubt that it was an aristocratic centre of the Dobunni; and the apparent occupation in the years following the invasion suggests tacit Roman approval for the tribal leader (see Wacher 1975, 292–3 for a summary of various earlier theories). The establishment of a Roman fort at Cirencester need not necessarily mark a change in Roman attitude (p 55).

The presence of such a high status site would doubtless have exerted a major influence on the contemporary settlement pattern of the Study Area of this project. The Whiteway may have been a pre-Roman ridgeway track leading off the Cotswolds towards a crossing of the River Churn at the later site of Cirencester (see below). It is conceivable that there may have been pre-Roman activity at the crossing, although excavated evidence to date suggests that this is unlikely to have been on any scale on the site later occupied by the Roman town. The only possible evidence of pre-Roman features found in excavations is a circle of stake holes, 2.4m in diameter, which predates the Leaholme fort (Wacher and McWhirr 1982, 28) and just possibly a stake palisade found adjacent to the *Verulamium* Gate (unless this is Roman military; J S Wacher pers comm). Reece (1990, 39–40) also considered that one of the features excavated at Kingshill might date to the late Iron Age period, but this is not certain.

No sites on the gravels of Siddington can be conclusively assigned to the late Iron Age, although this is undoubtedly a factor of the lack of fieldwork. In a recent survey of gravel sites Fulford (1992) has noted how settlements which are established in the early-middle Iron Age do not appear to continue beyond the first century AD, or rarely the second century AD. Conversely settlements which show evidence of structural continuity through the Roman period appear to commence in the late Iron Age, ie the first century BC–mid first century AD. Fulford speculates that the evidence for the abandonment of certain rural settlements in the early Roman period might be related to population drift to the newly

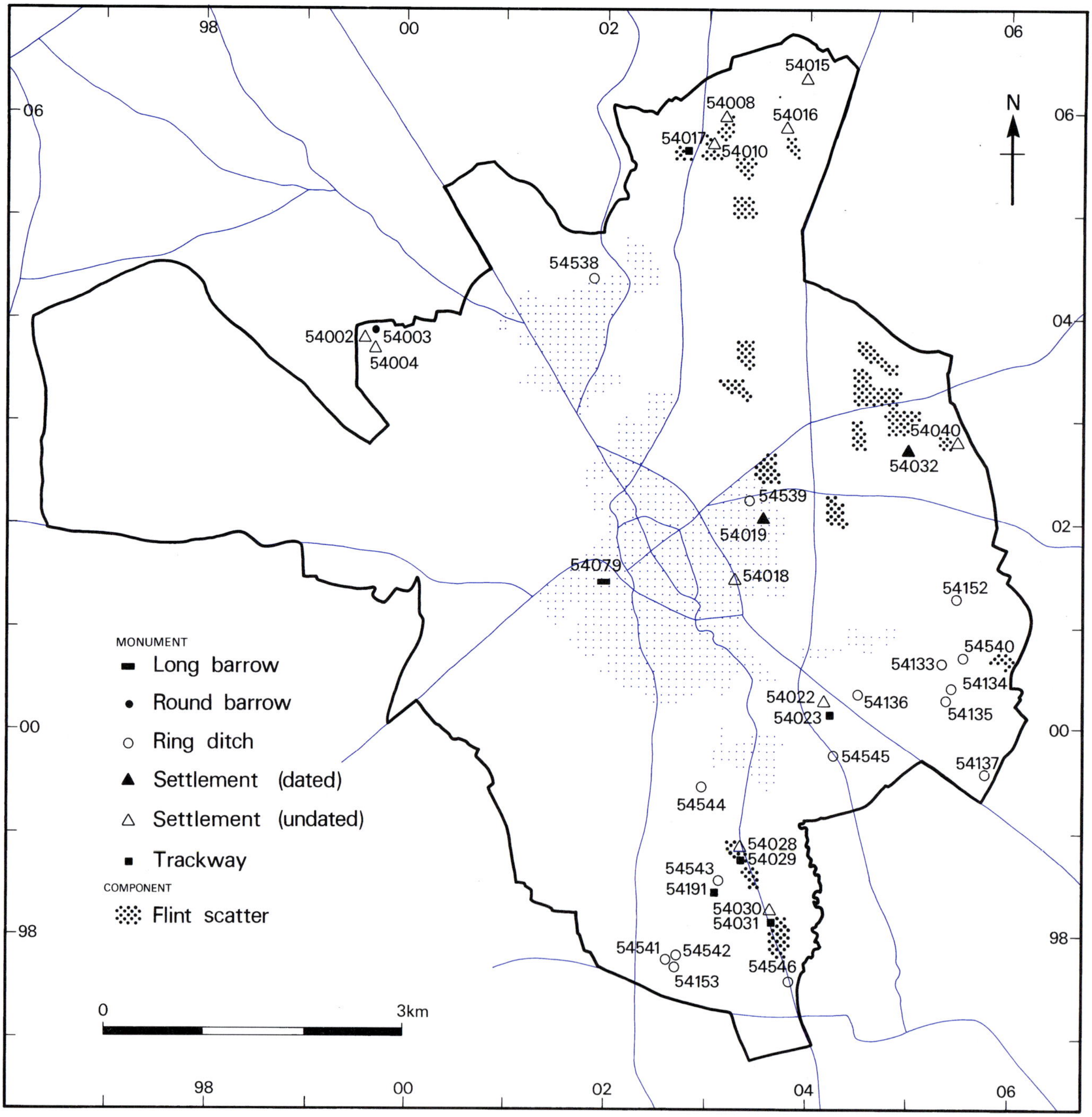

Figure 15
Prehistoric monuments in the Study Area

established towns and the imposition of Roman administration and taxes. At a local level the pattern seems to be represented in the excavations to the south of Siddington in Somerford Keynes, where the middle Iron Age Spratsgate Lane site appears to be abandoned, while at Cotswold Community a late Iron Age settlement with associated fieldsystems continued into the Roman period (Parry 1989; Wills 1990; Gardiner 1993, 15–16).

Pre-urban Roman (*c*AD 50–AD 100)

The main monuments examined in this section are the Roman road system and the evidence for Roman military occupation (Figure 16).

The road network

It is a commonly held view that the road network was established in southern Britain within a few years of the Conquest, although critical assessment shows that, in at least some cases, the earliest metalled surfaces detectable in excavation may date to some decades after the period of initial military activity. In the vicinity of Cirencester the following roads have been defined as monuments (see Figures 16 and 25):

Ermin Street: SE of Cirencester leading to Wanborough and Silchester (54292); NW of the town heading for Gloucester (Kingsholm) (54238)

Key to Figure 15:

54002	South of Wellhill Plantation	settlement (undated)
54003	South of Wellhill Plantation	round barrow
54004	South of Wellhill Plantation	settlement (undated)
54008	Baunton	settlement (undated)
54010	Baunton	settlement (undated)
54015	Baunton	settlement (undated)
54016	Baunton	settlement (undated)
54017	Baunton	trackway (prehistoric)
54018	Field at The Beeches	settlement (undated)
54019	Beeches Nursery Field	settlement (dated)
54022	East of Siddington House	settlement (undated)
54023	East of Siddington House	trackway (prehistoric)
54028	East of Ashton Road	settlement (undated)
54029	East of Ashton Road	trackway (prehistoric)
54030	Siddington	settlement (undated)
54031	Siddington	trackway (prehistoric)
54032	Preston	settlement
54040	Preston	settlement (undated)
54079	Long Barrow, The Querns	?long barrow
54133	Preston	ring ditch
54134	Preston	ring ditch
54135	Preston	ring ditch
54136	Preston	ring ditch
54137	Preston	ring ditch
54152	Preston	ring ditch
54153	Siddington	ring ditch
54191	West of Dryleaze Farm	trackway (prehistoric)
54538	Baunton	ring ditch
54539	Cirencester	ring ditch
54540	Preston	ring ditch
54541	Siddington	ring ditch
54542	Siddington	ring ditch
54543	Siddington	ring ditch
54544	Siddington	ring ditch
54545	Siddington	ring ditch
54546	Siddington	ring ditch
Not located:		
54437	Stratton Field	round barrow

Fosse Way: NE of Cirencester leading towards Bourton-on-the-Water and High Cross (54020); SW of Cirencester in the direction of Bath

Akeman Street: leading eastwards to Alchester and *Verulamium* (54452) and joining with the Fosse Way in the vicinity of the town

Kingshill Lane: apparently connecting the intersection of the Fosse Way/Akeman Street with Ermin Street (54021)

The Whiteway: leading northwards in the general direction of Andoversford/Wycomb (54143).

The absolute and relative chronology of these roads is a major research priority for the future as it may provide a telling insight into the early Roman occupation of Cirencester. There has been useful discussion of the problem (Wacher 1965, 99–101; Margary 1967, 146–50; Reece and Catling 1975, 3–6; Wacher and McWhirr 1982, 65–6) but fresh direct evidence is required to resolve outstanding problems.

By virtue of the incorporation of the Roman roads into the modern highway network opportunities for direct physical examination have been few. Field evaluation in advance of the proposed Cirencester Bypass led to trenching of the Fosse Way at Hare Bushes, although only the margin of the road was available for study as the remainder was overlain by post-medieval and modern surfaces. The Roman road proved to be built from local limestone rubble, and a flanking ditch might have served as a convenient source of roadstone. The ditch was filled in the second-third century. Some 4m beyond this quarry ditch lay a second shallow ditch which might have defined the limit of the area designated as road and thus in state control (CAT 1991, 129–30).

The status of the Whiteway as a Roman road requires closer examination, although a persuasive case can be made. Reece and Catling (1975, 3–5) stress its importance in the early Roman period, considering it to be a pre-Roman ridgeway track leading southwards off the Cotswolds to a crossing of the Churn at Cirencester, which lies at the point where the river valley widens out into the broad and (most probably) marshy floodplain of the upper Thames. The earliest course of the Whiteway as it approaches Cirencester is not as yet known with certainty; the modern road line is a reflection of the medieval and post-medieval development of the Abbey Grounds. To the north of the Study Area the Whiteway runs in straight lengths along the high ground until its junction with the Welsh Way when it adopts a sinuous and presumably later course (an agger is visible in North Plantation, North Cerney parish (RCHME 1976, 86)). Projecting the putative earlier alignment southwards provides a course heading for the *Verulamium* gate of the town and the earlier Leaholme fort. Close examination of this line revealed that a field boundary clearly rises over an earthwork feature near Exhibition Barn, and an evaluation trench cut to test the alignment revealed a single, well-cut ditch (containing no finds). No metalling was found in this trench, although the road need not have been metalled throughout its course, especially where it passes over firm limestone, as Marshall (1989) has discussed for a more northerly section of the road (CAT 1991, 53–4, 129).

Of the other roads Ermin Street displays a marked change in alignment at the point later occupied by the Silchester gate of the Roman town. Wacher and McWhirr (1982, 55) suggest that this might reflect the position of a military establishment which preceded the known Leaholme fort. Equally it could relate to the need for the road to cross the Churn and its floodplain at a suitable fording or bridging point. Recent work has elucidated somewhat the pre/early Roman course occupied by the Churn. Evaluation at City Bank, Watermoor in 1990 found a channel of the Churn with numerous intercutting subsidiary channels running on a broadly NW–SE alignment. First-early second century pottery was recovered from the sand and gravel fills of the channels, and a causeway, constructed from limestone blocks, traversed the area. The causeway seems quickly to have been covered by black organic deposits which denote a change in the river regime as the area progressively silted up and developed as marshland. Clearly the Churn no longer flowed through this area after the early second century (R King 1990e). A comparable picture was recovered from the evaluation at Kingsmeadow immediately south of the town in 1991 where silted, braided river channels were found to the SW of the present course of the Churn which here runs parallel with Ermin Street. At least one of these channels was still open in the second century (OAU 1991). Taken together the two evaluations point to a change in the riverine regime in the second century and this must surely be related to the canalisation of the Churn and its diversion around the outside of the north-east defences (see below). The general impression gained is that the Churn ran on a NNW–SSE alignment through Watermoor and Kingsmeadow in the early Roman period, in which case the change in alignment of Ermin Street could mark the original crossing point of the river. From this point Ermin Street heads north-westwards towards Gloucester (Kingsholm) and the Leaholme fort appears to straddle the road.

The alignment of the Fosse Way either side of Cirencester remains a puzzle. To the north-east the road follows an alignment heading directly towards

Cirencester until it makes a marked southward deviation at Raggedhedge Covert. Wacher (1965, 99–101) believed this latter section to be a diversion of an original course which would continue the road on a south-westward alignment to meet the north-east gate of the Leaholme fort, and subsequently to dictate the position of the *Verulamium* Gate which would have been sited upon it. Such an alignment was originally suggested by K M Kenyon (1948, 38) although in the absence of knowledge of the fort. In support we may note that Tar Barrows lie immediately adjacent to the projected alignment (occupied at this point by a field boundary (CAT 1991, 132)). It is conceivable that Tar Barrows are Roman rather than prehistoric in date (see below); if so it is of note that this class of monument is frequently early Roman in date and often adopts a roadside location (Collingwood and Richmond 1969, 169–70). If this hypothesis is correct it would suggest that Akeman Street and Kingshill Lane are later accretions to the road system.

The course of the Fosse Way to the south-west of the town also remains a problem, for once again after adopting a straight course the road undertakes a curious bend to enter the (known) Bath Gate. Excavation of a roadside building outside the Bath Gate indicates that this course was in existence before *c*AD 280 (McWhirr *et al* 1982, 46–9). Again this may also be a later development and formerly the road perhaps followed a continuation of its original alignment beneath modern Old Tetbury Road. Further observations are required to clarify the picture, although the discovery of first–second century cremation burials close to the point where Old Tetbury Road enters Cirencester, lends support to the notion of a road on this alignment at an early date (Reece 1962b).

In discussions of the road system much has been made of the importance of the Fosse Way, but as Margary (1967, 148) pointed out it is surely significant that the Leaholme fort is aligned upon the north-west extension of Ermin Street rather than the Fosse.

The fort and vicus

That there was a Roman military establishment in Cirencester is not in doubt; its form (or forms) and date are more problematical (Figure 16). Of the military occupation we know a little, reported in detail by Wacher and McWhirr (1982). The defences have been found on three sites. Excavation in 1961 on the site of the later *basilica* discovered a pair of parallel ditches (Figure 17). In 1964 similar ditches were located in Chester Mews, and the lip of a probable early ditch was observed at Price's Row in 1974; geophysical survey to locate the south-east defences unfortunately yielded inconclusive results. From these observations and a consideration of symmetry of other fort plans, Wacher and McWhirr reconstructed a fort (known as the Leaholme fort) with dimensions of 110m SE–NW along the *via principalis* and 165m NE–SW, giving an internal area of 1.8ha (4.5 acres) (54011). As the authors state these statistics are to varying degrees hypothesis and further evidence is required for certainty.

Internal buildings have been examined in small trenches in several locations; they were of timber construction, both individual posts and post-in-trench. In no case has sufficient of the plan been recovered for building functions to be adduced. At least three phases of internal buildings have been recognised and the excavators have sought to identify two phases to the defensive circuit. The putative first phase of the defences is represented by a pair of ditches 0.65m wide and 1.25m deep (one of the ditches was sealed by a later *intervallum* road). Consideration of the small size of the ditches led the excavators to suggest that they represent 'the presence of a campaign camp or *hiberna* (winter quarters) associated with the earlier years of the invasion and the initial military contact' (Wacher and McWhirr 1982, 78). Others may follow Fulford (1983) and wonder if this evidence alone is sufficient to suggest the existence of an earlier phase of military activity. The evidence for the ?military annexes is discussed elsewhere (p 67).

The proposed chronology of the Leaholme fort may be summarised: foundation *c*45–50; a large dump of pottery (some of it unused) in the fort ditch dated *c*60–65 is argued to relate to a change in garrison rather than abandonment as demolition and sealing deposits have yielded early Flavian material. Abandonment *c*75 is proposed. R Kenyon (1987, 38, table 22) in his tabulation of the small quantity of Claudian copied asses from Cirencester shows that the large heavy asses minted in the years immediately following the Invasion are largely absent from the town however, and Reece (1982) generally considered the assemblage to be consistent with a date after the late 40s. Foundation may not have occurred before *c*50 therefore. Regarding the life of the fort similarities in the pottery from Leaholme and that used at the Gloucester (Kingsholm) site are noteworthy, especially considering the lack of parallels with the pottery from the Gloucester (*colonia* site) fortress (Darling 1977, 64–7; Wacher and McWhirr 1982, 79). Abandonment of Kingsholm is currently dated to the mid–late 60s, which would accord with the date of the pottery from the Cirencester fort ditch. The dumping of quantities of pottery into the ditch terminals at a gate, by analogy with Cardean and Tiverton (Maxfield 1991, 67–8) points strongly to abandonment *of the site*. If this is

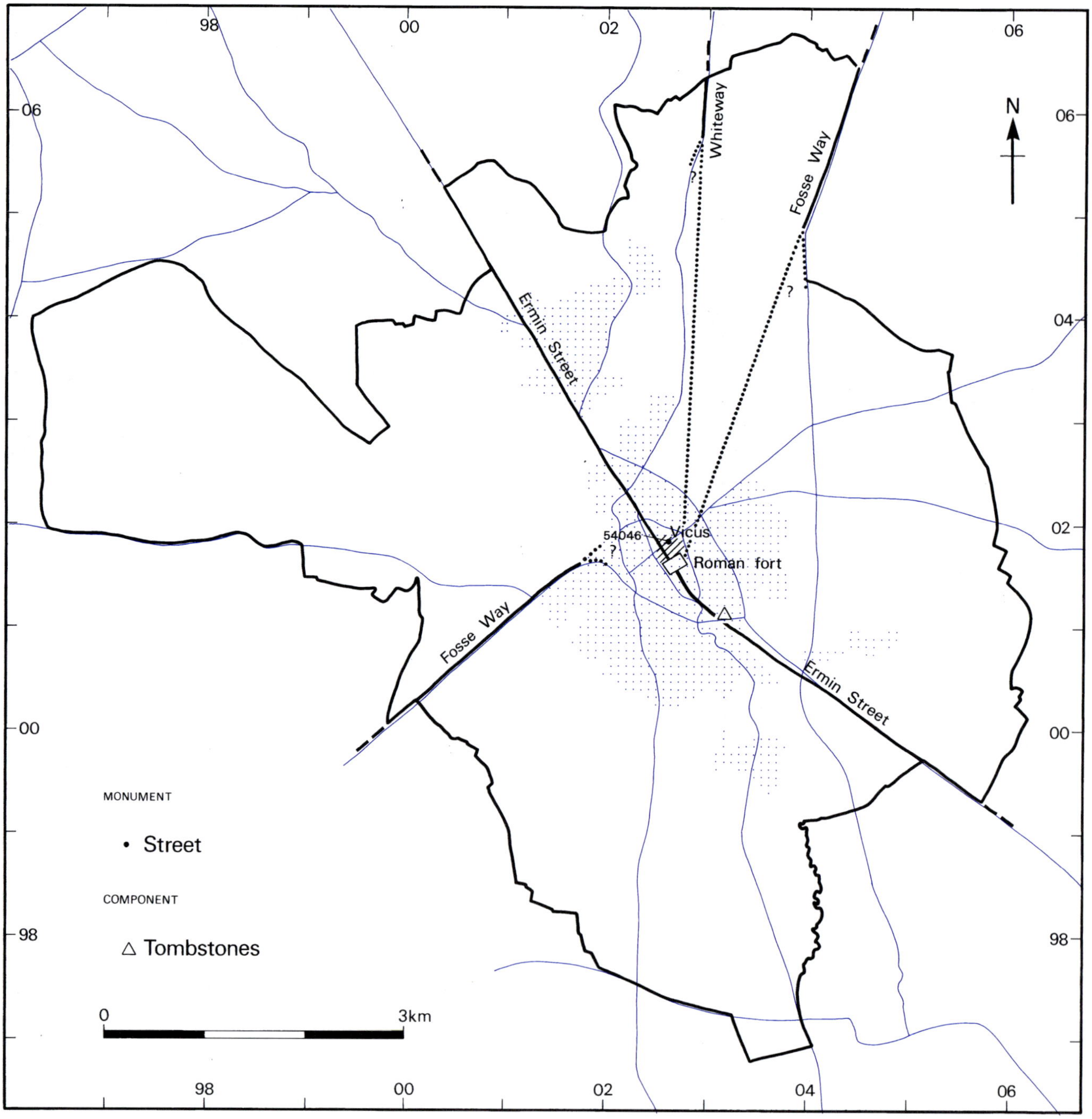

Figure 16
Pre-urban Roman monuments (*c*AD 50–AD 100)

Key to Figure 16:

54046	street (Romano-British)
Roman fort	54011
vicus	54414

Figure 17
Early ditches behind the rampart of the pre-urban fort, excavated at Leaholme in 1961 (Cirencester Excavation Committee)

so, a somewhat shorter period of military occupation, *c*50/55–65/70, might be proposed (the bulk of the early Flavian material, if that from the putative annexes is excluded, comes from layers sealing the military levels). The Leaholme fort may therefore have been occupied for little more than a decade, although there is seemingly evidence for at least two different cavalry regiments in garrison (Wacher and McWhirr 1982, 67–71).

The siting of a fort at Cirencester in relation to its proximity to Bagendon has been much discussed. To Wacher (1975, 30) the location was both tactical and political: the tactical control of a major bridging point of the Churn by two roads while also supervising the political capital a little to the north-west. Reece and Catling (1975, 3) stressed the importance of the Whiteway as a pre-Roman route and thus the policing of native traffic at the river crossing. Much depends on the relative chronologies of the two sites. If a late Claudian/Neronian date for the establishment of the fort is accepted then it is unlikely that it was established to police a potentially hostile native centre. Indeed the converse may be true, that it was sited to support a pro-Roman Dobunnic aristocrat during the unsettled conditions of the early Welsh campaigns, and perhaps to double as a reserve base for the ?legionary fortress at Kingsholm. Either way the establishment of a fort at Cirencester must reflect the perceived political importance of Bagendon and perhaps the developed systems of agricultural production which had evolved in its hinterland.

First century activity has been noted on a few sites outside the Leaholme fort. Excavations beneath the later *forum* piazza revealed timber post-trenches and a ditch overlain by a metalled street. Abraded pottery from beneath the road was pre-Flavian in character (Wacher and McWhirr 1982, 60–4); an associated pit produced a Flavian sherd. The street had been laid-out at right angles to Ermin Street; 64m distant, the *decumanus maximus* of the developed street plan was shown to have originated in the pre-Flavian period. At the Mycalex site in Ashcroft Road three rammed-gravel floors from timber buildings were noted in section; a small quantity of associated pottery suggested a date before the mid-Flavian period for their use (Reece 1976b). Levels containing early pottery have also been found at the Health Centre, Watermoor Road, and possibly in an evaluation test-pit in the Brewery Car Park in 1989 (Gerrard and Johnson 1989b, 12).

This material has been regarded as evidence for an extra-mural vicus contemporary with the fort. While this is highly plausible, and a number of Claudio-Neronian *vici* are known from southern Britain (Sommer 1984, 9–10) it is conceivable that some of this observed early activity might relate to a phase of post-military urban development which preceded the main public building programme in the later first century. Frere's (1983, 5–9) excavations at *Verulamium* have demonstrated how the town and street grid developed before the construction of the stone *forum* in the Flavian period.

Monument Discrimination

Of the early prehistoric monuments only a restricted number of monument classes have been identified and described. The major source types used in the recognition of monuments of this period, such as aerial photography, dictate a clear bias towards morphologically distinctive classes of monument which are easily picked out from the air. Thus, round barrows and trackways (which although frequently undated appear to be broadly prehistoric or early Roman) are particularly well represented and closely grouped in terms of importance. Those monuments which score highest tend to occur in clusters and in spatial association with contemporary monument classes (eg the Preston barrow cemetery). These monuments may be considered to be of regional importance.

Major late prehistoric monument classes which are not present or recognised within the study area include hillforts, cemeteries and field systems. The better known and authenticated Iron Age occupation sites such as Trewsbury and Bagendon which have upstanding earthworks lie just outside the boundaries of the Study Area. This under-representation of certain monument classes emphasises the artificiality of the modern administrative boundaries. Clearly, it would be an error to imply any administrative, social or cultural integrity to the Cirencester region or area at this period.

What little evidence we have of the early Iron Age in the Study Area is restricted to the ditched enclosure partially excavated at Beeches Nursery Field on the outskirts of the modern town (54019). There are no other sites with reliable dating evidence which may be confidently dated to the Iron Age.

Of the early Roman monuments, the fort (54011) scores high and may be considered as being of national importance. Although currently known by only very limited observations, should open area excavation ever occur the potential exists for the recovery of the plan, development and chronology of a Conquest-period fort. Too little is known of the *vicus* for meaningful evaluation. The roads may be considered to be of regional importance; although by virtue of their continued use into the present day, preservation of Roman features is likely to be generally poor. Nevertheless, they retain the potential to answer some of the questions posed above.

8. *CORINIUM DOBUNNORUM:* ROMAN *CIVITAS CAPITAL* AND PROVINCIAL CAPITAL

by Neil Holbrook

'Here they dig up antiquities every day, especially in the gardens; and in the plain fields, the tracks of foundations of houses and streets are evident enough. Here are found many mosaic pavements, rings, intaglio's and coins innumerable . . .'

William Stukeley (1724), diary entry for 23rd August 1721

Roman *Civitas Capital*

This is the earliest identifiable urban form at Cirencester (Figure 18). There is considerable archaeological evidence for the Roman town; that it was a *civitas capital* (ie the centre of a self-governing political unit frequently based upon a pre-existing tribal territory) is indicated by an entry in the Ravenna Cosmography which provides the tribal suffix (see below). Frere (1984a, 68) has suggested that Cirencester may also have been elevated to the status of a *municipium* (a self-governing chartered town) in the second century, although evidence is lacking. *Corinium* was therefore the administrative and political centre of the *Dobunni*, a territory which extended as far as we can tell over the modern counties of Gloucestershire, Avon, West Oxfordshire, North Wiltshire, Worcestershire and Herefordshire (for an attempt to define the topographical limits of the *civitas* see Branigan 1976, 112–14). Within this area the colonia of Gloucester and its accompanying *territorium* (for an estimate of the extent of which see Hurst 1988, 68–9) would have been self-governing and thus excluded from the control of *Corinium*. In the later Roman period it is possible that Kenchester may have assumed control of the western part of the *civitas* beyond the Severn (Wilmott 1980, 127–8).

The early development of the town

Military activity appears to have ended in Cirencester before *c*75 although the early development of the town is not entirely clear. The previously expressed view is that work commenced on the public building programme shortly after the departure of the military, although the possibility of a phase of civilian occupation between the departure of the army and before the construction of the main public buildings was raised above (p 56). Whatever the truth of the matter there was clearly a major programme of public building, the date of which will now be discussed. Excavations within the fort at Admiral's Walk showed military levels to be sealed by large dumps of refuse and silt, above which buildings which may be attributed to the town of *Corinium Dobunnorum* were built. The latest pottery from these dumps are a samian bowl dated 80–100 and a mortarium considered also to date to after *c*80 (Wacher and McWhirr 1982, fig 42, 5; fig 51, 68) (a small quantity of second-century material must be regarded as intrusive). A mortarium which probably dates to after *c*70 was recovered from *vicus* levels beneath the *forum* piazza (Wacher and McWhirr 1982, fig 65, 499). This evidence only provides for the earliest possible date of the building however, which when combined with other public buildings and streets may have taken several decades to complete. By way of analogy we may note that inscriptions suggest that the *forum* at *Lepcis Magna* was at least six years in the building (as Frere 1983, 9, n2 observed).

Further evidence for the date of the construction of the principal buildings comes from the stone quarries in the Querns, for the earliest (such as that beneath the amphitheatre) presumably date to this time; and also the evidence for gravel extraction. A number of quarry pits have been found beneath later civil buildings. These were presumably excavated to

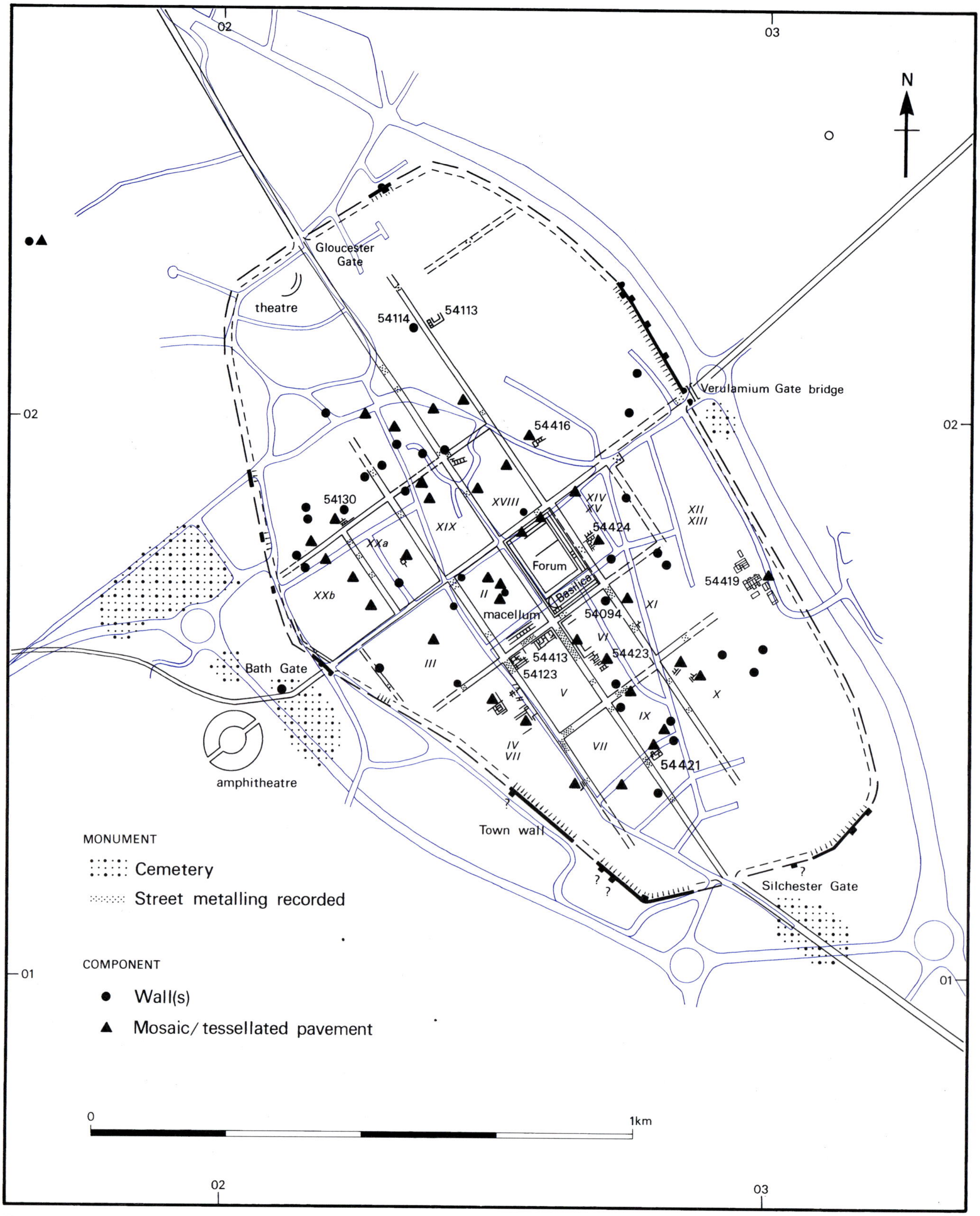

Figure 18
Monuments in the Roman *civitas capital*

Key to Figure 18:

54094	Chester Street	shops
54113	The Abbey	courtyard house
54114	The Abbey	courtyard house
54123	Price's Row, Watermoor Road	shops
54130	Mycalex	courtyard house
54413	Leaholme Gardens	shops
54416	Dyer Street	courtyard house
54419	Beeches Road	winged-corridor house
54423	Admiral's Walk	shops
54421	The Firs	winged-corridor house
54424	The Avenue	courtyard house

amphitheatre	54045	The Querns
basilica	54012	Watermoor House
forum	54009	Chester Lodge
macellum	54412	Leaholme Gardens
theatre	54115	41–43 Dollar Street
town wall (Romano-British)	54024	Cirencester

The street grid is defined by the discovery of street metalling at the following locations:

17 The Avenue	54014
19–23 Church Street	54333
28 Church Street	54330
30 Lewis Lane	54322
33 Sheep Street	54373
3–9 Church Street	54320
5–9 Ashcroft Road	54328
62 Victoria Road	54331
97 Victoria Road	54335
Abbey Car Park	54433
Abbey Grounds	54092
Ashcroft Road	54037
Ashcroft Road	54324
Bingham Hall	54051
Bingham Hall	54329
Brewery Car Park	54327
Brewery Car Park	54370
Chester Street	54095
Cotswold Mill	54035
Cotswold Mill	54242
Dyer Court	54001
Dyer Court House	54436
Dyer Street	54039
Dyer Street	54299
Garden of 45–61 Chester Street	54332
Gaumont Cinema	54093
Gosditch Street	54321
Grammar School Playing Field	54034
Leaholme Gardens	54013
Locks Timber Yard	54120
Old Railway Line, Sheep Street	54124
Orchard House, London Road	54149
Parallel to Cricklade St	54300
Parsonage Field	54132
Police Station	54006
Police Station	54007
Price's Row, Watermoor Road	54122
Purley Avenue	54047
Purley Road	54241
Querns Hill	54128
Querns Lane House	54033
Redlands, Queen Street	54334
Regal Cinema	54240
South of Dairy, Ashcroft Road	54325
South of Lewis Lane	54236
St John's Church	54052
St Michael's Field	54336
St Michael's Field	54357
St Michael's Field	54375
St Peter's Road	54326
Telephone Exchange	54050
The Avenue/Tower Street	54116
Trinity Church Gates	54036
Victoria Road	54027
Victoria Road	54038
Victoria Road	54048
Victoria Road	54294
Victoria Road	54295
Victoria Road	54359
Victoria Road	54434
Watermoor	54296
Watermoor Road	54239
Watermoor Road	54323
Watermoor School	54117
West Market Place	54121
West side of Watermoor Road	54237

provide gravel for street metalling and aggregate for mortar, and by virtue of their location and overlying stratigraphy ought to date to the earliest phase of the town's history. Once excavated the quarries made convenient rubbish pits and seem to have been quickly filled. In the centre of the town the sides of the fort ditches beneath the later *macellum* were exploited as convenient quarries, and the filling is dated *c*70–85 (Wacher and McWhirr 1982, 187–9). Four other quarry pits have been excavated by CAT in the last three years:

site	date of filling
Querns Road (context 22)	early–mid second century
60–62 Watermoor Rd (context 11)	early–mid second century
St Peter's Road	earlier second century
33 Sheep Street (context 36)	mid second century

These sites lie towards the periphery of the Roman town and suggest that construction of the street system may have been continuing well into the second century.

The evidence as a whole therefore suggests that the construction of the principal public buildings and developed street grid may have occurred over a period which may have lasted for as much as three or four decades either side of AD 100.

The street pattern

The process by which the street grid has been progressively reconstructed is chronicled in the earlier interim reports (Wacher 1962, 11–14 and successively thereafter). A previous attempt by Beecham (1887, map opposite page 250) was succinctly evaluated by Haverfield (1920, 173) 'he seems to have assumed, *a priori*, that the town must have been divided up this way [into regular *insulae*]. Of course this is likely enough, but we need specific proof that it was so divided'. The most recent plan shows four streets aligned NW–SE, and seven on the SW–NE axis. This produces approximately 30 *insulae* (and these have traditionally been numbered I–XXX; see McWhirr 1986, fig 2). It has to be recognised, however, that the street plan as generally depicted is highly generalised and is based on relatively few direct observations which allow precise alignments to be defined.

A new plan has therefore been produced (Figure 18) which attempts a more minimal level of reconstruction than previously. The street plan was founded upon the pre-existing line of Ermin Street which provided an orientation 34 degrees west of north for the grid (that a town did not always follow the orientation of a pre-existing highway is shown by *Verulamium* where Watling Street runs diagonally across the otherwise orthogonal grid). The alignment of Ermin Street proved in this case, however, to be a convenient orientation for *Corinium*: Vitruvius (I, 6) stressed the importance of excluding winds from the streets and the NW–SE plan of the town successfully masked the principal thoroughfares from the prevailing south-west wind. Ermin Street formed the principal NW–SE street of the town (the *cardo maximus*), with the *decumanus maximus* linking the later Bath and *Verulamium* gates. It is useful to split discussion of the *insulae* south-east of the *decumanus maximus* from those to the north-west. In addition to Ermin Street, two NW–SE streets are reasonably well attested in the south-eastern half of the town; a third (XV/XIII) was identified in Wacher's (1965, 101) work at the Gaumont Cinema. On the opposing axis the street bordering the long axis of the *basilica* is secure; the next to the SE has been moved about 20m further SE on the basis of Wilkinson's observations in St Michael's Park (Wilkinson 1984b, 224). This is of interest as the four central *insulae* (I, II, V and VI) can now be reconstructed with some confidence as being of almost identical size. Perhaps this represents the initial core of the town plan? To the NW of the *decumanus maximus*, it has already been noted that the NW–SE aligned streets are offset from their counterparts to the SE of the street (McWhirr 1978, 72–3). Recent watching-briefs conducted by CAT in Ashcroft Road and the Brewery Car Park suggest that street XIX/XX also displays this phenomenon (R King 1990f and g). The reasons for this dislocation remain unclear although it does suggest that the street grid developed by accretion (possibly over a number of decades) rather than being laid a *novo* in one go. Collecting together Beecham's records of street metalling suggests that a new NW–SE street should be added to the plan dividing *insula* XX. Two observations also point to the presence of a street or open area immediately inside the defences on the SW side of the town; probable street metalling was noted adjacent to the Bath Gate (McWhirr 1978, fig 4) and at Querns Road in 1992 (R King 1992, 20).

This more minimal plan highlights the gaps in our knowledge of the street grid; analysis of the observations which go to make up the plan also highlight a number of general points. Firstly that the rectilinear grid was probably not so regular as the process of reconstruction tends to make it appear. Secondly, that the overall axis of the street grid and the alignment of individual streets within it changes over the course of time. There are numerous examples of the shifting position of streets, most recently at 33 Sheep Street where a street was moved 2m to the NW in the second century (R King 1990f). There are also the large, apparently late Roman, metalled areas discovered in excavation at the Gaumont Cinema (Wacher 1965, 101) and Purley Avenue (McWhirr 1973, 202–3); in the former case the metalling sealed an earlier street. Thirdly, there are probably more streets within the grid than previously suspected. Nevertheless to ease reference with earlier work the traditional *insulae* numbers have been retained in the following sections.

Public buildings

The largest monuments recorded in *Corinium* are the *basilica* and *forum* (54012 and 54009 respectively). The former was first located in excavations directed and privately funded by Wilfred Cripps in 1897–8 (Figure 19) which produced a plan of the building (Cripps 1898a and b). Correspondence preserved in the Ashmolean Library between Helena Cripps, widow of Wilfred, and Haverfield indicates that 'To be quite correct the Basilica was discovered in the autumn of 1897'. The letter, dated 16th January 1918, is in praise of Haverfield's lecture on 'Roman Cirencester', read to the Society of Antiquaries on December 13th 1917 (Haverfield 1920), but also takes the opportunity to correct and append small details of fact or interpretation. Excavations by John Wacher in 1961 confirmed the position of the south-western end of the *basilica* (Wacher 1962, 5–8).

The *basilica* comprised an aisled hall approximately 85m long and 26m wide, with a paved apsidal recess at the south-west end which probably accommodated the tribunal. The hall was separated into nave and aisles by low sleeper walls which carried a colonnade; sculptured Corinthian capitals were found by Cripps. Beyond the south-east aisle lay a range of rooms which have been partly explored, flanked by an external veranda which returned around the south-west side of the hall. The arrangement of walls recorded by Cripps at the north-east end of the nave would preclude the presence of a corresponding apse at this end of the *basilica* and thus the building was of the long axis type (ie the main symmetrical design was on the long rather than short axis). The *basilicae* at Wroxeter and Leicester were probably also of this type (Bidwell 1979, 82).

The *basilica* suffered badly from subsidence over the infilled fort ditches and the colonnade walls were rebuilt in the mid-second century (Wacher 1962, 7). It is conceivable that the Corinthian capitals already mentioned date to this reconstruction, as it has been noted that they bear a marked similarity to the capitals used in the *basilicae* at Silchester and

Figure 19
Excavations in 1897–8 by Wilfred Cripps exposed the foundations of the *basilica*. This view, looking east, shows the south wall of the aisled hall (Corinium Museum)

Caerwent. The capitals from all three buildings display strong Rhineland influence (Blagg 1977, 64–9 following Kähler 1939). The stone *forum* at Silchester is dated *c*125–50 (Fulford 1985, 52–3); that at Caerwent appears to be Hadrianic (R Brewer 1990, 83 and pers comm). It is uncertain how long the Rhenish architectural fashion persisted, although as Blagg considered the Cirencester capitals to be typologically later than the other examples a broadly Hadrianic–Antonine date might be appropriate. Further repairs to the building in the fourth century are discussed below (p 75). Other elements of the decorative scheme used in the *basilica* are furnished by Cripps whose excavations produced fragments of Purbeck marble and Italian marble wall veneer. From the apse came a small fragment (depicting an eye) of a bronze (presumably Imperial) statue of super-human proportions (Cripps 1898a, 78).

Of the *forum* itself excavations by Wacher (1964a, 9–14) found a piazza 107m long by (an estimated) 84m wide to the NW of the *basilica*. It was surrounded on at least two sides by ranges of rooms with internal and external verandas. As designed the piazza was probably floored with flagstones, as were certainly used in its final phase. Later modifications include the walling-in of the inner portico on the north-west side and its flooring with tessellated pavement. The north-east range of the *forum* (with similar mosaic floors) was located in 1937 by Priestley and Matthews who also found a fragment of a Purbeck marble inscription which mentions the word *respublica*, 'the *civitas*' (Collingwood and Wright 1965, RIB 114). The *forum* is long in comparison to its width, although Wacher's excavations would seem to disprove any suggestion that there was a temple (*capitolium*) at the opposite end to the *basilica* in the manner of continental double-*fora* (a reasonable enough hypothesis if Cirencester was elevated to the status of *municipium* at some date (p 57), especially as the known *municipium* of *Verulmium* has produced this evidence; it is the only Romano-British town to have done so). Entrance to the *forum* may have been through the NE and SW sides. It is noteworthy that Beecham (1887, map) marks a street to the NE of the *forum* (traditionally XIV/XV; excluded from Figure 18 as the evidence for its existence is not explicit). An entrance into the *forum* at this point would find parallel at Leicester, and streets meeting the *forum* in comparable positions are known from Lincoln and Exeter. Further support for such a reconstruction at Cirencester is provided by the discovery of a (secondary but otherwise undated) cross-wall which divides the piazza into two parts (37m and 70m long respectively excluding porticoes) immediately SE of the postulated entrances.

A market place lay to the south-west of the *forum* and in its original phase appears to have been simply an area of open metalling (unless traces of any early timber buildings were obscured by the foundations of the later stone building in Wacher's (1962, 8–9) excavations). Open areas bordering the *forum* are known from a number of towns (such as Silchester, Leicester and Exeter; Bidwell 1979, 80–1) and they presumably served as market places for livestock, a trade hardly appropriate to the *forum* and normally kept separate (as in Rome). Boon (1974, 111) has suggested that the external verandas bordering *fora* and *basilicae* may have provided welcome shelter for traders, and the presence of 'nests' of pottery in a gutter drain at the Wroxeter *forum* points to the presence of market stalls beneath the veranda (Atkinson 1942, 122–4). In the second century a stone building with apparently timber internal partitions was constructed on the site. It comprised a range of regularly-sized rooms with an external colonnaded walk and internal corridor or veranda. A number of pits discovered both inside and outside the building were filled with sawn and cut animal bones, and the building has been interpreted as a meat market or *macellum* (54412). The building may therefore represent a formalisation of pre-existing activity on the site. The *macellum* was extensively repaired to a similar plan in the early fourth century. *Macella* have also been identified with varying degrees of confidence elsewhere in Britain at *Verulamium*, Leicester and Wroxeter (Wacher 1975, 60).

Another major public building (54115) has been tentatively identified in the north-west corner of the town. A number of observations combined to reconstruct a pair of concentric, curving walls, 1.8–2.7m wide; at two points narrower radial walls sprung from the inner curve. The radius of the inner wall was 21.5m; the diameter of the outer may be estimated at 58.5m (Brown and McWhirr 1967, 194–5; and Brown *et al* 1969, 235). Caution is required in accepting this structure unreservedly as a theatre, although no other interpretation fits the evidence (such as it is) as well. *If* a theatre, the concentric walls would define the passage which ran around the outside of the seating area (although this does seem very wide), with the radial walls marking walkways which lead to the inner arena. The diameter of 58.5m compares with 57m for the theatre at *Verulamium* (phase IV) and 66m for that at Canterbury (phase II) (Wacher 1975, figs 12, 13).

The amphitheatre, a major public building which lay outside the defences, is discussed below on p 79.

Commerce

Shops have been discovered in the central area, and are best known from the *insula* immediately south of the *basilica* which borders Ermin Street (*Insula* V). Excavations by Wacher in the northern corner of the *insula* in 1961 revealed timber shops with mortar floors and painted plaster (54413); because of later rebuildings relatively little can be made of their primary plan although the plot widths were in the region of 3m (Wacher 1962, 9–11). The shops were replaced in stone in a piecemeal fashion, and by the second century the Ermin Street frontage was equipped with a colonnade. The plan of this sector is best appreciated in its fourth-century form when some shops appear to possess double the frontage space of others. Small wells are known from the rear (living quarters) of two shops and one building was equipped with a channelled hypocaust. In this phase one or more ovens occurred in each shop, sometimes placed singly, sometimes in groups. Their small size suggested to the excavator that they are unlikely to have been bread ovens. Later excavations at the western corner of the *insula* in 1972 once again found a sequence of timber buildings replaced in stone (54123) (McWhirr 1973, 201–2). An alley-way leading from the inter-*insula* street was fronted by a row of six small shops; there were complex later developments. Finds from one room included late Roman buckles and belt-fittings, and a group of decorated stonework including altars and sculpture was recovered from a preliminary trench. When the report on excavations in this *insula* is available it is likely to yield important evidence for the patterns of trade and land-holdings over almost three centuries.

Elsewhere probable shops have been discovered in the *insula* (VI) on the opposite side of Ermin Street (54423) (McWhirr 1978, 74–7). Only the rear portion of the shops was available for study, and then only the latest phases. Nevertheless a picture of third-century living quarters to the rear of shops fronting onto Ermin Street has been obtained. The plot widths appear to be about 8m, and the shops were separated by yards and alleys. The living quarters were furnished with brick-mortar and mosaic floors. A collapsed internal dividing wall has yielded valuable evidence for the use of half-timbered panelling.

Housing

Turning to evidence of domestic housing McWhirr (1976a, 84–96; 1986) has summarised the evidence and there have been relatively few new observations of substance since he wrote. Of the earliest phase of domestic occupation little can be said. Fragmentary traces of timber buildings (presumably houses) were found in excavations in the Parsonage Field (*Insula* IV) underlying later stone houses; the timber buildings appear to have stood to around the middle of the second century (Rennie 1972, 73–4). In Victoria Road (*Insula* XI) building operations uncovered a second-century mosaic contained within a timber room with painted plaster rendering (Clifford 1949). In no case has it proved possible to recover the full plan of a late first-century/early second-century house, and in many cases the chronology of excavated structures is to a greater or lesser extent unclear. At the Police Station the earliest structure was built from plaster-faced clay walls sat upon masonry plinths, although little can be deduced of its plan. A new house (*Insula* XVIII, 1) was constructed in the early second century which comprised a simple row of five or more rooms with a corridor on the north-west side. Modifications continued into the fourth century (Wacher 1963, 16–19). Simple houses comprising linear ranges with flanking porticoes and corridors are a common feature of *civitas capitals* in the period before the mid–late second century (Walthew 1975, 189–95). Elsewhere second-century stone structures which are most probably houses include the Grammar School (X, 3; Reece 1970b); Victoria Rd (XI,1); Dyer Court House (XVIII, 1); Mycalex (XXI,1); Police Station (XXIII, 1) (see gazetteer in McWhirr 1986, 245–59 for further references). To these may be added the records of mosaics which are stylistically second century (D J Smith 1974); the majority presumably derive from houses.

Of the houses for which we have reasonably complete plans six achieve the status of courtyard house under the criteria used to define monuments adopted in this Project. This low number is largely a function of the method of investigation, for it is only in the course of more modern, open area excavations that the plan and sometimes the function of a building can be evaluated to enable designation to a specific monument class to be made. For that reason the numerous references to mosaics, tessellated pavements, walls and floors only attain the status of contexts and components rather than monuments. Nevertheless they provide an indication of the spread of occupation within the town and are mapped on Figure 18. Of the courtyard houses that at Mycalex (54130) included a simple range with corridor and courtyard (Reece 1976b); The Avenue house (54424) possessed a small central courtyard surrounded on two sides by corridored ranges (Brown *et al* 1969, 231–4); while Parsonage Field Building 3 was a simple block of rooms with associated courtyard/boundary wall (K M Richardson 1962).

The process by which disparate site records build to define a monument is well illustrated by the Dyer Street house (54416) (McWhirr 1976a, 88–90; 1986, 249–51, fig 169, for summaries of the evidence). In the course of laying a sewer pipe on the north side of Dyer Street in 1849 two substantial rooms set around by smaller rooms and corridors were exposed. Earl Bathurst paid for the lifting and display of the Hunting Dogs and Four Seasons mosaics in a purpose-built museum on Tetbury Road, and in so doing stimulated interest in the history of the town. Lysons (1817, Pl 7; Reece 1970, 175) records that in the cellar of an adjacent building a mosaic depicting a marine scene had been discovered in either 1783 or 1793. Subsequent twentieth-century observations furnish further details although the plan of the building is far from completely known. Two ranges at right angles have been identified, which have yielded 'arguably the best group of mosaics to have been found in a single house from any of the towns of Roman Britain' (McWhirr 1986, 251). The bulk of the mosaics date from the late second century or early third century; a poorly documented Orpheus mosaic, if it existed, must be considered as a fourth-century addition. A number of rooms were equipped with hypocausts, and column bases testify to a colonnade or veranda.

At Bingham Hall Gardens the fragmentary plan of a building complex of some opulence is known from various observations (McWhirr 1986, 191–205). A Roman building adjacent to a street which can now be recognised as Ermin Street was discovered during the construction of the Bingham Hall in 1908 (54421; Figure 20). From the plan made at the time of discovery it is clear that not all of the building was exposed, although the arrangement of rooms has the suggestion of a winged-corridor house furnished with hypocausts. Bravender in a letter to Haverfield (20–9–1915) which seems to refer to this site (see Haverfield 1920, 178, no 38) states 'we found several remains of small detached houses. Stones were burnt, rooms were small, each house with a small pavement, plain in the middle with an ornamental border – on the pavement there was generally 2 or 3 inches of ashes. Finds included coins (Constantine to Honorius), bronze objects, pins and brooches, and many stone roof tiles.' A short distance to the east a hypocausted room was discovered during the same works, and subsequent excavation in 1958 by Miss Rennie elucidated the plan further. The excavation revealed an octagonal room equipped with a channelled hypocaust; it was contained within a larger polygonal structure which also housed the furnace and a hypocausted apse in the south-west corner. To the south-east of this structure lay a second building which may confidently be interpreted as the hypocausted *caldarium* of a small domestic bath house with twin apses in its south-west wall.

These remains point tantalisingly towards a complex of some grandeur; a mosaic within the polygonal room is stylistically fourth century and the coins and pottery, although not usefully stratified, also point broadly to a late Roman date. Octagonal rooms are known from a number of south-western villas, frequently containing plunge baths (Branigan 1976, 56–7). In this particular case, however, an interpretation as a heated *triclinium*, as at Keynsham and some other sites, seems more likely (Russell 1985). Unfortunately it is difficult to reconstruct how

Figure 20
Construction of the Bingham Hall in King Street in 1908 revealed foundations of a winged-corridor house (Corinium Museum)

the different structural elements fit together, although if the octagonal room is connected with the winged-corridor house we might envisage a plan akin to that at Woolaston, Glos (Branigan 1976, 50) where an octagonal room lay to the rear of the corridored facade.

The house discovered beneath the medieval Abbey is of some interest (54113; McWhirr 1986, 222–33). The excavations revealed two wings with a third suspected; a central court was surrounded by verandas defined by large stylobate blocks with columns at approximately 3m spacings. Although fragmentary, the plan suggests a house in the peristyle tradition so prevalent in the Mediterranean provinces. The factor which distinguishes peristyle houses from courtyard houses is that the central courtyard must be conceived from the outset as an integral part of the architectural plan of the house (Hodgson forthcoming); courtyard houses often developed by accretion with four wings arranged around an open central area. The continuous stylobate in the Abbey house suggests that the courtyard was a designed-feature and thus the house may be considered to be in the peristyle tradition. Walthew (1975, 189–95) has observed that peristyle houses are well represented in British towns with a strong military connection (*colonia* such as Colchester and Gloucester, and the *civitas* at Caerwent) but are much rarer in other *civitas capitals*. He suggests that this essentially Mediterranean plan may have been introduced to the province by the army, a link still evident in the late Roman period (Hodgson forthcoming). The date of the Cirencester house is unclear, but it may be no earlier than the third century.

The most well-known house complex in Roman Cirencester is justly that excavated at Beeches Road in 1971–3 (54419), a full report on which is available (McWhirr 1986, 19–189). Baddeley had first identified the site as that of a Roman building in 1918 (Baddeley 1918a and b). The near complete plan of either one complex or two separate houses with associated outbuildings was recovered in the excavations. One house (XII, 1) originated as a simple rectangular structure although later additions were added on all four sides and included a bath-suite (see Figure 5). A rectangular outbuilding (barn?) lay immediately north-west of the house. Some 15m south-east of this first house lay a second building of winged corridor plan which has a similarly complicated structural sequence. It had three associated outbuildings.

Coins and pottery point clearly to the complex being constructed around, or shortly after, the middle of the fourth century on an apparently previously unoccupied site. Finds from the complex include an iron plough coulter and bone weaving tablets; iron smithing also appears to have been conducted.

The similarity in plan between this complex and rural villas has been highlighted and discussed, a link supported by the 'agricultural' artefacts. Indeed it has been dubbed *'villa in urbis'* (Wacher 1974, although *cf* the appended comment by Rivet which while accepting the general interpretation points out that the term cannot strictly be applied to this complex as the Latin word refers exclusively to a country house; the anglised 'urban farm' would make for a satisfactory compromise). It has therefore been proposed that this was a working agricultural complex farming land within, and perhaps also outside, the walls (excavations by Reece (1990, 39–44) 200m outside the town wall point to a reorganisation of the pattern of land holding hereabouts in the later Roman period).

The Beeches is also of note in that it lies on the very periphery of the defended area and is a late creation. Elsewhere excavations in the zone immediately within the walls have noted structures constructed in the third or fourth century (as at 33 Sheep Street (R King 1990f, 20), and Querns Road (R King 1992, 20 where a building overlay an earlier street). It is possible that the margins of the town were only developed to any great extent in the later Roman period when there appears to be a general trend towards larger houses more widely spaced. There also appear to have been considerable open areas around the periphery of the town; for example in the area of City Bank (R King 1990e) and apparently the Waterloo car-park (McWhirr 1986, 78). This would support the contention that the large area defended in the second century was an over-ambitious provision by the municipal authority.

Defences

The town defences have been investigated by over sixty separate events including excavations (both antiquarian and modern), watching briefs, recorded stray finds, documents, indirect records etc ranging from the sixteenth century to the present day. Despite this intensive investigation there are many unanswered questions relating to the defences, and the forthcoming publication of the CEC/CAT excavations will form the basis for future discussion. This present account is based solely on published interim reports.

The course of the defensive circuit in its final form has now been largely established. The monument today survives as an upstanding earthwork in the south-eastern quarter of the town in the area of City Bank and Watermoor, and a short section of the stone facing is exposed in the Abbey Grounds (54024) north-west of the *Verulamium* Gate. In about 1850 the Roman defences to the west of Sheep Street were described as an upstanding earthwork (Buckman and Newmarch 1850). Plans by Stukeley, Lysons, and

Skinner in 1721, 1817 and 1824 respectively indicate the survival of the circuit as almost complete, but by the turn of the nineteenth century much of the line had been denuded, and preserved only in property, road and estate boundaries. Subsequent records include chance observations, as for instance in 1917 when the foundations of the wall were found during sewerage work near Workhouse Lane, in Tetbury Road, at the foot of Cecily Hill, and near the bridge between Gloucester and Dollar Streets. The earliest purpose-designed excavation was in 1922 (Figure 21) when Baddeley speculated that the stones in the wall of the Workhouse Garden, on the south-western side of the circuit, were from the Roman town wall. Financed by Helena Cripps who had 'sent some unemployed to look for the town wall' Baddeley was able to test his theory and exposed a badly robbed 60m stretch of the curtain wall (Baddeley 1922a, 101–15). More recently Mary Rennie cut a single trench through the south-eastern defences at Watermoor in 1952 (Rennie 1957), but it was upon the establishment of the Cirencester Excavation Committee and work by Wacher (1961) in the vicinity of the *Verulamium* Gate that the principal phases of the evolution of the defences were identified. Excavations conducted by CEC in the 1960s and 1970s have located the wall at a sufficient number of points for the outline of the defences to be restored

Figure 21
Excavations by St Clair Baddeley in 1922 on the line of the defences in the grounds of the Union Workhouse (Corinium Museum)

with some confidence; and more recently evaluation test-pits by CAT confirmed the precise line of the rampart along Sheep Street. The area enclosed by the second century can therefore be stated with some confidence as approximately 96ha (240 acres), second only to London within the province in defended size.

The possibility of early (late first–early second century) town defences is worth considering. Traces of earthen rampart have been noted at two points which preclude their association with the Leaholme fort: at Watermoor Hospital Garden in 1963 and The Sands, Watermoor Road in 1966. In the former case the rampart was encapsulated within the later (mid-late second century) town defences; at The Sands it lay immediately inside the postulated position of the same defences (material sealing the ditch was interpreted as the tail of the rampart backing) (Wacher and McWhirr 1982, 55). Only a small sample of pottery was recovered from the Watermoor Hospital Garden section (none of it necessarily later than *c*70). At The Sands the latest material was dated *c*100–125; if (as the excavator believed) this material is considered to be intrusive then a date of *c*70–75 was suggested for construction. The mode of construction and date suggested to the excavators that these pieces of rampart belonged to a military fort, fortress or an annex to one of these. If an early Flavian date is accepted this suggests an episode of military activity after the abandonment of the Leaholme fort. If the Trajanic pottery is not disregarded then a military context must be precluded and the second possibility raised in the report has bearing: that the rampart belongs to a late first century/early second century town defence. Two further sightings have relevance to this discussion: in the Abbey Grounds in 1966 a clay, gravel and turf bank 1.8m high and 9.1m wide was found sealed beneath the later town defences. It was suggested in an interim report that this may have formed a containing dyke associated with the diversion of the Churn. No dating evidence was recovered from the bank, although sufficient time elapsed for a turf line to have developed on its surface before its incorporation into the later defences (Brown and McWhirr 1967, 188–91). Re-examination of the sections excavated by Wacher adjacent to the *Verulamium* Gate in 1960 now indicate the presence of the same bank there (J S Wacher pers comm; Wacher 1961, pl 18, section A–B, 38). The fact that all the observations are at points in immediate proximity to the line of the later second century defences suggests that the interpretation as early civil defences should be given greater consideration than has hitherto been the case. Late first–early second century town defences are known from other Romano-British towns, including the *coloniae*, the *municipium* of *Verulamium* and the *civitas capitals* of Silchester, Winchester and Chichester (Frere 1984a, 66). Such defensive circuits may be more commonplace than has previously been thought. As the interpretation of the Watermoor Hospital, The Sands and Abbey Grounds ramparts remains uncertain, for the purposes of this assessment they are classified as components of a larger, undefined, monument.

Turning to the better-attested defences, at some date a decision was taken to construct stone gates, apparently in advance of the construction of a new earthen rampart. Two gates have been investigated in recent times. The north-east (*Verulamium* Gate) was located in 1960 when only the north-west side was available for study (Wacher 1961, 65–7). Assuming perfect symmetry a gate some 30m wide equipped with projecting D-shaped drum-towers may be restored (Figures 22 and 23). The pattern of ruts visible in the street metalling suggested that there was a pair of carriageways on both sides of a central *spina*, four openings in all. Architectural fragments which may be assigned to the gate structure include fragments of column drum, string course and moulding.

The opposite gate, the Bath Gate, was found in 1974; known only from salvage recording the gate appears to be 22m wide and to be furnished with similar drum towers to the *Verulamium* Gate (McWhirr 1978, 71–2). A series of finely carved moulded blocks, perhaps from the parapet, were found in front of the gate. It seems clear that both gates preceded the construction of the stone wall, and at the *Verulamium* Gate it appeared that the rampart bank overlay the footings of the north gate tower. Strictly interpreted this should indicate that the gate was built before the bank, although it is always possible that a gap might have been left in the bank to accommodate the gate which was constructed subsequently (Frere 1984a, 69, n44). Indeed it is possible that the gates might have had timber predecessors, as has now been demonstrated at Silchester (north gate) (Frere 1992, 302) and Exeter (south gate) (Frere 1990, 348). In terms of their plan the *Verulamium* and Bath Gates find ready parallel with the London and Chester Gates at *Verulamium* which may also be attributed to the earthwork phase of defence (Frere 1983, 34–5).

A third gate (the Silchester Gate) is known only from passing accounts which record that a gate or wall foundations were found during construction of the Watermoor railway bridge, and in 1887 Beecham recalled of the Silchester Gate that 'many can recollect when a thick wall extended along the stream eastwards from the gate'. Baddeley records in his notebook that 'Mr Birch is said to have found two or more arches *in situ* a few years back at a point which corresponds with the probable site of the south gate'. The Gloucester Gate is likewise poorly documented,

Figure 22
The D-shaped drum-tower of the *Verulamium* Gate excavated in 1960, looking south (Cirencester Excavation Committee)

the only record being 'very substantial foundations' marked at the probable site on the 1921 OS map. In addition to these principal entrances other minor gates might exist, although none are known for sure. Baddeley thought he had found a gate in 1922 on the south-west defences (*in litt* 13–3–1922) although mention of a gate as such is dropped in his subsequent publication (1922a), which is a far from clear account of his excavations. A possible site for a minor gate has been speculated at the point where the putative original course of the Fosse Way would have met the defences (p 53; Wacher 1961, pl 19).

It would appear that stone interval towers were also contemporary with the earthwork phase of

Figure 23
The northern drum-tower of the *Verulamium* Gate, looking north along the line of the town wall (Cirencester Excavation Committee)

defence. Two towers have been found (there is a third possible example); on the north-east defences the tower foundations cut the earliest bank but apparently had the second (pre-stone wall) bank piled around them (Brown and McWhirr 1967, 188–91). As with the gates this suggests on face value that the towers were constructed before the rampart bank, although once again it is possible to interpret the sequence differently (if the walls were placed flush with the edge of a cut into the rampart then they could be an addition). This interpretation bears more conviction if Wacher's (1964a, 16) suggestion that a beam embedded in the rampart bank at Watermoor House marks a timber tower is correct.

Thus it is not impossible that the towers are a later (but pre-wall) addition to the earthwork defences. The sequence is even less clear at the tower excavated on the northern defences in 1965 although the fact that identical layers of banking were found inside and outside the tower suggests that the walls were inserted through these deposits (Brown and McWhirr 1966, 241–4). A third tower may exist on the south-west side where a wall 4.6m to the rear of the town wall was observed in a gas pipe trench (McWhirr 1973, 200).

Of the bank itself it is difficult to determine its original dimensions although it was at least 3m high. Beyond the bank there is evidence for at least one ditch which can be attributed to this phase (Wacher 1961, pl 18, section A–B). The co-existence of stone gates and earthwork defences is attested elsewhere in Britain at *Verulamium* and Silchester (Frere 1983, 34–5; Fulford 1984, 234–5); stone interval towers set in an earthwork bank are currently unique.

The date of the earthwork defences will rest upon an analysis of all the excavated evidence in the forthcoming report; until then nothing can be added to Hartley's (1983, 86) 'vaguely Antonine date' for the samian from the bank at Watermoor; the broadly second century date for the pottery from the CAT evaluation at Querns Road (R King 1992); and Wacher's (1961, 64) assessment that the bank in the Abbey Grounds may have been erected 'in the first half of the second century'.

The front face of the earthen rampart was subsequently cut back and a stone wall added. Where examined the wall has proved to be of varying thicknesses, and in the portion available for detailed study in the Abbey Grounds a number of different types of masonry facing have been identified. Although all the subtleties and complexities of the structural sequence relating to the stone defences have yet to be determined the following points at least seem to have been clarified.

i) On the north-east side of the town a 1.2m wide narrow curtain is the earliest walling. This was later replaced in part by thicker walling which varied from 2.3 to over 2.7m wide above the rear scarcements. In one section 2.3m 'wide' wall rested upon 'narrow wall' footings. This wider wall utilised a number of different masonry styles which could reflect different gang lengths or a protracted history of construction and reconstruction (Brown and McWhirr 1967, 190–1; Cullen 1970; Walker 1990).

ii) At one point on the north-west side of the town the pattern of robbing suggested that a narrower curtain had preceded the construction of broader wall (Brown *et al* 1969, 225–7). Examination of the wall footings (which were here almost 4m wide) immediately north of the *Verulamium* Gate found a tongue of natural undisturbed soil between the front and rear parts of the foundation, perhaps indicative of subsequent widening (Wacher 1961, pl 17, H–J–K).

iii) That narrow wall was not everywhere replaced is demonstrated by its discovery in sections at Watermoor (Wacher 1963, 22–3); northern defences (Brown and McWhirr 1966, 241); north-east defences (Brown and McWhirr 1967, 190); south-western side (McWhirr 1973, 200); and adjacent to the Bath Gate (McWhirr 1978, 71).

With the construction of the original stone curtain the earlier bank was heightened, and perhaps again when the narrower wall was replaced with broader curtain. At three places pitched stone slabs set in clay have been discovered – in section only at two points (Watermoor Hospital (Wacher 1964a, 16), and Querns Road (R King 1992, 16–17)) but on the north-east side the pitching had a width of about 4.8m (Wacher 1961, 67–8) and it was suggested that these may have been steps (*ascensus*) to provide access to the rampart walk. The discovery of such slabbing at three points suggests that this was a common phenomenon, however, and in an evaluation test-pit in Sheep Street the rampart was found to be capped with a substantial pitched limestone surface (Gerrard and Johnson 1989b, 7–9; cf Baddeley's 1922a, 110 'sloping saddle or track made from larger stones' which was 3.9m wide on the south-west side of town). It is conceivable therefore that rather than forming localised points of access the slabbing acted as a widespread revetment of the rampart bank to reduce the effects of erosion and slippage.

On the north-east side of the town two ditches were dug outside the wall; beyond these lay the canalised course of the Churn. As stated above (p 52) the Churn originally flowed on a NNW–SSE course through Watermoor and Kingsmeadow; pottery suggests a change to the riverine regime in the earlier second century and it seems probable that the Churn was diverted into a newly created canalised course to run around the outside of the north-east defences. It is uncertain whether this occurred when the postulated late first- or early second-century defences were built (p 67), or slightly later when the mid-late second century earthwork bank was constructed. Relief flood channels of the Churn may have occupied the innermost two ditches at the *Verulamium* Gate where they were crossed by a bridge (Wacher 1961, 65).

A consideration of the date of the construction and replacement of the stone wall must again await the forthcoming report, although a date 'before about AD 220' has been mentioned for the former event; the heightened bank at Watermoor Hospital yielded 'late second century pottery and a coin of Marcus Aurelius' (Wacher 1975, 302; 1964a, 16).

At some date external towers (or bastions) were added to the circuit. They are best known on the north-east side where four towers have been examined (Wacher 1961, 68–9; Brown and McWhirr 1966, 244; 1967, 190; Cullen 1970, 236–9). Bastions 1, 2, and 3 possessed square bases (bastions 1 and 2 were approximately 3.3m square; bastion 3 measured 6.4m × 6.0m). A number of splayed facing stones from the vicinity of bastion 2 suggests a polygonal superstructure above the square base. Bastion 4 was certainly polygonal, with sides angled at 144 and 126 degrees, and finds close parallel with a tower excavated on the northern defences in 1965 (Brown and McWhirr 1966, 244). Bastions are known with differing degrees of certainty from a number of other points around the walls (at Watermoor: Rennie 1957, reinterpreted by Wacher 1961, 68–9; R King 1990e, 15; and the south-western defences: Baddeley 1922a; McWhirr 1973, 200).

Differences in design and inconsistency in spacing are not exclusive to Cirencester. Caerwent, for example, lacks bastions on the west and eastern sides, the main approaches to the town. Some argue that this denotes a poor level of supervision in construction (Wacher 1975, 77), others that the provision of bastions was a piecemeal process reflecting the depleted nature of the fourth-century municipal treasury (Casey 1983). The provision of external towers brought the town defences into line with contemporary military architecture, although the concept of an actively defended 4km circuit is barely credible. The town may have played periodic host to detachments of the mobile field army during the fourth century however.

Evidence for the date of the external towers is sparse. Wacher (1961, 69) tentatively thought that a coin hoard from the inner ditch beside the *Verulamium* Gate might have some bearing as the construction of the towers necessitated the diversion of the river into the outer ditch and the consequent silting of the inner. As the hoard seems to date no later than AD 348 Wacher considered that the towers were constructed in the first half of fourth century. Whether this evidence can be directly related to the construction of the towers is not at all certain however, and generally only a broad fourth century date can be proposed for the towers based on evidence from other towns (Wacher 1975, 302 subsequently ascribed a date in the second half of fourth century for the towers).

Little-known, suspected and unlocated monuments

A number of monuments which may be expected have yet to be identified with certainty. These include the public baths. One possible location is in the *insula* (II) immediately south-west of the *forum* where a substantial, presumably public building, is known. The south-east part of the *insula* was occupied by the probable *macellum* (p 62) but further to the north-west recent observations in advance of redevelopment noted traces of a building equipped with hypocausts and brick mortar floors (Clews 1985, 230), and in 1987 further walls associated with gravel surfaces and similar flooring were found. Investigation was too limited for the determination of a meaningful plan. It is of interest that deposits survived here some 1.6m above the level of the *forum* suggesting a raised site (Frere 1988, 465–67). Three tessellated pavements have previously been recorded from this area (Haverfield 1920, 179, nos 29–31). This *insula* most probably also contains the discoveries recorded by Stukeley and Rudder. Visiting Cirencester in 1721 Stukeley (1776, 66) records an important discovery to the south of Lewis Lane

> 'Mr Richard Bishop, owner of the gardens [lewis grounds] . . . dug up a vault sixteen feet long and twelve broad, supported with square pillars of Roman brick three foot and a half high; on it a strong floor of terras: there are now several more vaults near it. . . I suppose these the foundations of a temple; for in the same place they found several stones of the shafts of pillars six foot long, and bases of stone . . .; these, with cornices very handsomely moulded and carved with modolions, and the like ornaments . . .: some of the stones of the bases were fastened together with cramps of iron: capitals of these pillars were likewise found, and a crooked cramp of iron ten or twelve foot long, which probably was for the architraves of a circular portico.'

It is conceivable that a fragment of a large modollion cornice contained within the collections of the Corinium Museum is a survivor of the pieces noted by Stukeley. Blagg (1977, 69; forthcoming) has noted that it is one of the largest and most elaborate cornices from Roman Britain and that it must have come from an important building, possibly a large temple in the classical tradition. New evidence which has come to light in the course of this project identifies the general location of this complex: the 'temple' is marked on Stukeley's sketch of Cirencester preserved in the Bodleian Library (Frontispiece). Although the sketch does not permit precise determination the 'temple' clearly lay adjacent to the site of the *forum*.

According to Rudder (1781, 346) the area of Stukeley's discoveries was re-examined in 1780 and the principal floor found to be 9.7m × 7.3m; there were four hypocaust arches in the walls which were 1m thick. Column fragments had evidently been reused in the hypocaust.

Taking the evidence as a whole the records of hypocausts and brick mortar flooring seem strongly suggestive of a bath-house, which at Leicester and Wroxeter also lay in *insulae* adjoining the *forum*. There may also have been another building in the classical tradition nearby. *If* a temple, it is worth noting that fragments of a bust and torso from a statue of Minerva have been found hereabouts.

Some further support for a bath-house in this vicinity is provided by a consideration of the water supply, of which a bath-house would have required a copious supply, doubtless provided by an aqueduct. A likely source of water would have been the rising ground to the north-east of the town (where springs are recorded in the post-medieval period; p 103). Timber water pipes with iron junction-collars have been found in excavation immediately inside the *Verulamium* Gate (Wacher 1961, fig 1) and at Purley Road (Wacher 1975, 300) which probably brought running water into the bath-house. A timber-lined box-drain running down the centre of Ermin Street between *insulae* IV/V (Wacher 1962, fig 5) might conceivably have been the principal outflow from the baths which fed into the Churn to the south of the Silchester Gate.

Another public building lay immediately south-east of the *basilica* (*Insula* V) where excavations have revealed a courtyard surrounded on three sides by an ambulatory which contained a mosaic in the south-east passage. The structure was built in the later second century on top of earlier timber structures. At some date a timber building was constructed in the courtyard before the area was given over to the dumping of rubbish. Unfortunately this building is only known from a narrow strip excavated across its width and its function remains uncertain (McWhirr 1978, 74; Darvill 1981a, 174). If it extended the full width of the *insula* it would have had dimensions of about 75m × 100m. Of any building(s) which lay to the north-east of the courtyard little can be said, although Beecham records Roman foundations from the vicinity of Chester Street, and Lysons lists a mosaic from the general area (Haverfield 1920, 177, no 32A). Wacher's (1965, 97–9) possible shop presumably fronted onto the inter-*insula* street. Interpretation of this building must necessarily be somewhat tentative, although one possibility is that the courtyard represents the *temenos* of a temple. As noted above (p 62) *Verulamium* is the only Romano-British town to have produced evidence of a temple (*capitolium*) within the *forum*, although at some towns such as Caerwent, Caistor-by-Norwich and Silchester a temple lay adjacent. Boon (1973, 108, n13) has suggested that these may have served as civic temples to some degree, a hypothesis supported at Silchester by the recovery of a collegiate inscription from the temple. The later developments which connected the ?*temenos* with the *basilica* (p 75) suggest a degree of civic ownership for this structure.

Although poorly known it seems probable that a building or complex of some significance existed in the vicinity of the area known as The Firs (which borders Victoria Road to the south-west and originally extended south of King Street). Chance finds from the area include fragments of Doric column, various Corinthian capitals, fragments from the base and shaft of a Jupiter column (see below), and architectural cornice and entablature. Haverfield (1920, 177–9) also lists a mosaic and tessellated pavements from the area. As McWhirr (1986, 191–2) has observed it is uncertain whether Haverfield's mosaics are the same as those marked by the Ordnance Survey in 1875, although this must be likely. Within the area of The Firs is the Bingham Gardens house complex mentioned above p 64; other buildings hereabouts are hardly known. Small scale evaluation work immediately north-west of King Street in 1985 found Roman walling and demolition deposits (Wilkinson 1986, 233), while a CAT watching brief noted Roman walling exposed in a pipe-trench in King Street (Barber 1992b, 17).

No temples can be located for certain within *Corinium*. M J T Lewis (1966, 125) cites three examples from the town under his heading of 'Other Temples Where No Structure Is Known'. Firstly a temple to the *Matres* (Mother Goddesses). A remarkable collection of sculpture was discovered during the construction of a cottage in Ashcroft in 1899 which included an altar (Collingwood and Wright 1965, RIB 105) dedicated to the *Suleuiae* by one Sulinus (who also dedicated an altar to the same gods in Bath where he describes himself as a sculptor; RIB 151); two reliefs of the *Matres*; a statue of a *Mater* and parts of another; two fragments of column and an uninscribed altar. Cripps (1900) considered the pieces to indicate the location of a workshop of Sulinus. Helena Cripps, in a letter to Haverfield (18–1–1918), wrote, 'one reason why we thought the carved *Deae Matres* were found in a sculptor's shop was that a partially finished column drum of Bath Stone was found with them'. Haverfield (1920, 180–4) preferred (but not dogmatically) to see them as coming from a temple or shrine. Lewis is more firm in his ascription to a temple which he gives a second-third century date.

Purely on the basis of sculptural finds Lewis also suggests temples dedicated to Mercury and Minerva which are certainly well represented in the sculptural record from the town, although as Toynbee's (1976) survey shows there are a greater number of Celtic reliefs. Few have useful provenances although the relief of Fortuna from the bath-suite of the Beeches house exemplifies that many probably came from domestic contexts (McWhirr 1986, 123).

Blagg (forthcoming) has undertaken a survey of the architectural carvings from the town, and several points are of note. *Corinium* has produced more carved Corinthian column capitals than any other site in Roman Britain, in terms of both variety and quantity. While such capitals were used in the aisles of the *forum basilica*, and others may have come from free-standing columns, certain capitals at least must testify to the existence of other buildings in *Corinium* in the classical tradition (temples and a theatre for example). Compared to the number of capitals, remains of entablature are poor with the exception of the modollion cornice mentioned above (p 71) and a sculptured relief which might have come from a pediment (of a temple?; Toynbee 1964b, 138–9, n6). A group of six miniature Corinthian capitals are noteworthy by virtue of their unusually early date, probably late-first century as Strong (1971, 14; Blagg 1980, 31) originally noted. It is interesting to speculate what kind of structure the columns came from; a stone peristyle house is unlikely at such an early a date, and thus a public building is probably indicated. The porch or ambulatory of a temple would be a plausible context.

Corinium has produced some of the best evidence for the cult of Jupiter in Britain. In 1891 a pedestal dedicated to Jupiter recording restoration by governor L Septimius [. . . (Collingwood and Wright 1965, RIB 103) was found 'near the corner of Mr Bingham's new building' [ie Bingham Hall] (Bravender *in litt* to Haverfield 20–9–1915). Bowly (1892–3) records that it was found in the garden of the Elms 'whether it was *in situ* is impossible to say'. The date and status of the dedicator of this inscription are of the utmost importance in a consideration of the status of fourth century *Corinium* and are fully discussed below (p 74). The stone can almost certainly be identified as the base of a Jupiter column, a monument which would have comprised a column shaft crowned by a capital carrying a sculpture of Jupiter (Figure 24). Probably also to be related to this cult is the well-known Corinthian capital, found in Gregory's Nursery (ie south of Lewis Lane) in 1838. The capital is of exceptional size, 1.06m high with a lower diameter of 0.59m and is unusual in being monolithic (capitals of this size were normally carved in two blocks). Between the volutes are four half figures, all drawn from the Bacchic repertoire. There has been considerable academic debate as to the nature of this capital, in particular whether it may be ascribed to a Jupiter column or not. One problem is its size, for most other capitals from such columns are less than a half, or even a quarter, of the height of the Cirencester example. In the most recent survey Phillips (1976, 40) concluded that 'a town of the size and importance of *Corinium* could conceivably have had an unusually large Jupiter column, which would have matched the scale of the nearby *forum* complex.' Jupiter columns

Figure 24
Pedestal from the base of a Jupiter column recording the restoration by governor *L Septimius [. . .*, discovered in 1891 (Corinium Museum)

are well-known in Gaul and Germany, and seem especially prevalent there in the late second-earlier third century. Phillips considers that the style of the Cirencester example would fit this period. Haverfield (1920, 192) observed that a fragmentary capital discovered in 1808 in the Leauses and recorded by Lysons might form a pair with the current example. Another very large Corinthian capital might also have crowned a votive column since there is a commensurate column drum carved with leaf decoration, a feature commonly (although not exclusively) associated with Jupiter columns. If correct this would have been the tallest column from Roman Britain, and also one of comparatively early date (late first–early second century) (Blagg forthcoming). Fragments of other column shafts with scale or leaf decoration have been recovered from The Firs, Grammar School Field and St Michael's Field (Wilkinson 1984b, 224). *Corinium* has thus produced substantial evidence of this cult, which is attested elsewhere in Britain by architectural fragments from a sprinkling of towns including London, Lincoln, Chichester, Winchester and Wroxeter amongst other sites (M Green 1982, 111).

Monuments currently unknown or unidentified include a *mansio* and fourth-century monuments which should be expected if *Corinium* was the capital of *Britannia Prima* (see below).

Roman Provincial Capital

The identification of Cirencester as a provincial capital is only hypothesis, and the evidence upon which the argument is based is not unchallenged.

In the Verona List compiled between AD 312 and 314 four provinces are grouped in a *dioecesis Britanniarum* (*Britannia Maxima Caesariensis, Prima, Secunda, Flavia Caesariensis*). It is generally believed that the four provinces were created from the existing Severan provinces of *Britannia Inferior* and *Britannia Superior* in the reign of Diocletian, or just possibly shortly earlier. *Prima* by analogy with other provinces will have been formed from old *Superior*, and as *Maxima* was the only one of the original four provinces to later possess a governor with the rank of *consularis* (as the *Notitia Dignitatum* shows) it is surely correct to centre that province upon London. *Prima* must therefore lie in the west. Was *Corinium* the capital of *Britannia Prima*? Two pieces of evidence have been advanced to champion its cause. Firstly that it was the largest town within the bounds of the suggested province (which are nowhere attested), and secondly *Corinium* has yielded the Jupiter column inscription mentioned above. Three faces of the pedestal base survive, although none fully. On the front there is a dedication by one L. Sep[timus . .], governor of *Britannia* [. .*Prima*?] to Jupiter; on the other two sides there is a verse which names the *rector* of *Britannia Prima* and records restoration of the column dedicated to 'the old religion'. *Rector* is a non-technical term which has generally been considered to be equivalent to *praeses*. It has been argued however (Birley 1981, 178–80, 315–7) that the interpretation of this inscription may not be entirely straight forward as it is possible that the use of *Britannia Prima* in the verse may be an informal slang term for *Britannia Superior* which was used to fit the hexameter prose-style (*Superior* would not scan). He also argues that the province named on the front face could just as easily be restored as *Britannia Superior* as *Britannia Prima*. If correct the inscription could then date to as early as the third century, a date which gains some support by the inclusion of a *praenomen* in the governor's name. Thus the reference to *Britannia Prima* is not beyond doubt (in the sense of the fourth-century province), and even if this is accepted it is by no means assured that Cirencester was the capital of the province (a governor could dedicate anywhere within his jurisdiction), or indeed necessarily that it lay within the bounds of *Prima* (Mann 1961, 319 citing the Digest notes that the 'one reason a governor was allowed to leave his province was to make a dedication'); this is further developed by Birley (1981, 317, n14) who suggests that *Prima* could have lain entirely to the west of the Severn.

On a different tack Reece (1991a, 33, following Burnett) notes that the CL mint mark on Carausian and Allectan coinage could in fact just as easily be read as GL which would indicate a mint at *Glevum* (Gloucester). Thus with a known mint at London it is conceivable that the division of *Britannia Superior* could have been effected under Carausius or Allectus and mints established at both provincial capitals (thus advancing the claim of Gloucester rather than *Corinium*).

Despite these caveats the majority of modern commentators favour the identification of Cirencester as the capital of *Britannia Prima*, although the evidence is more equivocal than is sometimes made out. Consequently a second Roman urban form for Cirencester has been identified in this Project (Figure 25). Whether the legal status of *Corinium* changed with the arrival of the governor and his court is unknown.

No monuments which can be directly attributed to the new administrative functions transferred to the town are known for certain, although Wacher (1975, 304–5) speculated that the modifications apparent in the *forum* (p 62) might be related to the installation of provincial control. Monuments which might be expected include a palace for the governor (*praeses*) and accommodation for accompanying bureaucrats and guards. We should also expect a church for the metropolitan bishop of *Britannia Prima*. In the acta of the church council of Arles in AD 314 the bishops of Britain are listed. By comparison with their Gaulish counterparts it can be proposed that the four British bishops were the metropolitans of each province (Mann 1961). Unfortunately the surviving text is corrupt but by a process of elimination it has been suggested that the province of *Prima* was represented by a priest (one Sacerdos) and a deacon (Arminus). By rights we should therefore expect a church for the metropolitan bishop of *Britannia Prima* in *Corinium* (although see Reece 1976a, 69; and Boon 1992, 42 for the difficulty in identifying fourth-century house-churches archaeologically).

Many of the monuments discussed in the previous section underwent modification and alteration in the fourth century and these have already been described. Others such as the Beeches Road complex were built afresh. None of these operations can be directly related to the increased administrative functions of *Corinium* with the possible exception of the area immediately behind the *basilica*. The external

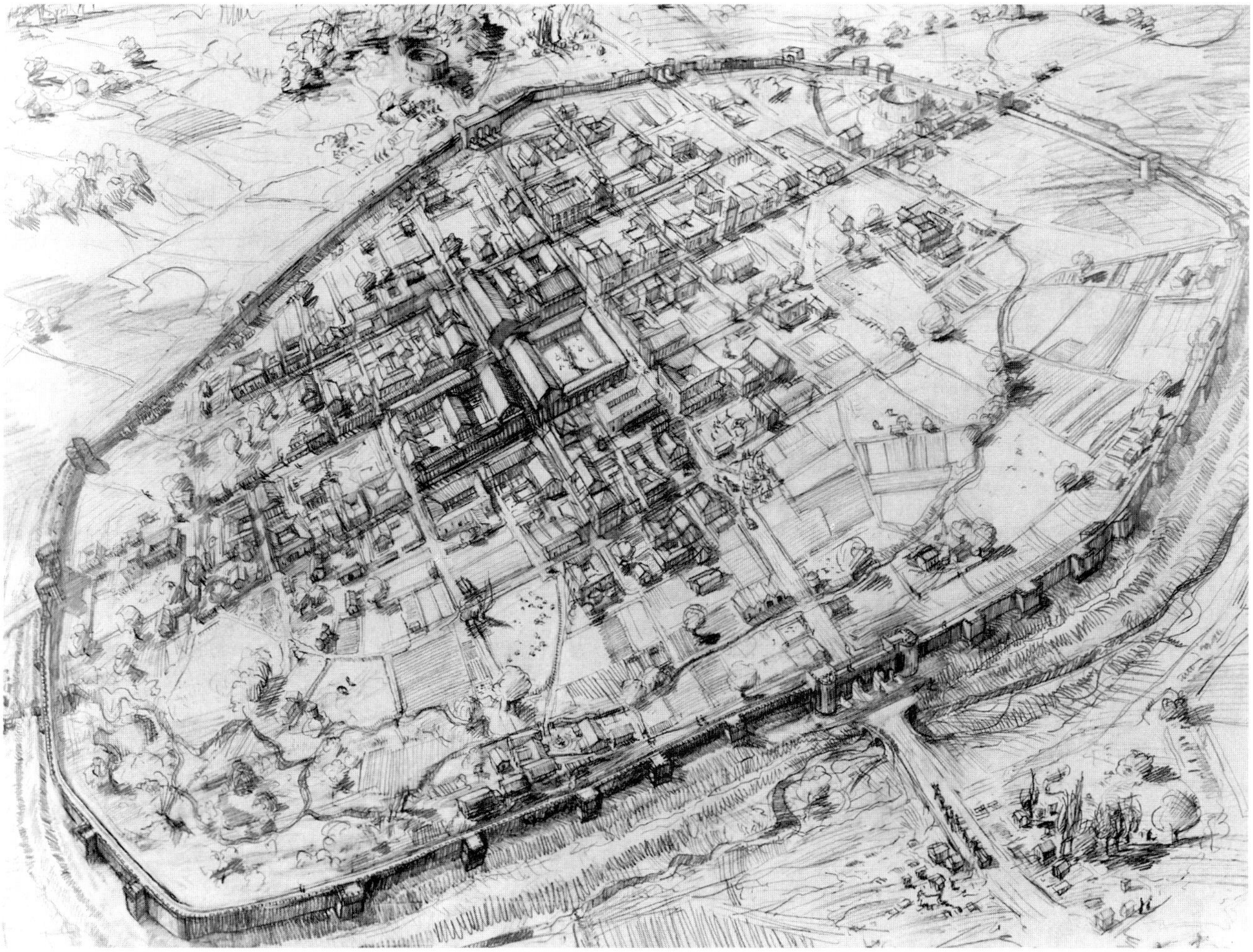

Figure 25
Imaginative reconstruction of the Roman townscape of the provincial capital (From an original drawing by Casper Johnson)

colonnade of the *basilica* was removed in the fourth century and the street behind the building blocked by a row of buildings at the point where it joined Ermin Street. A new open area was therefore created which extended across the former street into *Insula* VI where the public building (?temple) discussed above (p 72) lay. It is difficult on current evidence to evaluate the significance of these developments although the blocking of a street and creation of a new open area suggests official motivation. An apparently abortive attempt to construct a massive new building on the site of the *macellum* in the adjacent *insula* (II) in the fourth century might also be pertinent to this discussion (Wacher 1962, 8–9).

The nature of fourth-century *Corinium* is worthy of discussion from an archaeological standpoint as Reece (1980; 1988) has used the town to advance a general theory of the nature of late Roman towns in Britain, and indeed of the success of urbanism in the province as a whole. Reece believes that after the middle of the fourth century there was not a sufficient density of population for flourishing urban life to have continued. This is not to say that all building and occupation ceased, but rather that the character of towns had changed so much that they can no longer be considered as financial and commercial centres on the Mediterranean model, in whose likeness they were constructed in the first-second centuries. They probably retained their administrative functions to the end, but in his view it is debatable how much effect this activity had on the other inhabitants of the town.

Taking the evidence for *Corinium* on its merits the evidence for the fate of the *basilica* is unfortunately lacking, and the courtyard of the public building of unidentified function had become a rubbish dump in the late Roman period (p 72). Of the evidence for domestic housing there are a number of examples where demolition levels are directly overlain by dark earth. One such was the building excavated at Querns Lane by Reece where a collapsed roof was directly overlain by these accumulations; coin evidence points to a date of AD 340–50 for the collapse (Reece 1956; 1988, Trans 110). Such demolition deposits were also present above the shops in St Michael's Field, and although the evidence is not yet fully published Reece has considered (once again from coins) that this process can be put within, rather than after, the Roman period (1980, 83; 1991b, 14–17). Small scale excavations by CAT at 7 Corinium Gate found evidence for fourth-century demolition deposits, with two shallow pits containing charcoal and slag cut into the top of rubble deposits. The pits yielded pottery datable to the last quarter of the fourth century (Barber 1990d, 19–21). As Reece (1991b) has so clearly demonstrated the latest Roman coin issues (House of Theodosius) are extremely well represented in the town (St Michael's Field ranks third in terms of the ratio of Theodosian coins out of the 140 sites analysed) but where excavated the majority appear to come from unsealed deposits and dark earth. So far there are few published examples of Theodosian coins from construction and occupation levels, although a much better sample will be to hand when the CEC excavations reach publication. At present the following sites have produced unequivocal evidence for a prolonged history of occupation. In the Parsonage Field a coin of 388–95 was found in the make-up for the latest floor level, and as a number of other rooms appear to be contemporary with this one there was evidently major reconstruction at some date after 388 (Rennie 1971, 73). A second building near the centre of town (XIV, 3) produced coins of Valentinian II and of the House of Theodosius from beneath the latest floor (Brown *et al* 1969, 234–5). At the Beeches although there was relatively little stratification it seems clear that the complex continued to function right until the end of the fourth century; a rubbish deposit within one of the buildings was considered on the evidence of the coins it contained to have accumulated fairly rapidly around the year 400 (McWhirr 1986, 103–4). This deposit might relate to the final years of domestic activity at the Beeches.

Undoubtedly some houses were being actively maintained into the early years of the fifth century; the evidence from the public buildings is sadly lacking and it is uncertain at what date in the fourth century remetalling of the streets ceased. Equally some houses appear to have fallen out of domestic use before 400. How should the large quantities of the latest Roman coin issues be interpreted? Certainly it is a pattern at variance with many other towns, and finds closest correspondence with the pattern of coin loss on villas, rural settlements and temples (Reece 1991b). Whether this indicates that Cirencester had to all intents become a 'rural' site with few remaining commercial and financial functions by the closing decades of the fourth century, or for that matter a flourishing religious centre, remain interpretations of the established observation.

Accumulated deposits

These two forms are taken together for the purposes of defining importance and quality because they are archaeologically very difficult to separate and in many cases reflect continuous occupation and use of the same spaces and structures. The remains of these urban forms are extensive (*c*96ha) and locally represent considerable accumulations up to 3m thick. To the south of the line represented today by London Road, Lewis Lane and Querns Lane (the area known as Watermoor in post-medieval times) deposits relating to these two forms lie immediately below superficial deposits which vary in depth from as little as 0.3m (as in St Michael's Field) to more typically 0.5–0.6m. The depth of cover-deposits varies because much of Watermoor was used for market gardening in recent centuries. The lack of superimposed urban deposits in this southern part of the town reflects the restricted area of the post-Roman forms within the northern half of the area within the Roman defences. At the CAT evaluation at Querns Road in 1992 there was up to 1.10m of dark earth and overburden sealing Roman deposits (R King 1992); in Dyer Court Roman deposits lay 1.5m–2.4m below modern ground level (Webster 1959, 45), and similarly at the Police Station (Wacher 1963, 16).

Survival: The areas of highest survival are in the southern half of the modern town and/or where post-medieval disturbance has been minimal and where monuments are exceptionally robust. The defences on the east side of the town are still upstanding, those on the western and southern side have been truncated but where explored preserve their main features below ground level; at Querns Road, for example, the rampart bank survived to a height of 3m above natural gravel (R King 1992). Excavations at Beeches Road demonstrated how well fragile deposits such as mosaic floors and buildings can survive even at shallow depths. Recent excavations in Corinium Gate show how modern house foundations have often punctured but not necessarily greatly reduced the legibility of Roman deposits (Barber 1990d). In the central area of the town excavations at Dyer Court in 1957 revealed a

1.8m-2.4m thickness of Roman stratigraphy (Webster 1959, 45) and at the Police Station site a wall of a domestic house was preserved to a height of almost 1.8m with the internal plaster face still largely undamaged (Wacher 1963, 19).

Medium survival occurs in areas of shallow or localised disturbance, for example, under post-medieval buildings where cellars are not present. Zones of poor survival mainly coincide with areas of recent and intensive disturbance. The average depths of cellars recorded within the area of the medieval and post-medieval town is 2.5m and suggests that their construction will generally have little impact on the underlying Roman deposits. At School Lane and Dyer Street features visible in the cellar floors are probably of Roman date. Some elements of the Roman town plan can still be traced in the modern street pattern; for example the *decumanus maximus* is preserved by the line of London Road, Lewis Lane, and Querns Lane.

Potential: The areas of highest potential are mainly in the eastern and southern parts of the town. Here the effects of medieval and later occupation are minimal and the chances of waterlogged deposits greatest. Recent evaluation excavations at Abbey Nurseries resulted in the recovery of organic materials for the first time. The finds included plant material, branch-wood and timber, wooden artefacts including a writing tablet, leather shoes, and leatherworking waste (R King 1990e). Curiously, the reason for medieval and later neglect of this part of the town was the incidence of waterlogging – exactly the conditions that favour the preservation of the earlier deposits. Organic preservation may also be expected in the ditches outside the town defences; waterlogging is recorded from the north defences (Brown and McWhirr 1966, 244) and molluscan evidence was recovered from the ditch (Wacher 1961, 64). Potential is also high where post-Roman landscaping may have buried fragile features (eg in the Abbey Grounds). Medium potential applies to deep, undisturbed aerated deposits where fragile material such as wall plaster, mosaic may be well preserved. This especially refers to car parks such as the Waterloo and the Forum. Poor potential applies where extensive damage has already occurred.

One of the factors influencing potential is the distribution and age of the natural and man-made drainage systems of this section of the Churn Valley. Some progress has been made on this topic in recent years (p 52), but it is undoubtedly a future research topic of much potential.

Documentation (archaeological): A glance at the distribution of excavated sites (Wacher and McWhirr 1982, 19–21) reveals that many parts of the town have been subject to archaeological investigation at some stage, although the sum total of the area examined in detail is a very small fraction of the total extent of the forms as a whole. Much the same picture is apparent from the distribution of evaluations, watching briefs and other kinds of observations and record-generating events. Not all the work is yet fully published, but the first three volumes of Cirencester Excavations have been issued and three more are in active preparation. Typescript reports on recent evaluations and watching briefs are available for study.

Zones of highest archaeological documentation are St Michael's Field, Police Station, the Abbey Grounds section of the town wall, Tower Street/Lewis Lane. Medium archaeological documentation would apply to Cricklade Street, the Brewery car-park and Ashcroft Road. Zones of poor documentation apply to some of the larger open areas of the town such as the Abbey Grounds and the City Bank playing fields as well as the market place and those northern parts of the town beneath post-medieval buildings. These biases in the distribution of archaeological work are plainly apparent in Figure 18 which maps the recorded observations of Roman walls and mosaics/tessellated pavements. The apparent absence of sites in the northern sector and the Abbey Grounds is purely a reflection of the lack of archaeological endeavour in these areas.

Documentation (historical): This criterion can only be applied to the early urban forms in a general way because the level of expected documentation is minimal (for a convenient collection of the evidence see Rivet and Smith 1979, esp 321–2). Cirencester is referred to as *Corinium*, *Corinnium* and *Coronium*, the *polis* of the *Dobunni*, by Claudius Ptolemaeus, a mathematician and astronomer working in Alexandria in the second quarter of the second century AD, in Book II of his Geography. It has been clearly shown however that much of Ptolomey's information derived from earlier sources, and it is conceivable that the town may have taken its name from the *oppidum* of Bagendon (Corinion?; Rivet 1966, 102) or else have been newly given to the fort. The town is omitted by scribal error from the Antonine Itinerary, but occurs as *Cironium Dobunorum* in the Ravenna Cosmography, a document compiled from earlier sources in *c*AD 700. The name of the town is generally, and surely correctly, restored as *Corinium Dobunnorum* by modern scholars. From the town itself there is a small but significant collection of inscriptions, although few can be attributed to particular monuments or components within the town. A notable exception is the fragmentary inscription mentioning the word '*respublica*' from the *forum* (Collingwood and Wright 1965, RIB 114).

Group Value (clustering): At present there is generally little evidence for the localised repetition of monuments or major components within the town. Exceptions occur in the *insula* south-east of the *forum* where the rear of three strip buildings were examined during excavations between 1973 and 1976 on the site of Admiral's Walk in St Michael's Field (McWhirr 1978, 74–7) and in the *insula* on the opposite side of Ermin Street where a series of shops appear to occupy the whole of one frontage (Wacher 1962, 9–11; McWhirr 1973, 201–2). Thus zones of high Group Value (clustering) are rare but the present evidence is extremely restricted. The majority of the urban form must at present be considered as being of low Group Value (clustering).

Diversity (features): A common finding of excavations in Cirencester is that, once established, the main monuments and key components remain fairly constant over the course of time, being subject to remodelling but rarely major change. Thus few cases are presently known where one class of monument has been swept away to make room for another, although exceptions include the late walls cutting across the street south-east of the *basilica* (Wacher 1962, 8) and similarly at the Gaumont Cinema where the site of an earlier street was covered by a large tract of metalling in the late Roman period (Wacher 1965, 101–2). The public building of unidentified function south-east of the *basilica* was constructed in the later second century on the site of earlier timber buildings (p 72). At the Police Station a corridored house appears to have been demolished in the fourth century and a new building of uncertain function constructed on its site (Wacher 1963, 18–19). Likewise there was an apparently abortive attempt to construct a massive new building on the site of the *macellum* in the fourth century (Wacher 1962, 9). Generally there is ample evidence for houses constructed in the second century continuing in occupation as houses until at least the earlier part of the fourth century (see p 76). Although lying outside the walls, the area immediately outside the Bath Gate shows an interesting chronological progression from quarry to industrial workshop to cemetery (p 85).

Group Value (association): The north-eastern part of the town is a zone of high group value association because of the presence of later occupation. The south-eastern part of the town is a zone of medium group value association as only the two Roman forms are represented here. No areas of low group value association can be recognised.

Amenity Value: That fact that very little of these forms survives above ground level means that amenity value is generally rather low. Exceptions, which represent zones of high amenity value, include the defences on the eastern side of the town (where a programme of interpretation and display will occur in 1994) and the apsidal western end of the *basilica* which is marked out in the street tarmac. Zones of medium amenity value reflect the perpetuation of the Roman street patterns in the modern town (eg the London Road–Querns Lane axis). Much of the town, however, can only be regarded as being of low amenity value. A guide to the visible remains of Roman Cirencester has long been out of print (Viner 1973c).

The overall quality of Roman archaeology represented in Cirencester is very high, perhaps greater than the assessment of the deposits might suggest. It is one of only sixteen or so *civitas capitals* attested or inferred in Roman Britain, and very probably one of only four or five late Roman provincial capitals. *Corinium* therefore deserves to be considered as one of the major towns of the north-west provinces of the Roman Empire, and we may note that in terms of size *Corinium* finds ready parallel with *colonia Agrippinensis* (Cologne), one of the most important towns of Roman Germany. The town is well known for the abundance of mosaics discovered: approximately 90 separate pavements have been recorded over the last 100 years or so. One building in Dyer Street contains one of the most remarkable collections of mosaics known from a town house in Roman Britain. *Corinium* also makes a significant contribution to the sculptural record from the province. Although there is comparatively little to see of the Roman town today, the Roman amphitheatre is an exceptional example of its monument class. Overall as a resource for the study of the nature and form of Romano-British urbanisation Cirencester has considerable untapped and unexploited potential.

The Roman Countryside (*c*AD 80/100 to early fifth century AD)

A division may be made for convenience between those monuments which lay immediately outside the area of urban occupation later encompassed by defences ('the urban fringe'), and those which may be considered to lie within 'the countryside' (Figure 26).

The urban fringe

i) Civic pride and munificence
A bridge (54025) spanning the Churn (here on its second century and later diverted course; p 52) was discovered in 1960 immediately outside the *Verulamium* Gate (Wacher 1961, 65). The abutment comprised a 1m wide facing of large unmortared

stone-blocks standing at least five courses high. A similar facing retaining a rubble core was detected 4.2m from the abutment and interpreted as a pier. If the plan of the abutment has been correctly reconstructed, the spacing would narrow to a little over 2m at the centre of the gate, which suggests that this may have only been a subsidiary flood relief channel rather than the main river course of the Churn. The latter was probably bridged in the unexcavated area to the north-east. The robber trench of the abutment contained some moulded blocks and small tapering stones. No firm evidence was recovered for the form of the bridge superstructure, although stone-arched bridges are a notable rarity in southern Britain (Holbrook forthcoming).

An amphitheatre lay to the south-west of the town some 110m outside the Bath Gate (54045; Figure 27). The site was described by Rudder (1779, 349; 1800, 69–70) who was the first to identify it as an amphitheatre; he stated '. . . I am of the opinion, that there was originally rows of seats, or steps, one below the other, from top to bottom; but time has much defaced them'. Nineteenth-century investigations by Skinner and J Buckman proved relatively disappointing to their excavators and it was not until 1962 that Cirencester Excavation Committee commenced a programme of limited research excavations. It is from this work that the history and form of the amphitheatre may be sketched (Wacher 1963, 23–6; 1964a, 17–18; 1981; Brown and McWhirr 1967, 185–8). The site is popularly known as the 'Bull Ring' today, a name derived from its more recent use as an arena for bull-baiting (an eighteenth-century Cirencester Bull Club is attested).

As seen today the amphitheatre comprises an arena measuring about 47m along the long axis and 41m along the short. It is surrounded by earthen banks on average 30m wide. Excavations at the north-east entrance demonstrated that in its original form the great mass of the earthen banks was retained by timber posts and drystone walls. The date of the construction of the amphitheatre must await the final report, although broadly a second-century date seems likely. Later repairs include the reconstruction of the entrance in dressed stone where imposts for vaulting indicate that seating was carried over the entrance-way. Later still the dressed walls were dismantled and replaced by timber posts. At the same time two small chambers were built either side of the entrance with double-doors communicating directly with the arena; this treatment of the doors suggests that they served as beast-pens.

Examination of the bank showed it to be terraced with (presumably timber) seating placed upon low dry-stone walls. By comparison with better preserved structures Wacher suggests a capacity of 8–9000 (cf the estimate of 3640 seated or 7250 standing at the smaller timber amphitheatre at Silchester; Fulford 1989, 163). The arena was floored with sand and fine gravel.

At some date the width of the north-east entrance was drastically reduced to only 1.2m by the construction of rough stone walls. Whether this is a late or sub-Roman development must await publication of the excavations. The same applies to the date of a large post-built structure found within the arena, although for the views of the excavator see Wacher 1976, 16–17.

The amphitheatre is large by comparison with those at other British *civitas capitals*, (that at Dorchester is larger but this was dictated by the size of the reused Neolithic henge monument (see Fulford 1989, fig 80)), and is on the same axis as the street plan, by no means a typical arrangement (Fulford 1989, 179). A more telling statistic than pure area is to compare the area covered by the seating banks with that of the arena. This demonstrates that Cirencester, Dorchester and Chester stand apart from other Romano-British amphitheatres by having a ratio of roughly 2:1, whereas the ratios of other amphitheatres are roughly 1:1. Excluding Dorchester for the reasons mentioned above, this statistic places Cirencester between the legionary amphitheatres of Chester and Caerleon, and serves to emphasise that Cirencester probably had a greater crowd capacity than any other civilian amphitheatre in Britain (Wheeler 1992, fig 51).

ii) Cemeteries

Three cemeteries have so far been identified around the town, all beside main roads.

The Bath Gate cemetery is the largest and most extensively explored. A tombstone inscribed to Julia Casta was found before 1721 near the Querns. Stukeley (1776, 67) records that it was one of five similar stone-lined graves which lay in a row; there had been a second inscription but this had been destroyed before his day. A large stone coffin was dug up in *c*1760 on the side of the Tetbury Road 'in which was found a human skeleton, with the head between the legs' and a sword placed on the right side (Rudder 1779, 347). Eight small coffins were uncovered in 1867 on the cattle market site and workmen here 'constantly came across the evidence of numerous internments'(Beecham 1886, 257). In 1875 further evidence for a cemetery was uncovered at the Querns Hospital and a stone coffin was found in Cirencester Park. There are further twentieth-century references to coffins and skeletons, although by far the most useful information derives from the rescue excavations conducted outside the Bath Gate between 1969 and 1976 (fully reported in telling detail by McWhirr *et al* 1982).

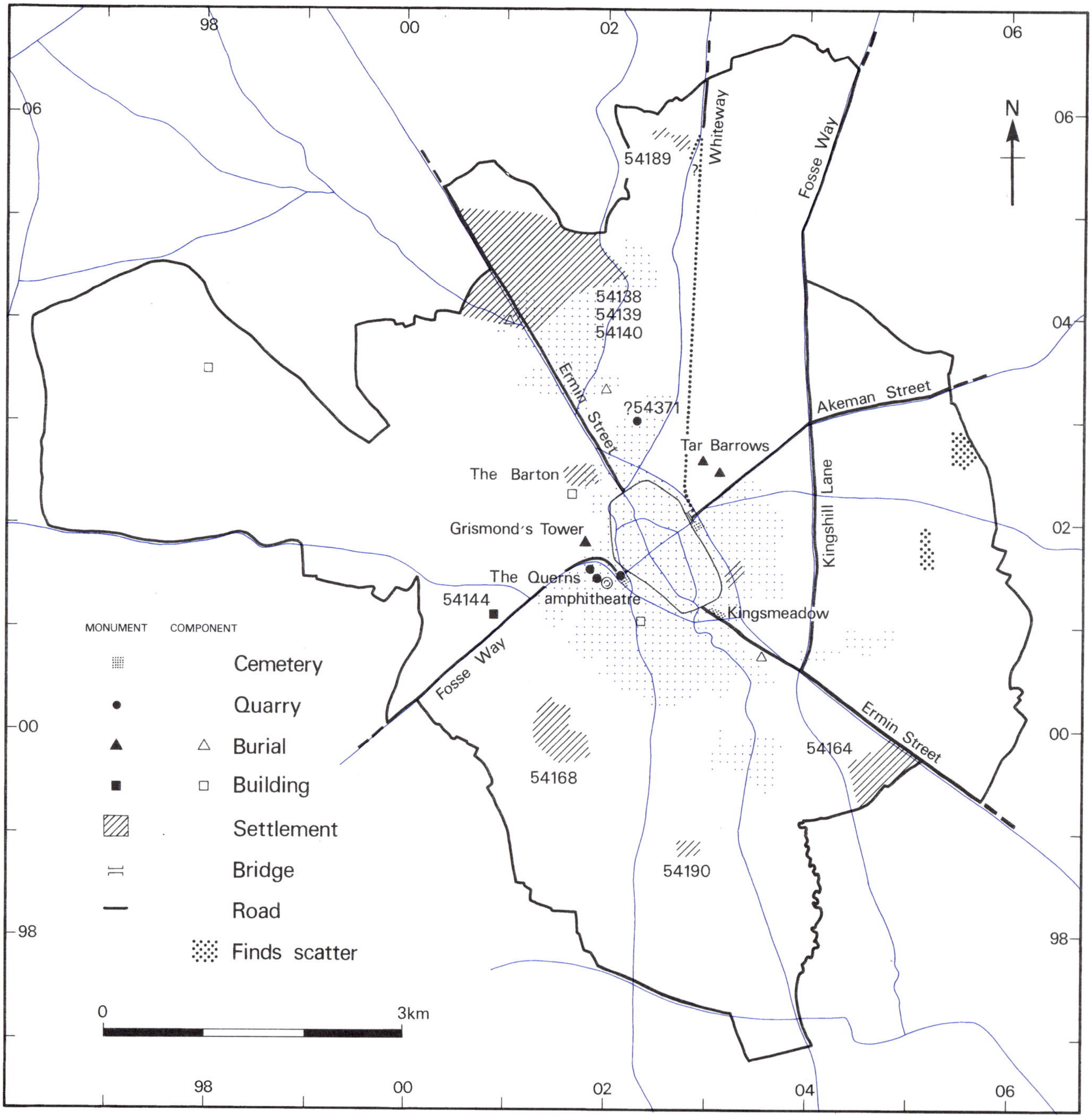

Figure 26
Romano-British monuments in the rural area (see Figure 18 for monuments within the urban form)

Some 453 burials were archaeologically recorded in the excavations and the extent of the cemetery appears to be about 60m north and south of the Fosse Way and laterally for at least 120m; a particular concentration lay on either side of the Fosse Way between the Bath Gate and the amphitheatre. In addition burial seems to have been prevalent in a line running between Querns House, the Cattle Market and Oakley Cottage (where Reece (1962b) recorded 45 cremations and inhumations buried with jewellery and metalwork). The density of cremations might suggest an early core and they possibly reflect the original course of the Fosse Way before it was diverted into the Bath Gate (see above). The salient points to mention in the present context are that the cemetery appears to date from the early fourth century and for burial to have continued throughout the century; a *siliqua* of Honorius from beneath the lumbar vertebrae of one burial points to continued deposition after AD 400. Many of the burials were aligned north–south and there was a complex sequence of later graves cutting earlier burials which hindered the recovery of a detailed chronology, as did the lack of grave goods. A few (25) higher status burials interred in stone coffins are known. Large fourth-century inhumation cemeteries are known from other towns such as Winchester (Lankhills) and Dorchester (Poundbury, Dorset). Where the third-century cemetery lay, if it existed on any scale, remains a problem.

Key to Figure 26:

54138	Sheep Dip, Cirencester	farmstead
54139	Sheep Dip, Cirencester	field system
54140	Sheep Dip, Cirencester	trackways
54144	Agricultural College	villa
54164	Worms Farm	settlement
54168	SE of Chesterton Farm	settlement
54189	Baunton Downs	settlement
54190	South of Clark's Lane	settlement
54371	Bowling Green Pits	quarry

Abbey Road Garages	54231	road (Romano-British)
Ambulance Station, The Querns	54188	quarry
Amphitheatre	54045	amphitheatre
Bath Gate	54118	road (Romano-British)
Bath Gate	54119	quarry
Ermin Street	54292	road (Romano-British)
Fosse Way	54020	road (Romano-British)
Gloucester Gate	54435	cemetery (Romano-British)
Ermin Street	54238	road (Romano-British)
Gloucester Street	54297	road (Romano-British)
Grismond's Tower	54217	?Roman barrow
Kingshill Lane	54021	road (Romano-British)
Kingsmeadow	54062	mausoleum
Kingsmeadow	54372	cemetery (Romano-British)
North of The Barton	54167	settlement
Phoenix Way	54126	road (Romano-British)
Phoenix Way	54159	road (Romano-British)
Preston	54041	settlement
Querns Kitchen Garden	54042	quarry (Romano-British)
Querns Kitchen Garden	54044	road (Romano-British)
Fosse Way	54125	road (Romano-British)
SW of Sandy Lane Farm	54166	settlement
Tar Barrow	54089	?Roman barrow
Tar Barrow	54220	?Roman barrow
Tar Barrow (?)	54219	?Roman barrow
The Querns/Bath Gate	54057	cemetery (Romano-British)
Verulamium Gate	54025	bridge
Verulamium Gate	54026	aqueduct
Verulamium Gate	54431	cemetery (Romano-British)
Whiteway	54143	road (Romano-British)

Figure 27
Aerial view of The Querns, with the amphitheatre centre left, and the Bath Gate cemetery excavation in the foreground during redevelopment in 1973 (Cirencester Excavation Committee)

Elsewhere evidence for burial seems heavily related to later factors such as the extent of ground disturbance and intensity of archaeological recording, although some general observations may be offered. Only 14 burials were recorded when the eastern ring road was constructed and this provides a ready contrast with the western route. The former included a number of inhumations on the east bank of the Churn immediately outside, and to the south of, the *Verulamium* Gate which might suggest a small cemetery hereabouts (McWhirr 1973, 195–7). Whether burial really was less prevalent on this side of town or simply lies further out in still undeveloped areas remains to be resolved. Stukeley (1776, 67) notes that a stone coffin burial was found during ploughing between Tar Barrows and the town, and F W Taylor recorded several discoveries of human bones hereabouts.

Some 600m from the *Verulamium* Gate are two barrows known as Tar Barrows (and anciently as *Thoreberuhe* or *Theoberuhe*; Beecham 1887, 83). They stand about 100m apart. The more easterly has a conical profile with indications of horizontal limestone coursing in the upper part of the mound (O'Neil and Grinsell 1960, 108). Stukeley (1776, 67) mentions that several Roman gold coins were dug-up at the mound, and Rudder (1800, 75) describes 'a large and lofty tumulus near the town called Tar-barrow-Hill which was opened about a dozen years ago [*c*1780], and nothing found in it but a small coin and a larger square stone, and should therefore think that it had been formerly exploited, and its contents taken away'. Baddeley records in his notebook a visit to view further excavations in 1935 directed by a Mr Groves who cut into the neck and shoulder of the mound at three points. Finds included a semi-circular fragment of worked stone which he considered to be Roman, and two fragments of pottery including a large rim from a 'pre-Roman cinerary pot'. Baddeley considered the mound to have been much altered in the Civil War, although the basis for this assertion is unclear. Taking the evidence as it stands, and considering especially the conical profile of the mound which is more a trait of Roman than prehistoric barrows, a Roman date may be tentatively proposed. Their location adjacent to the postulated early course of the Fosse Way has already been discussed (p 53).

Grismond's Tower which lies in Cirencester Park 90m from the town defences has also been considered to be a Roman rather than prehistoric barrow. Leland (Toulmin Smith 1964, 102) records that before 1540 two '*sepulcheres ex secto lapide*' were found, in one of which was 'a round vessel of leade covered and in hit ashes and peaces of bone'. 'Several very large urns, full of ashes and burnt bones' are said to have been found some years before 1780 (Rudder 1800). O'Neil and Grinsell (1960, 108) consider it more likely that Roman burials were inserted in a prehistoric mound, although it is hard to be conclusive on present evidence.

Early burial is indicated to the south of the town along Ermin Street. A green glass cremation urn containing ashes and burnt bones was dug up about 1710 in Kingsmead. This urn was placed in a stone coffin and covered with a flat stone, enclosed within a stone wall and covered with paving 'in the form of a very obtuse cone' (Rudder 1779, 347). In August 1793 'heaps of dead bodies, with bones much decayed' were discovered just outside the town and during the first half of the nineteenth century pre-Flavian military tombstones, dedicated to the cavalrymen Genialis (Figure 28), and Dannicus, were found adjacent to Cricklade Road and 700m south-east of the presumed location of the defences of the Leaholme fort (Leemans 1838). Later tombstones found dumped behind the town wall at Stepstairs in 1971 (awaiting reuse?) perhaps also originated from this cemetery (McWhirr 1973, 212–14). Evaluation at Kingsmeadow in 1991 found one possible cremation and areas of burning which were tentatively identified in a provisional report as a pyre (OAU 1991). A child burial was uncovered during sewer-pipe works in Cricklade Road opposite the Plume and Feathers pub in 1973.

There are unsubstantiated verbal accounts of a possible cemetery outside the Gloucester Gate, with recollections of 'bones' and 'vaults full of bones' discovered during extensions to the Texaco garage in

Figure 28
Tombstone dedicated to *Genialis*, discovered beside Ermin Street in 1835 (Corinium Museum)

the 1970s. It is uncertain how much credence should be given to these accounts. An outlying burial accompanied by an iron knife was found at Stratton Mill in 1927.

Reece and Catling have speculated on whether the medieval churches of St Lawrence and St Cecilia, which lie outside the defences, might have originated as late Roman cemetery churches (1975, 13). These are attested in the north-west provinces at places such as Bonn and Xanten, although a critical review of the evidence by Esmonde Cleary (1989, 36–8, 125–7) suggests they were predominately a fifth century phenomena in northern Gaul and consequently may not be as prevalent in Britain. Archaeologically the best evidence for an urban cemetery church is at Butt Road, Colchester, which also contained Christian mausolea; a similar mausoleum has also been found at the Poundbury cemetery, Dorchester. It is of note that neither of these sites had medieval successors around which settlement developed on the continental model, and the mechanism by which Reece and Catling seek to explain the northward shift of medieval Cirencester. Indeed the only good British parallel for the topographical shift proposed for Cirencester is St Albans where there is strong circumstantial evidence for a late Roman cemetery church preceding the medieval abbey. The pattern has also been suggested for a number of other British towns (such as Dorchester-on-Thames and Gloucester; p 93) although in an absence of firm evidence for a pre-existing Roman church.

iii) Industry

The local Great Oolite limestone was evidently much prized for the ease with which it could be worked for both building and sculpture. The main source was clearly the rising ground to the west of the town (known today as the Querns, a name derived from the old English *Crundel* meaning quarry) where irregular humps and hollows are still visible. Evidence for stone quarrying has been recovered from a number of observations, fully reported in McWhirr *et al* 1982. Excavations at Querns Hospital Kitchen Garden in 1978 demonstrated the method of extraction. Following initial opening, quarrying proceeded to a stepped face from which blocks were removed along their natural bedding and joint planes. Wedge and pick marks visible in the face testify to the tools used. Quarry waste was piled up into irregular mounds which still characterise the area. Quarrying took place on either side of the Fosse Way and covered in total an area of some 4ha. Metalled tracks serving the quarries have been located at several points.

The limestone was clearly being quarried from the early Roman period, as the sculptured military tombstones recovered from Watermoor testify (p 83). Excavation within the north-east entrance of the amphitheatre showed the arena to have been founded on the site of a pre-existing quarry which had already eaten into the spur of a low hill (Wacher 1981, 2). The construction of the amphitheatre is dated to the second century (p 79), and so the most likely context for the commencement of quarrying on any scale is the initiation of the public building programme at the end of the first century. A point of note, for which I am grateful to P T Bidwell, is that the amphitheatre was presumably constructed on 'public land', and thus the stone from the earlier quarry was presumably used for 'public' purposes, in short the civic building programme. At Querns Hospital Kitchen Garden (Figure 29) a quarry had been backfilled by the early fourth century at the latest, and generally the area on either side of the Fosse Way seems to have been given over to burial by this date. Bowling Green Pits (54371) to the north of the town may have been another Roman quarry although conclusive evidence is lacking.

Further evidence of industrial production is provided by the detached building excavated outside the Bath Gate in 1973–4. Here an apparently open-fronted rectangular stone building, 16m long by 7–7.5m wide with an internal partition, was found fronting onto the Fosse Way. It possessed a flagged stone floor and a small smithing hearth; the 2000 or so iron hobnails recovered from the site are best interpreted as products of the building (and perhaps also a timber predecessor) and suggest a workshop associated with the manufacture and salvage of footware. The building was constructed *c*AD 280 and abandoned before *c*330 (McWhirr *et al* 1982, 50–68).

To date no potteries or tile-making sites have been positively identified in the vicinity of the town, although petrological analysis of tiles stamped

Figure 29
Roman quarrying exposed in 1978 at The Querns (Cirencester Excavation Committee)

ARVERI and TPLF from the Beeches houses suggests that they were manufactured from local clays (McWhirr 1986, 127–9). The more prevalent tiles stamped TPF, TPFA, TPFP and LHS appear to originate from the known tile kilns at Minety, 12km south of Cirencester.

Study of the environs of Roman Cirencester is instructive in a number of regards. In particular, it is possible in the area outside the Bath Gate to observe a chronological progression of differing functional activities on the same site. Originally exploited as a limestone quarry, the quarries were utilised as convenient rubbish dumps upon disuse. Later, *c*AD 280, a building associated with footware manufacture was constructed, and abandoned in the early fourth century when the area was given over in favour of burial.

One notable result of this study is the lack of evidence for extra-mural occupation, particularly the ribbon development outside the principal gates apparent at some other large towns (Esmonde Cleary 1987, 45). This suggests that development and land holding within the walls may never have reached a state where there was pressure on the available land (and indeed there is evidence to this very effect; p 65).

The countryside

The current study area lies at the intersection of two distinct zones of Roman settlement: the Cotswolds, an area of dense villa settlement, and the Upper Thames valley where villas are hardly known. It was noted above (p 49) that there is considerable evidence for continuity of Late Iron Age sites into the Roman period on the terrace gravels of the Thames valley; less is known of the origin of Roman settlement on the Cotswold dip slope. It is beyond the scope of the current study to address general questions relating to the origin and patterning of settlement in these areas, and indeed the study area as defined for this urban project is manifestly unsuited to do so. Similarly, the study area is too small for useful discussion of the effect the development of *Corinium* had on the agricultural regime of the region. For example, it has been suggested that it was the growth of the town which led directly to a change in the economy of the rural settlement at Claydon Pike, 15km from *Corinium* (Robinson 1992, 58–9; Miles 1984). This section, dealing with the tract of Roman countryside contained within the study area, will be largely descriptive therefore, and will consider firstly villas (in the sense of rural structures constructed in the Roman tradition) and secondly other forms of settlement.

The spatial distribution of settlement in the environs of *Corinium* is worthy of comment. A view expressed by a number of earlier authors has been succinctly summarised by Branigan (1976, 27):

'There are relatively few [villas] close to the town itself, as one would expect since much of the land there must have been farmed from the town, but in the 8–16km zone villas are far more numerous and attest to a class of rural landowners who required the amenities of Cirencester to be close at hand.'

Thanks to the evidence collected by RCHME and this project we are now able to see that the environs of Cirencester were far from devoid of contemporary settlement. There are indications of high status buildings which might be termed villas in the immediate environs of the town, although unfortunately none are known to any great extent.

At The Barton, which lies 360m from the walls of the town, excavations in 1824, 1909 and 1937 revealed a fourth-century Orpheus mosaic, part of a column and fragments of painted wall plaster. At Somerford Road, Chesterton (350m from the walls) there are reports of a Roman building, including fragments of column (RCHME 1976, 31 (7)). Elsewhere Rudder (1800, 63–4) records a mosaic 'lately [found] at a place called Aing's ash in Oakley Wood' in Cirencester Park, and James Buckman (1866b, 292) mentions:

'I have only found one example of a quern made of this stone; it was found on the farm of the Agricultural College at Cirencester, having been turned up by the plough in an arable field, in which I had previously observed evidence of Roman occupation, besides finding the remains of a Roman Villa in another field on the same farm. Both sites are a little removed from Acman Street, about one-and-a-half miles from *Corinium*.'(54144)

A single tessera was recovered from fieldwalking at the south of Clark's Lane site (54190) to the south of the town (RCHME 1976, 102).

Too little is known for any meaningful discussion of the nature of these sites, although Esmonde Cleary has observed (1987, 173–4, 188) that high status sites lying within a short distance of the defences such as The Barton are known from other large towns (such as the Dagmar Road and Olga Road buildings, Dorchester (Dorset); Ilchester Mead, Ilchester; and the Norfolk Street complex, Leicester). Although frequently referred to as villas it is unclear whether these buildings were purely residential suburban homes or working agricultural complexes; indeed just the same debate applies to the Beeches Road complex within the walls (see p 65). We would be in a much better position to address these questions if more was known of The Barton; in particular whether the site originated in the period before the town defences, in which case its apparent location outside the defences is of little consequence. If a third or fourth century foundation, however, the evidence for tracts of undeveloped land within the town suggests that it is unlikely to have been pressure on space which led to its siting outside the defences.

Fleshing-out the picture significantly are the apparently non-villa settlements detected by fieldwalking and aerial photography in the vicinity of *Corinium*; these at once give the lie to the notion that the land surrounding the town was exclusively farmed from estates within the walls. Some 2.3km north of the town an extensive area of settlement is known on the high, well-drained land between Ermin Street and the Churn valley. Revealed by aerial photographs the site presents a confusing mass of cropmarks but appears to include linear trackways, several rectilinear enclosures and traces of field systems. Despite a number of difficulties in interpretation the cropmarks suggest a tract of managed agricultural landscape covering some 180ha (54138–54140). Although there is no direct dating evidence for the features, metal-detecting and fieldwalking finds from the general area including third-fourth century pottery and coins. Two inhumation burials, one containing Roman artefacts, immediately south-west of Ermin Street at this point should probably be related to this settlement (Anon 1887–8, 1). Further to the east on Baunton Downs and adjacent to the Whiteway a rectilinear enclosure (about 20m by 10m) is visible on aerial photographs (54189). Excavation and fieldwalking finds point firmly to a Roman date (finds include two uninscribed altars; no structural debris is recorded; RCHME 1976, 13). Other, apparently agricultural sites, are known from the south of the study area where elements of fieldsystems and track/droveways have been identified at three sites where Roman dating evidence has been forthcoming. To the east in Baunton parish two sites are known through surface collection: that adjacent to Witpit Copse has produced 36 fourth-century coins, late third-fourth century pottery and Roman tile (Anon 1981, 42). To the west of the town the lack of evidence is probably merely a reflection of the presence of Cirencester Park inhibiting arable agriculture which has led directly or indirectly to the discovery of the other sites.

Agricultural activity on the very fringe of Cirencester has been demonstrated by Reece's small excavation at Kingshill on the line of the Cirencester ring-road. Lying only 200m from the town wall the excavation suggested that occupation commenced around the mid first century AD. Features interpreted as palisades and ditches appear to have been filled in the third century before being covered by ploughsoil which yielded fourth-century pottery and coins. Finds of roofing tile and burnt daub in the filling of the ditches suggested the presence of a nearby building (Reece 1990, 39–44).

Of the agricultural economy of these sites we can say little. Bones recovered from the Kingshill excavation included cattle, sheep, horse and pig although in too small a quantity for meaningful statistics. Analysis of bone assemblages of late Iron Age/early Roman date from Bagendon and of late Roman date from the Beeches Road complex in Cirencester both point to the dominance of cattle over sheep in the meat supply, a pattern at variance with earlier Iron Age and high medieval assemblages where sheep are more prevalent (A King 1978).

Monument Discrimination

Large areas of the Roman town are scheduled as being of national importance. Specific monuments which score 'high' include the *forum* and *basilica*, the town wall with its component gates and towers, the *macellum*, and a number of town houses. It remains true that in areas of reasonable preservation within the walls, there is a good possibility that Roman deposits of national importance will be encountered. As additional data are gathered new Roman monuments of national importance will probably be elucidated.

Outside the walls, the cemeteries (54057, 54372, 54431, 54435) score high. Uncertainties over the identification and date of the Tar Barrows and Grismonds Tower as Roman burial mounds and the inadequate documentation of previous investigations on these sites tends to restrict their scoring at present but future research may change this. The amphitheatre (54045) is also of undoubted national importance, reflecting the rarity of this upstanding monument and its close association with a variety of other contemporary monuments of national and regional importance such as a cemetery, roads and quarries.

Of the rural sites the settlement at Kingshill may be classed as being of regional importance, especially considering that the early structures are covered by late Roman ploughsoil. The other rural settlements should probably be classed similarly, although little of substance is known of these sites. Depending upon the current state of preservation, the Roman building at The Barton may be classed of regional-national importance; too little is known of the other Roman 'villas' within the Study Area for meaningful assessment of their importance. Monuments not as yet recognised within the rural area include temples and potteries. These may exist elsewhere within the hinterland of the Roman town but have not so far been identified within the modern boundaries of the civil parishes chosen as appropriate units for this study.

9. *CYRNCEASTRE:* A ROYAL/ECCLESIASTICAL CENTRE IN THE EARLY MEDIEVAL PERIOD

by Christopher Gerrard

'Mr Smith, the fishmonger, had a stable there, and at a time when the cheapness of oysters made them a general article of diet, he used to deposit loads of oystershells there until they were inches deep on the road [*c*1870]. These shells now form the foundation of the present roadway, and it possible that centuries hence, when some scientific excavator comes across this deposit, he may frame an ingenious and convincing theory to account for the finding of marine remains so far inland.'

W Scotford Harmer, in Baddeley's *History of Cirencester* (1924, 328), highlights the dangers of interpretation of 'black earths'

This Chapter describes the archaeological evidence for the urban area between the end of the Roman period and the Norman Conquest. During this period the name of the town is variously recorded in the *Anglo-Saxon Chronicle* as *Cirenceaster* (sa 577), *Cirenceastre* (sa 628; A), *Cirnceastre* (E) and *Cyrenceastre* (sa 1020). Unlike the preceeding Roman period, the data available are scant and often questionable. Naturally, interpretations may be similarly flawed.

Certainly, the urban character of Cirencester in the early post-Roman period was very different from that of the preceding 400 years, in population size, structure and even location. While substantial Roman buildings must have remained standing and occupied, girdled by the town wall (and hence the '*caester*' name), initially there seems little to differentiate settlement in the town from settlements in the countryside. A number of Roman buildings have late features which suggest occupation into the fifth century, for example the winged-corridor villa at the Beeches (McWhirr 1986). Likewise, the heavy wear on paving stones at the *forum* has been taken to imply use 'to a late date' (*c*AD 430) while the lack of finds and debris suggested 'high standards of cleanliness' to its excavator (Wacher 1964a, 14; 1975). Viewed more dispassionately, it would be wrong to speculate how long buildings such as the *forum* might have continued to function and in what capacity.

After the mid fifth century there is precious little to go on. An undated ditch, of late Roman or possible early medieval date was discovered in 1961 on the Mycalex factory site (Reece 1976b; Wacher 1962, 11). Elsewhere, dubiously dated bodies found in the 'organic' fillings of ditches at Leaholme (McWhirr *et al* 1982, 207) and Dyer Court (Webster 1957; McWhirr *et al* 1982, 207) have fuelled speculation of fifth-century epidemics and 'unburied bodies left to rot in roadside ditches' (Wacher 1975, 313) inspired by the writings of Bede and Gildas (Colgrave and Mynors 1969). Between *c*AD 450 and AD 550, the earliest date for the artefacts from the Barton Farm cemetery, the gap is filled only by such undated and troublesome pieces of the puzzle as the black earths and the modifications to the amphitheatre.

The site of the Roman amphitheatre is the one candidate for early medieval housing within the study area and a fifth and sixth century fortified site has been suggested by the excavator. Late in its use the entrance passages were narrowed, flanking rooms blocked off and the entrance route improved. Crucially, excavations in the amphitheatre in 1963 uncovered a number of large holes together with rough cobbled floors and finds of fifth–eighth century pottery tempered with vegetal grog (Wacher 1964a, 18; 1981). The excavator interpreted these holes as being designed for the timber uprights of an Anglo-Saxon hall but insufficient of the plan was recovered to securely identify the monument. Photographs show that these holes might be better described as pits up to 1.5m across and, since the associated pottery was unstratified (Heighway pers comm) any further interpretation must await final publication.

The possible fortification of the amphitheatre is of great interest, not least because of the apparent importance of fortified bases to British military leaders of the post-Roman period, as shown by the re-use of hillforts in Somerset for example (Burrow 1981). The interpretation of the re-used amphitheatre as a chieftain's residence or place of shelter prior to the Battle of Dyrham in AD 577 has a seductive pseudo-historical authenticity but it may prove too exclusive an interpretation on the basis of so limited information.

Elsewhere the form and location of settlements are, if anything, even less certain. The field name 'Kingsmead' on the south-east periphery of the town had always been thought to hold some potential until recent evaluation proved negative (OAU 1991) but, tantalisingly, a possible Anglo-Saxon sunken featured building was identified but not recorded during a watching brief for the Cirencester ring road in 1973 (Reece pers comm). Away from the town, there is as yet no archaeological evidence to establish a pre-Conquest origin for any of the later medieval rural settlements, at least in their present locations, and it would be wrong to assert that Domesday Book tells us otherwise.

In 1886 an early medieval cemetery was discovered at The Barton (54420) where nine skeletons were found (P D C Brown 1976, 31–3). A number of discoveries have been made here including, in 1909, two shield bosses of pagan Anglo-Saxon type in association with one adult male and one child burial which had been cut down through a Roman Orpheus mosaic inside the former villa buildings (Figure 30; Baddeley 1924, 60–1). There is also an Anglo-Saxon pot decorated with stamped patterns, bosses and incised lines from this site. The extent and layout of the cemetery is quite unclear but has been dated to the sixth century (perhaps earlier than AD 550) on the basis of typological parallels with similar artefacts from the Upper Thames Valley (P D C Brown 1976). Nothing beyond selected skeletal remains and artefacts survives for study.

Figure 30
Skeleton of an adult male, cut through the Orpheus mosaic at The Barton, discovered in 1909 (Corinium Museum)

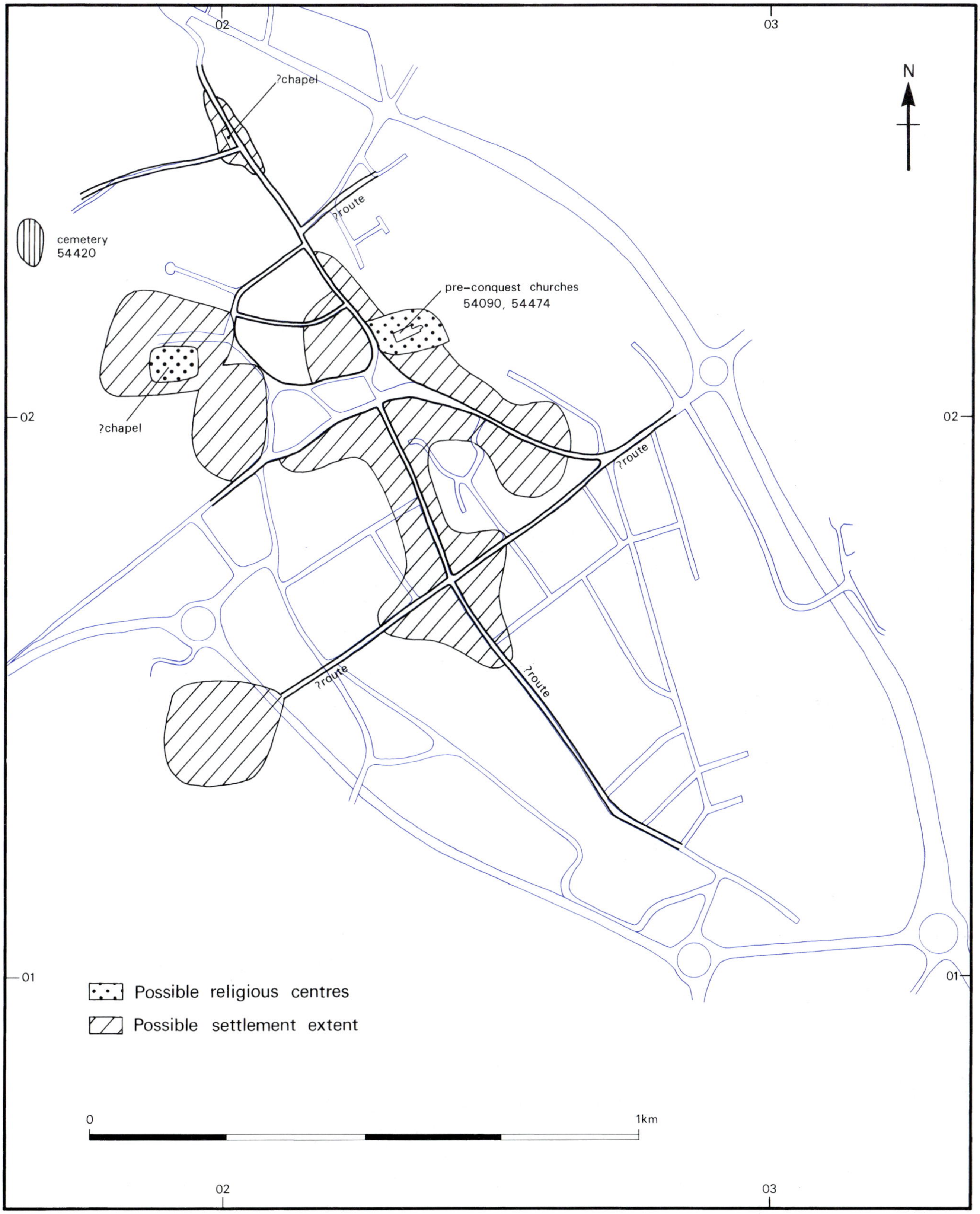

Figure 31
Monuments in the early medieval Royal/Ecclesiastical Centre
Key to Figure 31:
54090 The Abbey (1) pre-conquest church 54420 The Barton cemetery 54474 The Abbey (2) pre-conquest church

The historical evidence for Cirencester in the sixth and seventh centuries adds further complications. According to the *Anglo-Saxon Chronicle* in 577 Ceawlin is said to have defeated and killed the kings Conmail, Condidan and Fairinmail at the battle of Dyrham and to have taken Gloucester, Cirencester and Bath (Whitelock *et al* 1961). On the face of it a harmonious splicing of archaeological and historical evidence begins to look untenable in the face of mid sixth century material from the Barton cemetery which suggests Anglo-Saxon settlement around Cirencester well before AD 577. However, as Sims-Williams (1983) has pointed out, there are ways of reconciling the archaeology with the historical data. One could suppose, for example, that the artefacts in the Barton cemetery were already antiques when they were deposited or that the Britons had recovered the areas from the English before the 570s when they promptly lost them again. However, the chronology of the *Chronicle* must remain suspicious.

More generally, even if the dates cannot be given too much weight, the ninth-century compiler of the *Chronicle* presumably intends it to be understood that Cirencester was an important central place *c*400–600 AD (Yorke 1990). In 628 Cirencester again was fought over by Cynegils and Penda. This chiefly reflects the competition between the West Saxon and Mercian rulers to control the area but the forceful acquisition of administrative districts or *regiones* by Anglo-Saxons again implies a town of some status with a surrounding area dependent upon it.

A number of early medieval finds have been made in the town including pins, a buckle, a disc brooch, a mouthpiece from a sword scabbard, iron spearheads, a number of beads including imported examples, garter hooks, a pin beater (for work on a warp-weighted loom), and a carved bone tube (possibly a gaming piece) (P D C Brown 1976, fig 3.2, 23). Only one of these objects has a secure provenance but they do prove that artefacts from Ireland and possibly France were not unknown in the town before the seventh century and suggest bronze metal-working and weaving in the locality. Taken together, this information suggests at least intermittent activity in Cirencester in the immediate post-Roman period though there is little evidence for the continuity of town life after the mid fifth century judged by any satisfactory set of criteria. There was certainly trade and travel to and through the former Roman town but no recognisable urbanised form in Cirencester's continuing history of settlement.

There is considerable debate about whether Cirencester shows evidence for 'continuity' or not (eg Brooks 1986). Much depends on how the word 'continuity' is defined. It is probably true that there has been continuous use of the site and its environs from Roman times, perhaps because it was a river crossing on a major route or because the place carried a memory of its past, possibly an administrative identity, which was never forgotten. However, there have also been dramatic shifts in location, from Roman town to Anglo-Saxon ecclesiastical centre to medieval market town. Each urban form is so much an expression of a changed set of circumstances as to defy any argument for continuity.

Royal/Ecclesiastical Centre

By the mid seventh century Cirencester had probably re-emerged as an estate centre through the initiative and influence of the church and, later, royalty. How far this centre can be said to have had urban characteristics is debatable for, in common with many other towns and cities, few monuments have so far been identified from this form (Figure 31). It seems plausible that survival of the town was dependent more on administrative continuity than commercial or demographic growth which are arguably more visible in the archaeological record. One interpretation might envisage Cirencester retaining some limited 'central place functions' throughout the sub-Roman period and increasing commercial activity and population as a result of an early medieval role as an ecclesiastical centre.

What evidence is there for an effective urban centre after the ninth century? In general terms, the political and administrative complexity of the region in the pre-Conquest period as suggested by historical evidence is confirmed by considerable investment in later Anglo-Saxon rural programmes of church building and mill construction. Evidence for the nucleation of villages and the creation of open field systems might also be expected (C C Taylor 1983). The importance of the town itself is indicated by references in both Asser's *Life of Alfred* (Jane 1966) and the *Anglo-Saxon Chronicle* which describe how the Vikings moved camp from Chippenham to Cirencester in AD 879. The Vikings generally used royal '*tunas*' for their camps probably because they were centres of collection of royal '*feorm*' which were still probably paid in kind at this time. A big minster church would also have been a tempting attraction, if the proposed eighth century construction date can be accepted (Evans 1991).

In the tenth and eleventh centuries Cirencester did not have a mint, unlike Cricklade to the south and Gloucester or Winchcombe to the west and north-west (Loyn 1961) and does not feature in the Burghal Hidage (Hill 1978; Biddle 1976). In the absence of these attributes the relative importance of the town is difficult to gauge, though the layout of key topographic features is significant, as Haslam has remarked for Anglo-Saxon towns in Wiltshire

(Haslam 1984; see below). However, Cirencester's omission need not cause us to doubt the strength of the regional economy and the importance of Cirencester as a centre for Mercian and West Saxon royal administration should be recognised. There are sufficient references to show it was a royal *'tun'* and there were significant late Saxon assemblies here throughout the tenth century (Sawyer 1968; see Historical Documentation below for dates). It is quite possible that the main framework of the town was only established after the mid tenth century and that this may have been the town's most intense period of occupation since the Roman period with the growth of permanent tenements and ribbon developments (Astill 1991). In this respect, whilst never obtaining any known military status, Cirencester has much in common with the revival of towns elsewhere in southern Britain and it may be instructive that Cirencester is described as a 'new market' in the Domesday Book.

With so many interesting questions it is disappointing to report that archaeological information does not significantly increase what is known from other sources. With only one excavated monument, the unpublished late eighth century church site, and a small handful of artefacts only the most rudimentary assessment of this form is possible. Little investigation has taken place to the north of Lewis Lane where the greatest potential for fragile Saxon archaeology must lie. In part, medieval and post-medieval damage from cellarage and construction may be to blame, coupled with constraints of time and opportunity in past excavation programmes, exasperated perhaps by the lack of a clear chronology of ceramic traditions for this period.

The streets

The Roman road system had only a passive role in determining the layout of the early medieval town. The line of Lewis Lane, for example, may reflect a route straight through the town rather than to it and Cirencester's location at an important road junction must be one of the reasons why trade and town life reawakened. Within the Roman walled area, however, many minor streets were aligned differently from their Roman antecedents so that property boundaries and formal classical spaces were lost. Much of the area to the south of the modern alignment of Lewis Lane became redundant.

The alignments of Dyer Street, Castle Street, Park Street, Black Jack Street, and others, are all directed towards a clear activity focus, the church, and cut across the Roman streets. The accumulations of black earth (see below) would suggest that much of the Roman town, with the exception of the town walls and throughfares, was invisible to later inhabitants, buried beneath a thick mantle of soil.

Perhaps surprisingly, given the continued presence of a single, strong ecclesiastical lordship, there is no evidence of the deliberate reorganisation of the Roman topography though the proximity of the market place, church and, presumably, housing suggests a complex of features typical of a late Saxon urban centre. Elsewhere in the town whilst zones of 'plan-units', plots of regular size, shape and orientation, can be recognised on nineteenth-century maps along Gloucester Street, Cricklade Street, Dyer Street and on Cecily Hill, they cannot with any certainty be assigned an early medieval date (Conzen 1968). These units contrast with the sub-circular street blocks defined by modern Castle Street and Black Jack Street and may signal a different land-use history. Hopefully, archaeological excavation might in the future be of some assistance in dating particular blocks and recent work in Worcester (Baker *et al* 1992) shows the exciting potential of this kind of work.

Housing

Cyrnceastre was apparently confined to an area less than half that of the preceding Roman provincial capital and was located in the north-western part of the earlier town. Minor foci are possibly to be identified at Cecily Hill (medieval *Inchthorpe*) and at the site of St Lawrence's Hospital, as well as at unidentified sites outside the Roman town walls (see below).

No early medieval structures have been identified from the town but logically, structures might be grouped around the church sites and along the major arterial routes (especially those which differ in alignment from the late Roman street plan). Wooden structures of post-hole, post-in-trench or sill-beam construction might be expected (Rahtz 1976). These kinds of buildings are not easy to recognise in the archaeological record and might well have been missed in the past. Occupation may also have been very limited and, if Gloucester may be used as a model, parts of Cirencester may have been in agricultural use in the ninth and tenth centuries and occupation may have shifted around inside the urban area (Heighway 1984a). Sadly, given the lack of eighth to eleventh century recorded stray finds from Cirencester it is not possible to chart the growth of the town in a meaningful way.

A common feature of excavation is the accumulation of a homogenous black earth which may be partly ploughsoil, partly dumping and the accretion of compost from dying vegetation (McPhail 1981). Excavated Roman monuments within the town are commonly found to have been masked by these dark soils and, where they were formerly used to suggest the disuse, abandonment and decay of the Roman town, they are now suspected of containing valuable evidence of continuity for the period between the mid fifth century and the emergence of a convincing early medieval urban form. However, in Cirencester there is little dating evidence for these soils, which are thickest to the north of Lewis Lane, and much of this deposit may be medieval and post-medieval in date, as implied by the cautionary quote at the head of this chapter. Further micro-morphological studies are needed.

The historical evidence suggests a number of additional monuments about which we have no evidence at present. First, the assemblies of large numbers of important people in late Saxon Cirencester implies the ability to house them. At present there is no indication where this might have taken place, though it is notable that at Gloucester the 'palace' site at Kingsholm was outside the main town (Heighway 1984a and b). Second, there may be buried archaeological evidence for temporary Viking encampments and burials, as at Repton, Derbyshire (Biddle 1985).

Religious buildings

The massive foundations of a pre-conquest church (54090), incorporating robbed Roman masonry, were discovered in 1965 to the north of the present parish church. Later stone robbing, the lack of post-Roman artefacts and subsequent building caused some difficulties in interpretation and dating but the church, which is all of a single construction phase, had a 175ft (53.3m) nave with aisles to north and south divided into *porticus* and an apsidal east end with a crypt beneath (Figure 32). A number of burials were also excavated (P D C Brown 1976, 33–43; Brown and McWhirr 1966, 1967; Wilkinson and McWhirr, forthcoming), but ancilliary buildings, as possibly at Northampton (Williams *et al* 1984) were not recorded, though they should be expected nearby.

The probable existence of such a site, though often in the past misrepresented as a prebendal college (eg Leland (1535–1543) in Toulmin Smith 1964), is documented in the cartulary of Cirencester Abbey as well as by later historians (eg Collinson undated) although local opinion had previously placed the church below the Abbey House (Beecham 1887, 83).

The excavated church has been dated to the late eighth century and the presence of an early ecclesiastical centre seems as crucial for our understanding of the early medieval and later development of Cirencester as it does for Gloucester and Tewkesbury. The church clearly ranks amongst the known major Middle Saxon Mercian churches

Figure 32
The south wall of the apse of the Saxon church, with surviving parts of the robbed crypt to the left, and cut by a later tomb (Cirencester Excavation Committee)

such as Brixworth and must have been a minster with jurisdiction over a dependent surrounding area. This is reflected in later links which acknowledge the former dependency of daughter churches such as Baunton on the mother church at Cirencester.

The construction of this large church in the late eighth century raises questions about the earlier religious beliefs in this area. Were the inhabitants of the town non-Christian until the early eighth century? and if so, as Bassett inquires (1989), why are sources so silent about their eventual conversion? One likely alternative would be to envisage Cirencester, together with London, York and Lincoln as sites of late Roman/sub-Roman bishoprics with fluctuating roles as ecclesiastical centres throughout this period. By the seventh century, in spite of the large numbers of sees at former Roman cities, Cirencester was not amongst them, perhaps because of the town's location on the frontiers of unstable Anglo-Saxon kingdoms (see Bassett 1989 and 1992 for further discussion). If this interpretation is followed it seems quite possible that future work might reveal archaeological evidence of an early episcopal centre in the town which would later have been succeeded by the excavated church site. Quite possibly, our vision of a single church is false (Blair and Sharpe 1992) and there is more than one pre-Conquest church to be excavated within the Abbey Grounds. An alternative view, put forward by Evans (1991) would place the origins of the earliest church in Cirencester to the mid seventh century, the period of conversion of the Anglo-Saxon conquerors of the region.

Besides the status it afforded, the location of a church profoundly influenced the layout of all subsequent urban forms. Its construction is surely the single most important explanation as to why the northern half of the town came to be developed during this period. Sadly, its excavation gave us no clues as to why it might have been located in this particular spot. Was this cleared ground? Was there a pre-existing Roman religious site here (see Holbrook, Chapter 8)? Why were the sites of Roman official buildings such as the *forum* or public baths, surely a good source of quality building stone, not re-used as they were at Gloucester, Winchester and elsewhere?

The excavator's published interpretation is that this church of late seventh to ninth century date was taken down and replaced by a second, smaller pre-Conquest church (54474) some time before the Conquest (P D C Brown 1976, 33–43). In turn, this building was demolished to make way for the Abbey in the second half of the twelfth century and is presumably that mentioned in Domesday Book. Later re-interpretation of the stratigraphy seems likely to place this second church amongst remodellings of early thirteenth century date. The sequence is thus rather simplified with a large Saxon church, now redated to the late eighth century, replaced by the nave of the Abbey in the second half of the twelfth century (Wilkinson and McWhirr, forthcoming). To this crude sketch we should probably add subsidiary structures such as holy wells, cells for reading and praying, detached sleeping quarters, guesthouses, workshops and hermitages (Blair and Sharpe 1992).

Important recent work (Evans 1976, 1989, 1991) has made clear that there is no documentary evidence for the early church in Cirencester. The earliest mention of a group of canons seems to be in the charter of 1133 in which Henry I endowed the Abbey and there is little to connect the name of Regenbald, clerk to Edward the Confessor and William the Conqueror, with the site other than that he once owned the land. Regenbald was endowed with a number of minster churches on royal estates by Edward the Confessor and he probably took the greater part of the revenues and left priests to carry out the parochial duties. His acquisition of the Cirencester site is further confirmation for minster status for the site, since minsters were the normal form of endowment for royal priests. The distribution of his land holdings before and after Domesday, in which he is referred to once as 'Regenbald of Cirencester', suggests a strong association with the town and it may be that he settled down here and was buried in the church. His lands certainly form the basis of the group granted by Henry I to the foundation at Cirencester (Keynes 1987).

Two further chapels are shown on Figure 31 at the site of the medieval St Lawrence's Hospital and at the Chapel of St Cecilia. Reece suggests that both monuments may have their origins as late Roman cemetery churches and that this helps to activate a shift of settlement towards the north of the town by the medieval period (Reece and Catling 1975, 13). Something similar could be proposed for Gloucester where two leper hospitals overlie the Roman cemetery at Wotton Pitch (Heighway 1984a and b), and there are possible British and European parallels (eg Doggett 1986 for Dorchester-on-Thames; Biddle 1976). St Cecilia was also a popular Roman saint (Slater 1976a, 97) but it has to be said that there is no archaeological evidence whatsoever for these suggestions and, for that reason, no monuments have been marked on the map.

Accumulated deposits

This form is probably the least well understood in Cirencester's history. The kinds of evidence that might be expected contrast markedly with those available for the Roman town. Instead of stone walls and substantial and sometimes impressive floors the building techniques of the occupants of the town in the fifth–tenth centuries favoured timber and earth construction. It should not be assumed, however, that the changes in building technique represent a deterioration in the quality or impressive character of the structures. Timber buildings can be just as large and just as architecturally sophisticated as stone buildings, they simply do not survive as well in the long term. The most distinctive deposits of relevance to this period are the so-called dark earths, although visual comparison of the results of available site data suggest that there are several different kinds of dark earth in Cirencester, ranging from the locally famous oyster-shell level (see head of Chapter) to a relatively compact brown-black deposit immediately above later Roman structures.

With the exception of the cemetery, the majority of the deposits in this form are unclassifiable. There are no earthworks and the only known substantial building, the Saxon church site, is buried and mostly robbed out. The state of individual plots undoubtedly varies but the weakness of our understanding is such that it is not yet possible to say where there are stable deposits. More fragile elements may still exist away from street frontages under modern back gardens and where they have been buried under modern landscaping, for example in the Abbey Grounds.

Survival: Cirencester retains few visible clues as to the whereabouts of buried features in this urban form and so data for the assessment of survival is very limited. There are no zones of high survival. Zones of medium survival must include the Abbey Grounds and areas of open space around the market place. Dark earths which are thought to contain deposits of fifth to eleventh century date are present over much of the northern half of the urban area. The majority of the urban area must at present be considered of low survival because of the superimposition of later developments.

Potential: In spite of Cirencester's valley location and the potential for thick and/or waterlogged strata, there is no evidence so far to indicate any potential for wet recovery of artefacts at this date. Whilst casual stray finds from unknown locations indicate some general potential, the character and volume of deposits are poorly understood.

Documentation (archaeological): Relatively little detailed exploration of deposits of this period has taken place. Zones of high archaeological documentation are restricted to the area of the Anglo-Saxon church excavated in 1965–66 to the north of the modern parish church and miscellaneous stray finds, whose distribution shows no patterning. The remainder of the area of this form is of low archaeological documentation in spite of small-scale excavations and watching briefs which have helped to identify the presence of black earths.

Documentation (historical): The difficulties in handling the historical documentation for this period have been assessed by Sims-Williams (1983). Cirencester is mentioned in the ninth-century *Anglo-Saxon Chronicle* in the 577 Annal when the 'kings' of Cirencester, Bath and Gloucester are defeated at Dyrham. According to the same source, which may be questioned on many counts, Penda was victorious against the pagan West Saxon kings Cynegils and Cwichelm in a battle at Cirencester in 628 (Whitelock *et al* 1961). Afterwards the people known as the Hwicce came under Mercian lordship (Brooks 1989).

There are no Anglo-Saxon charters from within the study area, although portions of shared boundaries may be assumed from clauses in charters for the neighbouring lands of Kemble and South Cerney (Grundy 1935–6).

Cirencester was the site of a synodal council for Ethelred the Unready (991–993) as well as a council of King Canute. Significant late Saxon assemblies were held here in AD 935, AD 956, AD 985, and 1020 (Sawyer 1968). The town is listed in Domesday Book (Moore 1982).

Group Value (clustering): Knowledge of this form is so weak that no cases of repetitious monuments can be identified. Industrial zones, for example, have not been recognised. The whole form is zoned as poor in Group Value (clustering).

Diversity (features): There are no known cases of superimposed monument forms nor the re-use of Roman buildings such as the *forum*. However, the Roman buildings and streets have a passive role in determining the urban structure of the later town, particularly the major gateways. The whole form is zoned as poor.

Group Value (association): A large part of this form as presently understood can be regarded as of high Group Value (association) because it overlies the Roman forms and is in turn succeeded by the medieval and later forms. The putative north-eastern section of the form can be regarded as being a possible zone of medium Group Value (association) because it is overlain by the medieval town yet lies outside the walls of the Roman defences. The presence of the early medieval town in this area depends wholly upon the interpreted origins of the medieval suburbs along Gloucester Street and Cecily Hill which are poorly understood at present.

Amenity Value: With the exception of the amphitheatre, the survival of monuments of this period is generally poor and provides little visual amenity. It is not readily appreciated that the area of the post-Roman town is different from that of the preceding forms; there is no recognised 'old town' for example.

There are, however, some popular early medieval associations for the town. The fables of Holinshed and Geoffrey of Monmouth, amongst others, recount the antics of a certain Gurmund, described by some writers as 'King of the Africans' and by others as a Norwegian pirate (Beecham 1887, 12–13). In an attempt to take the city, he tied burning fibres to the feet of sparrows which nested in the eaves of the houses and so burnt the town to the ground. The legend appears on the shield of the present Town Council with the phoenix rising from the flames, and Grismond's Mount, though it has no known early medieval archaeology, is still a prominent earthwork just inside Cirencester Park.

Given the popularity of romantic legend it is slightly surprising that the medieval claim of Grismund's Mount as the coronation site of King Arthur, and of King Alfred living a year in Cirencester are forgotten today.

Overall, Cirencester is one of about 25 prime examples of Royal/Ecclesiastical Centres across England. However, there is little published archaeological data, especially when compared to the Roman or later medieval evidence for the town. Visitors to the town may leave quite unaware of even the existence of the early church site, the later history of Roman monuments such as the amphitheatre and the lasting influence of the pre-Conquest period upon modern land-use and town layout. Nevertheless, Cirencester has the potential to contribute to debate on a number of key issues in the early middle ages. These include our understanding of British powerbases following the end of Roman rule, the reasons for shifts in the focus of settlements, and the development of the later Saxon urban form.

Early medieval countryside

Administrative frameworks

Land ownership and administration is often invisible in the landscape but has an enormous influence on archaeology. For the early medieval period attention has been drawn to the existence of 'multiple estates', multi-vill manors dependent on head places or *caputs*. Cirencester shares miscellaneous characteristics in common with other head places: for example it was the head of a hundredal manor (a quarter of the shire); it is surrounded by subsidiary place-names such as Preston (meaning 'the priests' tun') and Siddington (meaning 'the place to the south'); it was a medieval royal demesne manor; it has a known early church site; and its medieval church had a number of dependent chapelries indicating earlier dependency. The overall pattern suggests that early estates approximated to the area of the Seven Hundreds of Cirencester and that this unit may have earlier, possibly even pre-Roman, antecedents. The territory of the Seven Hundreds as it existed in AD 900 has been reconstructed (Slater 1976a, 82–6) and implies an effective urban centre (Cooper 1986).

Although there are no Anglo-Saxon charters from within the study area, extant charters for South Cerney and Kemble-Ewen provide information for shared boundaries (Grundy 1935–6). In AD 909 King Aethelred (K703) granted 15 hides of land at South Cerney to the monastery at Abingdon, and the survey outlines the southern boundary of Siddington with South Cerney. Further to the west, the bounds of the former parish of Ewen are described in a charter of AD 931 (B671, 672, 673, K 355) whereby King Aethelstan granted 15 hides to Malmesbury Abbey. Here shared portions include the line of the Fosse, the line of the present parish boundaries between Cirencester–Kemble and the western edge of Siddington–Kemble.

Some monuments of known date are spatially related to boundaries and so help to date them. For example, the parish boundary between Preston and Cirencester follows the line of the Fosse Way and clearly post-dates it, as does the eastern margin of the parish of Baunton which also follows the road and is known to be a post-medieval invention. The only candidates for early boundaries are the Stratton–Cirencester boundary, the tything boundaries within Cirencester, the Siddington–Cirencester boundary and parts of the outer boundary of the Study Area. The Stratton–Cirencester boundary is particularly interesting because it is straddled by The Barton early medieval cemetery (54420). Similar cases elsewhere have been used to support the hypothesis that burials are deliberately placed on pre-existing or 'primary' economic boundaries in order to reinforce territorial claims (Goodier 1984). This would suggest a date before the mid sixth century for that part of the boundary line at least. Reece has argued that the medieval tythings are the heirs to late Roman farmsteads in or near the Roman town (Reece and Catling 1975).

By the tenth century these large administrative estates had fragmented into unicellular manors and the boundaries of some earlier economic units, like Stratton, became fossilised through the establishment of parishes.

Settlement, cemeteries and industry

The classic diagnostic features of Anglo-Saxon churches such as pilasters and long-and-short work are not to be found within the Study Area. However, the blocked remains of a Saxon doorway are still visible in the north wall of the nave in the pre-Conquest church of All Saints at Preston (54146). Upper and Lower Siddington (54438 and 54439) as well as Stratton (54440) are likely to have had pre-Conquest churches and are recorded as having a priest at the time of Domesday (Slater 1976a) (Figure 33). This evidence for Anglo-Saxon church sites around Cirencester must be seen in the context of a larger group identified by Taylor and Taylor (1968–78) including Bibury, Daglingworth and Coln Rogers amongst others. The reasons for such a grouping are unclear, substantial investments by late Saxon society are certainly indicated but whether this is a genuine 'cultural efflorescence' (Cooper 1986) or simply a misleading pattern which results from a lack of later medieval investment in

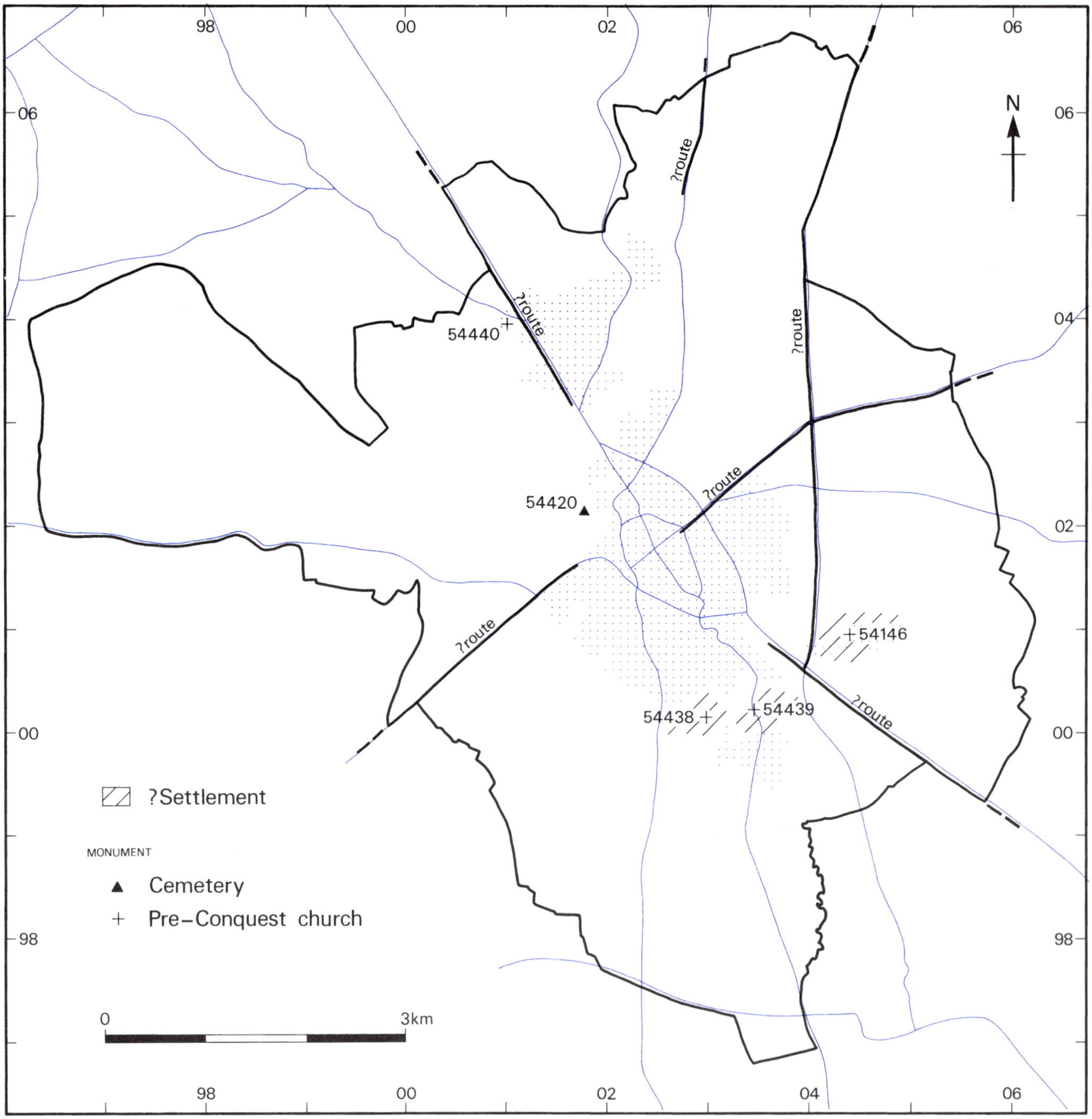

Figure 33
Early medieval monuments in the rural area (see Figure 31 for monuments within the urban form)

Key to Figure 33:

54146	Preston	pre-Conquest church
54420	The Barton	cemetery
54438	Upper Siddington	pre-Conquest church
54439	Lower Siddington	pre-Conquest church
54440	Stratton	pre-Conquest church

Not located:

54247	Stratton	mill
54374	Stratton	mill
54377	Cirencester	mill
54378	Cirencester	mill
54379	Cirencester	mill
54422	Siddington St Peter	mill
54425	Siddington St Mary	mill

church building outside of the major wool centres is unclear.

Domesday Book provides documentary reference to seven watermills lying within the four parishes. Three watermills recorded for Cirencester (54377–54379), valued together at 30 shillings, were part of the main manor, which Moore (1982) suggests was centred around Barton Farm. Archaeological evidence is lacking but one or more of these could be expected to be an antecedent for medieval watermills at The Barton and Gildenbridge. Assuming all seven were stream or river-driven, effective management of the river Churn can be envisaged, with two mills on its course to the north of Cirencester at Stratton (54247 and 54374), and two to the south in Siddington St Peter (54422), and Siddington St Mary (54425).

Environment

Organic clay deposits of possible Saxon date examined close to Trinity Mill showed good pollen preservation. Recorded in Domesday Book, the mill lies just outside the immediate study area in the parish of Bagendon, but illustrates well the potential for the survival of environmental evidence based on pollen analysis. A moderately diverse assemblage was identified including cereal pollen, grasses and herb pollen (buttercups, ribwort plantain, rat-tail plantains, Great Burnet), tree pollen (oak, ash) and shrubs (hazel and willow). This suggests a variety of vegetation environments typical of a species-rich water-meadow close to woods and farmland. Cereal grains may be derived either from adjacent arable areas or from crop processing associated with the mill (Scaife 1991), but too little material was available to provide accurate dating.

Monument Discrimination

The number of monuments identified in early medieval Cirencester is small in comparison with the previous Roman urban forms and the medieval market town. Only one identified monument has been investigated through techniques of modern excavation, the pre-Conquest church to the north of the present-day parish church of St John the Baptist. This monument ranks high. With the exception of the Anglo-Saxon cemetery site at The Barton, the existence of all the other monuments is only implied in written accounts such as Domesday Book. Their archaeological character is entirely unassessed.

10. *CIRENCESTRE:* A MEDIUM-SIZED MARKET TOWN IN THE MEDIEVAL PERIOD

by Christopher Gerrard

'Here was a castle on the south-west side of the town, and tho' I have not been able to discover when nor by whom it was built, our histories give us a more certain account of its destruction.'

Samuel Rudder, *A new history of Gloucestershire* (1779)

'There will always be uncertainty until there should chance to be, for some other purpose, any deep trenching, when the base of old foundations might be discovered.'

Rev E A Fuller discussing Cirencester Abbey Church (1892–3b, 52)

Medium-sized market town (medieval)

This Chapter gives an account of the archaeology of the post-Conquest town, from the eleventh century to the mid sixteenth century (Figure 34). During this period *Cirencestre* grew from the focus of the late Saxon town into a market and service centre for surrounding settlements, one of almost 1000 such communities of varying sizes spread across the country (EH 1992c).

Before the early fourteenth century, when the woollen industry and later the cloth industry began to create wealth and new markets, Cirencester probably remained little changed from the Domesday settlement, with the exception of the addition of the Augustinian Abbey. In rural areas this lack of investment has been observed in the striking lack of new building programmes in churches (Pounds 1988) and the consequent survival of Romanesque architecture generally on the Cotswolds. In the town itself archaeological evidence is ephemeral and most industries which process agricultural products have left few archaeological traces.

Throughout the medieval period the effects of surviving Roman fortifications and the Anglo-Saxon street plan had a continuing effect on the development of the town plan but new elements were added, such as the castle site and a wide range of public buildings which indicate a new urban life-style. The prosperity of the fourteenth, fifteenth and early sixteenth centuries is proudly symbolised by the parish church dedicated to St John the Baptist, built from the profits of the market place in which it stands. The market place, beyond the west precinct wall of the abbey, had become the dominant focus of the town. As we shall see, the archaeological evidence for this period is not inconsiderable and can act as a crude guide to medieval changes in the urban fabric.

The streets

The principal streets of the medieval urban area radiated from the market place. In only two instances does the medieval street pattern follow Roman alignments: in Dollar/Gosditch Street, and Querns Lane/Lewis Lane. However, the former Roman gateways remained as entrances to the town and so made an important contribution to the developing plan. The line of the Roman town wall was re-adopted as an administrative boundary for much of its length and, though ruinous, would have been sufficient to protect the collection of market tolls.

Many streets were defined as running between road bridges or street crosses and it is useful to locate these first. There are a number of bridges recorded within the urban area: *Gildenbrigge* (54314) was probably the later Bailiff's Bridge at the end of Gloucester Street (Fuller 1894a, 223); Clement's Bridge or Groomstoole (Gunstoole) Bridge (54251) at the bottom of Cecily Hill (Figure 35), and the Swyne Bridge in Gosditch Street (54170) both crossed the Gunstoole (Daglingworth) Brook. St John's Bridge

(54160) was at the northern end of Dollar Street, with New Bridge (54254) to the north of New Mills (Slater 1976a). No structural surveys of these bridges have been undertaken and it is not known if any of the medieval fabric survives. Fuller equates 'Walfrid Marescal's ford' with the site of a ford (54169) at the present Oxford Bridge, in London Road and it can be assumed that animals were washed down here on their way into the market just as they would have been at other horsepools and water troughs in the town.

None of these bridges are known to have had crosses or chapels but there was a series of standing crosses around the town, located mainly at road junctions. Of the six described by Pooley (1868, 34–8) only one survives, the High Cross, relocated to the West Market Place in 1927 after a sequence of moves since the eighteenth century. A document of 1413 refers to the High Cross (54084) as the *Nova Crux*, thus implying a predecessor. In 1795 the cross was removed to Cirencester Park (Figure 36) to a plantation known as Cathedral Firs in the northern sector of Oakley Wood where it stood for some years before being transferred to a spot near the Woodhouse. It originally occupied a space opposite the Ram Inn at the western end of the market place and 'stood on a base 10ft square, with four steps on each side with an octangular column or pillar supporting a capital which was much defaced' (Rudder 1800, 115–7).

Of the other five, the Pig Cross (54083) stood at the northern end of Dyer Street opposite the Waterloo Passage where the pig market was held (Fuller 1932; Slater 1976a, 101). In 1800 Rudder recalled a sundial fixed on a pillar at this spot which was taken down before 1795, and 'Site of Cross' is recorded on the 1875 Ordnance Survey of the town. In 1800 the round pedestal of the Dyer Street or London Road cross (54073), 'stood near the extremity of the borough at the first station of water at the end of Dyer Street'. Rudder also records the existence of the Churchyard Cross (54074) in the parish churchyard but it 'was not entire within living memory', whilst the round pedestal of the cross which stood at the junction of Tetbury Road/Park Lane/Castle Street was 'still remembered' although 'removed' (54078). The sixth recorded cross stood at the junction of Querns Lane and Cricklade Street (54077) and, together with the Sheep Street and London Road examples, demarcated the bounds of the township.

The streets which ran between the crosses and over the bridges had varying names and those listed in the Lady Chapel Register (1460) and the Minister's Accounts (1540) have been studied by Fuller (1893–4b) and more generally by A H Smith (1964). Some may be helpful in indicating the location of former monuments. *Castell Street* (54418) in 1540 is modern Castle Street and supposedly leads to the castle site. *Dyar Strete* in 1459 becomes *Chepingstrete* in 1540, modern Dyer Street (54104). Richard le Dyere is mentioned in 1341 tax records and the street name may indicate a developing industrial quarter centred on the wool and cloth industry (but see below); *Chepyng* suggests a market which we know to have existed here. *Bocherewe Row* (54097), later Butcher Row, and Shoe Lane (54151) were both streets threading their way between former buildings in The Shambles in the market place. *Dolehall Street* (54108) in 1540 is modern Dollar Street a name which must be derived from the Almonry or Almery gate or dole gate of the Augustinian Abbey. *Shoter Street* (54248) in 1540, modern Sheep Street, may indicate the site of the medieval archery butts (Slater 1976) or possibly, in its earlier form of *Schyttestrete*, the site of the public latrines. *Temple Street* (54101) in 1459 became *St John's Street* (1509) and is now Black Jack Street. This street began at the bottom of Cecily Hill and led to the parish church of St John the Baptist. According to Baddeley the Knights Hospitallers from the preceptory at Quenington had a courthouse (54252) in Black Jack Street where they succeeded the Templars (Baddeley's notebooks for 1935).

There have been many modifications during the evolution of modern street names: *Le Fosse* (54267) in 1540 became modern Lewis Lane and shows that the name Fosse was originally used inside the town; *New Street* (54268) is possibly the name used for Querns Lane in the 1460 Lady Chapel Register; Cecily Street (54102) was recorded as *Clack Hill* in 1202, *Inegthorpe* or *Inchstropp-street* in 1392 and 1428, *St Ceceyley Strete* in 1459, and *Inchthorpe Street* in 1540; *Lawegutter* (54426) is modern Park Lane; *St Lawrence Street* (54105) is modern Gloucester Street and ran from the *Gildenbrigge* to St John's Bridge (see below); *Raten Rewe* (54269) in 1459 or *Rotten Rewe* in 1540 is the medieval alignment of Spitalgate; fifteenth-century *Abbat Street* (54099) became *Abbot Street* by 1540 and is now Coxwell Street, renamed in the seventeenth century after a wealthy resident family of that name; *Batel Strete* in 1459 became *Battel Street* in 1540 (54098) and *Bartle Street* in 1619 but is now Thomas Street and named after the hospital. This street led from Clement's or Groomstole Bridge to the Dollar Street/Gloucester Street Bridge.

Some modern streets have retained their medieval names: Silver Street (54100); *Gosediche Street* (54110) in 1540, modern Gosditch Street, may be corrupted from *Foss-dyche Street*, or *Goose-ditch* (Slater (1976a, 102) and ran from Clements Bridge to the Swyne Bridge (Fuller 1874, 223); Cricklade Street (54109) was *Crekelade Strete* in 1540, running south from the market place beyond the cross which stood at the junction of Querns Lane/Cricklade Street towards Cricklade.

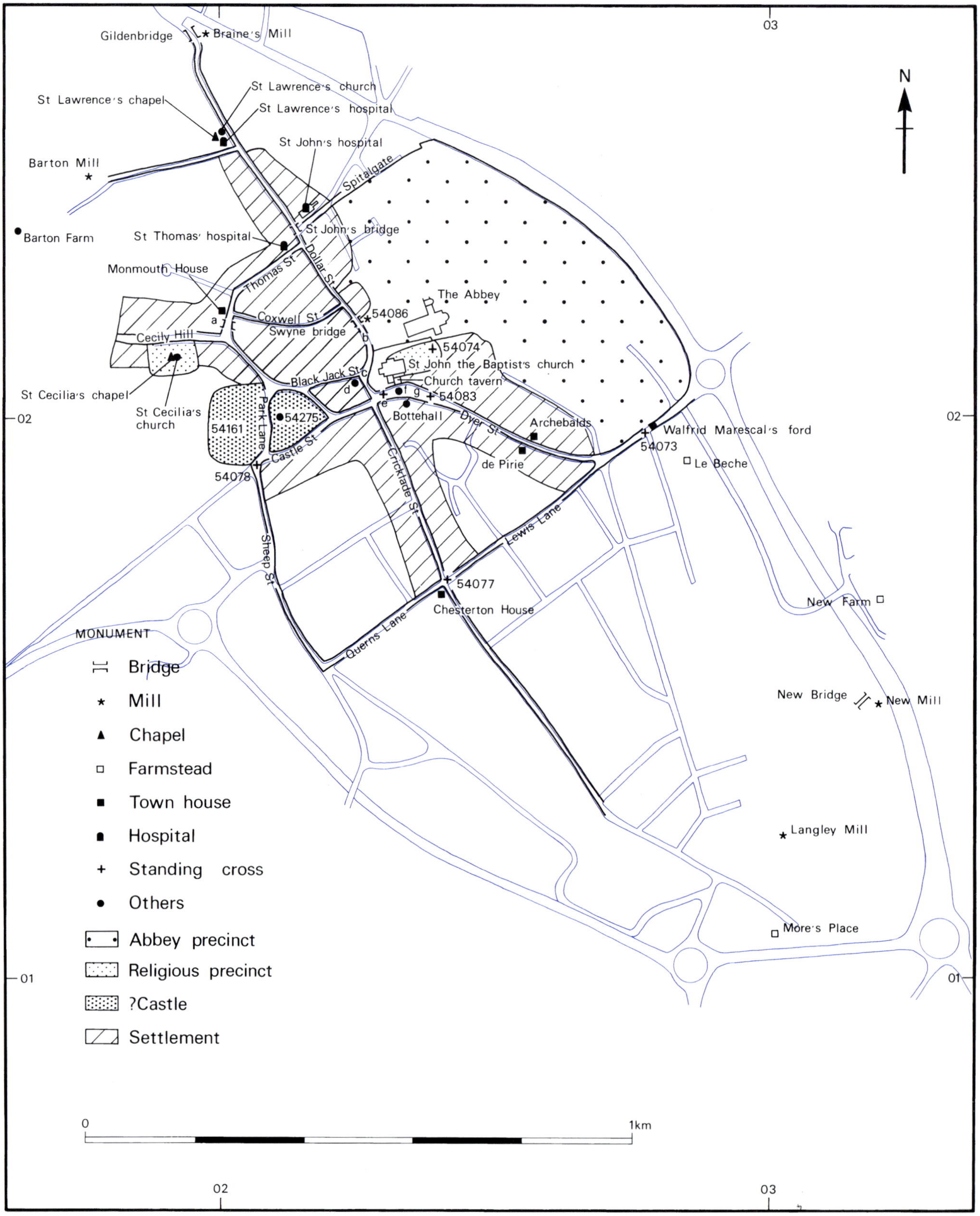

Figure 34
Monuments in the medieval Medium-Sized Market Town

Key to Figure 34:

54073	Dyer Street	standing cross
54074	Churchyard Cross	standing cross
54077	Lewis Lane/Querns Lane	standing cross
54078	Tetbury Road/Park Lane/Castle St	standing cross
54083	Dyer Street, Pig Cross	standing cross
54086	Mill, Dollar St	watermill (medieval)
54161	Park Street	motte and bailey castle
54275	School, Park Lane	school

a	54251	St Clement's Bridge	bridge
b	54110	Gosditch Street	street (medieval)
c	54215	The West Market Place	market place
d	54273	Dakker Gate Inn	inn
e	54084	High Cross	standing cross
f	54082	The Market Place	prison
	54088	The Market Place	stocks
	54097	Butcher Row	street (medieval)
	54151	Shoe Lane	street (medieval)
	54479	The Cage, Market Place	lock-up
g	54111	The Market Place	market place

Archebalds, Dyer Street	54000	town house (medieval)
Barton Farm	54293	grange
Barton Mill	54250	watermill (medieval)
Black Jack Street	54101	street (medieval)
Braine's Mill	54480	watermill (medieval)
Castle Street	54418	street (medieval)
Cecily Hill	54102	street (medieval)
Chesterton House	54207	town house (medieval)
Church Tavern, Market Place	54255	tavern
Coxwell Street	54099	street (medieval)
Cricklade Street	54109	street (medieval)
de Pirie, Dyer Street	54202	town house (medieval)
Dollar Street	54108	street (medieval)
Dyer Street	54104	street (medieval)
Gildenbridge	54314	bridge
Langley Mill	54186	watermill (medieval)
Lewis Lane	54267	street (medieval)
Monmouth House	54291	town house (medieval)
More's Place	54476	farmstead
New Bridge	54254	bridge
New Farm	54475	farmstead
New Mill	54187	watermill (medieval)
Park Lane	54426	street (medieval)
Querns Lane	54268	street (medieval)
Sheep Street	54248	street (medieval)
Spitalgate	54269	street (medieval)
St Cecilia's Church	54080	parochial church
St Cecilia's Chapel	54266	parochial chapel
St John the Baptist	54053	parochial church
St John's Bridge	54160	bridge
St John's Hospital	54076	hospital
St Lawrence's Chapel	54257	parochial chapel
St Lawrence's Church	54103	parochial church
St Lawrence's Hospital	54179	almshouses
St Lawrence's Hospital	54243	hospital
The Abbey	54087	monastery for men
Swyne Bridge	54170	bridge
Thomas Street	54098	street (medieval)
Walfrid Marescal's ford	54169	ford
St Thomas's Hospital	54096	hospital
'Bottehall'	54145	exchange
'Le Beches'	54477	farmstead

Not plotted/located:

54055	Gumstool Brook, Dollar Street	ducking stool
54081	South porch of Parish Church	guildhall
54100	Silver Street	street (medieval)
54105	Gloucester Street	street (medieval)
54252	Black Jack Street	courthouse
54478	Dyer Street	school
54481	Cecily Hill	watermill (medieval)

Figure 35
St Clement's Bridge at the bottom of Cecily Hill, with Monmouth House in the background (Corinium Museum)

Typically, historical debate over the evolution of street names in Cirencester has proved more distracting than details of greater significance such dates for street improvements (eg paving) or changes in alignments.

Public buildings and works

Of some of Cirencester's more important public buildings during the medieval period little can be said. The original south porch of the parish church of St John's has been suggested as being a guild meeting room before 1500 (54081) and it seems likely that the church served a variety of public functions before that date. An exchange (54145) in the market place, otherwise known as the Bottehall or Boot Hall, held a market on Fridays before 1800. Two further buildings are unlocated: Baddeley records a *saltewhiche* near the Boot Hall, presumably some kind of salt market, and the Tolsey was the meeting place of the Pie Powder Court which controlled the customs of the market.

Figure 36
The medieval High Cross removed to Cirencester Park (Corinium Museum)

Little more is known of the grammar school which is recorded in Cirencester as early as 1242 (54478). The site has not been located though Fuller thought it could have been in Dyer Street (Fuller 1886–7). The school in Park Lane (54275) was founded in 1457 by the Bishop of Lincoln, with the master living rent free in an attached house. The building, now much altered, ceased to be a school after 1881 (Fuller 1886–7; 1892–3d).

A single tavern is recorded, Church Tavern (54255), standing in the market place in the open space on the east side of the south porch of St John's Church. Before about 1500, when the present porch was built, the crypt may have been used as the cellar to the tavern. According to Fuller (1874) the Swan (54273) is recorded in 1540 as the Dakkar Gate Inn and travellers would have found shelter here as well as at the three hospitals and the Abbey granges or guest houses.

Miscreants might have spent time in the thirteenth-century 'Gaol' (54082), the 'Cage' or 'blind house' (perhaps some kind of temporary lock-up (54479)) or the stocks (54088) which were all to be found in the market place. The sites of the medieval pillory and gallows are unknown but there is documentary evidence to show that the Abbot had his own gallows after 1222 (Welsford 1987a). The ducking stool (54055) was at the mill pond at Swyne Bridge just outside the Abbey precinct or perhaps beside Clement's Bridge. This was presumably a chair fixed to a pole, called a gong stool (and hence the name Gunstool Brook) which could be lowered into the water (Slater 1976a).

The inhabitants of medieval Cirencester probably relied upon wells for their drinking water. From the late twelfth century the Abbey was provided with piped water supplied from a spring called Letherwell, possibly located east of the Gloucester Road near the Gildenbridge (Beecham 1887, 66; Evans 1991). There are legends in the town of a tunnel which connects the Spitalgate lodge there with the Abbey. Certainly, there are culverts, possibly of medieval origin, which were channelled past the former Abbey Mill site and led between the former buildings inside the precinct (see plan in Fuller 1892–3b; Evans 1991). Presumably they fed the reredorter and the *lavatorium* but this concern for hygiene does not appear to have been extended to the town, for example in the provision of public latrines, and town houses must have had their own cesspits.

The influence of watercourses on the urban topography is clear, for example in establishing the plot divisions at the rear of properties fronting onto Coxwell Street and Black Jack Street. Other urban streams are also indicated. A documentary reference of 1413 refers to the New Cross as being by a stream, while stones interpreted as a ford have been uncovered to the west of the parish church (Rudder 1779). Together this evidence has been taken to suggest that the River Churn, the so-called Inner Churn, ran along Gosditch Street by the Ram Inn and then down Cricklade Street. Such systems are well-known elsewhere (eg in Salisbury; Steane 1985) and the medieval system of water supply in Cirencester would benefit from further consideration.

Commerce and industry

At the heart of the town lay the market place (54111). The 'new market' recorded in 1086 was held on a Sunday. In a charter of Richard I the Abbots of the Augustinian Abbey were granted the market rights and weekly markets were held on Mondays and Fridays. The prosperity of the markets and the range of goods being traded within the town is reflected in a list of market tolls of 1321 which records over 80 items including cattle, horses, goats, bean and pea meal, cheese, butter, fish, salt, alum, iron, lead, tin, brass, linen, silk and cloth with gold (Welsford 1987a, 48–9; Fuller 1932).

Like many other Gloucestershire towns the market was situated in a widened section of the main street, and operated from temporary stalls set up in the open area between the site of the Pig Cross at the northern end of Dyer Street (formerly *Chepying* or *Chipping Street*) and the High Cross at the western end of the Market Place opposite the Ram Inn. In the course of time permanent buildings took their place, a process documented by the townspeople of Cirencester who complained in 1343 that the 'Abbots have encroached on the King's Highway since 1203, and built houses on the market place' (Slater 1976a, 101). Encroachments of this kind onto public spaces were a common feature of market towns but The Shambles, comprising Butter Row, Butchers Row and Shoe Lane, were eventually demolished in 1830. A second market represented by the placename West Market Place (54215) may also be identified to the north of the parish church.

In common with other market-based medieval towns dispersed markets did not develop in each sector of the town and residential areas were clearly demarcated from commercial sectors. Instead, all specialities were catered for within the central general market which was highly accessible and easily controlled. Like Fairford and unlike Tetbury or Stow, Cirencester's triangular market place does not seem to have been deliberately planned.

There is limited evidence for cloth-finishing processes in the medieval town, much of it based upon written evidence and the remains of structures rather than upon the study of tools used in textile manufacture. The name *Dyer Street* has been taken to imply an embryonic industrial quarter in the fourteenth century. However, there is good reason to doubt this interpretation on the grounds that there is no running water close to Dyer Street, which would have been needed to serve dyehouses and workshops. Given the lack of supporting archaeological evidence, best documented from the Lower Brook Street site in Winchester (Biddle 1990), it may be that the name, Dyer Street, was taken from a personal name, someone who may, or may not, have been employed as a dyer (see above).

The cleaning and thickening of the cloth was carried out at water-driven fulling mills, of which there are six recorded from the town. Barton Mill (54250), according to Baddeley was formerly called Chester Mill, and before that Maz, Mayesmille, Magres Mill or Peace Mill (Fuller 1932). From the early thirteenth century the tenant was Richard Clerk, hence the name Clerksmills, which may indicate two mills at this same site (Ross 1964). The modern name of Barton Mill came into use in the mid sixteenth century.

The Abbey Mill (54086), used by the monks of Cirencester Abbey, was situated on the Gunstool Brook just within the abbey precinct, in Gosditch Street. In 1559 it is recorded 'that a mill had stood at the first bridge from the church but that this had now been taken down'. Presumably the building was removed with the Abbey buildings at the Dissolution.

Built by Abbot Blake in *c*1530 St Mary's or New Mill (54187), continued as a cloth mill until about 1830 when it became a flock mill. In 1912/13 the mill portion was demolished although some part of the retaining walls of the mill do remain. On the line of the Roman town defences, Leland records that 'nere to the Place where the right goodly Clothing Mylle was set up a late by the Abbate, was broken down the Ruine of an old Tower toward making of the Mylle Waules' (Toulmin Smith 1964).

Langley Mill (54186), to the south of New Mill, shared the same water source with inevitable consequences. There is a documented dispute in 1561 between Langley Mill and New Mill, with Langley Mill claiming to be the older of the two sites and therefore with first claim to the stream (Walls 1986). The mill house still stands and a section cut across the mill pond in 1990 also identified associated yard surfaces (R King 1990e). Harmer (1924, 320) identifies a fifth mill site at the foot of Cecily Hill (54481).

Faced with a lack of work on documents, the broader significance of this evidence is hard to assess. Combing, spinning and weaving activities would have been housed in cottages and would be hard to identify. Progress in charting the fortunes of the Cirencester industry might best be made through detailed studies of artefacts such as spindle-whorls and tenter-hooks together with their distributions which might help to locate drying racks, for instance.

There is limited documentary evidence for the leather trade in medieval Cirencester. By the Gildenbrigge at the end of Gloucester Street there was a watermill, called Brain's Mill (54480), which was apparently in the possession of the Abbot by the end of the thirteenth century (Welsford 1987a). According to Harmer (1924, 320), tanning and malting were carried out here. It seems likely that the mill ground the oak bark used in the tanning process and this may indicate a tannery operating at some scale (Cherry 1991). Typically the archaeological evidence would comprise lime pits for defleshing, dung pits for de-lining and soaking pits for tanning (eg Shaw 1984 for Northampton). Sites are likely to be close to water and usually on the fringes of the town, so the Gloucester Street identification is not improbable.

A small hearth of late thirteenth- or fourteenth-century date discovered on the north side of Coxwell Street is thought to have been used for the working of bronze (Wacher 1963, 22). Evidence elsewhere suggests that the working of copper alloys was on a domestic scale and slag is common in excavations in medieval towns generally. Bronze was ideal for making small dress fitments, metal pots and jugs as well as larger and more specialised work like bell founding (Blair and Blair 1991). Examples of metalwork found in the town include buckles and brooches (eg fifteenth-century garter buckle in Partridge Way; and fifteenth-century belt clasp from the amphitheatre).

The accurate dating of archaeological sequences in the post-Conquest period underpins all interpretation. In Cirencester, few medieval sequences are datable with any degree of precision. Wooden and metal objects seem to be under-represented because of decay or the recycling of materials. The chronological and spatial distribution of these objects is unstudied but would doubtless reflect, at least in part, the inferior place of medieval studies in most excavation research designs. Medieval pottery has been recovered from a number of pits and robber trenches, eg south of Thomas Street (P D C Brown *et al* 1969, 235), but few stratified deposits have been recorded in the town and limited quantitative analysis of pottery has been carried out. In this respect the forthcoming publication of the medieval pottery from the Abbey excavations is of great importance but backlog material from other excavations would also benefit from re-examination. For example, some 'useful' groups of medieval pottery were obtained from the West Way area in 1963 (Wacher 1964a, 15).

The overall impression is that from the thirteenth century most coarse wares came from local centres of production making pottery tempered with limestone, such as Minety (Musty 1973). Occasional foreign imports are known from the Abbey excavations though this may not be typical for the rest of the town. A 'Moorish' jug, presumably a Spanish lustreware vessel, was found in a well in Watermoor but cannot now be located. Examples of stray finds include medieval jettons and coins, from Gloucester Street and Cricklade Street.

The limited range of archaeological evidence inhibits informed contribution to national debates, especially the question of decline in the late medieval town in the late fifteenth and early sixteenth centuries. Certainly, Cirencester did not benefit from industrial development as much as other nearby clothing towns, as the tax records show. In 1334 Cirencester paid five times as much tax as Bisley in the Stroud valley but by 1525 Bisley had a higher assessment (Carus-Wilson 1959–60). Evidence of any decline is more difficult to see in the archaeological record where the dispersal of material suggests widespread dumping and clearance in both medieval and post-medieval periods and is demonstrated conclusively by a single excavation at Orchard House, London Road, where sixteenth-century material had been used to raise ground levels (Guy 1986). At present, there is no suggestion of under-use of plots, rather continuous cycles of development and changing land-use.

Housing

Three town houses of the medieval period are named and documented. The first is *Archebalds*, a medieval manor house (54000), the residence of the Erchebauds at Domesday and by the sixteenth century the property of Richard Master. The precise location of this site seems uncertain but Fuller (1932) places it about a third of the way up Dyer Street opposite a second manor house, the de Pirie town house (54202). The manor house of Chesterton (54207) stood at the junction of Querns Lane and Watermoor Road.

The oldest standing secular building in Cirencester is the fifteenth-century Weavers' Hall in Thomas Street. According to the architectural survey of house facades undertaken by Reece and Catling (1975), Monmouth House (54291) may also date from the sixteenth century but it may seem surprising that a town so rich in quality freestone from Roman buildings should be so poor in medieval stone buildings. The lack of known medieval buildings may be a strong indication of the prosperity of a town in which housing was constantly rebuilt rather than repaired.

Almost nothing is known of household material culture during the medieval period, particularly for the lowest social classes. Portions of medieval structures including hearths, walling and rammed limestone surfaces have come to light in small evaluation trenches behind Castle Street (Gerrard *et al* 1989b) and 26 Dollar Street (McWhirr 1978, 79). Excavated medieval pits, often of impressive size, contain little more than re-deposited Roman material. There is therefore apparently little botanical or faunal evidence of reliable medieval date, though the questions of residual material could profitably be examined further. For example, we might consider if the Roman material has been found locally or imported, examine sherd size, cross-fits and so on. These methods ought to be more widely used although little real progress can be expected without fuller excavations of medieval sequences.

It has been assumed that the long, narrow parallel plots laid out at right angle to the main streets shown on nineteenth-century town plans reflect medieval land distribution. Each plot may have contained a house fronting the street with a yard or garden behind and access from a back lane running parallel to the main street. Pre-existing features certainly influenced the new layout, for example, the back line of the plots on the western side of Cricklade Street mirror the earlier alignment of the Roman street (Gerrard *et al* 1989b). It is worth asking the question as to how this is possible if so much Roman archaeology, including this particular Roman street, was masked from view by the accumulation of 'black earths' in the post-Roman period.

Boundary walls and associated surfaces dating to the medieval period were excavated at 26 Dollar Street between 1973 and 1976 (McWhirr 1978, 79), and south of Thomas Street in 1966 (Brown and McWhirr 1967, 195). None of these excavations uncovered sufficient to secure the identification of a monument or boundary sequence and it is quite possible that the real picture is not so static. Platt (1976) comments upon excavations in London, Winchester and elsewhere which demonstrate how larger plots can be subdivided into smaller ones with growing economic power and population numbers in a medieval town. Cirencester may have experienced similar transformations but, at present, little is known about how plot size and shape were related to different parts of the town at different dates although an example of sub-division has been illustrated by standing building recording at 45–49 Castle Street (D Smith 1976). Even around the parish church and market place, where greater continuity is to be expected, property boundaries have altered substantially.

Away from the main street frontages the patterns of medieval land-use are far from certain. Post-medieval cartographic evidence suggests that nurseries and orchards filled the southern half of the town and there is little archaeological evidence to prove otherwise. Areas of open land in the medieval town such as *Le Beche* (The Beeches), *Le Lewes* (later the Leauses), St John's Meade, *Ayshecroft*, and Barton Field are documented but not described (Fuller 1895–6; Slater 1976a). Slater proposes three 'farm houses' to the south of Lewis Lane at *New Farm* (54475), *More's Place* (54476) and *Le Beches* (54477) serving estates or sub-manors.

The question of possible zoning of medieval industrial and residential activities has scarcely been approached. Analysis of the geographical spread over which medieval material has been found might usefully indicate growth in the core and the suburbs and so establish an archaeological context for documentary references. The diversity of pottery assemblages might also act as a rough guide to the complexities and evolution of the medieval town but it should be remembered that local patterns of medieval occupations could be very fluid (eg Winchester; Keene 1990).

Looking at the town plan as a whole, Cirencester remained small. Table 5 shows that most space was taken up by tenements (39%), while the precinct of St Mary's Abbey covered almost the same area (36%). Areas designated as open space lay at the southern fringes of the town within the Roman walled area and may be more properly thought of as rural. Table 6 compares these results for Cirencester with those obtained for Tetbury and Gloucester (in EH 1992c). Cirencester lies half-way between Tetbury and Gloucester in overall size (525,888 sq m). Gloucester has a third more tenements than Cirencester but the area of its religious precincts is about the same.

Noticeably, it is the size of the religious precincts inCirencester and Gloucester which make these towns appear so much larger in area than Tetbury. The abnormally high figure for the area taken up by streets in Gloucester reflects the wide streets which were used for markets.

MONUMENT CLASSES	Sq. metres	% area
Tenements/cottages	204,436	39%
Religious houses	186,062	36%
Open space	82,250	16%
Streets	16,900	3%
Castle	21,500	4%
Churches and churchyards	9,812	2%
Bridges and gates	600	0.10%
Inns	300	0.05%
Public houses	225	0.04%
Market place	3,562	0.70%
Standing crosse	54	0.01%
School	187	0.03%
TOTALS	525,888	100%

TABLE 5 Distribution of monuments within the medieval medium-sized market town

Overall, the Cirencester plan is typical of many other medieval wool towns with ribbons of housing arranged down each side of the major routes and what is exceptional about the town plan is the lack of residential clustering around the major entrance-ways. Perhaps the lack of legal and social status for the town and its inhabitants impeded population growth generally.

The castle

The powerful and rich were drawn to the town edge. A castle (54161), most probably of motte and bailey

MONUMENT CLASS	CIRENCESTER		TETBURY		GLOUCESTER	
Tenements	204,436	39%	170,410	63%	311,450	39%
Religious houses	186,062	36%	–	–	196,000	25%
Open spaces	82,250	16%	44,000	16%	114,500	14%
Streets	16,900	3%	14,500	5%	77,810	10%
Castle	21,500	4%	–	–	54,500	7%
Churches	9,812	2%	9,000	3%	16,950	2%
Bridges	600	0.10%	900	1%	4,050	0.5%
Inns	300	0.05%	15,000	6%	3,210	0.4%
Public buildings	225	0.04%	–	–	790	0.1%
Market place	3,562	0.70%	15,000	6%	in streets	–
Standing crosses	54	0.01%	–	–	in streets	–
School	187	0.03%	–	–	–	–
Other	–	–	1,050	4.5%	–	–
TOTALS	525,888	–	278,600	–	796,760	–

TABLE 6 Comparison of the distribution of medieval monuments in three Gloucestershire towns: Cirencester, Tetbury and Gloucester

or ringwork type, was strengthened by Maud in 1142 during the Civil Wars with Stephen (Fuller 1890–91). Little is known of it except what can be gleaned from a single documentary reference in the *Gesti Stephani* (Potter 1976). Here we learn that the castle was near the Abbey and that, arriving in Cirencester, 'the keepers of the castle having secretly escaped in different directions, he [Stephen] found it empty; whereupon he gave it to the flames, and razed to the ground the rampart and the outworks'. There is a possibility that this castle is the 'new work' begun at Cirencester in 1117 (Evans 1991), in which case it stood for just twenty-five years, though the reference is usually taken to refer to the construction work for the Augustinian Abbey.

The precise position of the castle has been the subject of considerable speculation. F W Taylor, for example, thought the castle lay beneath the VWH Kennels, on the Tetbury Road. Today, a site to the west of the medieval town is favoured by most writers, in the vicinity of the present Cirencester Park mansion house and astride the Roman town wall. Slater (1976) provides some convincing supporting arguments: the borough boundary excludes this area from the township; Park Lane was once Lawditch Lane and suggests the line of a moat or ditch; St Cecilia's chapel may have originated as the castle chapel; while the medieval street name of Castle Street would link this area to the market place (Fuller 1890–91). Part of the castle is supposedly under the back garden of 10 Park Street where garden walls have subsided and the sub-rounded form of the two modern residential blocks framed by Castle Street, Black Jack Street, Park Street and Silver Street suggests the plan of two baileys. If so, there might be archaeological evidence for staked perimeter fences, rectangular wooden buildings, bridges, a timber tower and cobbled surfaces with cesspits and surface drains. The outer ditches, perhaps with inlet and outlet channels to prevent flooding, might survive.

Unlike Gloucester, where earlier gates into the town were rebuilt around the Conquest period (Heighway 1984a), no medieval defences are known in Cirencester apart from a large ditch of *c*1100 which was found to re-cut an earlier medieval ditch during excavations at the Mycalex factory (Reece 1976b). It is stretching the evidence too far to suggest that concern for Danish invasion in the early eleventh century or the Norman occupation of the town might provide the historical context for this work. Elsewhere, a single arrowhead of medieval date was found at 39 Purley Road but there is nothing to suggest that the Roman defences were adapted or strengthened in any way, though the precinct wall of the Abbey may have provided defence to the east. There is no evidence for medieval wall repairs, extensions or murage grants and, in any case, the northern suburbs of the town had already grown beyond the Roman circuit.

Religious buildings

It is the presence of the twelfth century Augustinian Abbey in Cirencester which dominates the archaeology of the medieval town, both physically and culturally (see reconstruction, Figure 37) and as a source of intermittent social tension for much of this period (Welsford 1987a, 50). The story of the foundation of Cirencester Abbey in about 1131 has recently been fully chronicled by Evans (1991) and the future publication of the excavations there may be expected to add significant detail (Wilkinson and McWhirr, forthcoming).

The Abbey of St Mary (54087) occupied much of the north-eastern half of the town. The key components of the monastery precinct were the great Abbey Church with its tower over the crossing (calculated by Fuller to be about the same size as Bristol Cathedral) erected, pre-1176, on the site of the demolished pre-Conquest church (Evans 1991); the claustral buildings lying to the north, comprising cloister, chapter house, library, muniment room, refectory or great hall, dormitory, infirmary etc; the service buildings such as the kitchen, the 'storehouse, the Styward's chambre, the Gesten chambre, the Abbot's lodging, stables, hayhouse, Abbey mill, the cellarer's chambre, the squier's chambre, the sextery, the wolhouse with the stabule by the mylle' (Toulmin-Smith 1964), barn; and the two gatehouses controlling access to the open space of the precinct with its fishponds, gardens and cloister garth (Fuller 1892–3b, 45). The precinct itself must have partially re-used the Roman town wall as its boundary line on its northern and eastern sides though no traces of medieval modifications were detected during excavation. Likewise, the twelfth-century site of the substantial temporary accommodation needed for the monastic community whilst its fifty-year church construction project was underway, is uncertain.

The monastery was visited by William of Worcester who noted the measurements of the Abbey buildings in *c*1460 (Harvey 1969). Leland, in *c*1540, commented on the new work of the nave and the eastern 'very old building' (Toulmin-Smith 1964) and some idea of the wealth and importance of the site is indicated by the 1535 tax record which shows Cirencester Abbey to be the richest Augustinian house in the country.

There were three granges which acted as centres for the extensive estates owned by the Augustinian Abbey. There were two farms within the walled precinct of the Abbey: Spyringate Grange and Almery Grange. A third grange called Barton Grange (54293) has a surviving dovecote and a seven-bay

Figure 37
Reconstruction of the medieval townscape of 1400 (From an original drawing by Casper Johnson)

barn. Other components such as gardens and agricultural buildings may once have existed.

Following the Dissolution the lead from the church, cloister and chapter house was granted to Roger Bassynge and demolition was so thorough that by the seventeenth century little remained (Figure 38). Ancillary buildings fared rather better so that in 1800 Rudder was able to record that two gateways and one 'very large' barn were still standing. Today only one component within the precinct remains as a visible standing structure: the Spitalgate, Hospital Gate, or Norman Arch, straddling the entrance to the precinct from the White Way. A gateway also led from the frontage of Dollar Street to the Almery Gate, which was demolished in 1826 and said to resemble the Spitalgate, though with rooms over the gate used

Figure 38
Extensive robbing of the claustral range of the Augustinian abbey in the area of the undercroft, looking south (Cirencester Excavation Committee)

as dwellings. In August 1721 Stukeley sketched the north-eastern elevation of the Spitalgate, and thus became the first of many to draw the gateway. His sketch is of interest in showing dormer windows in the roof and a southern, but ruinous, continuation of the precinct wall to the south of the main carriageway (Bodleian Library MS Top gen.d.13; Figure 39).

Speculation as to the location of what was once one of the richest Augustinian abbeys led Beecham, with William of Worcester's measurements, to publish a plan siting the abbey church beneath the Abbey House, a largely Victorian mansion built on the site of the Elizabethan house of the Master family (Beecham 1887, 83). A few years later Fuller published an alternative interpretation of the layout

Figure 39
Drawing of the Spitalgate by William Stukeley, 1721 (The Bodleian Library, MS Top.Gen.d.13)

using Kip's drawings as a basis (Fuller 1892–3b). Part of the cloister area was excavated by Baddeley in the early 1920s, and excavations by Reece in the spring of 1962 failed to locate the church (Reece 1962a). By the summer of 1964 Wacher had begun a campaign of excavation, continued by Brown and McWhirr in 1965 and 1966, which revealed not only the heavily robbed foundations of the Saxon church, but also the medieval Abbey church and some conventual buildings (Wacher 1965; Brown and McWhirr 1966, 1967; P D C Brown 1976).

These excavations sought to test, and were ultimately to disprove, Beecham's published hypothetical plan and placed the Abbey church far closer to the modern churchyard wall than had been suspected previously. Of the twelfth-century Abbey the apsidal plan of the chapter house was recovered together with the ash-covered floors of the adjacent undercroft of a possible calefactory, whose vaulted roof had fallen in filling the room beneath with limestone aggregate from the floors above. Only a small portion of the north range of the cloister was excavated as well as part of the north transept of the church. The excavation showed that by the Dissolution a number of structural changes had taken place including an enlargement of the north transept and the building of a polygonal chapter house where quantities of fine architectural masonry were found.

Architectural fragments from the Abbey precinct are to be found in the Abbey Grounds and scattered about the town: for example, there is fan-vaulting, possibly from the Abbey cloisters, in the ceiling of St Catherine's Chapel in the parish church of St John's, substantial blocks are to found in the garden of the Corinium Court Hotel, and also as fireplace and door surrounds in houses in Park Street, and Tower Street. Almost any unusual stone carving is usually attributed to the Abbey buildings, as perhaps is the inlaid medieval tile with griffin motif found in the former Workhouse in Trinity Road.

There are four recorded parish churches within the urban area. The church of St John the Baptist (54053), the largest parish church in Gloucestershire, still dominates the north side of the Market Place, and comprises a nave with aisles, chancel and adjoining chapels, north and south porches and embattled tower at the western end (for a plan see Fuller 1892–3a; Hill 1971). According to the most authoritative study available (Mclees 1988), there is some architectural evidence of a Norman church on the site, built to replace the earlier Anglo-Saxon church demolished to make way for the adjacent Abbey church. Later structural changes apparently incorporated Roman masonry in the chancel but there is no evidence of an earlier church on this site.

For over four hundred years the urban skyline would have been dominated by the bulk of two churches lying almost side by side. From the mid thirteenth to the early sixteenth centuries the prosperity of the wool town and the benefactions of its wealthier inhabitants was channelled into major extensions and renovations to the church fabric. A southern aisle, St Catherine's Chapel and the Lady Chapel were all added in the thirteenth century, the Trinity Chapel in the late fourteenth century, and the construction of the western tower was underway in 1402. Any attempts at phasing the different construction episodes are frustrated by later remodellings such as the rebuilding of the nave in the sixteenth century and the insertion of a vault into St Catherine's Chapel. The famous fifteenth-century south porch, once popularly termed the 'Vice' or 'Device' because of its architectural ingenuity, was rebuilt in *c*1830 (Fuller 1892–3a). One wonders how long this took because the porch is missing from both Kip's engraving of 1712 (Atkyns 1712) and the 1795 town map (Reece and Catling 1975) as well as Lysons' map of 1817 (1801–17, pl III).

A watching brief in 1990 confirmed the considerable extent of the mid nineteenth-century renovations and the re-use of the tombstones as floor supports. Re-cycling of materials is evidently not a new phenomenon; thirteenth-century stone coffin lids were found incorporated into the base of the north aisle wall fabric (Gerrard and Walker 1992, 8–9), as well as the western interior wall of the tower. Given the importance and complexity of this upstanding medieval monument it is surprising that fuller recording and phasing of the building have not so far been undertaken.

St Cecilia's stood on the southern side of Cecily Hill (54080), with its own graveyard. The parochial church later became a chapel of ease (54266) and so lost its rights of burial. The dedication is interesting and could suggest a Roman origin. Alternatively, it could be an early Norman dedication for a chapel linked to the castle but the foundation is not recorded (Leech 1981, 21; Slater 1976a, 97). The building probably ceased to be parochial before the mid thirteenth century, and was 'clene down' by the mid sixteenth century, according to Leland (Toulmin Smith 1964), apparently accidentally burnt in 1540–41. Its status as a church is suggested by the discovery of several skeletons closeby in Cirencester Park within the last twenty years, though these might possibly be of Roman date.

It is disputed whether a parish church or chapel of St Lawrence in Barton Lane (54103 and 54257) was converted into the hospital before the mid thirteenth century. Leland, Atkyns and Beecham all agree that there was a church site here. Rudder and Fuller disagreed and the balance of the present evidence is in their favour (Fuller 1892–3c).

There were three hospitals in the town, all alongside major routes. The Hospital of St John (54076; variously St John the Baptist and St John the Evangelist) was founded in 1168–9 for the destitute and sick, and permission was granted for a service to be held in the hospital in 1317–27 (Fuller 1883–4a). Evans (1991) has explored the early history of this building. Like many medieval hospitals St John's would have been dedicated to the health of people's souls as much as their bodies and so, as a dependency of the parish church, attracted the considerable charity and loyalty of the townsfolk. This building was the centre of a complaint made by the townsmen to Edward III that the Abbot had appropriated the hospital. It was Charles II who finally transferred it to the people of Cirencester and the recipients of the charity were housed in six tenements built within the arches that now remain.

Little is known of the original form of the structure but hospitals often include kitchens, cellars, courtyards and residences for wardens. The building as it survives today consists of two open arcades in late twelfth-century transitional style but excavations in 1971 and 1976 prior to landscaping and visual enhancement of the site led to the discovery of the north and south walls of the aisled infirmary hall (McWhirr 1973, 209–11; Leech and McWhirr 1982). The aisles may have been parallel dormitories for men and women with a chapel between the arcades. The cottages which stand to the east, partly rebuilt in 1821, may incorporate or be built upon the foundations of an aisle-less chapel built *c*1320.

St Thomas's Hospital, in Thomas Street (54096), is now better known as the Weavers' Hall and was built with money left by Sir William Nottingham in 1483

Figure 40
St Thomas's Hospital or Weavers' Hall (centre right), in Thomas Street, endowed by Sir William Nottingham in 1483 (Corinium Museum)

(Figure 40). It is probably the oldest secular building in Cirencester still inhabited, and continues to be administered by a charitable trust.

Most medieval towns had a leper house placed away from the heart of the town in isolation. St Lawrence's Hospital, on the corner of Gloucester Street and Barton Lane (54243), was founded by Edith Biset, Lady of Wiggold, as a leper hospital in the latter half of the thirteenth century, rather late in comparison to similar establishments elsewhere (Slater 1976a, 97). The position of this institution is useful in indicating the limits of settlement at this time. The hospital may have had its own burial ground, but the major components were open space, a chapel and the hospital buildings. The building was later seized by the Abbot of Cirencester and used as an almshouse (54179) to support two poor women (Fuller 1892–3c). This appropriation is cited as further evidence of the aggressive acquisitive nature of the Abbey but in fact it was quite common for smaller hospitals to merge with larger institutions after the threat of leprosy declined (Platt 1976, 37–8).

Accumulated deposits

As with many medium-sized market towns of this form there are inhabited buildings and structures which are still in use as well as buried below-ground deposits. The majority of the stone buildings and structures visible today may appear rather 'medieval' but mainly date to after 1650 and properly belong to the post-medieval period. Accordingly, what is really the present town of Cirencester is considered below as a sub-division of this form. The medieval medium-sized market town would certainly have had some stone buildings, and a few such as the church and hospitals still survive. Others would certainly be discovered if detailed interior surveys were untaken.

Like its predecessor, however, the majority of the buildings and structures will have been in wood and earth. The expected archaeological remains are therefore ephemeral traces of timber buildings together with the pits, middens, fences, hollow-ways, and wells that go with them. Judging the state of buried deposits is more difficult but considerable damage has been done from the extension of existing buildings and in the placement and replacement of services such as water, gas and telephones.

The principal features of the layout structure are well preserved (eg the market place, roads, parish church). However, other monuments such as shops, domestic architecture and gardens are very fragile and poorly recorded. These fragile elements must still exist where they are currently hidden within later buildings and gardens.

Survival: Although the morphological structure of the medieval town has remained largely intact further examination shows that few structures of this date survive. The main zone of high survival is around the market place with the parish church, roads, abbey precinct, market cross and Abbey mill all in close proximity. Medium survival may be expected in the vacant urban plots formerly occupied by medieval tenements and in the open spaces and gardens around modern housing. Poor survival is to be found where modern or post-medieval development has punctured, removed and disturbed medieval deposits or where archaeological excavation has taken place.

Potential: There is some potential for wet recovery close to the River Churn, along the Gunstool Brook, in the castle ditches, in the Abbey Grounds and in Watermoor but potential for the urban form is generally low.

Documentation (archaeological): Archaeological remains of the medieval period have rarely been uncovered during excavations. Most of the large-scale excavations over the last twenty years, with the exception of excavations on the site of the Augustinian Abbey, have been south of Lewis Lane, or on the periphery of the medieval town. Medieval archaeology has rarely been very high on the research agenda of these projects, and much relevant data is either published in interim reports or held as site archive. Recent evaluations at the Brewery car-park have, however, recorded remains of this date. There have been few detailed standing building recording exercises, the parish church and St John's Hospital for example have not been recorded in detail. It is anticipated that a number of timber-framed structures still survive behind stone or plaster facades and have yet to be discovered.

Documentation (historical): A checklist of Cirencester's historical documentation would include Domesday Book (Darby 1977), local government records (rentals, court rolls), fiscal records, ecclesiastical records (eg the published Cartulary of the Abbey; Ross 1964), private records (deeds, probate records), maps, illustrations, paintings, plans, antiquarian books and plans, newspapers, museum archives, amongst others. The whereabouts of these and other records is discussed in Chapters 3 and 5. Thanks largely to the work of Evans (1989; 1991), zones of high documentation include the Abbey Grounds, the parish church and the market place. The rest of the town ranks low. Documents have not been systematically studied and this material provides the greatest potential for future enhancement of our knowledge of medieval

Cirencester and the identification of new monument classes. Even published primary sources such as the Lay Subsidies (Sheail 1972; Glasscock 1975) have not been trawled for valuable data they may contain. New interdisciplinary studies which combine historical with archaeological expertise are sorely needed and must be planned for.

Group Value (clustering): Few repetitious monuments can be identified except the standing church crosses. Medieval tenements must be clustered but there is little archaeological evidence for this and the whole form must be zoned poor in Group Value (clustering).

Diversity (features): Examples of superimposed monument forms are the parochial church, the Abbey precinct and the castle but the general shapes of tenement blocks and street alignments appear to remain reasonably static so that the form as a whole scores low in Diversity (features).

Group Value (association): The central and southern parts of this form have a high Group Value (association) because they overlie the northern half of the Roman town. The northern part of the medieval town may have Anglo-Saxon origins and is of medium Group Value (association). There are no areas of low Group Value (association).

Amenity Value: General historical interest in the town is fairly high. Cirencester, most particularly the Abbey, can be associated with a number of important and well-known figures of the period, including: King Stephen (who destroyed the castle), King John (who is supposed to have visited the town five times), Henry III in 1218 (Henry III's sister-in-law, Sanchia of Provence, had her heart buried at the Abbey), Edward I in 1282, Edward II who spent Christmas 1321 in Cirencester, the Castilian Queen Isabella who visited the town with the future Edward III, and, finally, the Black Prince in 1353. The names of the more important abbots such as Hereward, Blake, Hakebourne and Estcote were all taken as the names of modern roads within the former abbey precinct. Cirencester took a minor role in national events including the Wars of the Roses. However, there are few visible traces of the associated archaeology, though zones of high Amenity Value might include the area of the market place and parish church.

The study of medieval archaeology in Cirencester is only just beginning and far more is known about the Roman town than its medieval successor. Without doubt, there are surviving structures of the highest quality, such as the parish church of St John's and St Thomas' hospital, but many important monuments survive only as buried deposits, such as the Augustinian Abbey, the castle, and St Cecilia's Chapel. There is considerable potential for the re-appraisal of existing material and for future excavations with a clearly stated medieval input to their research designs. The greatest need, however, is for detailed assessment of the written historical evidence and the complementary research of historians and archaeologists working together.

Medieval countryside

Communications

The mass of information on medieval rights of way requires detailed work (Figure 41). At the local level access would have been required to all parts of the common fields, meadow, woodland, wells and water supply and so on, as well as to the local church or chapel, mill, and manorial court. At the regional level attendance at the local market and fair in Cirencester and the hundredal court were no less important.

Of the more distant routes the Welsh Way, a sheep drover's road (54515), the Baunton to Cheltenham road (54517), and The Whiteway or Wiggoldway (54253), formerly a long-distance salt route (Slater 1976a), are presently recognised as separately numbered monuments (for further derivations see Fuller 1874). The former Baunton to Cheltenham medieval road, known as The Lynches trackway, has recently been sectioned. This confirmed a medieval date and produced evidence for several well-made superimposed metalled surfaces laid on to a levelled bedrock surface, revetted on the downslope edge (CAT 1991).

Roman arterial roads continued to provide lines of national communication, the Fosse is cited as one of the four great roads of the kingdom under Edward the Confessor. Evaluation trenches cutting the Fosse Way close to Hare Bushes on the north-eastern edge of the town revealed large quantities of gritty silt between Roman and post-medieval turnpike surfaces both in the wayside ditch and along the road. It is unclear whether this accumulation of material is imported bedding or ground down off the road surface. Whatever its origin, the absence of any medieval improvements is notable (CAT 1991).

The condition of Ermin Street is similarly uncertain. Fuller (1874) drew attention to a reference in the Minister's Accounts of 1540 to 'the Stoney road called Stone causeway, lying between the meadows Kingsmead and Bradenham'. This may refer to Ermin Street but, if so, implies the pitching was still visible in the mid sixteenth century.

No river crossings such as fords or bridges have been identified in the rural area, nor have various monuments associated with communications such as gates, stiles, hospitals, hermitages or chantry chapels.

Settlement

As elsewhere on the Cotswolds, the village plans of Siddington, Baunton, Preston and Stratton are worthy of further analysis. A strongly linear two-row plan is clearly visible at Preston, whereas the other settlements are polyfocal and appear to be irregular clusters of farms grouped at road intersections. The earthworks for settlement shrinkage at Upper Siddington (54443) illustrate the difficulties of plan analysis from map evidence alone. Nevertheless, whilst accepting that these plans have not remained static, and stating the argument somewhat crudely, there is a contrast to be made between the 'instantaneous' planned regular village and the 'agglomerated' irregular nucleus which may be relevant to differences in tenurial and agrarian circumstances. It may be pertinent to ask if the monks of St Peter's, Gloucester, could have extended their policies for urban organisation to rural manors in their ownership, like Preston? The future study of documentary sources such as rentals may shed light on the size of particular settlements but is generally less useful where settlement is dispersed.

Besides the existing villages there are settlement earthworks of presumed medieval date around the present Norcote Farm which are clearly visible from the air (54442). Norcote is interesting as a possible example of later colonisation of the open downland. The identification of medieval lower status settlements such as this within the study area may not be complete. There are visible indications of a deserted medieval ?farmstead site (54519) north of Witpit Copse, for example. One productive source of evidence would be the study of personal names in court rolls and taxation lists which often indicate the name of the settlement in which a person lived.

A moated mansion house site (54091) is described by Rudder near the church in Siddington St Peter 'but has long since been razed to the ground' (1779, 661). A map of *c*1778 shows water to the east of the church and disturbed medieval occupation has been excavated nearby (Barber 1991a). Moated sites were fashionable in the thirteenth and fourteenth centuries and this example at Siddington may be regarded as one further element in an evolving pattern of dispersed settlement. Further clues to the date of plan elements are provided by stray finds such as the fragments of medieval cooking pot found at Frazier's Folly, Siddington, and Stratton.

No farm buildings with surviving medieval fabrics are listed for the rural parishes with the exception of those mentioned above. The tendency for seventeenth century buildings to envelop and disguise their medieval ancestors should always be borne in mind but documents (such as *inquisitiones post mortem*) may yet provide more evidence of the clusters of structures present at the better documented manorial centres.

Manorial features include the site of the moot (54256), the meeting place for the hundred of Crowthorne and Minety which included Cirencester, which was formerly held by a bush in a common field known as 'Crowthorne'. According to Beecham (1887, 189) the View of Frankpledge was also held here, at which minor offences were tried and the constitution of tithings and breaches of regulations considered. The site has not been identified but is thought to lie on Court Hill at the Daglingworth-Gloucester Road crossroads (Fuller 1874). The View of Wardstaff was kept at *Sherston Brugge* (bridge) in Siddington St Peter, at *Wondenewell* in Siddington St Mary, at *Thwyselede Weye* in Baunton (Fuller 1874). The last two sites are unidentified.

The shifting pattern of manorial centres has proved difficult to trace. Perry Moor, in Cirencester Hundred at Domesday, cannot now be identified (though see Moore 1989). The same author recognises Prior's Court in Baunton as a separate manor as well as Chesterton, Cirencester, Preston, Siddington Langley manor in Siddington St Peter (centred at Home Close), Siddington St Mary manor (centred on Barton Farm), Siddington St Mary (at 'Bowley'), and Siddington House. The clustering of manorial sites south of the town at Siddington is worth highlighting but we have little inkling of what these places looked like – presumably they were farmsteads.

Baddeley (1924) associates the Tar Barrows with the site of the medieval gallows but there seems to be no good evidence for this besides its position near a major road and junction. If true, it is possible that there may also be a cemetery for executed criminals nearby.

Religious buildings

There are twenty medieval rural monuments identified and described from within the Study Area. Four of these are the parochial churches of All Saints, Preston (54444); St Peter's, Siddington (54216); St Mary's, Siddington (54075); and St Peter's, Stratton (54185) (Verey 1970). St Mary's, Siddington, was demolished in 1753 and the others were all heavily restored during the latter half of the nineteenth century. St Peter's, Siddington, is the more impressive of these for its location alongside the great thirteenth-century barn (54173) which is reputed to have been part of the former preceptory of the Knights of St John of Jerusalem (Figure 42). This building has recently been the subject of a detailed joint architectural and archaeological recording exercise and, though several phases of construction have been identified, there are dendrochronological dates of the mid thirteenth century for roof timbers associated with lapjoint carpentry. Relatively small

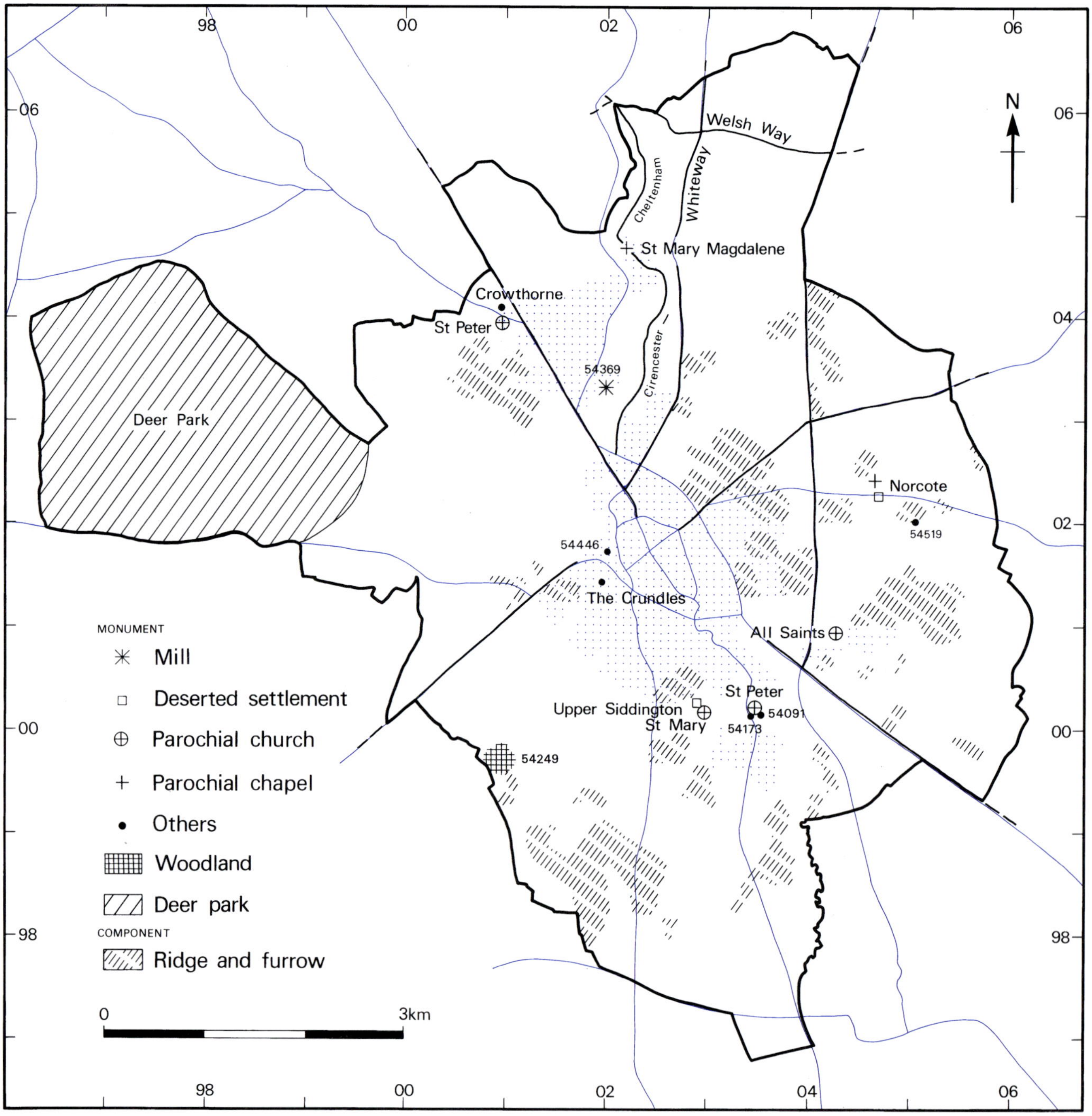

Figure 41
Medieval monuments in the rural area (see Figure 34 for monuments within the urban form)

Key to Figure 41:

54091	Siddington	moated site
54173	Siddington Barn	barn
54249	Chesterton Woods	wood
54369	Whiteway View	watermill
54446	Sheep Street	archery butts
54519	Witpit Copse	deserted farmstead

All Saints, Preston	54444	parochial church
Cirencester–Cheltenham	54517	road (medieval)
Crowthorne, Stratton	54256	moot
Deer Park, Cirencester	54112	deer park
Norcote	54441	parochial chapel
Norcote	54442	deserted village
St Mary Magdalene, Baunton	54259	parochial chapel
St Mary's, Siddington	54075	parochial church
St Peter's, Siddington	54216	parochial church
St Peter's, Stratton	54185	parochial church
The Crundles	54451	warren
Upper Siddington	54443	deserted village
Welsh Way	54515	road (medieval)
Whiteway	54253	road (medieval)

Figure 42
The spire of Siddington St Peter rising above the medieval barn (Thomas Collection, Bingham Library)

trees seem to have been used, probably obtained from several local woodlands, and there is evidence for several phases of repair and alterations (Hillam and Groves 1992). Excavation has established that the barn formerly extended further west with added bays and that the north porch may have been constructed in the fifteenth century, perhaps for a caretaker (Barber 1991a; Miles and Palmer 1987).

Former chapelries dependent on Cirencester were at St Mary Magdalene, Baunton (54259), which is known for its intact frescoes of St Christopher, and at Wiggold, which lies outside our study area but within the medieval parish of Cirencester. Norcote Farm is the site of a former post-Conquest chapelry (54441) dependent on Preston church. None of these would have had rights of burial and corpses would have been carried to the mother church, from Baunton to Cirencester, for example. However, some chapels would have played a fuller pastoral role (chapels-of-ease) than the private chapels which were sited conveniently close to manor house precincts. Both kinds served the needs of a dispersed community and it is possible that further examples remain to be recorded.

Where they survive the architectural merits of these churches and chapelries have been assessed (Verey 1970) but there would be much to be gained by a study of their wider topographical settings. For example, distinctions might be suggested by analysing the relationship between churches and manor houses, as well as the location of the church in the existing village.

Economy

The medieval deer park (54112), set aside for the management and hunting of deer and other wild animals, is one of two oval parks of wood-pasture which are today incorporated into the bounds of Cirencester Park. Documentary information relating to the royal deer park has yet to be systematically studied but it is known to have been given to the Abbey by Henry I and certainly maintained until the Dissolution. The pale still survives in sections as an impressive earthwork and can be traced for most of its sub-rectangular circuit except where it joins the post-medieval Lodge Park. The archaeological study of the park would reward closer attention, particularly in the identification of moats, park lodges, fishponds and warrens. Later landscaping may not have masked medieval features as completely as has been assumed, a 'fishpond' is marked on a map of the park dated 1852, for example.

Historians and archaeologists alike have ignored almost entirely any study of medieval agriculture around Cirencester. It is assumed that the basic features of open field agriculture were in place such as subdivided arable, rotated cultivation, and rights over waste and meadow. Examination of ridge and furrow on aerial photographs demonstrates a number of examples of medieval strips visible as zigzags in parish boundaries (eg between Siddington and Kemble) and as closely spaced (5–10m) curvilinear ridges of characteristic reversed-'S' shape (eg around Furzen Leaze Farm, Siddington). Several phases of ridge and furrow can be picked out and some straight, short and widely spaced strips may well be of post-medieval date (eg under Chesterton Park; west of Stratton). Typically, these later strips are bounded by straight, regular, enclosure hedges and may overlie earlier ridge and furrow. One example at Furzen Leaze Farm appears to show the tails of characteristic medieval ridges 'straightened' by later ploughing on a slightly different orientation.

Given the importance of Cirencester's trade in wool during the medieval period it is surprising that sites for sheep dips and sheep folds (perhaps with a shepherd's shelter and mangers inside) have not been recorded during documentary study or fieldwork. Drystone walling may provide evidence of early enclosure of land by agreement and possibly even earlier features. The publication of hedgerow studies around Cirencester is promised (Reece 1983, 1990).

Features and components such as ridge and furrow, orchards, gardens of minor tenants, banked paddocks (such as those around Manor Farm, Baunton; south of Norcote Farm, Preston), parish boundaries and the partial remnants of field systems have not been given monument numbers though there are a number of examples of fine upstanding earthworks (eg Witpit Copse near Preston).

The identification of blocks of common land and woodland has scarcely begun, although the medieval woods at Chesterton are classed as a monument (54249). The Querns area, the medieval *Crundles*, *Cronnes*, *Cornes*, amongst many other derivations, was common pasture, 'a thorny wood', until the thirteenth century when it was enclosed and used as a rabbit warren or coneygarth by the Abbot (54451). Leland mistook the site for that of the castle but in 1538 a 'keper of the game of conyes' is recorded as 'being within the lese or pasture called Corners' (Fuller 1890–1). Rabbits were kept for their fur and meat and principal components of a warren might typically include ditches, fences, hedges and artificial mounds or pillow mounds for breeding. The scheduled Neolithic 'long barrow' site may be just such a pillow mound.

Other rural monuments such as river fisheries and dovecotes seem likely in the area and documentary study would doubtless reveal examples. None have been recognised during fieldwork.

Industry

No medieval windmills are recorded, possibly because water power was abundant. A single watermill in Stratton (54369) is shown on the 1911 Beecham map in the Bingham Library, and is probably on the same site as the mill mentioned in Domesday Book.

There is no archaeological or historical evidence thus far for local crafts and industries such as blacksmiths, coopers, farriers, turners, charcoal burners, and so on. A large quantity of limestone-tempered green-glazed pottery has been recovered during fieldwalking programmes to the north of Preston. Geophysical survey and small-scale evaluation trenches failed to locate any kiln site but the quantity found is unusually high for it to be explained by manuring (CAT 1991). Pits containing medieval material have been recorded nearby.

Monument Discrimination

Monuments of recognised national importance inside the medieval urban area must include the entire precinct of the Augustinian Abbey (54087), the church of St John the Baptist (54053) with its cemetery, St John's Hospital (54076) on Spitalgate, St Thomas's Hospital (54096) in Thomas Street, and Langley Mill (54186).

Those of regional importance are the churches of St Cecilia and St Lawrence, the five other mill sites and Monmouth House. All of these require more thorough archaeological documentation to establish their nature and survival but have the potential to be elevated into the highest category of importance in the future. Likewise, the urban plots, the castle site, the bridges, *Archebalds* manor house, *de Piries* manor house, *Le Beches*, *More's Place*, *New Farm*, and the *Bottehall* are unknown but there is perhaps less potential for the recovery of intact archaeological deposits due to the impact of later post-medieval buildings.

For the countryside, the deer park (54112), the barn at Siddington (54173), and the parish churches (54185, 54216, 54259) are all monuments of national importance. Monuments such as the moot, portions of surviving open field system and Chesterton woods are judged to be of local archaeological importance only, though their interest may overlap with ecology and countryside issues. The short list of known monument classes largely reflects the lack of recent research into rural medieval monuments in the area.

Those medieval monuments which are not recognised at present include decoy ponds, industrial complexes, monastic granges, postmills, and potteries.

11. CIRENCESTER: A MEDIUM-SIZED MARKET TOWN IN THE POST-MEDIEVAL PERIOD

by Christopher Gerrard and Linda Viner

'On going to see my horse fed this morning, I noticed what I was not able to do last night, that this hospitarium or Inn was built on the model of that where Chaucer's Pilgrims assembled . . . galleries . . . supported on wooden pillars, carried backwards, to afford a communication with the apartments of the guests. Plans and drawings of such ancient buildings ought to be obtained; to illucidate the History of Past Times.'

Rev John Skinner (1824), diary entry for 11th November while staying at the Ram Inn

Medium-sized market town (post-medieval)

This Chapter considers the post-medieval development of Cirencester from the medieval period through to 1940 (Figure 43). The range and number of monuments is very considerable and discussion is highly selective. However, amongst the notable new landmarks are the mansions and gardens of Cirencester Park and the Abbey House, the arrival of the railways and canal, the re-building of many town houses in a 'Cotswold style' and numerous new public buildings and services.

Before the nineteenth century the overall topography of the town was little changed from the later medieval period. This may be somewhat surprising in view of the shift in ownership from the Church into private hands. Nevertheless, Cirencester Park and the grounds of the Abbey House merely replaced previous land units and did little to alter the shape of the town.

Real change occurred against a background of nineteenth-century population growth as development began to the south of Lewis Lane and Querns Lane. Nursery gardens and private estates, which had previously hemmed the town into its historic medieval core, were sold off and the town doubled its population and size. With development on the margins the core could be relieved of pressure and by 1830 the Market Place was cleared of its cluster of buildings, removing centuries of encroachment which had obscured views of the parish church and leaving the framework of the urban form which is still with us today.

The townscape presents a mixture of architectural styles, a point recorded by the Reverend John Skinner during his brief stay in November 1824. Notable examples of known sixteenth and seventeenth century jettied timber-framed buildings include The Bear in Dyer Street, The Fleece in the Market Place, 6 and 8 Dollar Street, and 17 and 19 Gosditch Street. All have visible external features, but it can be confidently predicted that many features remain hidden behind nineteenth-century facades and infillings. Many fine town houses were built with the characteristic features of stone mullions, transoms and drip moulding, beneath Cotswold stone slated roofs. These properties are survivors of private investments in the early post-medieval period which were common to many town communities, fuelled by the introduction of new design elements, and properties in Coxwell Street, Gosditch Street and Dollar Street typify the quintessential character of Cotswold vernacular expression.

During the eighteenth and nineteenth centuries many other timber buildings must have been refaced in stone, stucco or ashlar, and blocks of tenements cleared and replaced with substantial townhouses. Particularly notable examples of Cirencester's Neo-Classical style are Lloyd's Bank in Castle Street, and Gloucester House in Dyer Street with its gardens, orchards and summerhouse (Barker 1976).

In the Market Place the facades of buildings such as the Corn Hall and the former Wilts & Dorset Bank in the Market Place are notable nineteenth-century buildings. The introduction of brick, facilitated by the ease of transport by railway and canal, provided

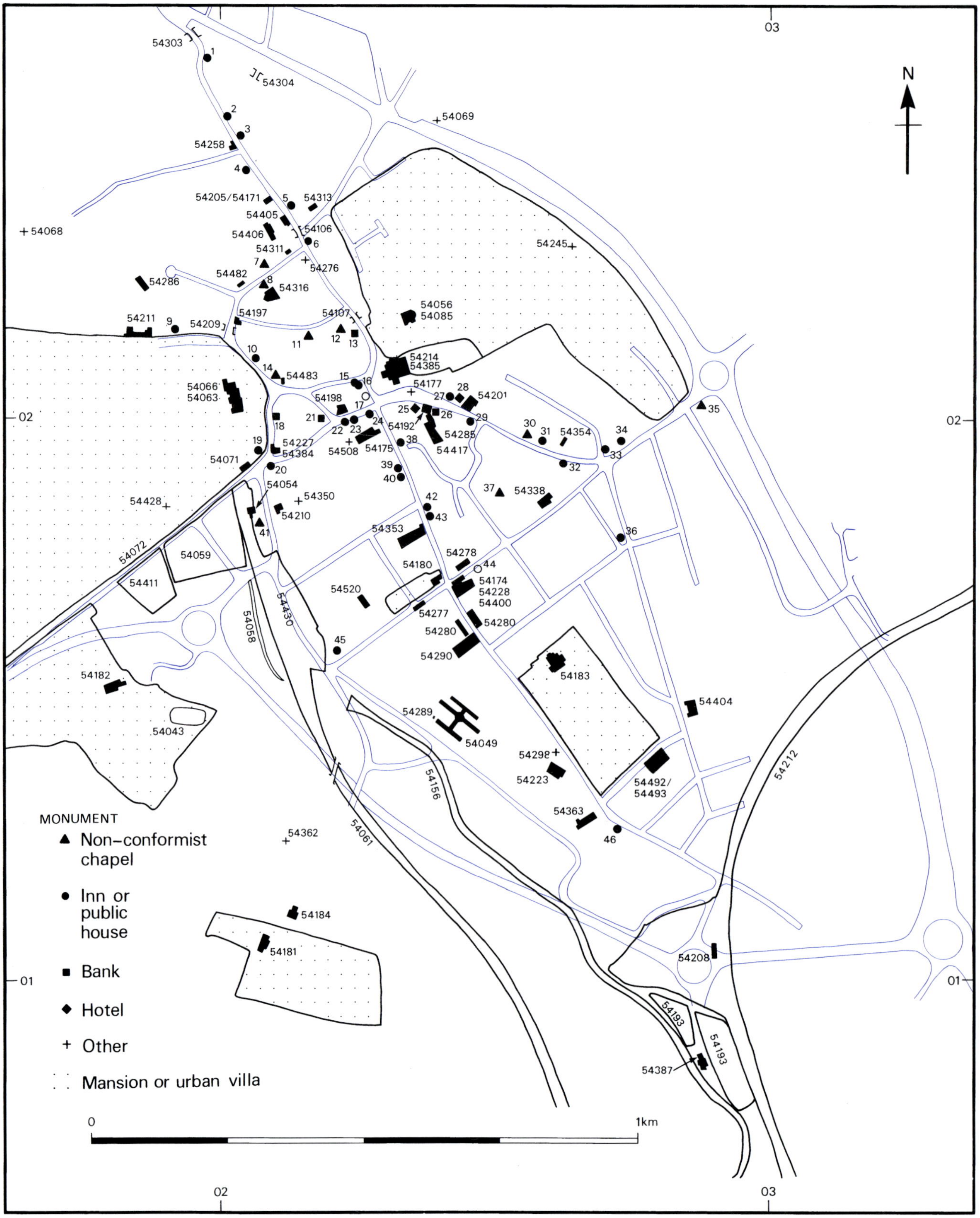

Figure 43
Monuments in the post-medieval Medium-Sized Market Town

Key to Figure 43:

54043	The Querns	kitchen garden
54049	Trinity Road	workhouse
54054	Brunel Station	railway station
54056	Abbey House (1)	town house (post-medieval)
54059	Cirencester Park	kitchen garden
54061	Great Western Railway	railway
54063	Cirencester House	town house (post-medieval)
54066	Oakley House	town house (post-medieval)
54068	Barton Mill	battery
54069	Spitalgate	fieldworks
54071	Museum, Tetbury Road	museum
54072	Cirencester Park	park
54085	Abbey House (2)	town house (post-medieval)
54106	Dollar Street	bridge
54107	Dollar Street	bridge
54156	Thames & Severn Canal	canal
54171	Gloucester Street	theatre
54174	Lewis Lane	waterworks
54175	Bowly's Brewery	brewery
54177	Market Place, Public Pump	public pump
54180	Ashcroft House	urban villa
54181	Chesterton House	urban villa
54182	The Querns	urban villa
54183	Watermoor House	urban villa
54184	Chesterton Museum	museum
54192	Corn Hall	exchange
54193	The Gas House	gasworks
54197	Thomas Street	exchange
54198	Castle Street, Post Office	post office
54201	Bingham Library	library
54208	Watermoor Station	railway station
54209	Park Lane/Thomas Street	bridge
54210	Cottage Hospital, Sheep St	hospital
54211	Barracks & Cecily Hill	armoury
54212	MSWJ Railway	railway
54214	Town Hall (Parish Church)	town hall
54223	Watermoor Church	parochial chapel
54227	Police Station, Park Lane	police station
54228	Coles Mill, Lewis Lane	mill
54245	Ice House, Abbey Grounds	icehouse
54258	St Lawrence's Almshouses	almshouses
54263	Primitive Methodist Chapel	non-conformist chapel
54277	Querns Lane, Almshouses	almshouses
54278	Lewis Lane, Almshouses	almshouses
54280	Almshouses, Watermoor Road	almshouses
54285	Subscription Library/Reading Room	library
54286	Swimming Baths	swimming baths
54289	Cirencester Workhouse	lock-up
54290	Burial Ground, Watermoor Road	burial ground
54298	Pest House, Watermoor Churchyard	pest house
54303	Gloucester Street Bridge	bridge
54304	Gooseacre Bridge, Gooseacre Lane	bridge
54311	4–6 Thomas Street, Almshouses	almshouses
54313	St John's Almshouses	almshouses
54316	Burial Ground, Thomas Street	burial ground
54338	County Junior School, Lewis Lane	school
54350	Memorial Hospital	air-raid shelter
54353	Cotswold Brewery	brewery
54354	Cotswold Foundry	iron works
54362	Cotswold Factory	factory
54363	Watermoor Infants School	school
54384	Police Station, Park Lane	court house
54385	South Porch, St John's Church	court house
54387	Infectious Diseases Hospital	hospital
54400	Pumping Station, Lewis Lane	pumping station
54404	Upper School Victoria Road	school
54405	Powell's School, Gloucester St	school

54406	Powell School, Watermoor	school
54411	Cattle Market	cattle market
54417	Corn Hall	concert hall
54428	Grismonds Tower	icehouse
54430	Great Western Railway	railway yard
54482	Cripps Museum, The Mead	museum
54483	Corinium Museum, Park Street	museum
54492	Bingham Hall	concert hall
54493	Bingham Hall	rifle range
54508	Brewery, Cricklade Street	air-raid shelter
54520	St Peter, Roman Catholic Church	non-conformist chapel

Monuments mapped as 1 to 46:

1	54302	Royal Oak Inn	public house
2	54309	Duke of York Inn	public house
3	54306	Nelson Inn	public house
4	54307	Anchor Inn	public house
5	54235	White Lion	public house
6	54312	Red Lion Inn	public house
7	54195	Temperance Hall, Thomas Street	non-conformist chapel
8	54265	Friends Meeting House	non-conformist chapel
9	54317	Dolphin Inn	public house
10	54498	Phoenix Inn	public house
11	54261	Baptist Chapel, Coxwell Street	non-conformist chapel
	54396	Baptist Chapel, Coxwell Street	non-conformist chapel
12	54203	Unitarian Church, Gosditch Street	non-conformist chapel
13	54282	Gloucestershire Banking Co	bank
14	54262	Chapel, Park Street	non-conformist chapel
15	54272	Crown Inn	public house
16	54273	Swan Inn	hotel
17	54070	Ram Inn, Market Place	inn
18	54283	Savings Bank, Park Lane	bank
19	54500	The Barley Mow	public house
20	54233	Three Compasses Inn	public house
21	54281	Lloyds Bank	bank
22	54497	The Black Horse	public house
23	54315	Kings Arms	public house
24	54213	Bell Hotel	hotel
25	54225	King's Head Hotel, Market Place	hotel
26	54141	Wilts and Dorset Bank	bank
27	54172	Sun Inn	public house
28	54196	The Fleece Hotel, Dyer Street	hotel
29	54349	Bear Inn	public house
30	54005	Congregational Church	non-conformist chapel
31	54356	Ship Inn	public house
32	54429	Old Bull Inn	public house
33	54150	The Nags Head	public house
34	54204	Waggon & Horses Inn	public house
35	54230	Catholic Chapel	non-conformist chapel
36	54337	Talbot Inn	public house
37	54263	Primitive Methodist Chapel	non-conformist chapel
38	54348	Kings Head Tap	public house
39	54200	Three Horseshoes	public house
40	54199	Bishop Blaize	public house
41	54060	Chapel, Sheep Street	non-conformist chapel
42	54342	Fox Inn	public house
43	54343	Wheatsheaf Inn	public house
44	54361	Twelve Bells	public house
45	54206	Great Western Inn	public house
46	54365	Queens Head	public house

Not mapped/located:

54308	187 Gloucester Street, at rear	smithy
54162	19 Park Street	cottages
54155	26 Gloucester Street	cottage
54305	95 Gloucester Street	smithy
54222	Abbey Grounds	culvert

54279	Almshouses, Gloucester Street	almshouses
54288	Armoury Hospital, Dollar Street	hospital
54287	Armoury Hospital, Silver Street	hospital
54064	Barton House	battery
54381	Bowly's Bank	bank
54407	British School, Sheep Street	school
54058	Canal Feeder, Hammond Way	canal
54347	Cecily Hill	road
54402	Cirencester Park	rifle range
54360	Cotswold Avenue	obelisk
54504	Cotswold Coffee Tavern	coffee house
54410	Coxwell Street	sewer
54394	Cricklade Street	mission room
54395	Cricklade Street	mission room
54065	Cricklade Way	battery
54380	Cripps Bank	bank
54386	Fishponds, Cirencester	fishponds
54340	Flagstaff	flagstaff
54271	Folly, Castle Street	folly
54226	Gaumont Cinema, London Road	cinema
54489	Girl's High School, The Avenue	school
54502	Globe Temperance Hotel	hotel
54067	Gloucester Street	battery
54310	Gloucester/Dollar/Spitalgate	post box
54276	Hodden House, Dollar Street	almshouses
54499	Hole in the Wall	public house
54408	Infants School, Thomas Street	school
54345	Iron Works, Ashcroft Road	iron works
54351	London Road	machine-gun nest
54205	Loyal Volunteer	public house
54391	Market Hall	market hall
54415	Market Place	battery
54490	Mechanics Institute	library
54486	Mr Webb's School, Coxwell St	school
54485	Mr Webb's School, Dyer Street	school
54194	Park Street	war defences
54319	Phoenix Public House	public house
54494	Picture House	cinema
54484	Police Station, Gloucester St	police station
54352	Post Box, Cricklade/Lewis Lane	post box
54355	Post Box, Dyer Street	post box
54284	Post Office, Black Jack Street	post office
54264	Presbyterian Chapel	non-conformist chapel
54127	Querns Hill	culvert
54488	School of Art, Dyer Street	school
54364	Smithy, 29 Church Street	smithy
54344	Smithy, Ashcroft Road	smithy
54341	Smithy, Cricklade Street	smithy
54318	Smithy, Park Street	smithy
54346	Smithy, Querns Lane	smithy
54358	St John's Hospital	passage
54270	Stocks, Market Place	stocks
54491	Subscription Library, Dyer St	library
54409	Sunday School, Cricklade Street	school
54399	Swimming Baths Pump	pump
54503	Temperance Coffee House	coffee house
54376	Tetbury Road	machine-gun nest
54398	The Flying Dutchman	public house
54495	The Regal, Lewis Lane	cinema
54496	The Swan	public house
54397	The Waterloo	passage
54389	The White Hart	public house
54224	Watermoor Church Hall	church hall
54487	Watermoor National School	school
54229	Wesleyan Chapel	non-conformist chapel
54501	Working Men's Club	men's club

cheap building materials for housing developments in Watermoor from the 1880s (Slater 1976c). At 32–38 Cricklade Street the detailed recording of late nineteenth century exterior facades, interior room dimensions, features and fitments prior to demolition illustrates the potential for detailed structural analysis and the assessment of changes in property boundaries within the post-medieval period (Gerrard and Johnson 1989a). Such studies are considerably enhanced by the opportunity to incorporate map regression analysis with the aid of First Edition Ordnance Survey maps, sale particulars where they may survive, early building plans and photographs (Figures 44 and 45).

Excluding the changes brought about by the dissolution of the ecclesiastical institutions in Cirencester there was little change in the physical size or general shape of the town until the late nineteenth century. Spare land which became available at the Dissolution was swallowed up by individual purchasers rather than being sold off for development. This is not to say that the fabric remained static; there was intense use of space, especially in plots behind the street frontages, and in the town growth took place by the infilling between plots of land rather than in the creation of suburbs. The notorious area of 'dark passage-ways among quasi-derelict cottages' called 'The Paen', to the west of St John's Hospital (54358), was cleared in *c*1850 (Baddeley 1923b). Conditions in many parts of the town gave rise to concern over public health, with outbreaks of smallpox and scarlet fever a common occurrence in the congested alleys and closes.

By the early nineteenth century, the concerted efforts of private developers, philanthropists and councillors instigated a review of housing and public sanitation to address the overcrowding and poor housing. The growth and development of the Victorian suburbs is admirably charted by Slater (1976b and c; 1977; 1978), supplementing the evidence first published by Beecham (1887). Expansion of residential housing began after 1826 with the sale of Watermoor Common and housing construction along Watermoor Road and Stepstairs Lane designed to re-house families moved from the market place and houses crowded around the south porch of the parish church.

Dramatic changes in the town plan continued in 1853 with the development of the Watermoor Nursery by the Master family. Within the space of fifteen years building plots for housing development in Tower Street, Corin Street (now The Avenue), New Road (renamed Victoria Road), Chester Street, and Church Street were laid out for sale. Considerable damage must have been done to the underlying archaeology, particularly by cellars. J Buckman (1853) records that 'remains of ancient buildings are so great that at depths ranging from 2–10 feet purchasers find enough stone . . . to build boundary walls'.

In the early nineteenth century elegant urban villas, set in their own landscaped grounds, satisfied the aspirations of the wealthy middle classes (Slater 1978; Verey 1970, 1976). Well proportioned and with spacious accommodation, they no longer retain their primary function and have since been converted or demolished: The Querns (54182), built in 1825 for Charles Lawrence, is now part of Cirencester Hospital; Chesterton House built 1813 (54181), and Watermoor House built 1825 (54183) have been converted to flats; whilst Ashcroft House (54180) built in 1775, was demolished in 1964.

In the middle of the eighteenth century the core of the town was bolstered by the estates of the two principal landholders – the Bathurst family to the west, and the Master family to the east. Of the two estates, Cirencester Park, with its extensive woodlands and home park dominates the higher ground to the west of the town. There is, unfortunately, very little surviving documentation relating to the development of either the park or the house and much of that which does survive is widely scattered in secondary accounts and record offices. Piecing together the information, the present-day Cirencester House (54063) was built *c*1713 by the first Earl Bathurst and later extended, probably incorporating parts of the earlier Oakley House (54066) within its core. This earlier Elizabethan house was sold to Sir Benjamin Bathurst by the Poole family in 1695, and it is this house which is depicted on Kip's view of Cirencester (Figure 46). The sixteenth-century house was built before 1592 when Queen Elizabeth was recorded as staying at 'Sir John Danvers' new house', the Danvers' selling the property to Henry Poole of Sapperton in 1615 (Kingsley 1989, 76).

The overall design of Cirencester Park as set out by Allen First Earl Bathurst in the early eighteenth century is specifically aligned on the tower of St John's church in the market place. From the Broad Ride, the longest avenue of trees in England, there are a number of vistas and rides which radiate out from clearings (eg at the Hexagon, the Seven Rides and the Ten Rides) through woodland and open parkland aligned on local landmarks such as the spire of Kemble church. Lord Bathurst took a keen interest in forestry, planting extensively inside the Park, and he is probably also responsible for the wonderful yew hedge which blocks views of the house from the town.

The woods are set with follies and buildings including Pope's Seat, Hartley's Temple, the Horse Temple, the Hexagon, the Venetian Building, Queen Anne's Monument, Alfred's Hall (Figure 47), and the Round Tower. Not all were built at the same time and

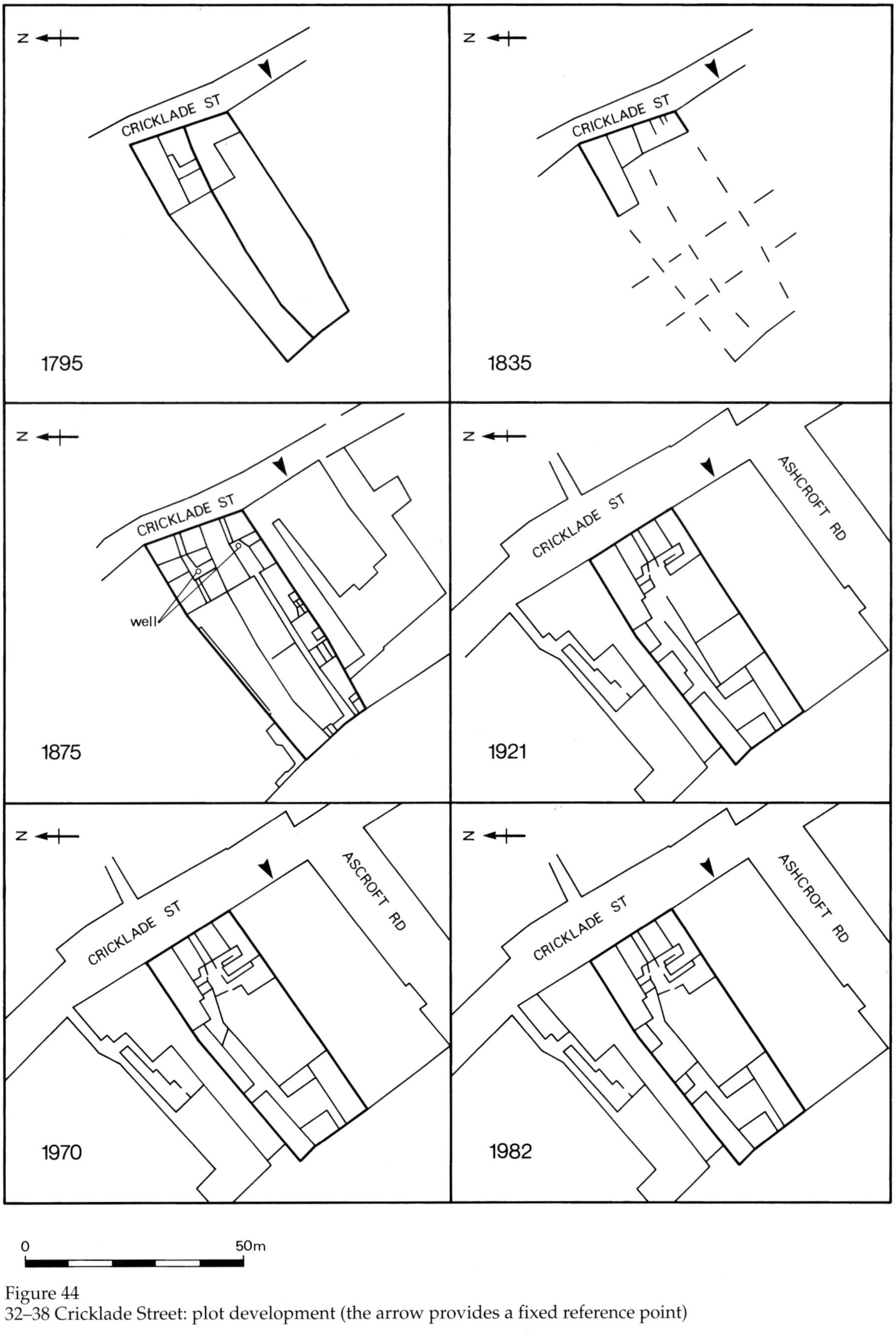

Figure 44
32–38 Cricklade Street: plot development (the arrow provides a fixed reference point)

Figure 45
32–38 Cricklade Street on the left, with the 1921 street frontage, looking north (Corinium Museum)

some, such as the Lion's Den and the Octagon, have since disappeared, if indeed they were ever constructed. However, the layout achieved effectively links semi-natural broad-leaved woodland with the house setting by means of a geometric pattern of rides. Pope called it 'the amiable simplicity of unadorned nature' and today this is the largest block of woodland on the Cotswolds supporting over 250 plant species as well as invertebrates, mammals and birds.

The principal landowner of estates to the east of the town was the Master family. Following the dissolution of the monasteries the first Abbey House (54056) to be built on the site of the cloisters of the former Augustinian Abbey was demolished in 1776 and replaced by one set in 'good gardens and spacious lawns' (54085; Kingsley 1989, 1992). While many of the medieval religious buildings were lost this conversion had the happy effect of preserving the former precinct intact as a single unit of property, while the Master family emulated the Bathursts, setting out rides and walks in parkland surrounding Hare Bushes and Tar Barrows.

Religious and charitable institutions

The rapid post-medieval expansion of the town with the development of residential and industrial areas to the south of Lewis Lane and Querns Lane called for a wider range of public services and utilities to be provided for the expanding population. The parish church of St John the Baptist continued to serve the community but by the mid nineteenth century the development of Watermoor necessitated the consecration of a parochial chapel, the Church of the Holy Trinity, in Watermoor Road (54223). Erected as a

Figure 46
View of Cirencester, engraved by Kip in 1712, showing the seat of Earl Bathurst

chapel-of-ease and opened for public worship in 1851, it was designed by Gilbert Scott in the Gothic style. The tower with its spire was added in 1852 and the south aisle was extended in 1876 to cater for the needs of an ever-expanding suburb.

Non-conformist worship was served by a number of chapels including the Baptist Chapel, Coxwell Street (54396), erected in 1856–57 in Italianate style with seating for 400 people, replacing an earlier chapel of *c*1650 (54261). Another Separatist Baptist Chapel in Park Street (54262) opened for worship in 1854, while the Independent or Congregational Chapel (54060) founded in Sheep Street in 1839 had seats for 400 people, and included a schoolroom under the chapel. Other denominations worshipped in the Wesleyan Methodist Chapel, Gloucester Street (54229); the Presbyterian Chapel, Gosditch Street (54264); the Unitarian Chapel, Gosditch Street (54203); the Congregational Chapel, Dyer Street (54005); and the Temperance Hall, Thomas Street (54195), built in 1864 as a Meeting House with seating for 600.

The Friends Meeting House in Thomas Street (54265) was formerly a dwelling house. Converted in

Figure 47
The Woodhouse, or Alfred's Hall, in Cirencester Park (Dennis Moss, Corinium Museum)

1673 into a place of worship and enlarged in 1810 it was capable of holding 700 people in 1887. Components of the Friends Meeting House include a caretaker's dwelling house, an infant school (not used after 1879), and a graveyard with no gravestones in accordance with Quaker traditions. The Roman Catholic community worshipped at a small Chapel in London Road (54230), before transferring to St Peter's Church in St Peter's Road, Ashcroft, built in 1896 by A J C Scoles (54520).

The churchyard of the parish church was extended in 1830–1840 from the more restricted area shown on Kip's view but despite this could not cater for the demands made upon it, and Chesterton Cemetery (54260), on the south side of Chesterton Lane, was laid out as an urban cemetery in 1871. Set in six acres of landscaped ground, the two Gothic chapels for Episcopalians and Non-Conformists, lodge and mortuary building were designed by Medland of Gloucester. Prior to 1871 the non-conformists used the small burial ground in Watermoor Road (54290), and the Friends burial ground in Thomas Street (54316).

Charities, established in previous centuries, endeavoured to help the poor, and wealthy, conscientious philanthropists continued to endow or renovate almshouses in the town. St Lawrence's Almshouses in Barton Lane (54258), on the site of the former church and hospital were converted after the sixteenth century into almshouse cottages. Hodden House in Dollar Street (54276), in use from 1620 to 1800, was replaced by almshouses in Querns Lane, built by John Wilkins (54277). In Lewis Lane, almshouses (54278), first mentioned in the original endowment of 1702 were taken down and new buildings erected. These were later re-endowed in 1874 by the 5th Earl Bathurst. Occupation of the earlier foundations at St Thomas' or Weaver's Hall (54311) and St John's Hospital (54313) continued and Christopher Bowly erected eight almshouses in Watermoor Road in 1837 (54280).

Public buildings and services

The growing prosperity of the town and dramatic increase in population placed considerable pressure on the public facilities, buildings and services demanded by the populace. For many years the south porch of the parish church fulfilled a variety of public functions, acting as town hall from 1672 (54214), and as the court house (54385) and seat of the administration of justice until the removal of the Petty Sessions and County Court to their own building in Park Lane in 1859 (54384). The Police Station shared the same site (54227), and included the Petty Sessional Court, Magistrates' Room, Police Superintendent's residence and his staff of police, replacing the 'old' police station located somewhere in Gloucester Street (54484; Harmer 1924, 322–3). Prior to 1859 malefactors and petty criminals had been detained either in the stocks (54270), reported as disused in 1887 when they were sited near The Shambles, opposite the entrance to the Waterloo Passage, or in the lock-up (54289), 'the dumpling house', a building with a chequered career and several physical re-locations which by the end of the nineteenth century was used as a lock-up for the refractory at the Union Workhouse.

Public services in the form of gas, electricity, and water supplies; the provision of health care and education; and the Victorian concern for social welfare necessitated a major building programme to satisfy the expanding population. It is estimated that by 1864 over ten miles of main piping led through the town from the Gas Works (54193) sited adjacent to the railway sidings of the Midland and South Western Junction Railway in Watermoor.

Domestic water supply was satisfied by private wells, many plotted on the 1875 Ordnance Survey map, with a public pump in the Market Place (54177) having a recorded depth of 25–26ft (7.6–7.9m). Following recurrent outbreaks of disease concern for the distribution of clean water to all householders led to the setting up of a private waterworks in Lewis Lane (54174). Located on the corner of Lewis Lane and Watermoor Road, the Cirencester Waterworks Company Ltd was formed in 1882, and taken over by the Urban District Council in 1898. A reservoir near the Farm Road in Cirencester Park (54401) with a 200,000 gallon capacity took water from the pumping station (54400) and supplied all parts of the town.

Health care was enhanced by the founding in 1875 of the Cottage Hospital (54210), a charitable hospital which benefited greatly from the support of Lady Bathurst. The Infectious Diseases Hospital (54387), established in 1878 by the Urban and Rural Sanitary Districts of Cirencester, was for obvious reasons located well to the south of the town near the canal, and replaced the earlier pesthouse (54298). Under the requirements of the Poor Law Act, the poor and destitute were served by the Workhouse (54049), constructed in 1836 with segregated male and female wards.

The educational reforms of the nineteenth century resulted in a reassessment of the facilities available to children within the town and the opening of new schools, especially in Watermoor. The fortunes of the Grammar School fluctuated during this period and the decision was taken to found the Upper School for Boys (54404). Opened in 1881 in New Road (now Victoria Road) the school was housed in an Elizabethan-style building, with a large playground. The Blue and Yellow Schools, founded in 1714 and 1722 respectively, were amalgamated in 1879 as the Powell Elementary School in Gloucester Street (54405). Too numerous to list here (see Appendix B), the governing boards of both private and public schools endeavoured to serve the needs of children of all ages. In addition, to satisfy the Victorian vogue for self-education and enlightenment, concerts, evening classes, lectures and library facilities were available at the Mechanics Institute (54490), and the Permanent Library and Subscription Room (54491) which opened in Dyer Street in 1835. The philanthropy and generosity of Daniel Bingham endowed the town with two major public facilities, the Bingham Library, opened in 1904 (54201), and the Bingham Hall in 1908 (54492).

Plays and entertainments were staged by theatres in Gloucester Street (54171) and the Corn Hall, attracting many famous actors to the town. With the advent of moving pictures, 'picture houses' were opened (54494) next to the Corn Hall in the Market Place, before the purpose-built construction of two cinemas, The Regal (54495) and The Gaumont (54226). More active pursuits were catered for by the open-air swimming bath (54286), constructed in 1885 and still in use today; a rifle range in the Bingham Hall, and sports facilities such as archery and cricket in Cirencester Park.

Following the discovery of the Hunting Dogs and Four Seasons mosaics in Dyer Street in 1849, the town acquired its first museum as a result of the generosity of Lord Bathurst. The museum in Tetbury Road, built especially for Roman antiquities (54071), was 'first got in order' in 1851 and opened in 1856. Private museums established by other antiquarians and collectors were opened to the public from time to time as adjuncts to private residences such as Rajah Brooks' at Chesterton House (54184).

Hotels, inns and public houses

Taking into account the number of hotels, inns and public houses recorded in Cirencester the town could not be accused of lacking in hospitality. No less than seventy-three public houses were recorded in the town in 1800 (Welsford 1987a, 116) and Kip's view of 1712 shows the Market Place crowded with inn signs (Atkyns 1712). This was the focus for the principal hotels and former coaching inns: the Fleece Hotel (54196); the King's Head Hotel (54225); the Bell (54213); and The Ram Inn (54070). Over the years their fortunes have waxed and waned, and the Ram illustrates this well. First mentioned in 1641, there is a print, reputedly by W Hogarth, dated 1779, which was used as a frontispiece by Rudder (1800), a history and guide to the town used by the Rev John Skinner when he visited the town in 1824 (see heading to this Chapter). The inn was later demolished and by 1887 only the stabling was retained.

Many of the public houses have survived to the present day, but those which have disappeared include the Sun (54172, walls and cobbled surfaces associated with this building were observed in 1985), Swan (54496), Bishop Blaize (54497), Flying Dutchman (54398), Phoenix (54498), Old Bull (54429), Dolphin (54317), Fox (54342) and Great Western (54206). The tee-total establishments have also declined: the Working Men's Club in Cricklade Street (54501); the Globe Temperance Hotel in Castle Street (54502); the Temperance Coffee House (54503), and the Cotswold Coffee Tavern (54504). The latter was established 'with the philanthropic object of providing an attractive resort for young men during winter evenings' (Beecham 1887).

Industry, trade and commerce

In the early post-medieval period Leland wrote that 'the town standeth by clothing' and the presence of supplies of Fuller's Earth nearby, together with the town's mills and good communications meant that Cirencester was well placed to benefit from wool manufacture. Clothiers bought raw wool and paid for the spinning, weaving and finishing processes, before selling and exporting the finished cloth. The wealth of prosperous clothiers such as Philip Marner, commemorated by a brass in the parish church (d1587), is reflected in the typical Cotswold-stone houses of Coxwell Street and Gloucester Street, often with warehouse storage attached (54197).

The woollen industry was essentially a home-based craft, and there is little direct archaeological evidence for the process itself. Documentary sources are therefore essential, not only for reference to woollen manufacture but also for related industries such as tanning, leather and horn trades. A contemporary manuscript compiled by John Smith of Nibley in 1608, listing all able-bodied men capable of serving in the militia, provides an indication of the occupations of citizens of the town and shows that over 18% were engaged in the woollen trade (Welsford 1987a, 75). Trades listed for woollen and cloth manufacture include clothier, weaver, cardmaker, dyer, tucker, glover, draper, and tailor; with leather and related trades represented by shoemaker, currier, sadler and tanner.

Government restrictions on distribution and competition from lighter worsted cloths led to a fall in the market and inevitable decline in the woollen trade. However, Daniel Defoe in 1724 in his *Tour through . . . Great Britain* was optimistic enough to describe Cirencester as 'A very good town, populous and rich, full of clothiers and driving a great trade in wool...They talk of 5,000 packs a year'. But by the late eighteenth century cloth manufacture was concentrated in the Stroud valleys, on sites with easy access to water to power the mills. Inevitably trade in Cirencester declined, with only one mill, New Mills, continuing to operate until the early nineteenth century, producing a worsted cloth called 'thin stuff' or 'chinas'.

The decline in the wool trade was compensated by a growing dependence on the manufacture of edge-tools such as curriers' knives and cutting blades. Agriculture, and its attendant trades, was always an important factor in the town's prosperity, and the manufacturing industry which existed in the town was primarily concerned with the supply of edge-tools for agricultural implements and machinery. Iron works in Ashcroft Road (54345), and the Cotswold Foundry (54354), complemented the smithies depicted on the 1875 Ordnance Survey map working on a smaller scale, in premises at the rear of properties in Gloucester Street, Park Street, Cricklade Street, Ashcroft Road, Querns Lane, and Church Street.

As the town developed, the processing of locally produced goods came to play an important factor in providing employment for the town and neighbouring villages. Breweries in Lewis Lane (Bowly, later bought by Cripps in 1882; 54175) and Cricklade Street (Cripps; 54353) made use of local produce, as did the Cotswold Bacon Factory (54362) at Chesterton. Coles Mill in Lewis Lane (54228) processed wheat and animal feeds. Increasing concern for public health and a shift of emphasis in trade from wool to corn led to the removal of the general market activity away from the town centre. The Market House (54391), erected by Earl Bathurst in 1819 to serve as a market hall, proved inadequate and much business was transacted in the open air or in neighbouring inns. The Corn Hall (54192), on the south side of the Market Place, opened in 1862, enabled the corn dealers to transact their business under cover for the first time. As with so many of the town's nineteenth-century public amenities the cattle market (54411) on Tetbury Road was constructed by Earl Bathurst in 1867. Paved with blue bricks and furnished with iron pens, its location adjacent to the Great Western Railway was a great advantage for farmers and dealers, and at the same time removed a public nuisance from the market place.

The demolition of The Shambles and the renovation of properties created a prosperous centre for commerce and trade, with many shops and small businesses established, many of which are still trading today. As commerce expanded so did the accompanying infrastructure with a number of private and commercial banks being founded at the end of the nineteenth century. The County of Gloucester Bank, in Castle Street (54281), formerly a private bank known as Bowly's Bank, was erected in the early nineteenth century, and today is more familiar as Lloyd's Bank. The Gloucestershire Banking Company, Gosditch Street (54282), built in 1880 took over Cripp's Bank. The Savings Bank started in 1817 and moved to premises in Park Lane (54283). The Wilts and Dorset Bank (54141) was established in the Market Place in 1899, in an impressive building designed by G M Silley, and constructed by a local building contractor, Sanderson and Sons.

Battle sites, militia and wartime

No town is immune to the effects of national and international events, and over the centuries Cirencester has been affected by and played its role in the wider sphere. During the Civil War, the inhabitants of the town supported the Parliamentarians and in January 1643 defended themselves with batteries and fieldworks (Paddock 1993). Barton Mill (54068) and Barton House (54064) were

Figure 48
The Armoury in Cecily Hill, built for the militia in 1856 with mock castellated facade, at the entrance to the Broad Ride of Cirencester Park (Corinium Museum)

strengthened, and batteries commanded Cricklade and Gloucester Streets (54065 and 54067). The Royalists established fieldworks 150 paces outside the Spitalgate (54069), and after fierce fighting on 2nd February 1643, Cirencester fell. Unlike many other towns, such as Gloucester, the Civil War seems to have had no dramatic effect on the topography of the town with no archaeological evidence for a remodelling of the defences, for example.

In the nineteenth century the armoury (54211), a castellated gothic building on Cecily Hill, served as an assembly point for the local militia (Figure 48). Erected in 1856, to designs by Fulljames and Waller of Gloucester, the impressive facade hides mess rooms, sergeants quarters, ammunition and clothing stores, and drill ground. At the outbreak of the First World War, members of the armed forces were billeted in the town, with a battalion of Gloucestershire Yeomanry encamped in Cirencester Park. Well-served by the railway system, the town became the focus of troop movements, with Watermoor Station acting as the reception point for wounded troops on their way to the Red Cross Hospital set up in the Bingham Hall in 1914. With the ending of the war in 1918, the town celebrated with 'heartfelt joy and gladness', and commemorated the deaths of over 200 inhabitants.

Cirencester prepared for invasion and attack in

Key to Figure 49:

54061	Great Western Railway	railway
54072	Cirencester Park	park
54129	Royal Agricultural College	quarry
54142	Hare Bushes Quarry	quarry
54147	Royal Agricultural College	college
54156	Thames & Severn Canal	canal
54178	Pit	quarry
54212	MSWJ Railway	railway
54218	Corner of Stratton Heights	windmill
54232	Dyer St/Grove Lane	toll booth
54234	Tetbury Rd/Stroud Rd	toll booth
54260	Chesterton Cemetery	urban cemetery
54274	Kingshill Quarries	quarry
54301	Chesterton	quarry
54339	East of Love Lane	quarry
54347	Cecily Hill–Park Corner	road
54366	Barton Gravel Pit	quarry
54367	Trinity Road	quarry
54368	Archery House	quarry
54383	Siddington	brickworks
54388	Greyhound Inn, Siddington	inn
54392	Stratton Mill	watermill
54393	Stratton Mill	watermill
54401	Cirencester Park	reservoir
54432	Baunton Pumping Station	pumping station
54445	St Mary Magdalene, Baunton	parochial church
54448	Siddington	water-meadows
54449	Village Farm, Preston	farmstead
54450	Church Farm, Preston	farmstead
54453	Dilley's Farm, Baunton	farmstead
54454	Merrillhill Farm, Preston	farmstead
54455	Norcote Farm, Preston	farmstead
54456	St Augustine's Farm, Preston	farmstead
54457	Ermin Farm, Preston	farmstead
54458	Bowling Green Farm	farmstead
54459	Whiteway Farm	farmstead
54460	Cranhams Farm	farmstead
54461	Chesterton Farm	farmstead
54462	Manor Farm, Baunton	farmstead
54463	Church Farm, Siddington	farmstead
54464	Barton Farm, Siddington	farmstead
54465	Plummer's Farm, Siddington	farmstead
54466	Worm's Farm, Siddington	farmstead
54467	Sandy Lane Farm, Siddington	farmstead
54468	Furzen Leaze, Siddington	farmstead
54469	North Furzen Leaze Farm	farmstead
54470	Bowley's Farm, Siddington	farmstead
54471	Dryleaze Farm, Siddington	farmstead
54472	Preston Forty Farm, Preston	farmstead
54473	New Farm, Cirencester	farmstead
54505	Baunton	water-meadows
54506	Preston	water-meadows
54507	Whiteway realignment	road
54509	Preston Place, Preston	vicarage
54510	School, Siddington	school
54511	School, Baunton	school
54512	Preston Mill	watermill
54513	Salutation Gate	tool booth
54514	Siddington	?windmill
54516	Cirencester–Stroud	road
54521	Siddington Field Farm	farmstead
54522	College Farm	farmstead
54523	Siddington Mill	watermill
54525	Stratton	quarry
54526	Preston	school
54527	Stratton	school
54528	Ivy Lodge	farmstead
54529	Cirencester–Fairford	road
54530	Cirencester–Gloucester	road
54531	Cirencester–Burford	road
54532	Cirencester–Stow	road
54533	Cirencester–Swindon	road
54534	Cirencester–Tetbury	road
54535	Cirencester–Cheltenham	road
54536	Cirencester–Stroud	road
54537	Cirencester	water-meadows

Not plotted/located:

54148	Cranhams Lane	culvert
54390	Stratton Maltings	maltings
54403	Baunton	rifle range
54447	Siddington	maltings
54524	Cheltenham Road	limekiln

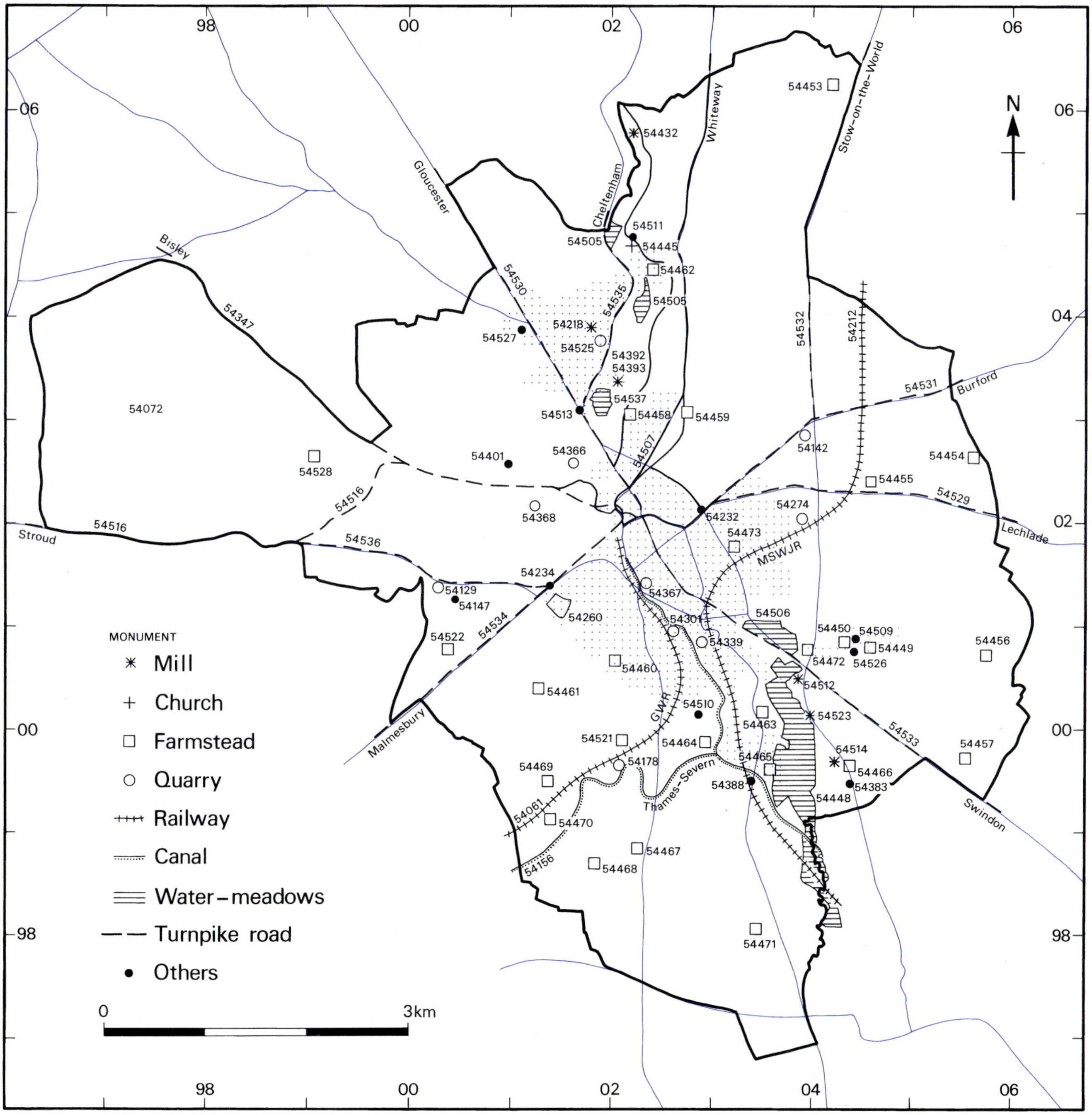

Figure 49
Post-medieval monuments in the rural area (see Figure 43 for monuments within the urban form)

1939. Second World War air raid shelters were built behind the Memorial Hospital (54350) and on the Cricklade Street premises of the Cirencester Brewery Co (54508), while a number of basements to private houses and building premises were prepared in the event of air raids over the town. Two machine gun nests in the London Road (54351) and the Bath Road (54376) monitored the road approaches, and tank trap sockets were placed at the foot of Cecily Hill. The Local Defence Volunteers, later renamed the Home Guard, formed the 3rd Glos (Cirencester) Battalion Home Guard, and consisted of six companies with their headquarters in The Barracks, at the top of Cecily Hill.

The town did not experience any direct hits, but was witness to troop movements and general civilian precautions and reception of evacuees. In March 1944 officers and men of the United States 15th Hospital Center arrived to organise and administer fourteen hospitals in the south of England, establishing their base in the Bingham Hall before moving to the Stratton House Hotel. Typical of the hospitals administered from the 15th Center were the 188th and 192nd US General Hospitals in Cirencester Park, and the 111th General near Daglingworth on the Gloucester Road. The latter became a Polish Refugee Camp at the end of the war.

Accumulated deposits

This sub-division of the medium-sized market town form is very much the town that is visible today and which is represented archaeologically by numerous standing buildings and structures as well as by buried deposits. The early drawings and plans of the town show the main changes that have taken place within the currency of the form. The railways and the canal have come and gone, notable buildings in the market place and elsewhere are no longer present and former fields and gardens have been built-over as infilling has taken place. All of these changes have resulted in a translation of the built environment into an archaeological resource. For this last identified form, however, the process is incomplete and while there are certainly aspects of the post-medieval history of the town which are now an essentially archaeological phenomenon and therefore of archaeological interest and importance the overall picture is not susceptible to the kind of deposit discrimination that has been applied to earlier forms.

This sub-division of the medium-sized market town form relates to the relatively recent history of the town's evolution (Welsford 1987a and b). The exterior facades of the post-medieval buildings have been documented by Reece and Catling (1975), and the overall development of the town is discussed in detail in the series of essays entitled *Studies in the archaeology and history of Cirencester* (McWhirr 1976b). The original layout and arrangement of monuments is clearly shown on the 1795, 1817, 1835 and 1875 maps of the town.

Post-medieval countryside

A large number of medieval and earlier monuments are also present in the post-medieval period. Antecedent forms of monuments such as churches, bridges and roads, for example, are still important in later rural landscapes. Only where these monuments are significantly restructured or renamed have they been assigned new monument numbers (Figure 49).

The village communities

The identification and recording of listed buildings was not part of this Project. However, the historic core of each of the parishes encapsulates a number of individual buildings of considerable architectural merit. It would be invidious to list each but of passing note are Roberts House, Siddington; Manor Farm, Baunton; and Church Farm, Siddington. Of the ecclesiastical buildings, the chapel of St Mary Magdalene, Baunton (54445) gained parochial rights in 1625 and a burial ground was consecrated, an important step towards becoming an independent parish. In contrast the eighteenth century was to witness the consolidation of Siddington St Mary and Siddington St Peter with the demolition of St Mary's church in the 1750s.

To suit a more specialist need and reflecting the Victorian interest in science and agriculture, the Royal Agricultural College (54147) was opened to students in 1846. Lord Bathurst gave a farm of 400 acres with an existing farmhouse and Daukes designed an impressive college comprising a chapel, college farm, lodge, labourers cottages, botanical gardens, dairy and within the main complex of buildings, a library and reading room, dining hall, students studies, theatre, laboratory, gymnasium, quadrangle, museum, council rooms, and dormitories.

Elementary education in the parishes was enabled by the building of Victorian schools, in line with new teaching practices in the middle of the nineteenth century. Schools, often with the schoolmaster's house attached, were built at Siddington (54510), Baunton (54511), Preston (54526), and Stratton (54527).

Roads, canal and railways

The Highways Act of 1555 transferred responsibility for the upkeep of the King's highways to the parishes, who were required to provide labour, materials and a surveyor to maintain the parish roads. Until the seventeenth century wheeled traffic was rare, but increased wear and tear from trade and travel by carriage lead to the degeneration of the surface, especially in winter, and parishes were unable to maintain standards for the comfort of travellers. To improve conditions private Turnpike Acts enabled the setting-up of Trusts who were responsible for a defined stretch of road, and in return for its proper maintenance, the Trust was entitled to collect a toll from which to defray its costs. Under a Private Act of Parliament in 1727 the first local Turnpike Trust was formed to administer the road from Cirencester to Lechlade via Fairford (54529). A tollhouse (54232) was constructed at the London Road-Grove Lane junction to control and collect tolls for vehicular, pedestrian and animal traffic, and milestones erected along its course (Hartland 1984–5).

Successive Acts resulted in a network of turnpike roads radiating from Cirencester: 1747, Cirencester to Gloucester via Birdlip (54530); 1751, to Bisley via Park Corner (54347); 1752, to Stroud via Minchinhampton and Rodborough (54516); 1753, to Burford via Barnsley, Bibury and Aldsworth (54531); 1755, to Stow-on-the-Wold via Northleach (54532); and 1758, to Swindon via Cricklade (54533), and to Malmesbury via Tetbury (54534). The present Cirencester to Cheltenham road (54535), with a tollhouse at the junction with the Gloucester Road (54513), followed the line of the River Churn and was not opened until 1827, after an Act of Parliament had consolidated all the Turnpike Trusts into the Cirencester District of Roads.

During the early nineteenth century two important routes into the town were rerouted. The road to Stroud via Minchinhampton left the town from the top of Cecily Hill (54516) and originally shared a course through Cirencester Park with the Bisley road (54537), before diverting to cross the line of the Broad Ride in the centre of the Park near the Round Tower. In order to divert the road, the present Stroud road near the Agricultural College was constructed in 1818 along the southern boundary of Oakley Wood (54536), and a turnpike house, The Octagon, constructed at the junction with the Tetbury Road (54234; Figure 50). The Whiteway once led directly to the town through the Spitalgate but the road was diverted 1817–35 (54507) as it approached Cirencester and now survives in part as an upstanding earthwork or hollow-way.

Coach and mail services to surrounding towns and to London were improved, but from the late eighteenth century road transport faced increasing competition, first from the canals and later from the railways. The Thames and Severn Canal (54156) connected the Stroudwater Canal (completed 1779) with the River Thames at Inglesham, near Lechlade. It was opened in 1789, and a short branch at Siddington connected the town with the main canal. The basin with its wharfhouse at the foot of Querns Hill was a focal point of trade. Although beset with problems, the canal continued to operate until 1933. Water levels fluctuated, particularly at its summit, and in Cirencester it was necessary to take water from the Daglingworth Brook, via a feeder (54058), which was culverted for much of its length (54127).

By the end of the nineteenth century Cirencester was served by two railways, providing north-south and east-west links to the rest of the country. The Great Western Railway in Tetbury Road (54061) was opened in 1841 as the terminus of a branch line with connections at Kemble to the Cheltenham-Swindon line. The station building was designed by Brunel (54054), and the yards provided easy access to the Cattle Market on the western outskirts of the town, to the benefit of local farmers and merchants. The line was closed in 1964. The Midland and South Western Junction Railway (54212) in Watermoor opened in 1883 and survived until 1961. The station (54208) was surrounded by extensive marshalling yards and sidings, and played a vital part in the social and economic development of the Watermoor area.

Agriculture

Changes in agriculture during the post-medieval period were aimed at increased yields. There are three visible aspects to this in the archaeological record within the rural area around Cirencester: the effects of the enclosure movement on boundaries and field shapes; the development of new techniques of drainage and irrigation; and new buildings and farms.

It is unlikely that the Parliamentary Acts of Enclosure of the late eighteenth century (1768 in Baunton and 1771 in Stratton) involved the removal of entire common field systems around Cirencester for this was the end of a piecemeal process of enclosure which had continued for centuries by private agreement. The formation of Cirencester Park is a good example of the gradual accumulation of blocks of land through purchase. Nor would there have been many changes of land use following enclosure, pasture remained dominant. Most dramatic was the division of upland areas by drystone walls into large land parcels and the changing patterns of ownership. Rudder (1779) complains about the 'laying of two or three farms into one' and the subsequent desertion of rural farmsteads in Gloucestershire. No such deserted farmsteads have been securely identified inside the Study Area though shrinkage around Norcote Farm may be of post-medieval date. Pre-enclosure maps, such as the surviving survey for Siddington, provide useful clues to boundary dating and rural settlement.

Figure 50
Tollhouse at the junction of the Tetbury and Stroud Roads (Corinium Museum)

The most obvious signs of post-medieval land improvements are the seventeenth- and eighteenth-century water-meadows at Baunton (54505), Siddington (54448) and Preston (54506). Water was allowed to flood the fields in a controlled fashion as a means of improving lowland pasture, ensuring an early grass crop. The Preston meadows are described enthusiastically by Rudder (1779) as 'very rich meadows on the side of the Churn, which are occasionally covered with water, by means of trenches cut from that river, and drained again at pleasure, whereby vegetation is surprisingly strong and early'. The remains of the Baunton water meadows in the vicinity of Trinity Mill, which are shared with Bagendon parish, were recorded and interpreted by the Royal Commission in 1990 (CAT 1990). Possible wet ponds for withy beds have also been identified south of Trinity Mill, and drainage improvements are visible on aerial photographs south of Whiteway View in Stratton.

A number of Cotswold barns have drawn attention because of their architectural merit. The earliest in date within the study area is the late seventeenth-century barn near Forty Farmhouse in Preston. There are many more examples of late eighteenth century and early nineteenth century date, including the field barn at Lower Norcote Farm which is of particular interest for its relationship to enclosure boundaries.

A study by Celia Miller has highlighted a number of 'model' farms in Gloucestershire (Miller 1990), of which two, College Farm and The Ivy Lodge in Cirencester Park, are of particular note. In the eighteenth century many owners of landed estates developed an interest in agriculture, and introduced improved standards and design in farm buildings, often a necessary adaptation to accommodate changes in farm practice. The Ivy Lodge, one of the earliest 'improved' farms, dates from 1715 and uses a decorative Gothic facade to blend functional farm buildings within a picturesque park landscape.

The Victorian concept of a 'model' farm was less concerned with architectural impact. Farms were seen as 'a processing plant for livestock and crops' and layout needed to be functional. College Farm, as first conceived and built in 1845, was a typical example with farm office, weighbridge, carpenter's shop, smithy, slaughterhouse, stables, pigsties and yards, covered sheep pens for fattening sheep, feeding house, yards for loose cattle surrounded by open-fronted shelter sheds, barn, and steam engine house. Originally known as Port Farm, College Farm formed an integral link to the neighbouring Royal Agricultural College, and served as a teaching and research base for the College's students as well as a working farm.

Industry

The principal source of employment was centred on farming but a number of rural industries supported the needs of the urban and farming communities of the area. A small brickworks is recorded at Siddington (54383) in the nineteenth century. At the maltings at Stratton (54390) and Siddington (54447) barley was dried in a kiln, allowed to germinate and placed in tanks to produce malt. Limited excavation at the eighteenth-nineteenth century maltings in the north porch of Siddington barn produced evidence for hearth activity (Barber 1991a). Structural analysis has demonstrated several adaptations but it seems that the typical oast house roof commonly seen in the south-east of England never existed here.

As in previous centuries, the natural resources of the area were harnessed and exploited to provide power. The watermills at Preston and Siddington on the River Churn are of seventeenth-nineteenth century date (54512, 54523). There were two mills at Stratton (54392 and 54393), both of which closed in the mid-nineteenth century. Sadly, archaeological attention to all these sites has been insignificant. There was a windmill at the corner of Stratton Heights (54218) but the site and form of construction are unknown.

Quarrying continued to be important locally with a number of quarries indicated on the Ordnance Survey maps. Individual quarries were favoured for particular rock types, for example at The Barton for gravel (54366), the Kingshill quarries (54274) for Forest Marble, whilst the Hare Bushes quarry (54142) was famous for Great Oolite exposures and the discovery of fossil eggs (J Buckman 1858). More general-purpose quarries were worked at Stratton, west of the Cheltenham Road (see Figure 8), in the Chesterton area of Cirencester, and adjacent to the Royal Agricultural College.

It is likely that post-medieval limekilns remain to be identified. Cartographic evidence indicates one at Stratton, to the west of the Cheltenham Road (54524), associated with a large quarry. Lime was used in construction, tanning and as a soil dressing. Many farmers probably quarried for limestone on a small scale and Beecham (1887) mentions quarry waste at St John's Meadow, Shepherds Piece, the Bowling Green and Bowling Green Pits.

Monument Discrimination

For the post-medieval period there is a good deal of surviving architectural heritage and it becomes progressively more difficult to define what is meant by the archaeological importance of identified monuments. Cirencester Park (54072), with its follies, stables, outbuildings and icehouse, would seem to be of national importance, although further work is needed to establish its many phases of development in any detail. The Market Place (54111), West Market Place (54215) and St Lawrence Almshouses (54179) contain the urban deposits with the highest potential for this and earlier periods. Other monuments of regional importance might include the museums, the inns, the public houses, the schools, the maltings, the breweries, the gas works, the toll houses, and so on. Candidates for promotion to the higher level of recognised national importance might be the water-meadows, the canal and the railways, but further archaeological documentation is required first.

12. ARCHAEOLOGICAL SENSITIVITY

'The representation of the Church is execrable: a lower building, possibly a charnel house, appears to have been built against the East end, but the beautiful South Porch is omitted, the object of the artist being to show the Bathurst and Master mansions and estates adjacent.'

K J Beecham in his *History of Cirencester* (1887) on Kip's engraving of Cirencester in Robert Atkyns' *Ancient and present state of Glostershire* (1712)

In the foregoing Chapters attention has been given to the importance of identifiable monuments and to the discrimination of accumulated deposits relating to particular urban forms. Here, attention is directed towards an overall evaluation of deposit importance by taking into account all the deposits within defined areas. In doing this there is of course the danger that some things of interest and importance will be omitted in order to show other things, as Kip is accused of doing in the quotation at the head of the Chapter while making his engraving of the town in the early eighteenth century. It is hoped, however, that this problem is avoided through attention to detail and the systematic nature of the analysis that leads to the grading of accumulated deposits. One of the strengths of the 'Cotswold system' of recording sites and monuments and of looking at accumulated deposits is that the analysis is repeatable and capable of further refinement as more and improved data become available.

For the analysis of all accumulated deposits the standard set of eight discrimination criteria is used (see Chapter 2). Strictly speaking, not all urban forms have been taken into account as post-medieval remains have been omitted from the analysis. The reason for this is two-fold. First, the majority of remaining evidence for this phase in the town's history is preserved as standing buildings, many of which are still in use, rather than archaeological monuments and deposits. Moreover, the nature of the remains relating to the latest phase of development is not always susceptible to archaeological investigation. Secondly, the generally better survival of recent remains compared with those of earlier forms means that inclusion of the latest form would distort the picture of the earlier, now essentially archaeological, deposits. Thirdly, whilst it is acknowledged that post-medieval structures are equally at risk, it may be that the protection of most post-medieval monuments is best achieved through building and planning legislation, for example through the listing process and the maintenance of conservation areas.

Survival

Survival is the continuing existence of the stratigraphic sequence in relation to the number and characteristics of the forms represented and in the light of the degree of recent disturbance. The appreciation and identification of areas of disturbance in the town comes from a combination of cellar survey information coupled with land-use data and a review of the available sites data, in particular the location of potentially destructive modern excavations.

High These areas contain either thick deposits or are known to be lightly disturbed by later activities. Areas under car-parks, gardens, and open spaces are all included such as the Watermoor area, the Forum car-park, the Waterloo car-park, St Michael's Field, Paternoster School area, the area south of Querns Lane, the Brewery car-park, and the area south of St Peter's Road.

Medium These areas contain a roughly average thickness given the range of forms represented. This includes those areas of the town under post-medieval and modern development and housing where the buildings are known not to have basements or cellars and where potentially damaging or disturbing groundworks have not taken place.

Low These areas have been badly disturbed by later activities and include buildings with cellars, archaeological excavations, churchyards and burial grounds. In particular, the area of Tower Street, Leaholme Court, St Peter's Road, Ashcroft Gardens, Ashcroft Road, and the edges of the major streets leading into the Market Place.

Potential

This criterion is intended to measure the abundance of contexts likely to offer exceptional prospects for the preservation of archaeological evidence. This might include areas with deep stratification or waterlogging, for example. Potential is graded on a three point scale although no areas of low potential have been identified in Cirencester, except in the sense that deposits no longer exist in some parts of the town.

High Zones of high potential in Cirencester include those areas on the urban fringes at Watermoor where waterlogged deposits are known to exist, and in the Abbey Grounds where deep stratification occurs in an area undamaged by later post-medieval urban activity. St Michael's Field, the area south of Querns Lane, the Forum and Brewery car-parks are also considered to be of high potential with above average circumstances for the preservation of structural, artefactual and ecofactual evidence.

Medium The remainder of the town has only average circumstances for the preservation of archaeological evidence.

Group Value (association)

This criterion in the urban context is taken to mean the association of earlier and/or later periods of urban occupation: the superimposition of evidence for a succession of forms. In Cirencester mapping this criterion requires the overlaying of the four urban form maps and identifying those areas where there is overlap in the forms represented. The degree of association may be graded on a three point scale as follows:

High Areas with four or more superimposed forms present are restricted to the northern half of the modern town where the two Roman period forms, the early medieval, and medieval forms coincide. North of Lewis Lane two areas within the line of the Roman town wall are excluded: an area to the north of Dyer Street and east of Gosditch/Dollar Street; and an area to the west of Cricklade Street and south of Castle Street.

Medium Areas with three superimposed forms include those areas mentioned above and a tongue of possible Anglo-Saxon occupation running southwards down either side of Watermoor Road. Areas with two superimposed forms include the remainder of the southern half of the town and two more envelopes on the northern edge of the town which take in both the Gloucester Road and Cecily Hill where the early medieval and medieval forms coincide.

Low Within the Roman town walls there are no areas of low group value but outside there are two strips where medieval activity may have exceeded the limits of any previous early medieval occupation. These areas are at the possible site of the castle in Cirencester Park, and on either side of Gloucester Street where tenements extend back perpendicular to the street.

Group Value (clustering)

Clustering of monuments of the same class can occur at a single time (for example shops), and through time (for example where medieval and post-medieval tenements overlie each other). Group Value (clustering) therefore picks out those parts of the urban area in which there is areal or chronological continuity of similar activities. There is a three point grading.

High There are very few areas in Cirencester where five or more successive examples of monuments are clustered. Certain Roman roads such as Watermoor Road, for example, are thought to have existed throughout the Roman, early medieval, medieval and post-medieval periods. There are also zones within the northern half of the town where houses appear to have existed from the Roman period onwards so that there are strong spatial as well as stratigraphic associations between monument categories and classes.

Medium Slight clustering of related monuments such as tenement plots are judged to have existed over much of the area of the medieval town. Exceptions occur in those areas where unique monuments break the pattern of repetitious, contiguous or related monuments, for example the parish church of St John the Baptist.

Low Areas with low or no marked clustering of similar monuments occur in most of the southern half of the town, particularly towards the fringes of the urban area, and also in the Abbey precinct.

Diversity (features)

This criterion is a measure of change in the range of elements, especially components and monuments. Grades are determined by adding the numbers of elements which are known or suspected as being superimposed one above the other. Diversity is graded on a three point scale as follows:

High There is only one area in Cirencester where five or more monuments are superimposed. This occurs at the junction of Cricklade Street and Lewis Lane where the site of a medieval standing cross overlies the medieval road and early medieval, Roman and pre-urban *vicus* deposits.

Medium Three or four superimposed monuments coincide in a number of small patches particularly in the northern half of the town. Four monuments overlie each other only within the *vicus* area. Three monuments are superimposed where wall foundations and mosaics of Roman date have been identified within the assumed area of the early medieval and medieval occupation.

Low Two or less superimposed monuments are found over most of the town area and especially to the south of Lewis Lane where no monuments are recognised at all toward the fringes of the Roman town.

Documentation (archaeological)

Archaeological documentation falls into three categories: archaeological investigation; survey and recording; and environmental analysis. The volume of work achieved in any one area is not as important as the quality of the contribution made towards our understanding of the urban area. The grades are as follows:

Good Abundant archaeological documentation in Cirencester exists where modern excavation, recorded observations, watching briefs and antiquarian excavations combine to provide a quality archive for the monuments, components and features cited. In particular these areas reflect the investigations of the Cirencester Excavation Committee and the Cotswold Archaeological Trust. Particularly good documentation exists near the *forum*, fort and *basilica* sites around Tower Street and St Michael's Field. Other excavations such as the Abbey/Saxon Church, parts of the town wall, Watermoor, and the Police Station site all score good.

Medium For these areas the quality of archaeological documentation derived from antiquarian and modern excavations is considered of medium quality only. Generally, this reflects the publication record for the site and the degree to which all archaeological deposits were adequately investigated.

Low Here the archaeological documentation is derived from indirect records and recorded observations. The quality of the record is not sufficient to accurately pinpoint or describe the features noted. In particular, in Cirencester this reflects the nineteenth-century development of the area to the south of Lewis Lane.

Documentation (historical)

The level of historical documentation for any part of an urban area will depend on what has survived and been researched. Only those records which are considered to represent a net gain in our understanding of the urban area can contribute to elevating the selected grade. The quantity of documentation is therefore not necessarily any guide to the grade. There is a three point scale.

Good Since there is historical documentation in Cirencester for only two periods, medieval and post-medieval, the well documented areas are confined mainly to the northern half of the town. These include St John's Church with the High Cross, St John's Hospital, the Pig Cross and some components of the Abbey precinct, such as the gatehouses and Abbey Church, described by Leland and in the medieval cartulary. These monuments are also mentioned in traveller's accounts, national surveys such as Domesday Book, national fiscal records, ecclesiastical records, inscriptions, ancient maps and antiquarian books.

Medium An average level of documentation exists for the Abbey precinct, the medieval roads, and the churches of St Lawrence and St Cecilia. These are mentioned in local fiscal records, ecclesiastical records, antiquarian books and are identified on ancient maps.

Low Little or no historical documentation exists for the rest of the town although there is some appropriate cartographic documentation.

Amenity Value

Amenity value can be enhanced either because a part of the urban area retains visible and accessible features or because there are strong historical associations through links with known people and events. An appreciation of Amenity Value for education and display is assessed on a three point scale.

High Those areas with extant monuments which are good examples of their class or have strong historical associations are: the Roman amphitheatre, the Watermoor and Abbey Grounds sections of the Roman town wall, the parish church of St John the Baptist, and St John's Hospital.

Medium Areas of limited access or with more generalised historical associations will include the possible prehistoric long barrow, the Roman *basilica* site marked in the road, the medieval and post-medieval Cirencester Park, the remainder of the Abbey precinct, and the medieval Hospital of St Thomas.

Low The remainder of the urban area will rank low in amenity value. This directly reflects the lack of upstanding archaeology in the town.

Archaeological interest in the urban area

The zoned discrimination criteria described in the last section provide a basic representation of the main factors reflecting the importance of the archaeological resource viewed as a series of accumulated deposits. In order to achieve an overall view of archaeological interest/sensitivity the information on all the maps can be combined to produce a single zoned plot. The methods of doing this are described elsewhere (EH 1992c).

Three grades of interest are defined: high, medium and low. The distribution and extent of each is shown on Figure 51. It should be emphasised, however, that any judgements made concerning the boundaries between the different zones should be checked by reference to plans at a larger scale. Post-medieval features, for example, might be usefully checked with reference to a nineteenth-century Ordnance Survey map together with the gazetteer in this document. In addition, the importance placed on any one part of the town reflects only the values that can be attached to the chosen discrimination criteria at the time of the analysis. The map will change if the criteria are altered or if the assigned values change. For example, an excavation will increase the Documentation (archaeological) in any one area but at the same time decrease the Survival. With these caveats, however, the three zones can be briefly summarised as follows:

High Sensitivity These are zones which are archaeologically sensitive and contain deposits which may be considered as being of national importance. In general these zones contain deposits where Survival and/or Potential are good and Documentation (archaeological) is sufficient to confirm the high quality of the remains.

The identified zones of high sensitivity include Watermoor, most of the Abbey Grounds, the Bowling Green and parts of the Brewery car-park, the area around the Gaumont Cinema site, the area of Paternoster School, Watermoor Church, the area south of Querns Lane, the Forum car-park, and parts of Tower Street. Approximately 32% of the urban area of Cirencester falls into this grade of sensitivity.

Medium Sensitivity These zones contain archaeological deposits which are likely to have been partially damaged through unsympathetic land-use, particularly building foundations. But valuable information could still be gained in these areas, and between localised areas of damage Survival and Potential may be good. Documentation (archaeological) may be low to medium and could be enhanced.

Areas zoned as being of medium interest also include land whose precise archaeological interest is difficult to determine because of a paucity of data. Some such areas would, upon evaluation, undoubtedly prove to be of high interest, other parts would probably prove to be of low interest.

The main areas of medium sensitivity are: the areas either side of Victoria Road, Stepstairs Lane, Dyer Street, Cricklade Street, Castle Street, Park Lane, Coxwell Street and Thomas Street. Approximately 63% of the urban area of Cirencester falls into this grade of sensitivity.

Low Sensitivity In these zones archaeological stratigraphy no longer exists or survives only in very poor condition. Generally this is because such deposits have been removed or punctured or otherwise damaged during archaeological excavations or when digging out cellars for medieval and later buildings.

The main areas of low sensitivity include: parts of Chester Street, St Peter's Road, Ashcroft Gardens, Leaholme Court, Tower Street, part of St Michael's Field, Tesco's, the fringes of the Market Place, the area of the Abbey excavations and the parish church of St John the Baptist. Approximately 5% of the urban area of Cirencester falls into this grade of sensitivity.

Archaeological interest in the rural area

Another way of looking at the non-urban archaeological resource is to focus on the presence and extent of archaeological deposits rather then defined monuments. This takes account of isolated components and features which cannot be defined as monuments and encourages a broader consideration of the landscape beyond the constraints of strict monument definition. In this way it is possible to identify zones of varying archaeological interest. The discrimination criteria used to study individual monuments can be adapted to deal with generalised deposits and the scores so obtained combined (using the same formula) to produce maps of overall archaeological interest. Figure 52 shows the map produced in this way, the contours being drawn to reflect the position and extent of three broad grades of interest:

High These are zones which are of greatest archaeological interest, where Survival and Potential

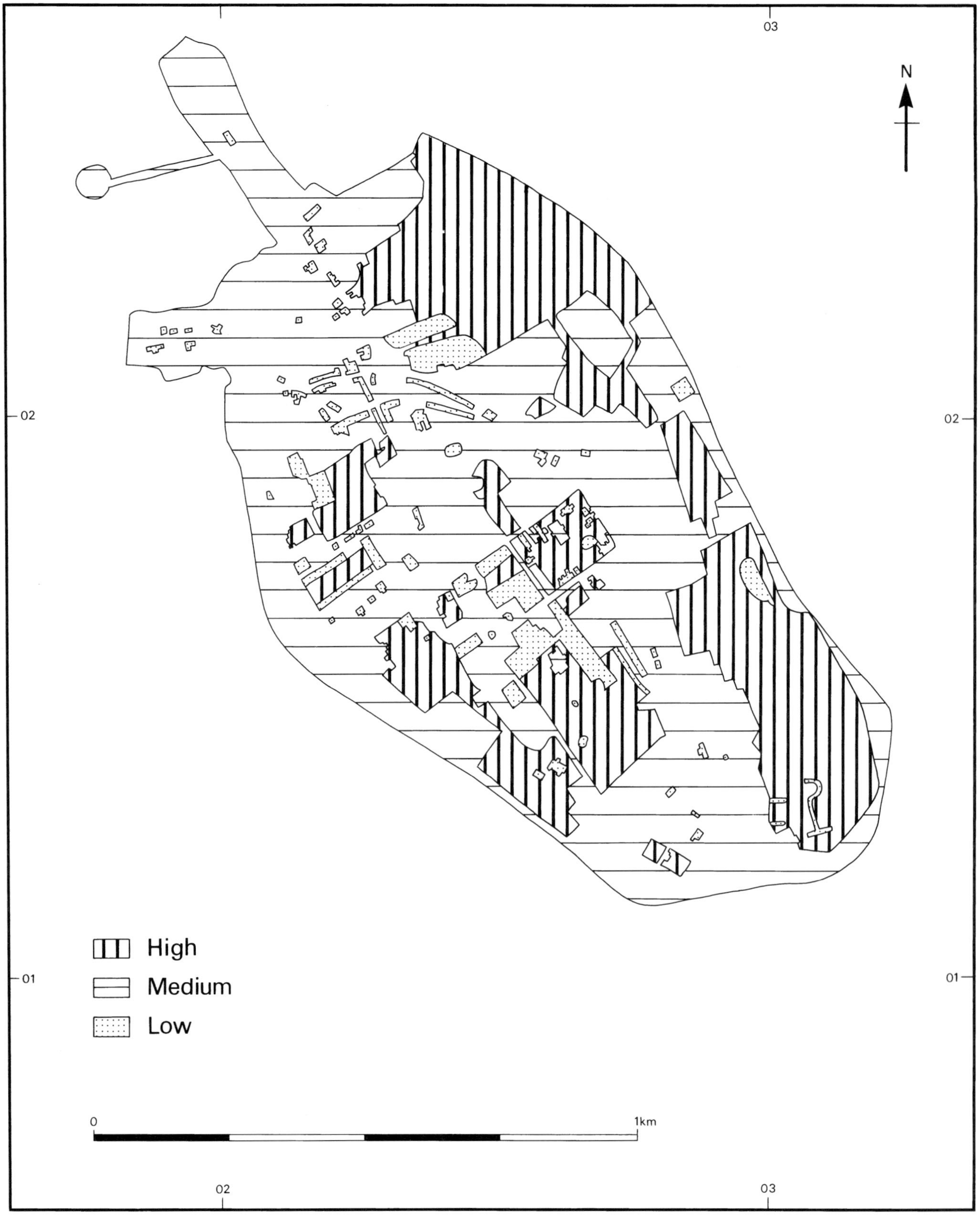

Figure 51
Zones of archaeological interest in the urban area

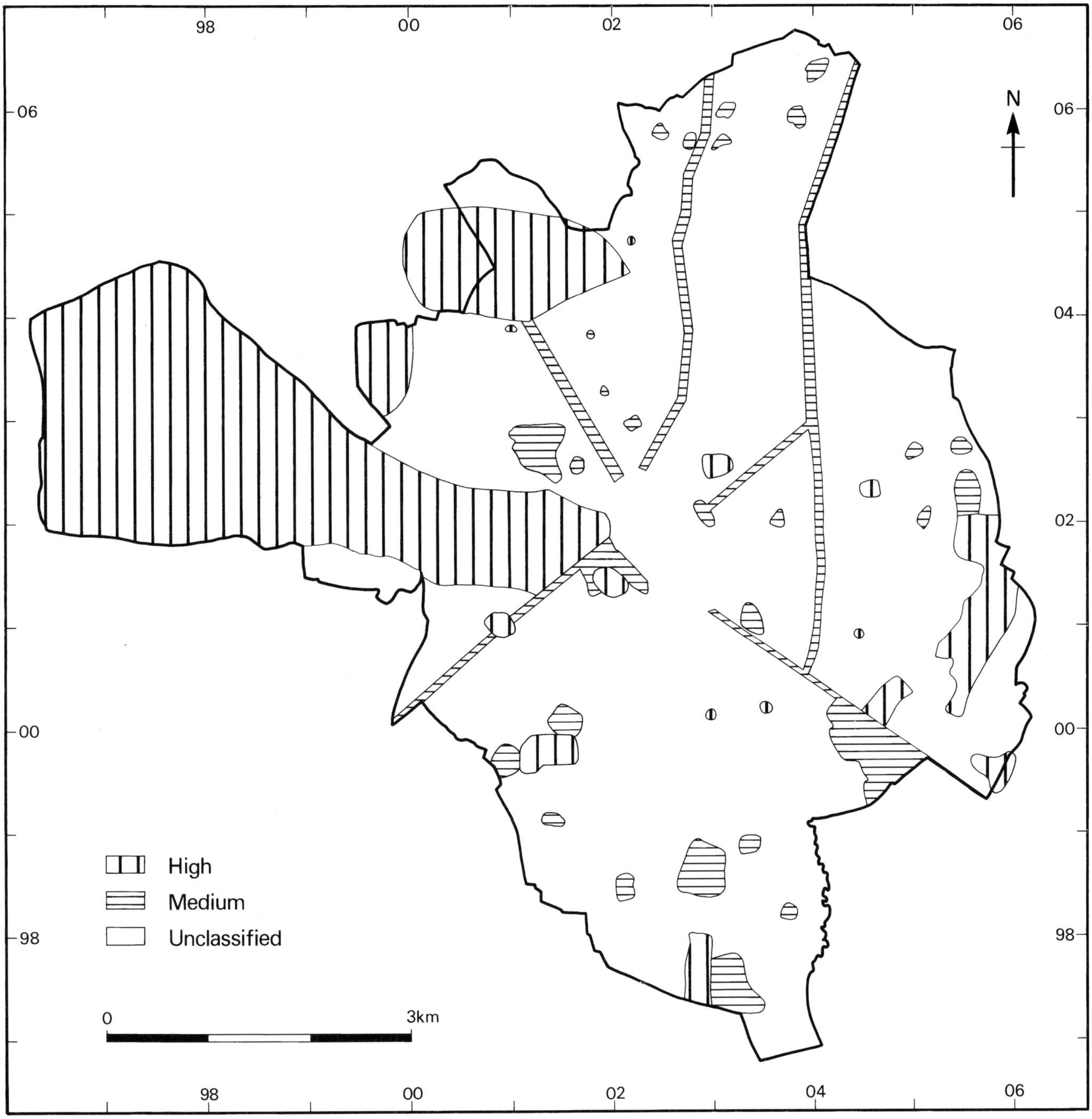

Figure 52
Zones of archaeological interest in the rural area

are high and Documentation (archaeological) is sufficient to suggest high quality deposits. Academic interest will be high. In the four rural parishes these zones include Cirencester Park, two areas of prehistoric activity near Wellhill Plantation, the Roman amphitheatre, the Tar Barrows, the deserted medieval settlement at Norcote Farm, areas of dense prehistoric activity near Siddington House, the southern tip of Siddington parish, the area in the vicinity of St Augustine's Farm, and the sites of parish churches and chapels.

Medium Here the archaeological deposits are likely to have been partially damaged through unsympathetic land-use, particularly intensive agriculture and extractive industries such as quarrying. Valuable information could still be gained in these areas. Archaeological documentation may be low to medium and could be enhanced. Areas of medium interest in the rural areas include various prehistoric sites located during fieldwalking in Baunton parish, the Romano-British settlement at Siddington, the Roman cemetery areas on the fringes of the Roman town, the Barton gravel pits, quarry sites, undated features west of Barton gravel pits, Chesterton Woods, all the arterial roads, and a small area at Kingshill.

Unclassified deposits Most of the rural area consists of unclassified deposits between recognised and defined monuments. This is not the same as saying that there is no archaeology in these areas, merely that no archaeology is at present known here. This may occur for a variety of reasons, the area may genuinely be 'blank' or the archaeological deposits may not have been recorded either because no archaeological work has been done or because sites are masked by later colluvial or alluvial deposits, for example.

Excluding the urban area of Cirencester, about 28% of the total area (*c*1280ha) is judged to be of high sensitivity; 3% (*c*130ha) is medium sensitivity, and 69% is unclassified. The figure of 28% high sensitivity is higher than might be expected because of the inclusion of Cirencester Park. The parish of Preston is perhaps more typical of a rural Cotswold parish being 12% high sensitivity, 1% medium and 87% unclassified.

PART IV
ARCHAEOLOGY AND DEVELOPMENT

13. FRAMEWORKS FOR THE FUTURE

'. . . with the efforts that are being made for the success of small holdings and the more profitable use and development of the land, it seems desirable that the town should have some control over its extension within a reasonable radius, whereby all would be benefited.'

K J Beecham (1887, 30)

'The next [mosaics] brought to light were the celebrated pavements in digging for a sewer in Dyer-street, in 1849, the first in the month of August, the second and larger one...in the following month, through a trial hole having first been sunk outside the line of the sewer. A great deal of the first was destroyed before its nature was ascertained, and the second is incomplete in consequence of its extending beneath the foundations of Gloucester House.'

K J Beecham (1887, 269)

Managing change

The future of the archaeological resource in Cirencester and its environs is intimately bound up with the inexorable processes of economic and social change that affect the town, the countryside, and the life of the local community. The archaeological resource described and examined in the foregoing Chapters cannot look after itself, rather it requires active management as one component of the wider environment.

Achieving successful management provokes an obvious dilemma: historic urban areas and their surroundings cannot simply be fossilised at some arbitrarily defined point in time like an insect trapped in amber, but, equally, today's economic growth and prosperity cannot be allowed to rob present and future generations of their past. Resolving this dilemma presents a considerable challenge. It involves on the one hand a willingness to accept controlled change through balancing competing demands, and, on the other, a disposition towards the retention of those things which are most valued. Participating in, influencing, and in some cases stimulating controlled change with concerns for the archaeological heritage to the fore is known as Archaeological Resource Management and this is the focus of the present Chapter.

The detailed analysis of the archaeological resource presented in earlier Chapters allows the interest and importance of individual monuments and whole tracts of accumulated deposits to be determined in a logical and consistent way. This in turn provides the foundation upon which a strategy for the future management of the resource can be built. English Heritage have recently published a position statement on the management of the urban archaeological resource (EH 1992a), in which they identify three key elements: the urban database, the urban assessment, and the urban strategy document. This report has described the urban database established for Cirencester (maintained at the Corinium Museum) and is itself the urban archaeological assessment. In due course, and after careful consideration of all the relevant factors, an urban strategy will be developed, perhaps to link in with the Local Plan. This chapter is not, therefore, a strategy *per se* but rather the framework from which a formal urban strategy will be developed. As such it represents the views and thoughts of the authors rather than the policies of either of the two sponsors of the Cirencester Urban Assessment Project.

Fundamental to the effective management of the urban archaeological resource are the following four factors (EH 1992a, 4):

(1) **Frameworks**. Clear legal, planning, policy, and academic frameworks are essential for a structured and consistent approach to the urban archaeological resource. These frameworks operate within the broader context of prevailing opinions and circumstances and it is important that a good consensual framework is established to resolve conflicts of interest.

(2) **Information**. Good decision-making about the future of the archaeological resource requires

quality information to be readily available to those who have to take or to contribute to making decisions affecting the resource.

(3) **Expertise**. Urban archaeology is a specialised field, and the management of the urban archaeological resource requires appropriately qualified and experienced staff.

(4) **Resources**. Resources are needed to support the development of frameworks, the gathering of information, and the maintenance and development of expertise; to support appropriate archaeological input to decision-making which affects the resource; and to carry out appropriate management action.

In the following sections these requirements are considered in more detail as they relate to the situation in and around Cirencester. First, however, consideration is given as to why the archaeological resource in and around historic towns is of value.

Why is archaeology important?

Archaeological deposits are expressions of particular kinds of social, economic, political, cultural, and symbolic actions that were undertaken by individuals and communities at some time in the past. They represent the successes, achievements, and failures of our forebears.

In environmental terms, archaeological remains represent man-made capital, that is they are resources that have been created or brought about through the activities of human communities. In many cases their formation has taken place over a very long period of time. Their creation is unique in the sense that the particular events, processes, and conditions that provide the context of their emergence will never be repeated. As such, archaeological deposits are a finite and non-renewable resource.

In seeking to define values which attach to archaeological remains there are three main areas of interest: use value, option value, and existence value. These are explored in the following sections with specific reference to urban areas, but the same principles apply to all kinds of archaeological remains (Darvill 1993).

Use value

Urban areas as archaeological resources are already widely used for a variety of purposes. Archaeologically, they are the sole sources of data about the development of urban settlement. The key parameters of interest are space and time, reflected archaeologically by horizontal and vertical stratigraphy respectively. Among the many thematic interests that have been identified for study are: town planning and vestiges of authority, military works, church organisation, crafts and commerce, and the urban environment.

Educational interests are served by archaeological remains in urban areas in the general sense of providing the raw materials and case studies for the exploration of such subjects as urban sociology, geography, environment, and so on, as well as in the restricted sense of being the raw materials for teaching urban history and archaeology itself. Both visible and invisible remains are relevant to these uses.

Urban areas are, of course, not only valued for the archaeological information they contain, but also for their individual buildings and their townscape appeal. This is especially true of the more recent forms and those earlier forms which have survived well into modern times. Particularly important is the plan of an urban area because it will often preserve spatial articulations, an indication of the scale of the place, and a record of the disposition of single monuments through the patterns of roads and spaces.

The sense of history implicit in many urban areas, 'the presence of place', is currently used heavily for commercial and aesthetic purposes. New shopping centres in historic towns, holidays, guided tours, tourism, leisure activities and so on take the very spirit of what is essentially the archaeological resource as their raw materials. The past, though it is often a corrupted version, is successfully used to validate the present, and attempts may even be made to quantify this through environmental audits.

Option value

Although present uses of the urban resource are considerable it is quite impossible to gauge what uses may be required in the future. Such a diverse resource may potentially be susceptible to many uses and contain many options which future generations may wish to exploit. Might the experience of an electronic vision of the past city be a means of alleviating stress, for example?

Existence value

The very existence of urban areas which have a clear historical identity is something which some people value in its own right. This overlaps considerably with the current uses which are made of the strong presence of place that ancient urban areas acquire. In the more general context it is perhaps relevant to contrast the popular images of Milton Keynes or

Basingstoke as against those of York or Cirencester. Such perceptions betray deep-seated emotional attachments to what may again be regarded as an essentially archaeological resource; the feeling of knowing that many centuries of history lie beneath the streets and buildings, that important events have happened here, or that well-known individuals have travelled along a certain street or occupied a particular building. Familiarity with the past can make the present more comfortable by increasing a sense of continuity and enhancing communal identity.

Existing measures and policies (Figures 53 and 54)

The basic framework within which archaeological resource management takes place comprises prevailing legislation and planning policy guidance. A number of levels can be identified ranging from the national through to the local. There are no monuments in the Study Area included on the World Heritage List established by UNESCO. Archaeology is represented not only in specifically Ancient Monuments Legislation but also in a wide range of other Acts of Parliament, most notably those concerned with Town and Country Planning.

Scheduled Monuments

The purpose of scheduling, which applies only to monuments regarded as being of National Importance, is to protect and preserve the archaeological integrity of the monument. A monument does not have to be 'old' for it to be on the Schedule; some World War II defence works are included, for example. The main criterion for the selection of monuments for protection through scheduling is that candidates should be of National Importance (Darvill *et al* 1987). Scheduled Monument Consent (SMC) is required from the Secretary of State for the National Heritage before any works are carried out which would have the effect of demolishing, destroying, damaging, removing, repairing, altering, adding to, flooding, or covering-up the monument (EH, no date). If consent is not obtained, or the terms and conditions are not complied with, then a criminal offence has been committed. The conservation of Scheduled Monuments is encouraged through the provision of discretionary management agreements by English Heritage, and reports are regularly made by Field Monument Wardens on the condition of Scheduled Monuments. Application for Scheduled Monument Consent is a completely separate procedure to the application for planning permission. There is no obligation to give public access to Scheduled Monuments.

The following eight monuments in the Study Area are currently designated as Scheduled Monuments under the terms of Section 1 of the *Ancient Monuments and Archaeological Areas Act 1979* (as amended in England):

Glos 39	Long barrow and Roman amphitheatre and cemetery, Cirencester
Glos 267	Wellhill Copse round barrow, Cirencester
Glos 268	Tar barrows, Cirencester (×2 items)
Glos 361	Corinium Roman Town, Cirencester (×26 items)
Glos 372	St John's Hospital Chantry, Cirencester
Glos 397	Churchyard Cross, Cirencester
Glos 464	Settlement SE of Chesterton Farm, Cirencester / Siddington
Glos 475	Siddington Tithe Barn, Siddington

At the time of preparing this report the Monuments Protection Programme (MPP) being carried out by English Heritage is reviewing all monuments recorded to date in England with a view to recommending for scheduling any monuments that are not already scheduled and where scheduling is considered appropriate. It is understood that some presently unscheduled monuments within the Study Area are likely to be recommended for scheduling in due course.

The existing use of scheduling and the identification of scheduled areas in Cirencester are both unusual. The entry in the Schedule is simply for 'Corinium Roman Town', although only certain areas of the town have been notified and entered in the local land charge register, and the use of scheduling, which is a discretionary power, is more extensive than for other Roman towns now covered by modern settlement. Modern thinking concerning the protection of archaeological remains in major historic towns (Startin 1991; EH 1992a) would favour a more defined use of scheduling and an emphasis on the use of planning powers under PPG16. Accordingly, it is expected that scheduling in Cirencester will be rationalised under the MPP, in parallel with the development of clear strategies for the management of the archaeological resource throughout the Study Area.

Areas of Archaeological Importance

Cirencester is not one of the Areas of Archaeological Importance (AAIs) defined under the terms of section 33 of the *Ancient Monuments and Archaeological Areas Act 1979* (as amended in England). It is understood that there are no plans to extend the initial group of five towns (Canterbury, Chester, Exeter, Hereford and York) designated in this way, this part of the legislation having been overtaken by PPG16.

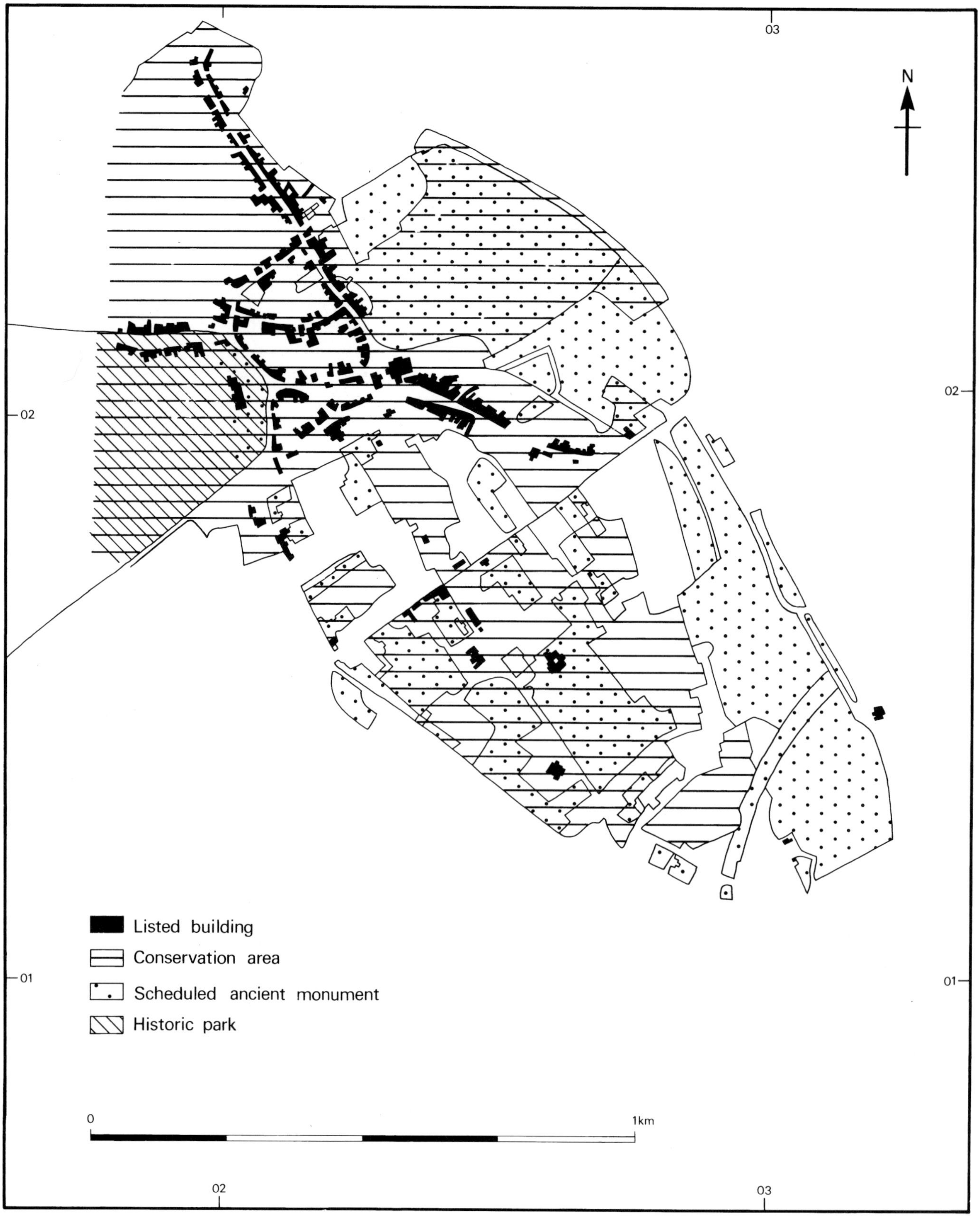

Figure 53
Designations in the urban area (sources: various)

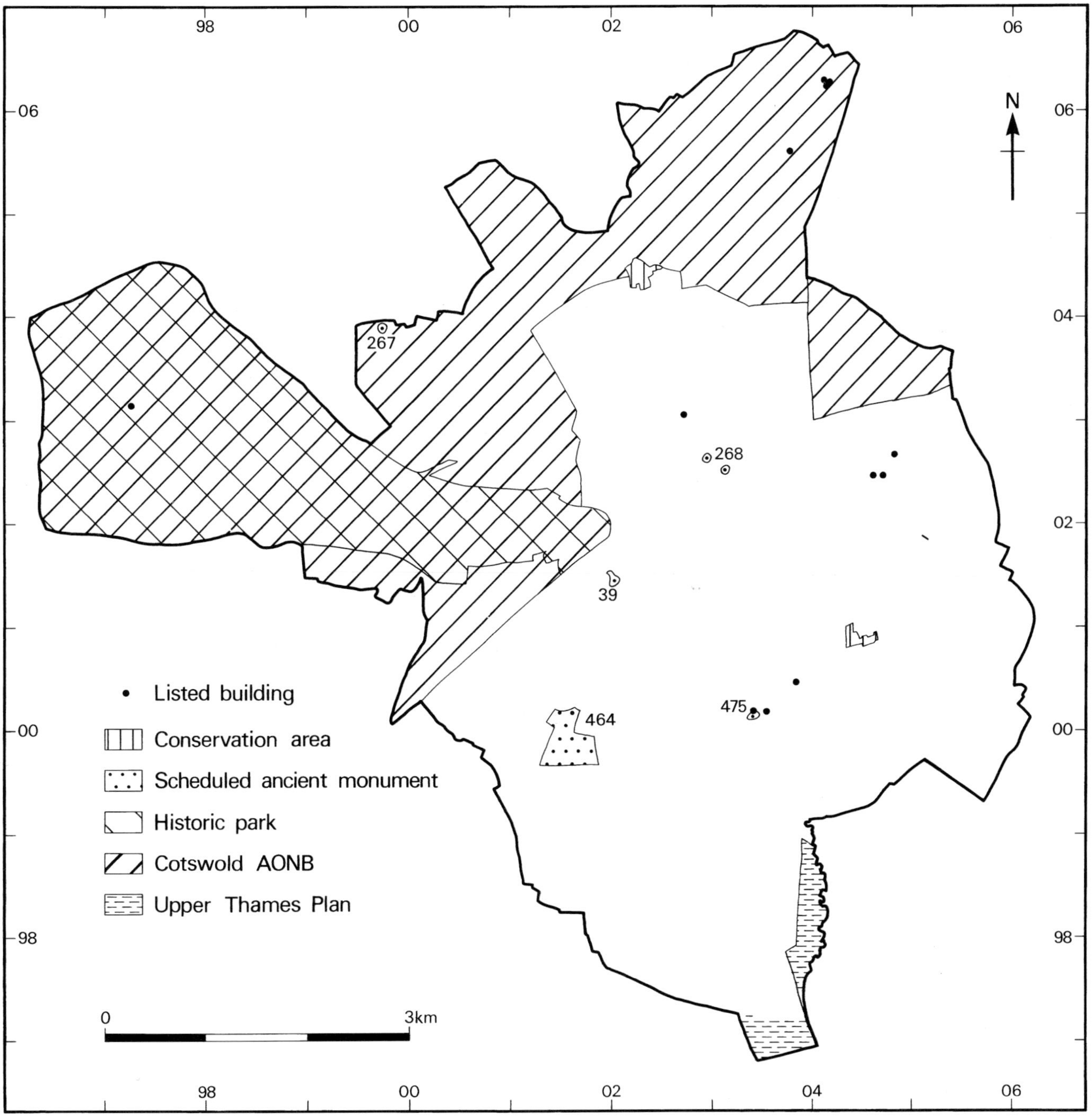

Figure 54
Designations in the rural area (sources: various)

Guardianship Monuments

The purpose of Guardianship is to secure the maintenance and preservation of monuments and their amenities. There is currently just one Guardianship Monument within the Study Area: the Roman amphitheatre at The Querns. This monument is in the custody of the State under the terms of Sections 12 and 13 of the *Ancient Monuments and Archaeological Areas Act 1979* (as amended in England).

In the Study Area there are no instances where a local authority has exercised its power to take monuments into Guardianship, although there are cases where archaeological monuments are recorded on land which is in public ownership. The most notable examples of this are the Roman town wall and medieval monastery for men in the Abbey Grounds, Cirencester.

Cotswold Area of Outstanding Natural Beauty

Any area that appears to the Countryside Commission to be of outstanding natural beauty may be designated by the Commission (subject to confirmation by the Secretary of State) as an Area of Outstanding Natural Beauty (AONB) under the terms of the *National Parks and Countryside Act 1949*. Part of the Cotswolds AONB (designated in 1966) lies within the Study Area.

Inside designated AONBs planning control is strengthened to give extra protection to the landscape and to conserve natural beauty (Smart and Anderson 1990). The preparation of management plans for estates and land-holdings within AONBs is actively encouraged. There has been much discussion as to what comprises 'natural beauty', but the 1990 Policy Statement by the Countryside Commission states that the primary purpose of designation is

> '. . . the conservation and enhancement of natural beauty, which includes protecting flora, fauna and geological as well as landscape features. Man's influence too has shaped the landscape and conservation of archaeological, architectural and vernacular features is also important.' (Countryside Commission 1990, 2).

Conservation Areas

Conservation Areas can be designated by Local Authorities under the *Planning (Listed Buildings and Conservation Areas) Act 1990* for the purposes of protecting the architectural and historic character of defined parts of towns and villages. Conservation areas have been defined within the parishes of Cirencester, Baunton and Preston.

Within Conservation Areas there are enhanced provisions for forward planning and development control (Hennessey *et al* 1990). None of these provisions is specifically archaeological, except in the sense that some aspects of the built environment are physically contiguous with the buried archaeological resource (eg the present standing building may be the most recent refurbishment of a much lengthier sequence of development which relates to earlier features such as pits, boundaries, yards and so on which would be regarded as purely archaeological). The constraints on above-ground development which are consequent on Conservation Area status have the effect of reducing below-ground disturbance and thus serve to protect buried archaeological remains.

Listed Buildings

Buildings of character which make an important contribution to parts of the countryside or townscape can be Listed under the terms of the *Planning (Listed Buildings and Conservation Areas) Act 1990*. Three grades are used according to the quality and age of the building. Within the Study Area there are 3 Grade I listed buildings, 37 of II*, and 378 Grade II.

The main effect of Listing a building is that it becomes an offence to demolish, alter or extend it so as to effect its character as a building of special architectural or historic interest without the written grant of consent – Listed Building Consent – from the local planning authority or the Secretary of State. Some listed buildings are themselves of direct archaeological interest, and may also be defined as Scheduled Monuments. For example, two listed buildings in the Study Area, St John's Hospital Chantry and Siddington Tithe Barn, are also Scheduled Monuments. Others, while not of direct archaeological interest may overlie or be set within archaeological deposits. Thus the restrictions placed on works to listed buildings have the indirect effect of protecting archaeological deposits. Specific advice on the care and maintenance of historic buildings may be issued by English Heritage from time to time (eg EH 1991b).

Burial Grounds

Legislation relating to the discovery of human burials and development over known burial grounds is contained in the *Burial Act 1857*, the *Disused Burial Grounds Act 1884* and the *Disused Burial Grounds (Amendment) Act 1981*. A useful summary of the complicated field of legislation relating to human burials has recently been published (Garratt-Frost 1992). In general, an exhumation licence is required from the Home Office before human remains can be lifted. Development is not permitted over known burial grounds unless formal notification procedures have been carried out and the ground itself has been cleared of human remains.

Parks and Gardens

A non-statutory register of parks and gardens dating to before 1939 and of special historic interest has been compiled by English Heritage to draw attention to important historic gardens and parks as an essential part of the nation's heritage. The register contains one entry relating to property within the Study Area; Cirencester Park.

No special controls exist with respect to parks and gardens in the register, although some will contain buildings of special architectural or historic interest and/or Scheduled Monuments. Inclusion in the register does not afford rights of access. The main purpose of the register is to draw attention to the existence of important parks and gardens. Like Listed Buildings, a series of three grades (I, II*, and II) is used to differentiate examples of varying quality.

National Planning Legislation and Policy Guidance

Development in England and Wales is governed by the *Town and Country Planning Act 1990*. There is a presumption in favour of allowing applications for development unless that development would cause demonstrable harm to interests of acknowledged importance. In making a decision as to whether to grant or refuse planning permission, a Local Planning Authority has to take into consideration a range of such interests. The fact that Cirencester contains a number of Scheduled Monuments and that there is a high level of public interest and awareness of the historical character of the town clearly indicates that archaeology is an established interest of acknowledged importance.

Planning decisions must also have regard to any material considerations which relate to an application. The provisions of a Development Plan provide one of the main material considerations, but with reference to archaeological matters Planning Circular 8/87, issued by the Department of the Environment in March 1987, established that 'Where application is made for planning permission to carry out development which would affect an ancient monument, whether scheduled or unscheduled, the desirability of preserving the monument and its setting is of course a material consideration' (DoE 1987, S.52). Local authorities could then ask for further archaeological information about a particular application under the terms of the *Town and Country Planning Act 1971*. This was followed by the *Town and Country Planning General Development Order 1988* which restated a widened definition for a 'site of archaeological interest' as 'land . . . within a site registered in any record kept by a County Council and known as the County Sites and Monuments Record'.

All these matters are codified in the most recent piece of planning policy guidance in respect of archaeology, PPG16, entitled *Archaeology and planning* (DoE 1990). This document begins by stating clearly that the archaeological resource is an important one:

> 'Archaeological remains should be seen as a finite and non-renewable resource, in many cases highly fragile and vulnerable to damage and destruction. Appropriate management is therefore essential to ensure that they survive in good condition. In particular, care must be taken to ensure that archaeological remains are not needlessly or thoughtlessly destroyed. They contain irreplaceable information about our past and the potential for an increase in future knowledge. They are part of our sense of national identity and are valuable both for their own sake and for their role in education, leisure and tourism' (paragraph 6)
>
> 'Where nationally important archaeological remains, whether scheduled or not, and their settings, are affected by proposed development there should be a presumption in favour of their physical preservation' (paragraph 8)

Positive planning is seen as one of the main ways in which the archaeological resource should be managed, and guidance is given on the archaeological content of development plans:

> 'Development plans should reconcile the need for development with the interests of conservation including archaeology. Detailed development plans (ie local plans and unitary development plans) should include policies for the protection, enhancement and preservation of sites of archaeological interest and of their settings. The proposals map should define the areas and sites to which the policies and proposals apply. These policies will provide an important part of the framework for the consideration of individual proposals for development which affect archaeological remains and they will help guide developers preparing planning applications' (paragraph 15)
>
> 'Archaeological remains identified and scheduled as being of national importance should normally be earmarked in development plans for preservation. Authorities should bear in mind that not all nationally important remains meriting preservation will necessarily be scheduled; such remains and, in appropriate circumstances, other unscheduled archaeological remains of more local importance, may also be identified in development plans as particularly worthy of preservation' (paragraph 16)

The sections dealing with development control and applications for planning permission also provide guidance on the appropriate information that should be supplied to a local planning authority. Early consultation with the local planning authority is recommended. Two kinds of survey are proposed: Archaeological Assessments which normally involve desk-based studies of existing information (paragraph 20), and Field Evaluations which normally involve ground surveys and small-scale trial trenching (paragraph 21).

> 'Local planning authorities can expect developers to provide the results of such assessments and evaluations as part of their application for sites where there is good reason to believe there are remains of archaeological importance. If developers are not prepared to do so voluntarily, the planning authority may wish to . . . direct the applicant to supply further information under the provisions of Regulation 4 of the *Town and Country Planning (Applications) Regulations 1988* and if necessary authorities will need to consider refusing permission for proposals which are inadequately documented. In some circumstances a formal Environmental Assessment may be necessary' (paragraph 22)

Extensive guidance is given in relation to the kinds of development control that may be exercised when there are archaeological considerations:

> 'The desirability of preserving an ancient monument and its setting is a material consideration in determining planning applications whether that monument is scheduled or unscheduled' (paragraph 18)
>
> 'If physical preservation *in situ* is not feasible, an archaeological excavation for the purposes of 'preservation by record' may be an acceptable alternative' (paragraph 13)
>
> 'Where planning authorities decide that the physical preservation *in situ* of archaeological remains is not justified in the circumstances of the case and that development resulting in the destruction of the archaeological remains should proceed, it would be entirely reasonable for the planning authority to satisfy itself before granting planning permission, that the developer has made appropriate and satisfactory provision for the excavation and recording of the remains. Such excavation and recording should be carried out before development commences, working to a project brief prepared by the planning authority and taking advice from archaeological consultants. This can be achieved through agreements reached between the developer, the archaeologist and the planning authority. Such agreements should also provide for the subsequent publication of the results of the excavation. In the absence of such agreements planning authorities can secure excavation and recording by imposing conditions' (paragraph 25)
>
> 'Planning authorities should seek to ensure that potential conflicts are resolved and agreements with developers concluded before planning permission is granted. Where the use of planning conditions is necessary, authorities should ensure that, in accordance with DoE Circular 1/85, they are fair, reasonable and practicable' (paragraph 29)
>
> 'In cases when planning authorities have decided that planning permission may be granted but wish to secure the provision of archaeological excavation and the subsequent recording of the remains, it is open to them to do so by the use of a negative condition, ie a condition prohibiting the carrying out of a development until such time as works or other action, eg an excavation, have been carried out by a third party. In such cases the following model is suggested:
>
> No development shall take place within the area indicated (this would be the area of archaeological interest) until the applicant has secured the implementation of a programme of archaeological work in accordance with a written scheme of investigation which has been submitted by the applicant and approved by the Planning Authority' (paragraph 30)

In summary, when a Local Planning Authority is faced with a development proposal which has an impact on archaeological remains it can take a variety of steps to secure the protection, enhancement or preservation of the remains: planning permission can be refused; the application can be approved subject to certain specified conditions (including negative conditions); or the application can be approved subject to a formal agreement between the Authority and the applicant (under Section 106 of the *Town and Country Planning Act 1990*). A number of assessments of the practical implications of PPG16 have now been published (Pugh-Smith and Samuels 1993; Lane and Vaughan 1992).

Environmental Assessment

The EC Directive on *The assessment of the effects of certain public and private projects on the environment* (85/337/EEC) was adopted in June 1985 and came into effect in July 1988. This required member states to introduce legislation making environmental assessments compulsory for certain types of development and discretionary for others. In Britain the Directive has been implemented through the *Town and Country Planning (Assessment of Environmental Effects) Regulations 1988* (Statutory Instrument 1199) and associated regulations relating to the specific kinds of development. A guide to procedures has been published (DoE 1989). An Environmental Assessment (EA) must consider the likely significant effects, direct and indirect, of a proposed development and report them as an Environmental Statement (ES). Among the subjects to be considered during the assessment is the matter of 'cultural heritage' which will include archaeological remains. The archaeological heritage is referred to specifically in Annex III to Council Directive 85/337/EEC.

In general, any development project likely to have

significant effects on the environment because of its size, location or nature should be subject to an EA. The legislation identifies two groups of development projects which are listed under separate schedules. Schedule 1 covers developments for which EA is mandatory, as for example with oil refineries, power stations, radio-active waste facilities, and special roads and railways. Schedule 2 covers developments for which EA is discretionary, for example mineral extraction, urban development projects, industrial estate development, oil or gas pipeline installations, and holiday villages or hotel complexes. The Local Planning Authority has the role of determining whether an EA is required for development projects of the kind listed in Schedule 2. DoE Circular 15/88 provides guidance on when a Schedule 2 development requires an EA to be carried out and highlights three main situations:

(i) where a major project has more than local importance, principally in terms of physical size;

(ii) where a project is proposed for a particularly sensitive or vulnerable location; or

(iii) where a project has an unusually complex and potentially adverse environment effect.

In general only large-scale projects will merit an EA, although it is recognised that an area or monument of major archaeological importance may well be considered a sensitive location (DoE 1989, 5). Thus an EA might, for example, be appropriate where archaeological deposits might be affected by an urban development.

County Planning Policy

The County Structure Plan for Gloucestershire is the statutory planning document controlling development in the County. The Plan was approved in October 1981 (GCC 1982) and has since been revised as the First Alteration (GCC 1992). A survey report covering the Built and Historic Environment was published in 1979 (GCC 1979).

Archaeological matters are covered in the section dealing with the Built and Historic Environment (BHE: GCC 1992), the policies are:

BHE.7 THE COUNTY COUNCIL IN ASSOCIATION WITH THE DISTRICT COUNCILS WILL SEEK TO ENSURE THE PROTECTION OF SITES OF ARCHAEOLOGICAL AND HISTORIC INTEREST.

BHE.8 DEVELOPMENT WILL NOT NORMALLY BE PERMITTED WHICH WOULD ADVERSELY AFFECT SCHEDULED ANCIENT MONUMENTS AND THEIR IMMEDIATE SETTINGS, OR SITES OF LOCAL ARCHAEOLOGICAL INTEREST WHICH ARE RECOGNISED AS WORTHY OF PRESERVATION BECAUSE OF THEIR COMPLETENESS, EXTENT, QUALITY, RARITY OR FRAGILITY.

WHERE EXCEPTIONS TO THE ABOVE ARE MADE, IT WILL BE NECESSARY TO ENSURE MINIMAL DAMAGE TO THE ARCHAEOLOGY AND TO FULLY INVESTIGATE AND RECORD THE ARCHAEOLOGY WHICH WILL BE LOST AS A RESULT OF THE DEVELOPMENT.

BHE.9 FULL ACCOUNT WILL BE TAKEN OF THE LOCAL ARCHAEOLOGY WHEN CONSIDERING A DEVELOPMENT PROPOSAL NOT SUBJECT TO BHE.8 INCLUDING:

(A) ITS PROXIMITY TO SITES OF KNOWN ARCHAEOLOGICAL INTEREST AND ITS HISTORICAL CONTEXT; AND

(B) THE PHYSICAL CHARACTERISTICS OF THE SITE.

THE COUNTY COUNCIL IN ASSOCIATION WITH THE DISTRICT COUNCILS, WILL CONSIDER THE NEED AND SEEK TO ENSURE THAT PROVISION IS MADE FOR ARCHAEOLOGICAL INVESTIGATION BEFORE AND DURING DEVELOPMENT, WHERE APPROPRIATE.

BHE.10 THE COUNTY COUNCIL IN ASSOCIATION WITH DISTRICT COUNCILS, WILL SEEK TO ENCOURAGE AND DEVELOP THE EDUCATIONAL, RECREATIONAL AND TOURIST POTENTIAL OF SITES OF ARCHAEOLOGICAL INTEREST.

Local Planning Policy

The local planning context for the Study Area is currently provided by the Cirencester Local Plan which was adopted in May 1984 (CDC 1984). Since then a district-wide Local Plan has been researched and published as a deposit draft in August 1993 (CDC 1993). This new Plan provides a comprehensive approach to the preservation, enhancement and protection of archaeological remains based in part on the results of this Archaeological Assessment and in accordance with English Heritage advice (EH 1992b). Archaeological matters are covered by section 15 of the draft plan which includes the following policy which is tied to map inserts which show the limits of the 'Archaeological Urban Area' and 'Areas of High Sensitivity':

Policy 7.29: Archaeology in Cirencester

1. Proposals for development, which would damage or destroy monuments or deposits within areas of high archaeological interest, will not be permitted. Any application affecting such a site must be accompanied by a full assessment of its implications and applicants will be required to show how its archaeological interest will be protected.

2. Elsewhere within the Archaeological Urban Area, applicants may be required to carry out an assessment of the archaeological implications of a proposed development before the Council will determine the application.

3. Where development is likely to affect archaeological remains, but not to the extent that permission should be refused, the Council will impose conditions, or seek a planning obligation, to ensure archaeological investigation prior to construction starting, or inspection during construction, the recording of finds and their after-care.

A small part of the southern end of the Study Area lies within the area covered by the Upper Thames Plan which is a subject plan for minerals and interrelated subjects. The plan was adopted in 1988 (GCC 1989). Archaeology is covered in the section dealing with conservation. The relevant main policies are:

UT A.1
PLANNING PERMISSION WILL NOT NORMALLY BE GRANTED FOR DEVELOPMENT WHICH WOULD AFFECT ADVERSELY IMPORTANT ARCHAEOLOGICAL SITES OR AREAS WHICH, BECAUSE OF THEIR COMPLETENESS, EXTENT OR QUALITY ARE RECOGNISED AS WORTHY OF PRESERVATION.

UT A.2
DEVELOPMENT WHICH MIGHT AFFECT ADVERSELY SITES OF KNOWN OR POTENTIAL ARCHAEOLOGICAL INTEREST WILL NOT NORMALLY BE PERMITTED WITHOUT ADEQUATE PROVISION FOR THE RECORDING OF THE ARCHAEOLOGY

There are, in addition, three supporting policies as follows:

UT A.S (i)
The County Council will encourage the provision of facilities to provide archaeological information and site interpretation at suitable locations.

UT A.S (ii)
The County Council supports the principles of the Code of Practice for Mineral Operators sponsored by the Confederation of British Industry in co-operation with the Council for British Archaeology and the Department of the Environment.

UT A.S (iii)
Where tree planting or other forms of landscaping treatment are envisaged, the County Council will expect measures to be taken to ensure that archaeological features are not damaged or destroyed without record.

Archaeological matters are also mentioned in connection with policies relating to the release of land for sand and gravel working (UT M.7 and UT M.10).

Other legislation

A number of pieces of legislation additional to those mentioned above contain significant clauses which relate to archaeology (see Darvill 1987b, 173).

Getting the right information

Integrating archaeological considerations into the development process is made easier if appropriate information is available to key groups of people at the right time. This extends from the developer needing to be aware of the possibility of general archaeological constraints at an early stage in considering the viability of the project, through to the elected members of the local Planning Committee needing to know the impact of development proposals, and in some cases on to the Secretary of State and his/her advisors when they determine an application for Scheduled Monument Consent. Along the way there may be many others too, among them members of the professional team engaged in designing a development (engineers, architects, project managers etc) and of course the general public whose support is often crucial in achieving smooth progress.

Measures such as the Environmental Assessment regulations outlined in the previous section provide one means of getting the right information, as too the powers available to Local Planning Authorities to request specific information before determining a planning application (eg Regulation 4 of the *Town and Country Planning (Applications) Regulations 1988*). These are, however, formal channels and in some cases have restricted or last-resort application. PPG16 advocates a pragmatic voluntary approach to the gathering and presentation of relevant information through two stages: **Archaeological Assessment** and **Field Evaluation**. In the following sub-sections these stages are discussed in more detail in the context of a simple step-by-step model which allows the development process to be integrated with archaeological resource management from initial conception through to completion (and see Darvill and Gerrard 1990). Figure 55 provides a diagrammatic summary of the five main stages involved. Using this approach helps to minimise the risk of extra costs and delays to the developer.

Appraisal

This stage involves a preliminary search to determine whether or not there is an archaeological dimension to a project. This is sometimes done before a plot of land is purchased and in such circumstances the work is often initiated or commissioned by consultants engaged by the developer, his land agent or planning consultants. On other occasions the

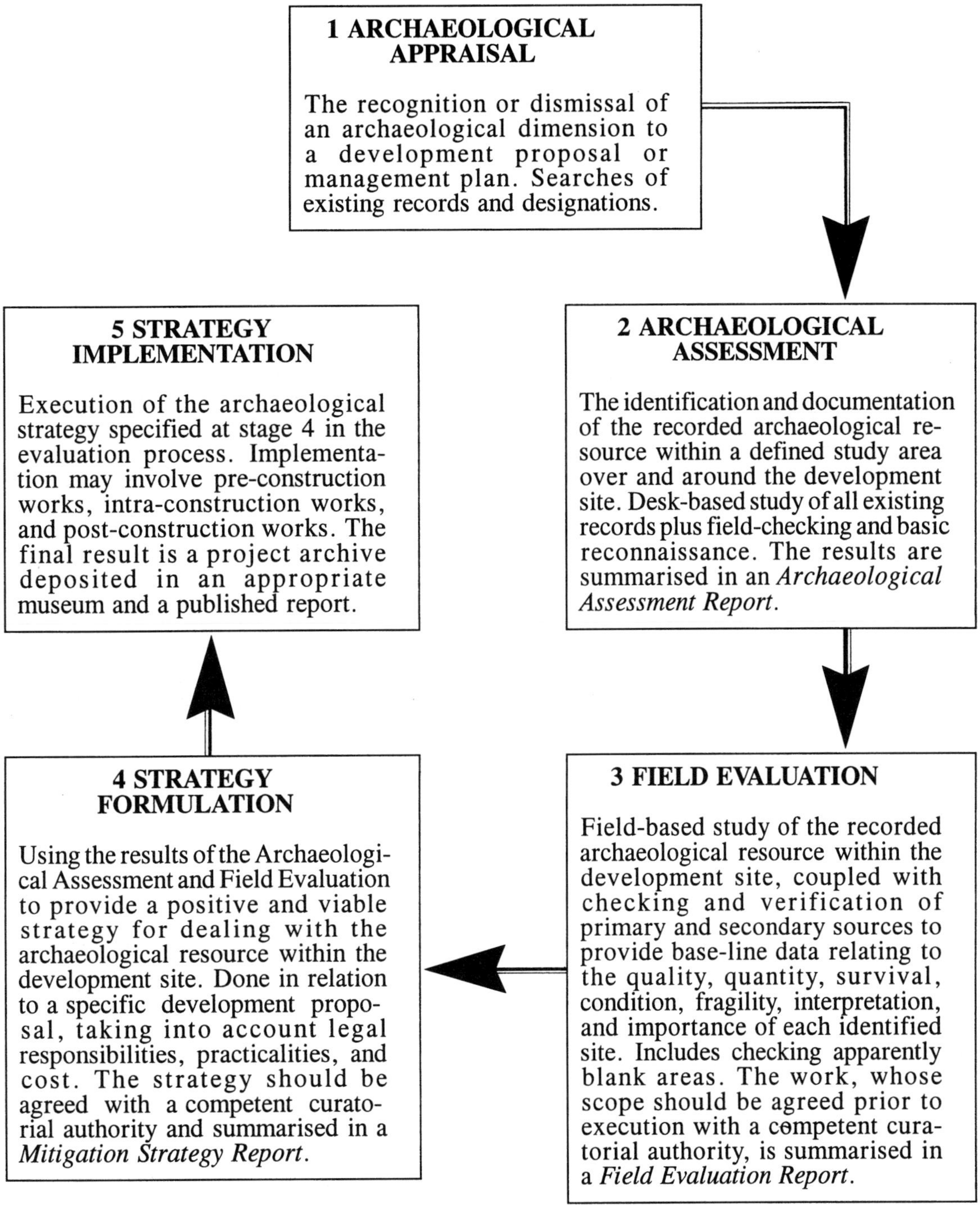

Figure 55
Diagram showing the main stages in integrating archaeological responses with the development process (after Darvill and Gerrard 1990, fig 1)

Appraisal stage forms part of the planning process when planning applications are scanned to check for archaeological implications.

The main sources of information used at the Appraisal stage include: a site visit, a scan of the local Sites and Monuments Record data for the site and its neighbourhood, and a brief check of the main published material for the area in question. Professional judgements on the likelihood of there being unrecorded archaeological deposits may also be important, for example, in areas where no previous fieldwork has been undertaken or where deposits may be buried beneath colluvium.

A short report or letter will suffice to outline the nature and extent of known, probable, or possible archaeological implications and the requirement for further work. An Appraisal of this kind should conform with the need to have early consultations between developers and planning authorities (DoE 1990, paragraph 18).

Archaeological Assessment

An Archaeological Assessment is essentially a desk-based exercise involving a detailed search of existing and available primary and secondary records and sources. Occasionally, in rural situations, extensive fieldwalking (as opposed to intensive gridded fieldwalking) may form part of the data-collection. The overall purpose of the Assessment is to review and consolidate existing information for presentation as a factual report.

An Archaeological Assessment is usually undertaken on behalf of a developer or land agent at their cost. It may be commissioned independently from consultants acting for the developer or his representatives, or in response to a brief issued by or approved by an archaeologist working in a curatorial capacity, usually an inspector with English Heritage or the county/borough/district archaeological officer.

The starting point for any Archaeological Assessment is the local Sites and Monuments Record. For Cirencester, the databases and records compiled during the course of this study provide a useful index to more detailed data which may be needed for particular cases. Machine-based, map-based, and supporting paper records are accessed and studied, and the references and source material are followed-up and checked wherever possible. In addition, available aerial photographs are examined and sketch-plotted (Palmer and Cox 1993), local museum collections and accession records are checked, available records in the local history library are scanned and transcribed (especially cartographic sources, place-names, fieldnames and street names; a map regression exercise is usual), local special interest groups, experts and landowners are contacted (often to establish the depth and extent of recent ground disturbance), and discussions are held with the county archaeologist and English Heritage inspector as appropriate.

The site itself is examined visually in some detail to check for upstanding features and the condition/survival of any above-ground remains. In urban areas this includes checking cellars and collating information about other sub-surface structures (such as drains and services) and geotechnical information (boreholes, engineering data etc). The potential for the application of more intensive survey techniques, detailed fieldwalking, auguring, geophysical survey, ground radar, and ditch-side surveys should be examined.

The product of the Archaeological Assessment is a factual report on the accumulated background information together with a synthesis of the archaeological data and notes on the local, regional, and national context as appropriate. Comments on the quality and reliability of the available information and the likely reasons and implications for any gaps in the coverage achieved will be noted.

Either as part of the same report, or as a separate document, there will be a consideration of the need for, content, and scope of the next stage which will variously be Field Evaluation where further information is needed to complement or supplement that already available, or Strategy Formulation where detailed data is already available.

The Archaeological Assessment report might typically provide a suitable document for use in applying for outline planning permission and, where appropriate, for Scheduled Monument Consent relating to the Field Evaluation stage. Often the Assessment Report will assist in the design of a development at a time when the basic footprint of the scheme is being worked out. An Archaeological Assessment of this sort conforms with the requirements of PPG16 (DoE 1990, paragraph 20).

Field Evaluation

This stage involves the close examination of the archaeological resource, sometimes through intervention by excavation, to determine, as far as practicable, the principal physical characteristics of the quality, extent, survival, condition, potential, and fragility of the deposits, as well as details of the form, interpretation, date, and archaeological value and potential of the remains.

Field Evaluation is applied in areas of known and unknown archaeology, although in general it is better to avoid duplication in the recovery of data at sites where some investigations have been carried out previously. Such cases will have been identified at the Archaeological Assessment stage.

No two Field Evaluations are the same, and the brief/specification for an evaluation will ideally be drawn up as part of the Archaeological Assessment stage and approved by an archaeologist working in a curatorial role.

Typically, a Field Evaluation will include: detailed fieldwalking (10m to 20m grid collection with trend surface mapping and detailed analysis of the collection) where circumstances permit; detailed topographic surveys at a large scale of upstanding ancient buildings and monuments; detailed plotting of aerial photographs to the same scale as topographic or field-survey plots; balloon or remote-controlled aerial photography to fill gaps in existing cover (Renow 1985); ditch-side surveys of drainage channels and boundary ditches; auger surveys to gauge depths of overburden and the thickness of deposits; review and analysis of historical documentation revealed in the searches undertaken at the Archaeological Assessment stage; geophysical survey and/or ground radar survey in selected areas defined during the Archaeological Assessment or as a result of other tasks within the Field Evaluation stage (Gaffney and Gater 1991; Gurney 1985); hand-dug test-pits in areas of known archaeology; and machine dug test-pits in 'blank' areas with no known archaeological or environmental deposits.

At this stage great emphasis is placed on the results from hand excavated test-pits. No specific sampling strategy can be recommended to determine how many such pits are needed or what area as a fraction of the site should be studied. Rather the intention should be to achieve a general coverage according to the shape and size of a site, what is proposed (and here the importance of feeding the Archaeological Assessment results into the design of the development footprint is important), and what constraints exist.

Field Evaluation is ideally needed before full Planning Permission for a development is given and this often means working round or within existing buildings. The proximity of neighbouring buildings, the presence of drains and known sub-surface disturbances (eg cellars), and the need for continuing site access also provide constraints on the position of the test-pits.

Generally between 1% and 2% of deposits by volume are examined, a small but practical sample which, it is accepted, is unlikely to be wholly reflective of small-scale structuring in archaeological deposits over a large area, but which will at least give some indication of broad patterns. Prescriptive formulae for evaluation design are unhelpful because they fail to take account of the Assessment or previous archaeological work in the locality. It is also important to recognise that test-pitting should not be too destructive of the archaeological resource since experience suggests that not all sites which are evaluated are developed or redeveloped immediately.

Test-pit work involves ground disturbance and Scheduled Monument Consent will be necessary in Scheduled areas, as well as permission from the land-owners if they are not the clients.

Sometimes there are opportunities to include specific research objectives on the list of factors influencing the position of test-pits, especially where the Archaeological Assessment has highlighted the potential to contribute evidence to the resolution of particular questions.

The archaeological deposits recovered in a test pit must generally be regarded as expendable and the principle accepted that their loss can be set against the information gained as a result. The intention is to study the intrinsic nature of the deposits themselves rather than provide intricate interpretations of any remains revealed. For this reason, a test-pit excavated as part of an archaeological evaluation should sample the entire stratigraphic sequence from top to bottom. It is equally important to gauge the quality and extent of what could be preserved as what might be lost in the course of development. Thus, although a test-pit might show that a development proposal involving the removal of the uppermost 1m of deposits in a 3m deep sequence is archaeologically acceptable because the top 1m is heavily disturbed, it is also important to know that any overcutting beyond 1m would, for example, involve loss of medieval structural evidence, Roman floors, or whatever.

The product of a Field Evaluation is a factual report on the work, usually arranged into sections relating to each methodology applied, and including appropriate plans, sections, elevations, photographs etc, together with a chronological and/or areal summary of the findings. Specialist reports on the main categories of finds and samples are also included, although the emphasis in such reports is directed towards the description of quality and potential of the material. The factual report produced by a Field Evaluation programme provides supporting documentation for a full planning application, a Scheduled Monument Consent application for the development as a whole, or an Environmental Statement (where it would probably represent a technical appendix). Such a report would conform with or exceed the specification for a Field Evaluation described in PPG16 (DoE 1990, paragraph 21).

Strategy Formulation

With the results of the Archaeological Assessment and, if appropriate, the Field Evaluation to hand a strategy can be formulated to deal with the archaeological dimension of the whole site or for each sector or part of a large development area. Details of the main available management options are discussed in the next section. Effective use of the Archaeological Assessment report at the stage of preparing the footprint for a development usually enhances the opportunities for maximising the application of the preservation and conservation options.

Decisions about which options to pursue for any particular area will be based not just on the level of impact envisaged but also on practicality (including health and safety factors, the phasing of development, purchase agreements etc), legal status (eg whether Scheduled or not), and cost (including actual cost of archaeological investigations, hidden costs caused by delays to construction programme, changes to layout or foundation design, and offsetting agricultural or commercial loss during strategy implementation).

Archaeological strategies for an individual site may comprise the application of a single-option strategy or a multi-option strategy according to the size of the site and the degree of diversity of impact across the site. Multi-option strategies can usefully be summarised as zoned plans. Once a strategy has been formulated and agreed among interested parties it can be used as part of an Environmental Statement (ie mitigation measures based on the factual reports noted above), and/or in applying for Scheduled Monument Consent and full Planning Permission.

In choosing options, however, it is important to balance the general objectives of archaeological resource management relating to urban areas. These can be summarised as follows (Darvill 1987b, 25):

(a) to retain the rich diversity of archaeological remains that is known to exist in urban areas

(b) to consider demands made upon the archaeological heritage by society as a whole

(c) to reconcile conflict and competition for the use of land within urban areas that contain archaeological deposits.

Translated into specific objectives the following intentions may be defined:

(a) preserving archaeological deposits *in situ* wherever possible

(b) recording in advance of their destruction any archaeological deposits that cannot be preserved

(c) identifying and resolving conflicts of interest at an early stage

(d) recognising and communicating the importance and nature of the archaeological resource to a wide general public

(e) carrying out programmes of archaeological research to enhance understanding of the resource.

Strategy Implementation

The final stage is Strategy Implementation, and here too the results of work undertaken as part of the evaluation programme are important for the interpretation and programming of tasks. Generally, implementation proceeds in three blocks, details of which would be included in the project design.

Pre-construction works: This usually includes preparatory works for the preservation or conservation of deposits, and the total or selective excavation of areas of high and very high impact before groundworks get underway (eg lift shafts, basements, underground car-parking).

Intra-construction works: This involves small-scale excavations, watching briefs, and recorded observations undertaken in parallel with groundworks and the activities of construction contractors on the site.

Post-construction works: This involves archaeological operations after the development is complete and may include on-site operations such as the establishment and maintenance of long-term conservation or preservation measures, or off-site operations such as the analysis of finds and records from earlier phases of archaeological work, the conservation of fragile finds, the preparation of general and academic reports and accounts of the work, and the deposition of the archive and finds in an appropriate museum.

Management options

The range of management options that can be pursued with reference to any given site is considerable. In the following sections short summary descriptions of three main sets of options are provided together with notes on the applicability of each: Preservation, Exploitation, and Recording.

In general, the selection of an appropriate option or options will be based on the legislative frameworks, financial considerations, engineering constraints, and the use and design of the building. There is, however, another ingredient in the equation relating to the kind of response that is appropriate, and that is the question of research objectives.

Much is already known about Cirencester and its

hinterland, but there are many unanswered questions and inevitably a study such as this focuses attention on both the known and the unknown. In archaeology, the accumulation of further knowledge proceeds in two main ways. Firstly through chance unexpected discoveries; and secondly through planned and considered research. Both are important, but while much publicity has been given to the former a proper balance needs to be maintained and due weight given to the pursuit and implementation of research objectives. Such objectives are particularly important when choices have to be made between competing demands for time and money and in framing the questions to be asked of a particular archaeological project or recording exercise. APPENDIX C sets out a research framework for Cirencester and its surroundings.

Preservation

The preservation of the archaeological resource is widely recognised as the primary objective in the ancient monuments legislation, in planning guidance, in the minds of a significant sector of the population, and in professional ethics. Many options are open, although some are less often stated than others, such as moving a monument (eg the Cirencester Lock-Up (54289)), reinstating a monument (eg the Roman town wall (54024) in the Abbey Grounds), adapting a monument (eg the Great Western Railway Station (54054)), even copying or duplicating a monument (eg the South Porch of St John the Baptist's Church (54053)). More usually preservation as an option falls into two main spheres: conservation and protection.

Conservation establishes a positive relationship between processes of change and the maintenance of the archaeological resource. Typically this involves the adoption of land management regimes which promote the stability of buried or upstanding archaeological deposits (eg through Countryside Stewardship schemes or management agreements), and preventing anything that might accelerate the decay of such remains.

Protection minimises or guards against the adverse effects of some identifiable threat to the archaeological resource usually through planning or ancient monuments legislation. The main threat in urban areas comes from the disturbance of the ground in which structures and deposits may lie. Construction works such as the excavation of basements, foundations, soak-aways, drains, lift-shafts are all common causes of such disturbance, as too is the laying of shallow pipelines or groundworks connected with the creation of large level surfaces for car-parks and playing fields. Here the balance that has to be achieved is the economical construction of buildings within the constraints (archaeological and otherwise) of the site.

There are a number of ways in which the preservation of archaeological deposits can be achieved, many of which require an engineering solution to the problem of supporting large structures on small but strong foundations. The precise details will of course be site-specific, but two general considerations can be identified.

Firstly, careful design of the footprint of a scheme is essential. Experience shows that architects and planners, unfamiliar with archaeological constraints, may not have considered redesigning the layout of a scheme to avoid contact with archaeological deposits altogether. On many smaller urban sites this may not be possible but basements, deep pits for soak-aways or lift shafts can be sited in areas of previous disturbance. The very process of Field Evaluation may archaeologically sterilise a few areas which can be incorporated into the design of the structure.

Secondly, when considering possible foundation designs the aim should be to leave intact as much of the archaeological deposit as possible, accepting that a suitable engineering solution may require the loss of a small proportion of deposits in order to achieve the preservation of the remainder. A study of foundation design in York suggested that a 5% loss of deposits to achieve an engineering solution to the construction of new buildings was archaeologically acceptable and in design terms practicable (Ove Arup 1992, 48). However, when designing foundation structures it must be remembered that the value of archaeological remains is reduced if the deposits themselves become dissected into small blocks making it very difficult to relate one set of deposits with another. The development of foundation schemes with the widest possible spacing between supports curbs the damage.

At Cirencester the depth of made-ground representing accumulated archaeological deposits varies greatly within and around the town, the greatest depths being in the central area (Market Place/Brewery Car-Park/Forum Car-Park) where up to 4m of deposits are commonly found. Some of the more common foundation arrangements and their strengths and weaknesses with reference to the preservation of archaeological deposits are reviewed in the following sub-sections. Figure 56 illustrates some of the configurations considered.

Above-ground construction

In some cases it is possible to found structures, hardstandings and landscaping works on top of the present ground surface. Removal of the vegetation cover is usually acceptable, but the aim is to preserve the topsoil as a buffer between the new development and underlying deposits. Relatively light structures such as roads and car-parks can be constructed in this way, if necessary introducing a geotextile mat to separate existing deposits from aggregates and form foundations on which to build new structures. In some cases new structures can be set on a fully raised aggregate or redeposited bedrock foundation. This is especially useful for lightly-used roads and tracks which are in effect constructed as a causeway over the top of buried deposits.

Above-ground construction is a good way of preserving buried archaeological remains and where it can be used involves only careful design and slight modifications to construction methods so that groundworks do not disturb underlying deposits. Engineering considerations will include the weight of traffic and the fall of drainage.

Strip foundations

Where the overburden (including archaeological deposits) is relatively thin, and the underlying bedrock firm, reinforced concrete strip foundations can be used to support and transmit the loads of heavy walls. (Figure 56.A). This is probably the most commonly used kind of foundation structure, especially for houses and smaller buildings, and also for extensions and garages. The area of loss to foundation trenches as a proportion of the total deposit is generally high, as too the degree of fragmentation of the archaeological deposits. In general, this kind of foundation is not a good method of preserving archaeological deposits and should be avoided wherever possible. Strip foundations are not practical where deep deposits and/or poor bedrock is encountered.

Pad foundations

This type of foundation is used to support and transmit loads from piers and columns which form the frame of a building or superstructure. (Figure 56.B). The most economic plan shape is to set the pads on a regular square lattice, although near site boundaries and in special circumstances a rectangular lattice may be possible. The pads are set in pits either machine or hand dug according to conditions. Such pits may be up to 2m square, their depth will depend on ground conditions and the expected movements and shear forces. Normally, such pads are excavated down to or into the top of the bedrock. Although less destructive of archaeological deposits than strip foundations, the areal loss through pad construction can amount to 20% of the area of the site with substantial accompanying groundworks and soil removal during excavation.

Rafts

Where load-spreading is important, some kind of raft is appropriate. Three main kinds are currently in use: solid slab, beam and slab, and cellular (Chudley 1982, 156). (Figure 56.C–E). Solid slab rafts are constructed of uniform thickness over the whole raft whereas beam and slab rafts are generally better on poor soils as the beams can distribute loads over the raft with the result that the slab thickness can be reduced. The beams can be upstand or downstand, the upstand variety being preferable in terms of the preservation of archaeological deposits because ground penetration can be minimised if the slab is founded more or less at ground surface level. For architectural reasons it is often considered desirable to conceal a raft below ground level, but this is not actually necessary. The slab can be cast directly on subsoil or on a thin layer of binding concrete (Tomlinson 1986, 262). Cellular rafts are most appropriate where a reasonable bearing capacity subsoil can only be found at depths where beam and slab techniques become uneconomic. The construction is similar to reinforced concrete basements except that the internal walls are used to spread the load of the superstructure. In general, cellular rafts are not appropriate foundations for the extensive preservation of archaeological deposits.

Piled foundations

For thicker deposits and less firm bedrock piles provide another alternative to strip foundations, pad foundations or rafts. Piles are relatively long and slender members used to transmit foundation loads through soil strata of low bearing capacity to deeper soil and rock strata with a high bearing capacity. They are also used in normal ground conditions to resist heavy uplift forces or in poor soil conditions to resist horizontal loads (Tomlinson 1986, 398). From an archaeological point of view piles are important because they have the effect of relieving archaeological deposits of the loads imposed by overlying buildings and structures.

Piles normally work in one of two ways. (Figure 56.F). If the bearing stratum is a hard and relatively impenetrable material, such as rock or a very dense sand or gravel, then piles will derive most of their carrying capacity from the resistance of the material at the bottom or toe of the pile. These are known as end-bearing or toe-bearing piles. Alternatively, if the deposit through which piles are constructed does not itself have much resistance then the carrying capacity of the piles is derived partly from end-bearing and partly from friction between the embedded surface of the pile and the surrounding soil. These are called friction piles. For the preservation of archaeological deposits end-bearing piles are the most important as these produce less stress and strain within the deposits through which the piles pass.

Five main ways of constructing piles are currently used (Tomlinson 1986, 398):

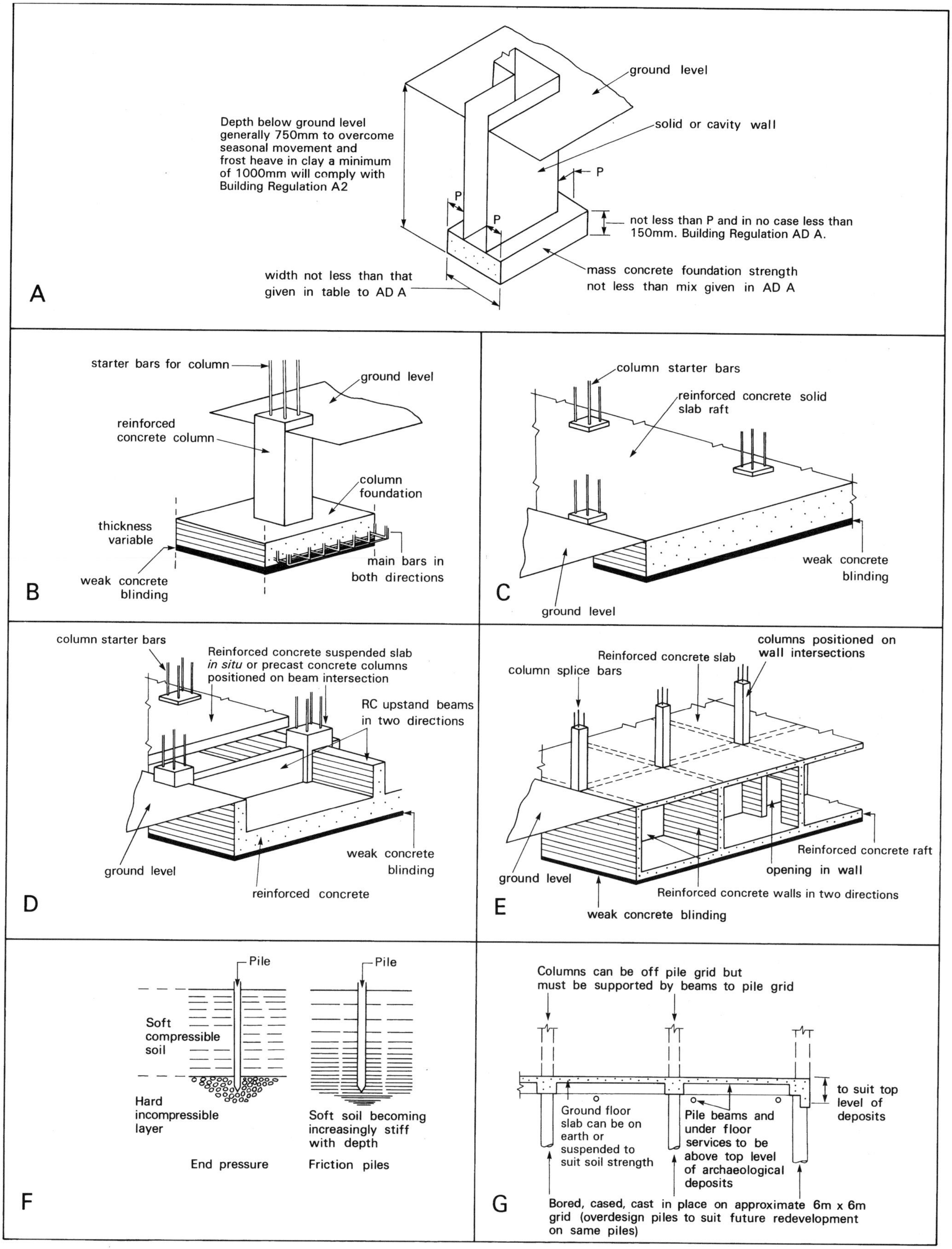

Figure 56
Common foundation arrangements: A. Strip foundations; B. Pad foundations; C–E. Raft foundations; F. Pile types; G. Pile and slab foundations (sources: various)

(a) Driven piles. Pre-formed units driven into the soil by a mechanical hammer or pile-driver.

(b) Driven and cast-in-place piles. Formed by driving a tube with a closed end into the soil and filling the tube with concrete. The tube may or may not be withdrawn.

(c) Jacked piles. Steel or concrete piles jacked into the ground.

(d) Bored and cast-in-place piles. Piles formed by drilling a hole into the ground to the required depth and then filling it with concrete. Two kinds of boring are commonly used: rotary bored piles (flight auger or helical auger) or percussion bored (drop hammer, single acting hammer, double acting hammer, diesel hammer).

(e) Composite piles. Combinations of two or more of the preceding types or combinations of different materials in the same type of pile.

The first three methods are sometimes called displacement piles because soil is displaced by the pile when it is driven or jacked into the ground. This causes some localised disruption of stratigraphy around the pile, mainly through compaction and deflection. Bored piles may be regarded as replacement piles as material is physically removed by the drill and later replaced with concrete. Generally, replacement piles are preferable to driven piles in terms of the preservation of archaeological deposits. Calculating the carrying capacity of piled foundations is a complicated process (Tomlinson 1986, chapter 7) and while bored and cast-in-place end-bearing piles are archaeologically preferable compromises may have to be made depending on ground conditions.

The degree of preservation achieved by piling also depends on the size of the piles and their spacing. Table 7 shows in general terms the projected loss of deposits from a range of pile sizes set out on a 6m by 6m grid on the basis of studies in York. Preservation is improved by using widely spaced piles even though the piles themselves have to be of larger diameter.

Constructing piles through archaeological deposits is not always as straightforward as it might seem. One technical problem with constructing replacement piles occurs when major obstructions are met with in the hole being drilled to take the pile. The temptation that many piling contractors succumb to involves using a Hy-mac excavator or similar to dig down and remove the obstruction. The result is extensive damage to archaeological deposits. To achieve good archaeological preservation other means of overcoming the problem need to be found. Good field evaluation is one way of minimising the risk in the first place, but even this is not infallible. Where an unexpected obstacle is encountered two possible solutions can be tried. The first is to use an appropriate drill-head, or percussion boring. Second is to hand-excavate a square hole through which the upper part of the pile will pass, the remainder of the pile being drilled down from the bottom of the excavation.

Whatever pile arrangement is used the top of the piles are set in a reinforced cast *in situ* concrete pile cap. This is what takes the load of the superstructure. The pile caps may be linked by ground-beams to support walls or a cast slab floor. As with rafting, there is a tendency to sink the ground beams below ground level for cosmetic reasons, but again this is not strictly necessary and it is quite possible to found the ground beams on an artificially-raised ground level which effectively seals underlying deposits.

Pile diameter (mm)	Allowable load (kN)	Cross sectional area (m^2)	% of Grid Area occupied by piles on a 6m × 6m grid	% of Grid Area occupied by pile plus
450	1300	0.16	0.5	0.75
600	2300	0.28	0.8	1.2
750	3600	0.44	1.2	1.8
900	5250	0.64	1.8	2.7
1050	7100	0.87	2.4	3.6
1200	9300	1.13	3.1	4.7

TABLE 7 Minimum site area affected by piles of different diameter (after Ove Arup 1992)

Exploitation

There are many demands placed upon the archaeological resource by today's society. These range from access to ancient monuments for educational and recreational use, promotion of the archaeological heritage as a tourist attraction and visitor facility, and the exploration of the past through research and study. All represent perfectly legitimate claims on the resource and need to be taken into account when considering its long-term future. Intensive exploitation of the archaeological resource through excavation or restoration for public display can be as destructive as developing the land for a completely non-archaeological purpose.

There are two main exploitative options which merit consideration in the context of the present state of Cirencester's archaeology:

Presentation

At present there is relatively little to see of Cirencester's archaeological heritage except for the displays in the Corinium Museum and the standing buildings reflecting the more recent forms (eg medium-sized market town). The main visible monuments of earlier times are the Roman amphitheatre, the town wall in the Abbey Grounds; the eastern apse of the basilica marked in the road at the south end of Tower Street; and various small pieces of masonry set up around the town (eg opposite the Police Station). Plans are in hand to improve the presentation of the town wall in the Abbey Grounds.

Opportunities which allow improved access to some of the more tangible remains of Cirencester's past may present themselves as part of development proposals and should be considered on their merits. Large companies particularly will have stated long-term environmental goals which may aspire to conservation benefits, even if policies are not backed-up by quantified targets or reviewed through auditing procedures. Bearing in mind this likely increase in concern, there is probably scope for making some additional Roman remains accessible to the public in the central area of the town. Presentational work need not always involve archaeologically destructive operations. There is enough visible already in and around the town to allow the creation of a 'Roman Trail' (the existing *Roman Trail* booklet available at the Museum has now sold out), and a 'Medieval Trail', and successful day-schools are run regularly to cope with this educational demand. Careful signboarding coupled with a trail leaflet would probably be adequate and the Civic Society have recently gone some way towards this by funding a number of new plaques around the town, for example at the site of the Bath Gate. There have been signboards at the site of the Augustinian Abbey and the *basilica* for some years as well as an English Heritage board discreetly placed at the amphitheatre.

Initiatives for the conservation and restoration of distinctive historic landscapes and features also include the Countryside Commission's 'Countryside Stewardship Scheme' and English Heritage's 'Survey Grants for Presentation'. Both these schemes recognise the importance of informal access to well-managed sites. MAFF also offer a range of grants such as the 'Farm Diversification Grant Scheme', 'Farm and Conservation Grant Schemes', 'Environmentally Sensitive Areas', and 'Set-Aside' which can be used to help attract visitors. Estate management plans may also be expected to feature archaeology especially where proposals are put forward for inclusion in the local plan.

Research excavation

No research excavations have been carried out in Cirencester since the work at the amphitheatre in 1962–3 and 1966. Two main reasons explain this dearth. First the lack of a coherent research framework for the town which points-up questions. Second, the fact that rescue recording has led to the excavation of many sites and fully occupied the staff resources that might otherwise have been available for research. In this respect Cirencester is not unique, many other archaeologically-rich urban areas find themselves in the same position, but archaeological knowledge about the town is certainly poorer.

One way of improving knowledge of the archaeology of the town is by making the best of available opportunities. In 1990, the Cotswold Archaeological Trust published a provisional research framework to help guide the allocation of time and resource (Darvill 1990, 9). That framework has since been expanded and is set out in APPENDIX C of this report. Any opportunities to explore these questions should be exploited if supported by adequate resources.

Recording

Where the preservation of a monument or part of it is not feasible and remains are likely to be destroyed in the course of development some sort of record should be made in advance of and during destruction. This work is normally restricted to the minimum compatible with the extent of destruction, but there may be arguments in certain cases for recording more comprehensively to ensure that the intelligibility of the remains is not compromised. Archaeological work will always be undertaken in a way which maximises the information retrieval and makes the results available to the academic world and the general public.

Recording work can be expensive, particularly in deeply stratified urban sites. In recent years the onus of meeting the costs of such work has increasingly shifted to the landowner or developer, and most now accept a level of responsibility to carry out an agreed programme of works within the development programme. The money from central government, administered by English Heritage, which was used to cover the cost of recording until the mid 1980s is still available, but is deployed in a slightly different way. Grants are still given under the terms of section 45 of the *Ancient Monuments and Archaeological Areas Act 1979* (as amended in England) to 'undertake or assist in or defray or contribute towards the cost of an archaeological investigation of any land in England which [English Heritage] consider[s] may contain an ancient monument or anything else of archaeological or historical interest'. A policy statement (EH 1991c, 33–4) on the dispersement of such grants issued in June 1991 sets out three main areas where funds will be applied:

(1) For recording those archaeological sites which cannot be preserved and whose destruction is taking place beyond the control of the agencies with the power and resources to deal with the problem.

(2) For undertaking projects which in the view of English Heritage and that of their advisors, should be undertaken to enable English Heritage to carry out its statutory duties, including the direction of funding towards particular problems with this in view.

(3) For assisting, subject to the availability of funds, with the financing of projects where it is not practical for a developer to make full provision for archaeological work required by a local planning authority. Such cases normally fall into two types: where a developer is demonstrably unable to make full provision in the budget for the level of recording demanded by the quality of a threatened site; and where (despite properly designed and conducted evaluation) unpredicted and important evidence has emerged subsequent to the granting of planning permission and beyond the resources already put aside for archaeological work.

There are three main recording options regularly used in archaeological work, some more far-reaching than others:

Rescue excavation
This involves the complete systematic investigation, recording, and removal of archaeological deposits according to the normal principles of stratigraphic excavation. The size of a rescue excavation may vary from the examination of holes to take piles or foundations (small-scale excavation) through to extensive trenches in excess of 100 square metres in extent (open area excavation). Rescue excavations do not always involve the complete removal of deposits, their size and depth is usually determined by the extent of expected destruction.

Watching brief
This involves the presence of a qualified archaeologist during the digging of holes or foundations by machine. The work is undertaken slightly more slowly and with a little more care than usual so that any archaeological remains that come to light can be seen and recorded. Recording is usually by written descriptions, plans and photographs. Finds are recovered as time and safety constraints permit. If very spectacular finds come to light (eg a mosaic) work may need to be halted for a short period to allow a record to be compiled. In the case of human burials being uncovered the normal procedures have to be followed. The loss of deposits during a watching brief is fairly high and the information yield generally rather low. It is unlikely that remains will be uncovered in an undamaged state. Generally, watching briefs should only be used on deposits considered to be of medium or low importance.

Recorded observation
This is the minimum level of active archaeological recording for groundworks and the disturbance of archaeological layers. Usually it involves a qualified archaeologist visiting the site at intervals to simply observe any holes that have been dug, make notes on what is visible, and collect any finds that have come to light during the course of the work. Good relations with the contractors and workmen makes this option much easier to implement. The frequency of visits depends on the speed of progress and the nature of the operations. The loss of deposits is very high and the information retrieved of generally low quality.

Monument and deposit importance in Cirencester

One key factor in selecting appropriate management options is the perceived value and importance of the resource itself. In general four main levels of importance are recognised:

International Importance:
Archaeological remains recognised by the international community as being of world-wide significance and interest (eg World Heritage Sites designated by UNESCO).

National Importance:
Archaeological remains recognised as being of special significance and interest in terms of the history and development of the British nation (eg Scheduled Monuments).

Regional Importance:
Archaeological remains recognised as being of less than national importance but representative of more regionalised traditions or historical developments and of interest and significance for those reasons.

Local Importance:
Archaeological remains recognised as being of interest and significance only in the context of their local manifestation of generally common and widespread traditions or historical developments.

In addition to these four levels it is appropriate to recognise one further category, that of non-antiquities. This category covers natural or fake features which are credited with having a relevance to the history of development within a given area but in fact have no such links.

Assigning individual monuments or blocks of accumulated deposits to a place within this hierarchy of importance has largely been covered in Chapters 7–11 above. At present no parts of the study area can justifiably be claimed as being of International Importance, although as a former Roman Provincial Capital the future discovery of significant remains of international importance cannot be ruled out. Such discoveries would place Cirencester on a par with the fourteen defined World Heritage Sites which include Stonehenge and Avebury, Hadrian's Wall, the City of Bath, the Tower of London, and Canterbury Cathedral. Monuments and deposits of National, Regional and Local Importance can however by identified from present data.

Monuments
Single monuments in non-urban situations and those identified within defined urban forms were described and discussed in Chapters 7–11. A detailed analysis of all single monuments revealed that there were a total of 29 monuments which can be recognised as being of National Importance. Of these 13 (44%) are in non-urban situations, the remainder can be tied to defined urban forms. The number of Nationally Important examples represents about 13% of all identified medieval and earlier monuments. Of those identified as being Nationally Important some 27% are currently Scheduled.

The following monuments have been identified as being of National Importance in the foregoing analysis (those marked * are currently Scheduled Monuments):

(1) Non-urban situations

54003	S. Wellhill Plantation	round barrow*
54079	The Querns	?long barrow*
54011	Tower Street	fort (Roman)
54045	The Querns	amphitheatre*
54057	The Querns	cemetery (Romano-British)*
54089	Tar Barrow	?Roman barrow*
54219	Tar Barrow	?Roman barrow*
54217	Grismond's Tower	?Roman barrow
54220	Tar Barrow	?Roman barrow
54372	Kingsmeadow	cemetery (Romano-British)
54435	Gloucester Gate	cemetery (Romano-British)
54112	Deer Park	deer park
54173	Siddington Barn	barn*

(2) Within identified urban forms

54009	Chester Lodge	*forum*
54012	Watermoor House	*basilica*
54024	Watermoor	town wall (Romano-British)*
54113	Abbey	courtyard house
54114	Abbey	courtyard house
54416	Dyer Street	courtyard house
54419	Beeches Road	winged corridor villa
54424	The Avenue	courtyard house
54053	St John the Baptist	parochial church
54076	St John's Hospital	hospital*
54087	The Abbey	monastery for men
54096	Thomas Street	hospital
54111	Market Place	market place
54179	St Lawrence's Hospital	almshouses
54186	Langley Mill	watermill (medieval)
54215	West Market Place	market place

Approximately 34% of medieval and earlier monuments may be identified as being of Regional Importance, the remaining 53% being of only Local Importance.

Accumulated deposits
The main characteristics of the total accumulation of archaeological deposits within the urban area at Cirencester were discussed and described in Chapter 12. Three main levels of archaeological interest were defined. These three levels can be taken as indicators of archaeological importance in view of the fact that it was achieved by combining the discrimination criteria to arrive at the result.

Approximately 32% of the urban area of Cirencester was considered to be of high sensitivity.

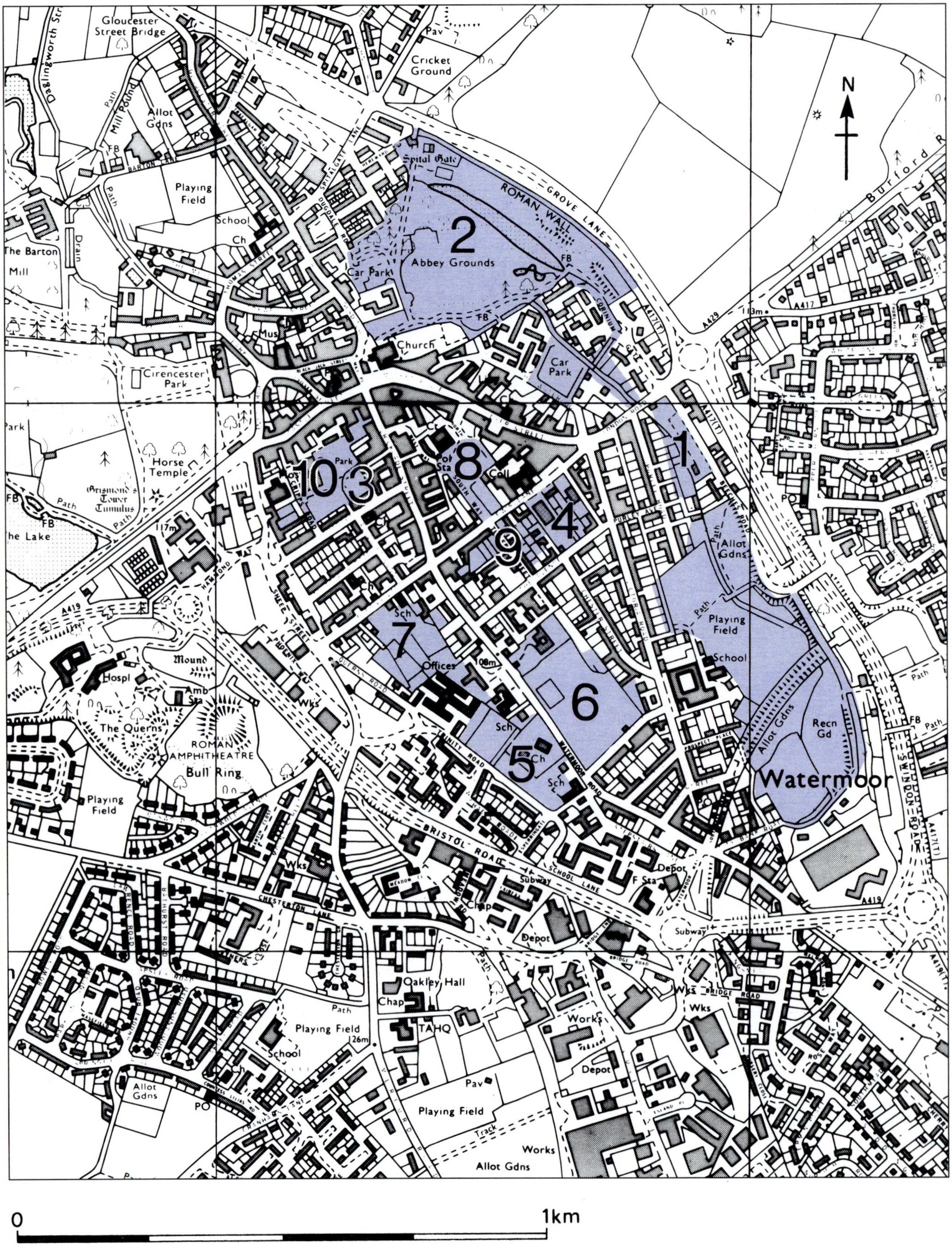

Figure 57
Zones of high archaeological interest in the urban area (Reproduced from the Ordnance Survey's 1:10,000 map of 1983 with the permission of the Controller of Her Majesty's Stationery Office, © Crown copyright)

This comprised the following ten main blocks (see Figure 57 for extent of areas):

(1) **Watermoor / City Bank / Beeches Road car-park**: This is an area of open playing fields, allotments, and former nursery area running from New Mill to City Bank Road. It includes areas to the north and south of the former railway line and contains upstanding sections of the Roman town defences, New Mill and Langley Mill. The area is sensitive because it has remained undeveloped since Roman times and parts of the area are known to be waterlogged. The potential for the preservation of organic materials in anaerobic conditions has been demonstrated during recent evaluation work.

(2) **Abbey Grounds/Corinium Gate**: The Abbey Grounds are an area of public open space to the north-east of the parish church, bounded by Grove Lane on the eastern side and Spitalgate to the north. There is evidence for two Roman courtyard houses, the upstanding Roman town defences (with a variety of components), the Anglo-Saxon church, the buildings of the Abbey precinct (including barns, gateways, church, fishponds, collegiate and hospitate buildings), and the post-medieval landscaped gardens and site of the Abbey House.

(3) **Bowling Green**: The Bowling Green lies to the west of Cricklade Street and to the south of Castle Street. It is an area of undisturbed ground which is outside the presumed limits of the Anglo-Saxon and medieval town but within the post-medieval landscaped grounds of the Ashcroft estate. There is certainly a north-south Roman street here, the possibility of shops and strip houses, and the earlier *vicus* settlement.

(4) **Gaumont Cinema and car-park**: The cinema is on the south side of Lewis Lane. The Roman *forum* lies here with the *basilica* to the south. This block is bounded by Roman *insulae* streets and well-appointed courtyard houses with mosaics. The early and later medieval urban forms do not extend into this part of the town. In the post-medieval period Chester Lodge was located here with its landscaped grounds and gardens.

(5) **Paternoster School**: The school lies to the west of Watermoor Road. There are foundations and mosaics of well-appointed buildings together with streets on the edge of the Roman defences. The early and later medieval urban forms do not extend into this area. This was an area of open space in the post-medieval period.

(6) **St Michael's Field**: An area of open playing fields and parkland, formerly the grounds of Watermoor House to the south of The Avenue and east of Watermoor Road. In the Roman period there is evidence for the Roman fort, later strip houses, streets, and possibly an additional market or temple. The early and later medieval urban forms do not extend so far south. The area was included in the landscaped grounds of Watermoor House in the post-medieval period and survival is generally good.

(7) **South of Querns Lane**: This area, which lies to the south of Lewis Lane and west of Watermoor Road has been gardens and paddocks since at least the post-medieval period. In the Roman period there are known to be well-appointed buildings in this area and survival is good.

(8) **Forum car-park**: This area lies to the north of Lewis Lane and to the north of the *forum* in the Roman period. The pre-urban *vicus* settlement must lie in this area and excavations at Dyer Court revealed well preserved wall foundations and Roman streets. It is likely to have been open space outside of the main settlement areas in the early and late medieval periods. There is some post-medieval housing, now demolished, along the southern edge of the area.

(9) **Tower Street area**: Tower Street runs between Lewis Lane and The Avenue and includes the gardens to the west of Tower Street. The Roman *forum* lies here with the *basilica* to the south. This block is bounded by Roman *insulae* streets and Ermin Street with the *macellum* to the west. The early and later medieval urban forms do not extend into this part of the town. It was an area of Nurseries in the post-medieval period and developed in the 1850s.

(10) **Brewery car-park**: The Brewery car-park lies to the west of Cricklade Street and to the south of Castle Street.

Key to Figure 57:

1 Watermoor / City Bank / Beeches Road Car-Park
2 Abbey Grounds / Corinium Gate
3 Bowling Green
4 Gaumont Cinema and Car-Park
5 Paternoster School
6 St Michael's Field
7 Area south of Querns Lane
8 Forum Car-Park
9 Tower Street Area
10 Brewery Car-Park

It is an area of partially disturbed ground which is outside the presumed limits of the Anglo-Saxon and medieval town but within the post-medieval landscaped grounds of the Ashcroft estate. There is certainly a north-south Roman street here, the possibility of shops and strip houses, and the earlier *vicus* settlement.

Taken together, the areas of high archaeological interest comprise what appears to be a fairly representative sample of historic Cirencester, at least in spatial terms. Central areas of the town as well as peripheral areas are represented. Several monuments which are unique within the town for certain forms are represented (eg the *forum*; the abbey); equally, repetitive monuments such as domestic structures and defences should be included. It is impossible to gauge the validity of the sample of zones of high interest with reference to unknown but anticipated monuments.

The boundaries of existing Scheduled Monuments do not correspond with the extents of areas of high archaeological sensitivity. Scheduling is a discretionary power and has not been used to identify all nationally important remains within the built environment. In addition, the existing scheduling was undertaken some years ago, without the benefit of much of the data which is now available, and without the kind of systematic analysis presented in the previous Chapters. English Heritage will review the extent of scheduled areas as part of the development of a strategy for the management of the archaeological resource throughout the Study Area.

Zones of medium interest within the town are relatively hard to define and at present account for only 5% of the area of the town. At present, areas of low interest and areas where interest cannot be easily determined account for 63% of the town. Within this, however, there is likely to be areas of medium and high interest which have yet to be identified. Only field evaluation will help with the closer definition of these areas.

Dealing with the unexpected

There will of course always be occasions when, despite the most careful planning and detailed site investigations, something unexpected turns up. When this happens it is important not to panic, but rather to have anticipated the remote possibility and make provisions accordingly. This may simply involve established lines of advice and decision-making. Close working relationships with a local archaeological contractor can be important here, encouraging a rational view of the situation and appropriate action. Where unexpectedly discovered remains are of national importance help may be available from English Heritage provided that the full assessment and field evaluation procedures have been followed. In all cases, however, the range of options which are available is often considerable and it is usually possible to make alternative arrangements that allow a development to continue while also safeguarding or recording the archaeological remains.

Who does what

The range of organisations involved in archaeological matters and the administration or operationalising of archaeological legislation can appear bewildering. In general there are two main sets of roles fulfilled by archaeologists. The first is what is called the 'curatorial' function, that is looking after or taking care of the archaeological resource as a whole through the administration of the legislation and the implementation of policies. The second is what is called the 'contractor' function, that is the carrying out of archaeological work such as evaluation programmes or management options (see above). A third group can also be distinguished, consultants, who act on behalf of clients faced with archaeological matters. Figure 58 is a flow chart designed to show the archaeological management cycle alongside the planning procedure and indicates the roles of principal organisations.

In the following sections the main archaeological curators and contractors relevant to Cirencester are briefly described. It should be noted, however, that archaeological contractors operate on a commercial basis and that while each tends to have a home operating territory most are able and willing to work in other areas too. The *Directory of Members* published by the Institute of Field Archaeologists includes advertisements for archaeological contractors and consultants.

Cotswold District Council

As the Local Planning Authority, Cotswold District Council is the principal archaeological curator for Cirencester and the Cotswold District. They are responsible for the formulation of the Local Plan, and for the implementation of PPG16 and the archaeological elements contained in the planning process. Together with English Heritage the District Council plays an important role in developing scheduling and management strategies to feed into the working of PPG16. As a District Authority the task of formulating archaeological advice involves internal consultations between the Planning Department and the Cotswold Museums Service, and also receipt of external advice from Gloucestershire County Council and English Heritage as appropriate.

Gloucestershire County Council

As the County Planning Authority, Gloucestershire County Council is the principal archaeological

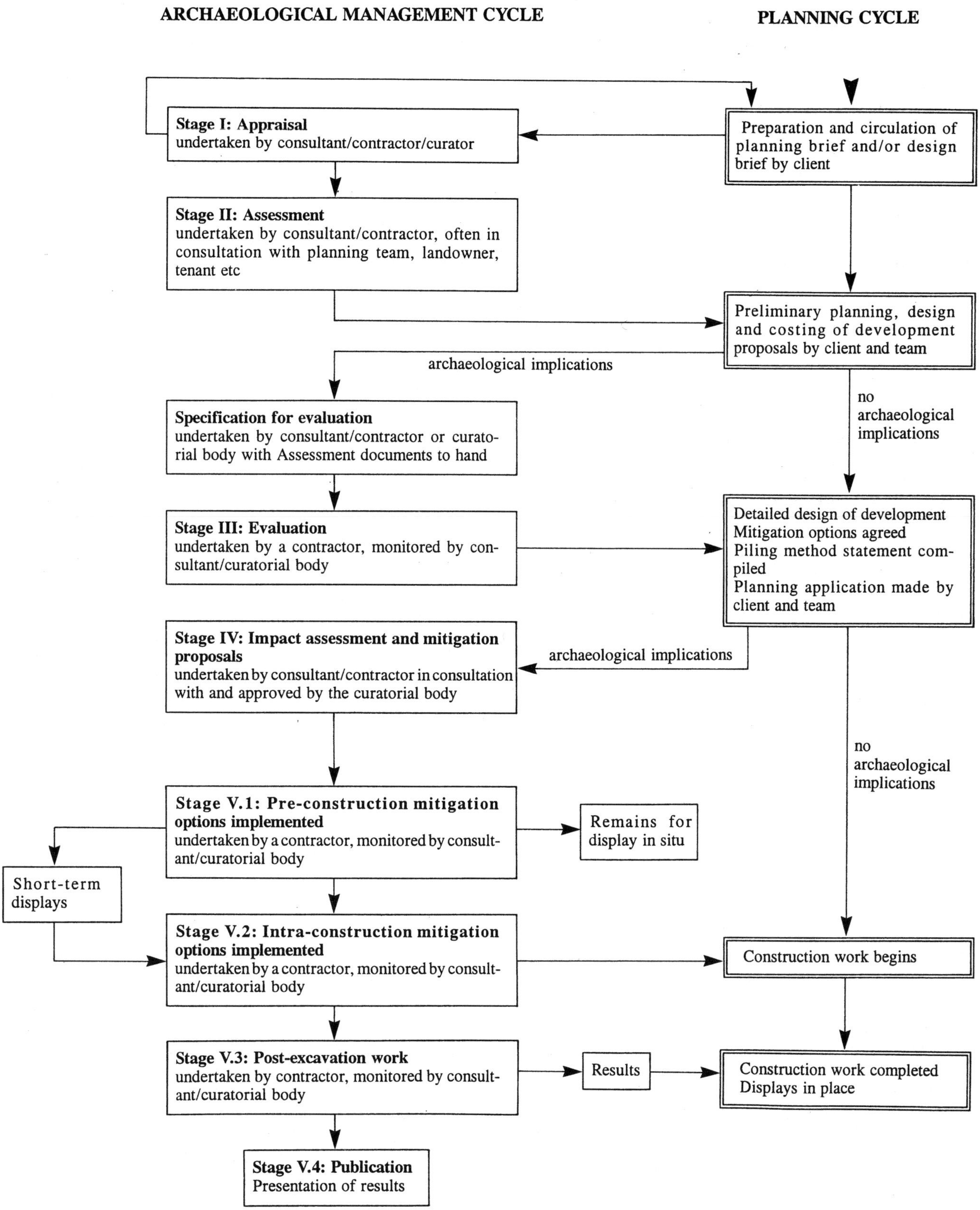

Figure 58
Flow chart to show the archaeological management cycle alongside the planning process

curator in respect of certain reserved planning matters (eg minerals), and is responsible for the formulation of archaeological policies within the County Structure Plan. A county-wide SMR is maintained within the Planning Department and advice is given to District Authorities as appropriate.

English Heritage
The Historic Buildings and Monuments Commission (England) or English Heritage as it is generally known, was created by the *National Heritage Act 1983.* It is the principal archaeological curator in terms of the national archaeological resource and the main adviser to central and local government. In relation to the operation of PPG16 and the integration of archaeology in the planning process, English Heritage assists and, wherever possible, works in association with the Local Planning Authority in order to achieve practical and relevant scheduling and management strategies. English Heritage is responsible for the care of ancient monuments which are in Guardianship. It gives grants for archaeological projects and for assisting with the management of monuments. Although the Secretary of State for the National Heritage retains statutory roles in relation to the Scheduling of Ancient Monuments and the granting of Scheduled Monument Consent for works affecting monuments, he/she is advised by English Heritage on these matters. English Heritage also has responsibilities in respect of Listed Buildings and Conservation Areas.

Cotswold Archaeological Trust
The Cotswold Archaeological Trust was formed in 1989 as a direct successor to the Cirencester Excavation Committee which had been carrying out archaeological investigations in and around Cirencester since 1958. The Trust is the only archaeological contractor based in Cotswold District and, although organisationally separate, has close links with Cotswold District Council through the Cotswold Museums Service. From its formation to the end of 1993, Cotswold Archaeological Trust has carried out over 50 archaeological projects in and around Cirencester, with many others elsewhere in Gloucestershire and further afield.

Other organisations
A number of other archaeological contractors have worked in and around Cirencester over the last few years, including the Oxford Archaeological Unit based in Oxford and Wessex Archaeology based in Salisbury. Mention may also be made of the Royal Commission on the Historical Monuments of England who take national responsibility for the creation and maintenance of SMRs and who operate a National Archaeological Record and a National Library of Aerial Photographs. A number of consultancies also offer archaeological advice on planning and management and may act in a useful independent role between curatorial and contractual bodies.

Standards of archaeological service

Archaeology is a self-regulating profession. Some aspects of archaeological work are prescribed by statute, for example those dealing with Scheduled Monuments or human burials. All archaeological work should be carried out to accepted professional standards and curators, contractors, consultants and specialists should adhere to these. Archaeological curators in particular have a duty to monitor standards in the execution of work programmes.

The professional institute which covers archaeologists is the Institute of Field Archaeologists (IFA). It recognises three classes of corporate membership according to levels of training and experience: Practitioner, Associate, and Member. Membership classes carry the distinctions PIFA, AIFA and MIFA. All members of the Institute subscribe to a Code of Conduct, and there are other by-laws dealing with such matters as the regulation of contract archaeology and competitive tendering. A series of 'standards' documents relating to specific areas of archaeological endeavour (eg Archaeological Assessment) have been produced.

There are two industry-sponsored codes of practice relevant to archaeological work. The first was established by the British Archaeologists' and Developers' Liaison Group (1986, reprinted 1991) and concerns the integration of archaeology in property development. The second was established by the Confederation for British Industry (CBI 1991) and deals with mineral operators.

Standards of project management in archaeology are assessed with reference to a manual published by English Heritage: *Management of Archaeological Projects* (EH 1991a).

Conclusion

The main thrust of this Urban Archaeological Assessment has been to report in summary form something of the nature, extent, and importance of the archaeological resource represented in the Cirencester area and to put this into its context in respect of the way that the resource is managed. But this is only one element in the range of outcomes from the project as a whole.

Underpinning everything that is included here is the urban archaeological database. This detailed record is kept in the Corinium Museum, with a copy in the county SMR. As new data comes to light it will be added to this record.

Developing out of the Cirencester Urban Assessment there will be a series of further initiatives taken forward by a number of organisations. English Heritage will, in due course, consider the nature and extent of scheduling within Cirencester. Cotswold District Council will, as part of its work on the Local Plan for the District, develop appropriate policies to deal with the protection and management of the archaeological resource. English Heritage and Cotswold District Council together will hopefully develop and endorse an urban archaeological strategy for Cirencester which is consistent with similar strategies being developed elsewhere. Finally, the Cotswold Archaeological Trust will continue to work for and with others to take forward best practice in the investigation, enhancement and management of the rich archaeological resource in and around Cirencester for the benefit of all those interested in sharing or learning about its history.

GLOSSARY

Ancient Monument: As defined by the *Ancient Monuments and Archaeological Areas Act 1979* this term means:

> '(a) any scheduled monument; and (b) any other monument which in the opinion of the Secretary of State is of public interest by reason of the historic, architectural, traditional, artistic or archaeological interest attaching to it'.

In the context of responsibilities delegated to HBMC under the *National Heritage Act 1983*, however, this term means:

> 'any structure, work, site, garden, or area which in the Commission's [ie HBMC's] opinion is of historic, architectural, traditional, artistic or archaeological interest' (Ch.47, S33 (8)).

Antiquarian Excavation: (AE) Site type. Excavation undertaken before 1940.

Appraisal: The recognition of an archaeological dimension to a development proposal or management plan. An appraisal is the first stage in preparing a detailed archaeological response to development or management proposals.

The appraisal is a preliminary 'look-see' to determine whether there is an archaeological dimension, based usually on SMR data, published sources, and a brief field-visit.

Archaeology: Archaeology is taken to mean the study of past human societies through their material remains, from prehistoric times to the modern era. No rigid upper date limit has been set but AD 1940 is used as a general cut-off point. It is accepted that some undated sites of slightly later date will unavoidably be included in the absence of firm evidence of date.

Archaeological Assessment: The identification and documenting of the recorded archaeological resource within the study area. Desk-based study of all existing records plus field-checking and basic reconnaissance.

Archaeological Excavation: see Excavation, Antiquarian Excavations, Modern Excavation.

Artefact: Man-made object.

Cartographic Depiction: (CD) Site type. Map-based source of information.

Category: General descriptive term covering a group of monument classes related by function, origin or purpose: mill, megalithic tomb, village, burials, houses, round barrows, bridges. The category 'megalithic tomb' encompasses the classes portal dolmen, simple passage grave, entrance grave etc.

Characterisation Criteria: Criteria which deal with the description and definition of specific single monument classes, relict landscape forms, or urban area forms. The characterisation criteria are:

Period (currency),
Rarity
Diversity (form)
Period (representativity)

Class: Descriptive term applied to a group of monuments which share common visible features of design, layout, construction and use: eg moat, windmill, stone circle, portal dolmen, simple passage grave, entrance grave, Roman fort, motte and bailey caste, fish pond, amphitheatre.

Class Characterisation Stage: The part of the evaluation procedure during which the characterisation criteria are applied to single monument classes.

Component: Descriptive term applied to any constituent part of a recognised class or type of monument: eg components of a moat include: gatehouse, ditch, causeway, bridge, island, internal bank, external bank, leat, pond, well, dam, house and other internal structures.

Context: A context in archaeological terms may be regarded as the smallest definable stratigraphic unit, other than a removable object, about which useful information can be recorded. For example: a gravel surface, burnt clay spread, cremation, ploughsoil, old turf line.

Corpora: Corpora and gazetteers are of varying quality. Compiled on a regional or national scale they can include information derived from non-local sources. The information tends to be superficial and often derives from secondary sources.

Descriptive text – primary: Primary published sources comprise original reports on research, excavation, and finds: eg three volumes published by CEC, original papers in *TBGAS, Archaeologia* etc.

Descriptive text – secondary: Secondary sources are published accounts based on previously published reports. Archaeological sites and finds have been included in general histories and gazetteers since the eighteenth century, although it must be recognised that the details reported may be vague, ambiguous, and sometimes inaccurate.

Descriptor: Qualifying term providing information about a specific monument which is additional to the class and type definitions. This information is usually related to function, ownership, status or usage rather than morphology. For example, a monument which falls into the class of Watermill may have the descriptor 'corn-mill' because of the material processed. This same descriptor may of course also apply to a Windmill used for the same purpose.

Discrimination Criteria: Criteria which deal with the characteristics of individual monuments and which allow the relative importance of any site to be evaluated by reference to other examples of the same class or form. The discrimination criteria are:

Group Value (association)
Survival
Potential
Documentation (archaeological)
Documentation (historical)
Diversity (features)
Group Value (clustering)
Amenity Value

Direct observation: This type of evidence largely comprises extant artefacts (finds) or sightings of structural remains and/or objects (observations) that have come to light by engineering works or other forms of ground disturbance, and which were brought to the attention of an archaeologist who was able to record basic information such as the position and depth of the find or structure. In some cases such information may be derived from a non-specialist eye-witness or the person who made the discovery. The range of information recorded varies greatly, as does its accuracy.

Documentary Record Unit: (DRU) Site type.

Evaluation: The assessment or appraisal of a monument or groups of related monuments for the purpose of determining their importance, quality, or value. See also field evaluation.

Evaluation Excavation: (EE) Site type.

Excavation: Excavation is the complete systematic investigation, recording and removal of archaeological deposits according to the normal principles of stratigraphic excavation. The size of an excavation may vary from the examination of holes to take piles or foundations (small-scale excavation) through to open-area excavation involving one or more trenches covering anything in excess of 100 square metres.

Techniques and standards of excavation have changed over the last fifty years and any excavation, therefore, must be seen in the context of professional standards prevailing at the time of its execution.

Normally the records of an excavation include plans, sections, notes, descriptions of individual layers and features, photographs, catalogues of finds recovered.

Feature: Groups of associated contexts which can be recognised as stratigraphically connected in recognised patterns may be defined as features. For example: beam slot, cess pit, floor, hypocaust etc.

Field Evaluation: Field-based study of the recorded archaeological resource coupled with checking and verification of primary and secondary sources to provide base-line data relating to the quality, quantity, survival, condition, fragility, interpretation, and importance of each identified site. Includes checking apparently blank areas.

Field survey: See Geophysical Survey Unit, and Systematic Surface Collection Unit.

Form: The term 'form' is used within MPP in two ways:

(1) In its general sense the term is used to describe patterns of survival, at any level of abstraction, which are considered archaeologically meaningful. Thus, the total archaeological resource can be seen as comprising three main forms of monuments: SINGLE MONUMENTS, RELICT CULTURAL LANDSCAPES, and URBAN AREAS, while recognised sub-divisions of each of these (eg classes, forms, types and variants) are also generally referred to as 'forms' (as in the criterion 'Diversity (form)').

(2) In its specific sense the term is used to describe the various ways in which monuments survive as field evidence as part of the assessment of the 'Condition' criterion (eg standing building, earthwork etc). Specific uses of the term will be obvious from the contexts in which they occur.

Form Characterisation Stage: The part of the evaluation procedure during which the characterisation criteria are applied to urban areas or relict landscapes.

Geophysical Survey Unit: (GSU) Site type. Area surveyed by remote sensing devices.

Interpretation and Mapping Unit: (IMU) Site type. Site perceived by analysis of one or more aerial photographs.

Indirect Observation: (IR) Site type. This is the least satisfactory type of evidence available and mostly comprises secondary accounts of discoveries based on gossip, rumour, memories, and knowledge passed on by word of mouth. Naturally such records are often imprecise or garbled, and on occasion can even be invented to satisfy an enquiry. Indirect records may relate to extant artefacts (finds) or sightings of structural remains and/or objects (observations).

Management Appraisal Criteria: Criteria which deal with the situation, physical condition and site management at a monument. These are taken into consideration when determining the most appropriate immediate course of action or the preservation of a monument. The management appraisal criteria are:

Condition
Fragility
Vulnerability
Conservation value

Management Appraisal Stage: The part of the evaluation procedure when the management appraisal criteria are applied to individual single monuments, or relict landscapes, or urban areas.

Modern Excavation: (ME) Site type.

Monument: As defined by the *Ancient Monuments and Archaeological Areas Act 1979*, this term means:

(a) 'any building, structure or work, whether above or below the surface of the land, and any cave or excavation;
(b) any site comprising the remains of any such building, structure or work or of any cave or excavation; and
(c) any site comprising, or comprising the remains of, any vehicle, vessel, aircraft or other movable structure of part thereof which neither constitutes nor forms part of any work which is a monument within paragraph (a) above; and any machinery attached to a monument shall be regarded as part of the monument if it could not be detached without being dismantled' (Ch.46, S61(7)).
References in the Act to a monument includes reference to: (A) the site of the monument in question; and (B) to a group of monuments or any part of a monument or group of monuments (Ch.46, S61(10).

Within this definition, the MPP recognises the survival of monuments in three main forms: single monuments, relict landscapes, and urban areas. Under the 1979 Act, the term 'Monument' does not apply to any ecclesiastical building for the time being used for ecclesiastical purposes, nor to any vessel which is protected by an order under section 1 of the *Protection of Wrecks Act 1973* designating an area round the site as a restricted area (Ch.46, S61(8)).

Monument Discrimination Stage: The part of the evaluation procedure during which the discrimination criteria are applied to single monuments, relict landscapes, or urban areas.

MPP: Monuments Protection Programme.

National Importance: Under Section 1 of the *Ancient Monuments and Archaeological Areas Act 1979*, the Secretary of State may include in the Schedule any monument which appears to him to be of NATIONAL IMPORTANCE. Before doing so for monuments in England he is required to consult English Heritage. In practice, English Heritage takes the initiative and recommends monuments for inclusion to the Secretary of State.

The characteristics which make a monument of national importance are frequently not readily visible and their identification and the consequent inclusion of a monument in the Schedule (or rejection from it) are based on informed judgement. The criteria governing this informed judgement were published in November 1983. These are framed on two main guiding principles. Firstly, that the Schedule should be representative of the range of known monuments and their associations and thus properly reflect the history of the country.

Secondly, that the best surviving examples of any given class of monument and those with the highest archaeological potential will be worthy of preservation.

At any point in time, informed professional judgement is based on the best contemporary interpretation of the data then currently available. Accordingly, judgements require adjustment through time as archaeological interpretations improve and more data becomes available.

Period: A chronologically, culturally, or technologically definable episode or phase within the overall calendar of human existence from earliest times to the present day. Specific uses of the term will be obvious from the contexts in which they occur.

Pictorial Unit: (PU) Site type. A site type which includes pictorial and photographic representations: prints, drawings, photographs etc.

Placename Evidence: (PN) Site type.

Plot: Area of land within a site, whether or not bounded by fences, walls etc.

Recorded Observation: (RO) Site type. This is the minimum level of active archaeological recording for groundworks and the disturbance of archaeological levels. Usually it involves a qualified archaeologist visiting the site at intervals to simply observe any holes that have been dug, make notes on what is visible, and collect any finds that may come to light during the course of the work. The loss of deposits is very high and the information retrieval very low.

In some cases the information may be derived from a non-specialist eye-witness or the person who made the discovery. The range of information and the quality/accuracy of record will vary, eg mosaics and burials are by nature more noticeable in the ground than coins, pottery, hearths etc.

See also unrecorded finds/observations, and indirect records of finds or observations.

Recorded Stray Find: (RSF) Site type. Finds made by individuals where the circumstances of discovery are known.

Relict Cultural Landscape: One of the three recognised forms in which monuments survive. A relict cultural landscape is a tract of countryside which has survived in a relatively unaltered state since its period of use and which exhibits sufficient traces to allow its structure and arrangement to be wholly or partly interpreted. Relict cultural landscapes as here defined do not simply comprise extensive monuments or groups of monuments, but rather show themselves as repetitive patterns of recurrently associated groups of monuments. The key concept is that the landscape is built up from a number of discrete units (groups of sites) which are complete in themselves but which taken together provide insights into the organisation and structure of the landscape as a whole rather than just their own neighbourhood. These repetitive patterns of recurrently associated groups are almost always linked together, or articulated, by a common feature(s) which may be archaeological, such as a linear earthwork or boundary dyke, or natural, such as a coastline, river-system, escarpment, or valley. The absolute size of a relict landscape is not important as this varies greatly according to the scale of the monuments involved and the degree of repetition preserved. In plan, most relict landscapes will contain gaps between groups of monuments, but these will in many cases be occupied by natural features (rivers, lakes, marshes, etc.). Classified by FORM and VARIANT.

Scheduled Monument: Any monument which is for the time being included in the Schedule maintained by the Secretary of State for the Environment under the terms of the *Ancient Monuments and Archaeological Areas Act 1979* (Ch.46, S1(11)). The power to schedule 'does not apply to any structure which is occupied as a dwelling house by any person other than a person employed as the caretaker thereof or his family' (Ch.46, S2(4)).

Single Monument: One of the three recognised forms in which monuments survive. Single monuments can be identified as separate, self-defining entities which may be classified on the basis of morphological similarities and the interpretation of function. A number of component parts can usually be recognised, some not always present, but all of which are integral to the overall design. Classified by CATEGORY, CLASS, TYPE, and COMPONENT.

Site: An area of land, which may be of any size from a few square metres upwards to include monuments covering hundreds of hectares, within which there has been some recognised observation, 'sight', or window onto the archaeological resource which lies on and/or under the ground.

Site Type: Recognised kinds of encounter or observation of the archaeological resource, eg excavation, evaluation, watching brief, direct observation, indirect observation etc.

Strategy Formulation: Using the results of the Archaeological Assessment and Field Evaluation to provide a positive and viable strategy for dealing with the archaeological resource within the development site. Done in relation to a specific development proposal, taking into account legal responsibilities, practicalities, and cost.

Strategy Implementation: Execution of the archaeological strategy formulated as a result of the evaluation process. Implementation may involve pre-construction works, intra-construction works, and post-construction works.

Systematic Surface Collection Unit: (SSCU) Site type. Fieldwalking in a systematic pattern.

Topographical Survey Unit: (TSU) Site type. This includes all levels of survey from basic sketch plotting through to a full interpretative EDM plot.

Type: Descriptive term applied to identifiable variations within any class of monument. The basis for identifying types is usually the morphology of the monuments themselves, for example differences in ground-plan, construction, or size: eg a post mill is a type within the class of windmill.

Unclassifiable sites, monuments and deposits: Sites which cannot be classified (except at the most general level) because of special circumstances of preservation. Such sites are not unclassifiable because they are poorly preserved (many of these would probably be classifiable to category if nothing else), but because very little is known about their morphology, plan, design, layout, or construction, or because they cannot be seen.

Unclassifiable monuments may occasionally be single monuments, as for example some cropmark sites, or areas of buried land surface, details of which cannot be obtained without destroying it through excavation.

More common, is the presence of unclassifiable deposits within relict landscapes and urban areas. In the former deposits between the individual monuments (inter-stratified deposits) may not be classifiable because they are not fully documented even though they are known to exist. In the latter, the presence of deposits is again known, but without investigation their nature and composition in terms of the classes of monuments represented is quite impossible to gauge: eg buried land surfaces, interstratified urban deposits.

Unclassified sites: Unclassified sites are sites which can be classified but which for some reason have not yet been considered, perhaps because of poor records. These sites cannot be evaluated at the moment, but they can at least be identified for further study with a view to improving the level of information recorded about them.

Unpublished manuscripts: Unpublished manuscripts, eg theses, dissertations, diaries, reports, assessment reports, reports on watching briefs. As archive sources, unpublished manuscripts are to be found in museums, libraries, record offices, private possession.

Unrecorded destruction: This involves the removal of archaeological deposits without any form of observation or recording. Loss is great, the information return nil.

Unrecorded stray find: (USF). Site type. This kind of evidence comprises extant artefacts or objects that have come to light during engineering works or other forms of ground disturbance but which were not recorded at the time by an archaeologist or other interested person. By the time such finds come to the attention of a qualified archaeologist any information about the position of the findspot, who made the find, when, and under what circumstances, may have been lost completely or become garbled. It is often difficult to know how much reliance to place on what is reported.

Typical of sites that fall into this kind of evidence are

those with no contemporary or eye-witness accounts of the discovery and no supporting documentation to allow cross-checking.

Eg objects donated to the Corinium Museum with a minimum of accompanying documentation, in some cases the findspot may be given as a broad geographic area only (eg Ashcroft, Watermoor).

Unsystematic Surface Collection Unit: (USCU). Site type. Fieldwalking for the collection of finds in which objects are related to field or area only.

Urban Areas: One of the three recognised forms in which monuments survive. Urban areas comprise distinctive patterns of spatially and stratigraphically associated single monuments linked by deposits of an essentially unclassifiable nature, such as accumulate as a result of intensive occupation in towns and cities. The term is not used to imply that the remains of a settlement had any particular legal or functional 'urban' status, but only in an archaeological sense to refer to extensive accumulations of interconnected, stratified, settlement debris. Urban areas can be evaluated as successive, period-specific, units. Classified by FORM and VARIANT.

Variant: Term used to describe the main subdivisions identified within forms of relict landscape or urban area. Such subdivisions are usually identified on the basis of morphological traits and variations in the range of single monuments represented.

Visible Feature: (VF) Site type. All features, components and monuments which exist in such a form as to be apparent to the naked eye in the field.

Watching Brief: (WB) Site type. This involves a qualified archaeologist monitoring the excavation of a hole by a building contractor. During the work the archaeologist records any evidence that comes to light by way of plans, sections, and photographs. Watching briefs are mainly used where the nature and extent of the deposits are not fully known, where the holes to be dug are small, or where the extent of damage to archaeologically sensitive deposits is insufficient to warrant a full investigation. During most watching briefs it is difficult to be precise about the alignment of structural features such as walls or ditches which come to light, and any finds are often difficult to relate to the deposits in which they originally lay. Thus although a general picture can be glimpsed, the detail that can be recorded is very much less complete than with a full excavation.

APPENDIX A

Databases and Record Structure

Records and databases

Three records were designed to facilitate the recording and interpretation of data gathered in the course of the Project: Sources Record, Site Record, and Monument Record. Specific fields within individual records are controlled by glossaries, and all three are inter-linked by one or more fields.

Five databases have been compiled as part of the Urban Assessment Project. These represent one of the defined outcomes of the project and in that sense constitute the research archive. They are also the starting point for the ongoing active maintenance of the Archaeological Record for Cirencester and its environs. The content of the five databases can be summarised as follows:

1. A **Sources Record** database which can be sorted and indexed as desired by author, date, title, theme, etc. All information is generated from a master list which currently comprises 1210 sources which is maintained in a DOS environment using dBase III software.

2. A **Site Record** for the study area currently comprising 3473 items (to August 1991). This takes the form of a paper record at present, its maintenance for future use is under consideration.

3. An **Abbreviated Site Record** version of the Site Record (2 above) with a shortened list of fields or tags, known as 'Lords', is available in a DOS environment using dBase III software, as well as a paper record in a variety of sorted outputs.

4. A provisional **Monument Record** for the study area currently comprising 538 items. This takes the form of a paper record at present; its maintenance for future use is under consideration.

5. An **Abbreviated Monument Record** version of the Monument Record (4 above) with a shortened list of fields or tags. This record, known as 'Oval', is available in a DOS environment using dBase III software, as well as a paper record in a variety of sorted outputs.

The five databases are related to a series of **map overlays** whose coverage and scale are listed below:

Coverage			Scale	Quantity
1.	Present topography		1:25000	1
2.	Contour profile		1:25000	1
3.	Geological map		1:25000	1
4.	Hydrology map		1:25000	1
5.	Agricultural and Classification		1:25000	1
6.	Land-use	(urban area)	1:500	30
7.		(study area)	1:2500	43
8.		(study area)	1:25000	1
9.	Constraints	(urban area)	1:500	30
10.		(study area)	1:2500	43
11.	Sites maps	(urban area)	1:500	30
12.		(rural area)	1:2500	43
Monuments:				
13.	Undetermined		1:2500	43
14.	Prehistoric		1:2500	43
15.	Roman		1:2500	43
16.	Early medieval		1:2500	43

Coverage	Scale	Quantity
17. Late medieval	1:2500	43
18. Post-medieval	1:2500	43
19. Modern	1:2500	43
Monuments by Urban Form:		
20. Roman *civitas capital*	1:2500	1
21. Roman provincial capital	1:2500	1
22. Royal/ecclesiastical centre	1:2500	1
23. Medium-sized market town (medieval)	1:2500	1
24. Medium-sized market town (post-medieval)	1:2500	1
Monument Discrimination for the urban area:		
25. Survival	1:2500	1
26. Potential	1:2500	1
27. Group Value (association)	1:2500	1
28. Documentation (archaeological)	1:2500	1
29. Documentation (historical)	1:2500	1
30. Group Value (clustering)	1:2500	1
31. Diversity (features)	1:2500	1
32. Amenity Value	1:2500	1
33. Monument Interest Values (urban area)	1:2500	1
34. Monument Interest Values (rural area)	1:2500	1
Urban Form Discrimination:		
35. Survival	1:2500	1
36. Potential	1:2500	1
37. Documentation (archaeological)	1:2500	1
38. Documentation (historical)	1:2500	1
39. Group Value (clustering)	1:2500	1
40. Diversity (features)	1:2500	1
41. Group Value (association)	1:2500	1
42. Amenity Value	1:2500	1
43. Urban zones of archaeological sensitivity	1:2500	1
44. Rural zones of archaeological sensitivity	1:2500	1

SOURCES RECORD

The following fields have been defined:

Source number
Author
Date
Year
Title
Source
Volume
Pages
Publisher
Place of publication
Edition
Collection
Ref
Type
Consulted
Copy
Subject
Notes

SITE RECORD

The following fields have been defined:

General
- Site record number
- Site location
- Site recognition type
- Date of recognition
- Site description (cross-referenced to the Sources field)

Locational and Background
- Parish (civil)
- Parish (ecclesiastical)
- District
- National Grid Reference
- Map references (1:10000/1:2500/1:500)
- Height (OD)
- Land classification 1945
- Land-use 1990
- Surface geology
- Soils
- Topography
- Aspect
- Area

- Cross Reference
  - NAR number
  - NEI number
  - SAM number
  - OS Record number
  - Glos SMR number
  - Constraints

- Discrimination Criteria
  - Survival
    - Depth of deposits (m)
    - Thickness of deposits (m)
    - Volume of deposits (cubic m)
    - Survival is: poor/medium/good
    - Preservation is: sterilised/wet/dry/robbed out
  - Potential
    - Potential is: poor/medium/high
  - Documentation (archaeological)
    - Quality is: low/medium/high
  - Documentation (historical)
    - Quality is: low/medium/high
  - Diversity (elements)
    - Diversity is: low/medium/high

- Element List
  - Artefacts/material/period general/period specific
  - Contexts/period general/period specific
  - Features/period general/period specific
  - Components/period general/period specific
  - Monuments/period general/period specific

- Sources
  - Source number< >

- Compilation
  - Visitor/organisation
  - Date
  - Record compiler
  - Date

The Cirencester Archaeological Record is, as far as possible, compatible with the Gloucestershire County Council's Sites and Monuments Record (1991). Some of the fields identified above are controlled by glossaries designed by the Gloucester record.

The site numbers allocated by Gloucester Sites and Monuments Record for the Cirencester database begin at 50,000 and are mapped at a scale of 1:500 for the urban area and 1:2500 for rural areas with appropriate symbols.

MONUMENT RECORD

Monument Records have some sections in common with the Site Records described above. The full list of fields on the Monument Record is as follows:

- General
  - Monument Record Number

- Locational
  - Name
  - Parish (civil)
  - Parish (ecclesiastical)
  - District
  - County
  - National Grid Reference (centred on)
  - Map references (1:10000/1:2500/1:500)

- Background
  - Land classification 1945
  - Land-use 1990
  - Height (OD)
  - Surface geology
  - Soil
  - Topography
  - Aspect
  - Owner(s)
  - Occupier(s)

- Cross Reference
  - NAR number
  - SAM number
  - Glos SMR number
  - Constraints

- Archaeological Classification
  - Category
  - Class
  - Type
  - Descriptor
  - Components
  - Period general
  - Period specific
  - Site references

- Description
  - [Free text]

- Characterisation Criteria
  - Currency
  - Rarity
  - Diversity
  - Representativity
  - CIV

- Discrimination Criteria
  - Survival
    - Depth (m)
    - Thickness (m)
    - Preservation is: sterilised/wet/dry/robbed out
    - Volume of deposits (cubic m)
    - % survival
    - Survival is: poor/medium/good
    - Score
  - Potential
    - Potential is: low/medium/high
    - Score
  - Group Value (association)
    - Associated monuments
    - Association is: low/medium/high
    - Score
  - Documentation (archaeological)
    - Documentation is: poor/medium/good
    - Score
  - Documentation (historical)
    - Documentation is: poor/medium/good
    - Score

Figure 59
Sites recorded to the south of The Avenue

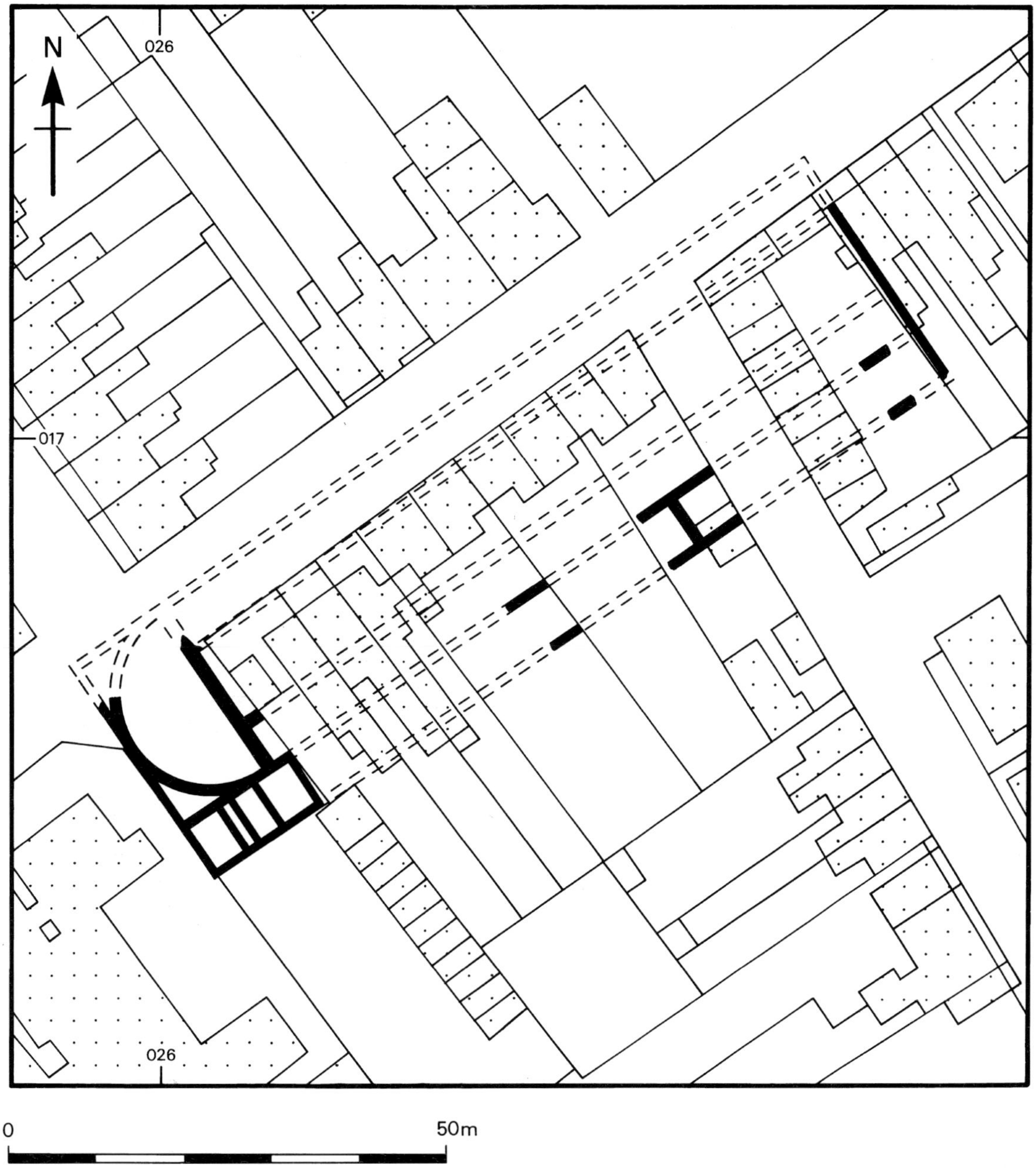

Figure 60
Defining the monument : the *basilica*

Group Value (clustering)
Group value is: low/medium/high
Score
Diversity (features)
Diversity is: low/medium/high
Score
Amenity Value
Amenity value is: low/medium/high
Score

Value
MIV

Management Appraisal Criteria
Condition
Form
State is: unknown/bad/medium/good
Stability is: unknown/stable/unstable/deteriorating
Fragility
Comment
Vulnerability
Comment
Conservation value
Conservation value is: zero/low/medium/high/very high
Comment

Sources
Source number < >

Compilation
Visitor/organisation
Date
Record compiler
Date

Single monuments were allocated numbers in sequence from 54000, and mapped at 1:2500, by period.

FROM SITES TO MONUMENT

The following provides a summary of the process leading to monument recognition. The record structure for each stage is as outlined above, but is summarised for the purposes of this worked example.

Site recording

The gathering of data from a number of sources forms the basis for the identification and recording of specific site types, with a mapped element to record the physical extent of each site (Figure 59).

Site Record 50022
Antiquarian excavation (AE) in 1897–8 by W J Cripps revealed walls, floors, pottery, coins etc.
Source: Cripps 1898a, 1898b, with plans and photographs; Haverfield 1920.

Site Record 50023
Modern excavation (ME) in 1962, directed by J S Wacher, revealed pits, walls, floors, postholes etc and confirmed the position of levels recorded by Cripps in 1897–8.
Source: Wacher 1962; excavation archive deposited in the Corinium Museum.

Site Record 50024
Unrecorded stray find (USF), found in 1905, consisting of Roman coins.
Source: Corinium Museum accession register.

Site Record 50035
Recorded stray find (RSF), *c*1890, of a Corinthian capital recorded by Cripps 'on the west wall of Mr Crook's'.
Source: Cripps 1898a, marked on plan.

Site Record 50327
Cartographic depiction (CD), 1875 Ordnance Survey plan, depicts 'Capital (found here)'.
Source: 1875 OS map, at 1:500.

Site Record 50781
Antiquarian excavation (AE), in 1897–8, by W J Cripps, who describes a number of walls which were 'traced' in the gardens of neighbouring properties.
Source: Cripps 1898a.

Site Record 51384
Unrecorded stray find (USF), of an 'altar found to the east of the basilica in a drain'. Date and exact location of find are unknown, and the site record therefore is plotted with the appropriate symbol.
Source: Corinium Museum Accession A343.

Site Record 51422
Antiquarian excavations (AE), in 1897–8, by W J Cripps to trace walls (see Site Record 50781 for comparable activity to the west of Chester Street).
Source: Cripps 1898a.

Site Record 53622
Cartographic depiction (CD), recording 'Site of basilica'. Plotted by F W Taylor, acting as surveyor for Wilfred Cripps. The plan originally formed part of the displays in Cripps' museum in The Mead.
Source: Corinium Museum.

Monument definition

With one or more Site Records to hand, the definition and description of individual monuments can be facilitated, and a Monument Record form compiled for each. Within this particular example, the Site Records described briefly above can be used in total or in part to define the Roman *basilica* (54012; Figure 60). The interpretation of the basic data contained within the Site Record enables the information to be ascribed to a particular monument. The hierarchy and structure created within the two records provides flexibility for the addition of new site records and subsequent reassessment and enhancement of the monument description.

As a single monument defined by the parameters set out within the Monuments Protection Programme, the Roman *basilica* comprised an aisled hall approximately 85m long and 26m wide, with an apsidal end. Finds of architectural fragments, veneers, stonework etc would suggest an elaborate structure (see Chapter 8 for fuller description).

APPENDIX B

List of defined monuments in the study area

The following lists summarise the monuments identified as part of the Cirencester Urban Assessment project up to October 1991. Further monuments have been identified since and details have been added to the Monument Record. Accordingly these lists should be regarded as interim summaries.

The sections are arranged chronologically, with subdivision according to location within the urban form or environs.

The three columns within each section are:
1) Monument Record Number, within the range 54000–54537
2) Summary location/provenance in the modern landscape
3) Single monument class designation as defined within MPP (Monuments Protection Programme)

Prehistoric monuments

Figure 15.

54002	South of Wellhill Plantation	settlement (undated)
54003	South of Wellhill Plantation	round barrow
54004	South of Wellhill Plantation	settlement (undated)
54008	Baunton	settlement (undated)
54010	Baunton	settlement (undated)
54015	Baunton	settlement (undated)
54016	Baunton	settlement (undated)
54017	Baunton	trackway (prehistoric)
54018	Field at The Beeches	settlement (undated)
54019	Beeches Nursery Field	settlement (dated)
54022	East of Siddington House	settlement (undated)
54023	East of Siddington House	trackway (prehistoric)
54028	East of Ashton Road	settlement (undated)
54029	East of Ashton Road	trackway (prehistoric)
54030	Siddington	settlement (undated)
54031	Siddington	trackway (prehistoric)
54032	Preston	settlement
54040	Preston	settlement (undated)
54079	Long Barrow, The Querns	?long barrow
54133	Preston	ring ditch
54134	Preston	ring ditch
54135	Preston	ring ditch
54136	Preston	ring ditch
54137	Preston	ring ditch
54152	Preston	ring ditch
54153	Siddington	ring ditch
54191	West of Dryleaze Farm	trackway (prehistoric)
54437	Stratton Field	round barrow
54538	Baunton	ring ditch
54539	Cirencester	ring ditch
54540	Preston	ring ditch

54541	Siddington	ring ditch
54542	Siddington	ring ditch
54543	Siddington	ring ditch
54544	Siddington	ring ditch
54545	Siddington	ring ditch
54546	Siddington	ring ditch

Pre-urban Romano-British monuments

Figure 16.

54011	Tower Street	fort (Roman)
54046	Lewis Lane/The Avenue	street (Romano-British)
54414	Lewis Lane/The Avenue	*vicus*

Monuments within the urban form defined as the Roman *Civitas Capital*

Figure 18.

54001	Dyer Court	street (Romano-British)
54006	Police Station	street (Romano-British)
54007	Police Station	street (Romano-British)
54009	Chester Lodge	*forum*
54012	Watermoor House	*basilica*
54013	Leaholme Gardens	street (Romano-British)
54014	17 The Avenue	street (Romano-British)
54024	Cirencester	town wall (Romano-British)
54027	Victoria Road	street (Romano-British)
54033	Querns Lane House	street (Romano-British)
54034	Grammar School Playing Field	street (Romano-British)
54035	Cotswold Mill	street (Romano-British)
54036	Trinity Church Gates	street (Romano-British)
54037	Ashcroft Road	street (Romano-British)
54038	Victoria Road	street (Romano-British)
54039	Dyer Street	street (Romano-British)
54047	Purley Avenue	street (Romano-British)
54048	Victoria Road	street (Romano-British)
54050	Telephone Exchange	street (Romano-British)
54051	Bingham Hall	street (Romano-British)
54052	St John's Church	street (Romano-British)
54092	Abbey Grounds	street (Romano-British)
54093	Gaumont Cinema	street (Romano-British)
54094	Chester Street	shops
54095	Chester Street	street (Romano-British)
54113	The Abbey	courtyard house
54114	The Abbey	courtyard house
54115	41-43 Dollar Street	theatre
54116	The Avenue, Tower Street Nursery	street (Romano-British)
54117	Watermoor School	street (Romano-British)
54120	Locks Timber Yard	street (Romano-British)
54121	West Market Place	street (Romano-British)
54122	Price's Row, Watermoor Road	street (Romano-British)
54123	Price's Row, Watermoor Road	shops
54124	Old Railway Line, Sheep Street	street (Romano-British)
54128	Querns Hill	street (Romano-British)
54130	Mycalex	courtyard house
54132	Parsonage Field	street (Romano-British)
54149	Orchard House, London Road	street (Romano-British)
54236	South of Lewis Lane	street (Romano-British)
54237	West side of Watermoor Road	street (Romano-British)
54239	Watermoor Road	street (Romano-British)
54240	Regal Cinema	street (Romano-British)
54241	Purley Road	street (Romano-British)

54242	Cotswold Mill	street (Romano-British)
54294	Victoria Road	street (Romano-British)
54295	Victoria Road	street (Romano-British)
54296	Watermoor	street (Romano-British)
54299	Dyer Street	street (Romano-British)
54300	Parallel to Cricklade St	street (Romano-British)
54320	3-9 Church Street	street (Romano-British)
54321	Gosditch Street	street (Romano-British)
54322	30 Lewis Lane	street (Romano-British)
54323	Watermoor Road	street (Romano-British)
54324	Ashcroft Road	street (Romano-British)
54325	South of Dairy, Ashcroft Road	street (Romano-British)
54326	St Peter's Road	street (Romano-British)
54327	Brewery Car Park	street (Romano-British)
54328	5-9 Ashcroft Road	street (Romano-British)
54329	Bingham Hall	street (Romano-British)
54330	28 Church Street	street (Romano-British)
54331	62 Victoria Road	street (Romano-British)
54332	Garden of 45-61 Chester Street	street (Romano-British)
54333	19-23 Church Street	street (Romano-British)
54334	Redlands, Queen Street	street (Romano-British)
54335	97 Victoria Road	street (Romano-British)
54336	St Michael's Field	street (Romano-British)
54357	St Michael's Field	street (Romano-British)
54359	Victoria Road	street (Romano-British)
54370	Brewery Car Park	street (Romano-British)
54373	33 Sheep Street	street (Romano-British)
54375	St Michael's Field	street (Romano-British)
54412	Leaholme Gardens	*macellum*
54413	Leaholme Gardens	shops
54416	Dyer Street	courtyard house
54419	Beeches Road	winged-corridor house
54421	The Firs	winged-corridor house
54423	Admiral's Walk	shops
54424	The Avenue	courtyard house
54433	Abbey Car Park	street (Romano-British)
54434	Victoria Road	street (Romano-British)
54436	Dyer Court House	street (Romano-British)

Monuments within the urban form defined as the Roman Provincial Capital

The monuments for this form are the same as for the *civitas capital* listed above.

Romano-British monuments in the environs of the urban forms Roman *Civitas Capital* and Roman Provincial Capital

Figure 26.

54020	Fosse Way	road (Romano-British)
54021	Kingshill Lane	road (Romano-British)
54025	Verulamium Gate	bridge
54026	Verulamium Gate	?aqueduct
54041	Preston	settlement
54042	Querns Kitchen Garden	quarry (Romano-British)
54044	Querns Kitchen Garden	road (Romano-British)
54045	Amphitheatre	amphitheatre
54057	The Querns/Bath Gate	cemetery (Romano-British)
54062	Kingsmeadow	mausoleum
54089	Tar Barrow	?Roman barrow
54118	Bath Gate	road (Romano-British)
54119	Bath Gate	quarry
54125	Querns Maternity Hospital	road (Romano-British)
54126	Phoenix Way	road (Romano-British)
54138	Sheep Dip, Cirencester	farmstead

54139	Sheep Dip, Cirencester	field system
54140	Sheep Dip, Cirencester	trackways
54143	Whiteway	road (Romano-British)
54144	Agricultural College	villa
54159	Phoenix Way	road (Romano-British)
54164	Worms Farm	settlement
54166	SW of Sandy Lane Farm	settlement
54167	North of The Barton	settlement
54168	SE of Chesterton Farm	settlement
54188	Ambulance Station, The Querns	quarry
54189	Baunton Downs	settlement
54190	South of Clark's Lane	settlement
54217	Grismond's Tower	?Roman barrow
54219	Tar Barrow (one of)	?Roman barrow
54220	Tar Barrow	?Roman barrow
54231	Abbey Road Garages	road (Romano-British)
54238	Gloucester Street	road (Romano-British)
54292	Ermin Street	road (Romano-British)
54297	Gloucester Street	road (Romano-British)
54371	Bowling Green Pits	quarry
54372	Kingsmeadow	cemetery (Romano-British)
54431	Verulamium Gate	cemetery (Romano-British)
54435	Gloucester Gate	cemetery (Romano-British)

Early medieval monuments within the urban form defined as the Royal/Ecclesiastical Centre

Figure 31.

54090	The Abbey (1)	pre-conquest church
54420	The Barton	cemetery
54474	The Abbey (2)	pre-conquest church

Early medieval monuments in the environs of the urban form Royal/Ecclesiastical Centre

Figure 33.

54146	Preston	pre-Conquest church
54247	Stratton	mill
54374	Stratton	mill
54377	Cirencester	mill
54378	Cirencester	mill
54379	Cirencester	mill
54420	The Barton	cemetery
54438	Upper Siddington	pre-Conquest church
54439	Lower Siddington	pre-Conquest church
54440	Stratton	pre-Conquest church
54422	Siddington St Peter	mill
54425	Siddington St Mary	mill

Monuments within the urban form defined as the Medium-Sized Market Town (Medieval)

Figure 34.

54000	Archebalds, Dyer Street	town house (medieval)
54053	St John the Baptist	parochial church
54055	Gumstool Brook, Dollar St	ducking stool
54073	Dyer Street	standing cross
54074	Churchyard Cross	standing cross
54076	St John's Hospital	hospital
54077	Lewis Lane/Querns Lane	standing cross
54078	Tetbury Road/Park Lane/Castle St	standing cross
54080	St Cecilia's, Cecily Hill	parochial church
54081	South porch of Parish Church	guildhall

54082	Market Place	prison
54083	Dyer Street, Pig Cross	standing cross
54084	High Cross	standing cross
54086	Mill, Dollar St	watermill (medieval)
54087	St Mary's Abbey	monastery for men
54088	The Market Place	stocks
54096	Weavers' Hall, Thomas Street	hospital
54097	Butcher Row	street (medieval)
54098	Thomas Street	street (medieval)
54099	Coxwell Street	street (medieval)
54100	Silver Street	street (medieval)
54101	Black Jack Street	street (medieval)
54102	Cecily Hill	street (medieval)
54103	St Lawrence's Church	parochial church
54104	Dyer Street	street (medieval)
54105	Gloucester Street	street (medieval)
54108	Dollar Street	street (medieval)
54109	Cricklade Street	street (medieval)
54110	Gosditch Street	street (medieval)
54111	The Market Place	market place
54145	'Bottehall'	exchange
54151	Shoe Lane	street (medieval)
54160	St John's Bridge	bridge
54161	Park Street	motte and bailey castle
54169	Walfrid Marescal's ford	ford
54170	Swyne Bridge	bridge
54179	St Lawrence's Hospital	almshouses
54186	Langley Mill	watermill (medieval)
54187	New Mill	watermill (medieval)
54202	de Pirie, Dyer Street	town house (medieval)
54207	Chesterton House	town house (medieval)
54215	The West Market Place	market place
54243	St Lawrence's Hospital	hospital
54248	Sheep Street	street (medieval)
54250	Barton Mill	watermill (medieval)
54251	St Clements Bridge	bridge
54252	Black Jack Street	courthouse
54254	New Bridge	bridge
54255	Church Tavern, Market Place	tavern
54257	St Lawrence's Chapel	parochial chapel
54266	St Cecilia's, Cecily Hill	parochial chapel
54267	Lewis Lane	street (medieval)
54268	Querns Lane	street (medieval)
54269	Spitalgate	street (medieval)
54273	Dakker Gate Inn	inn
54275	School, Park Lane	school
54291	Monmouth House	town house (medieval)
54293	Barton Farm	grange
54314	'Gildenbrigge'	bridge
54418	Castle Street	street (medieval)
54426	Park Lane	street (medieval)
54475	New Farm	farmstead
54476	More's Place	farmstead
54477	'Le Beches'	farmstead
54478	Dyer Street	school
54479	The Cage, Market Place	lock-up
54480	Braine's Mill	watermill (medieval)
54481	Cecily Hill	watermill (medieval)

Medieval monuments in the environs of the urban form Medium-Sized Market Town (Medieval)

Figure 41.

54075	St Mary's, Siddington	parochial church
54091	Siddington	moated site
54112	Deer Park, Cirencester	deer park
54173	Siddington Barn	barn
54185	St Peter's, Stratton	parochial church
54216	St Peter's, Siddington	parochial church
54249	Chesterton Woods	wood
54253	Whiteway	road (medieval)
54256	Crowthorne, Stratton	moot
54259	St Mary Magdalene, Baunton	parochial chapel
54369	Whiteway View	watermill
54441	Norcote	parochial chapel
54442	Norcote	deserted village
54443	Upper Siddington	deserted village
54444	All Saints, Preston	parochial church
54446	Sheep Street	archery butts
54451	The Crundles	warren
54515	Welsh Way	road (medieval)
54517	Cirencester-Cheltenham	road (medieval)
54519	Witpit Copse	deserted farmstead

Monuments within the urban sub-form defined as the Medium-Sized Market Town (Post-Medieval)

Figure 43.

54005	Congregational Church	non-conformist chapel
54043	The Querns	kitchen garden
54049	Trinity Road	workhouse
54054	Brunel Station	railway station
54056	Abbey House (1)	town house (post-medieval)
54058	Canal Feeder, Hammond Way	canal
54059	Cirencester Park	kitchen garden
54060	Chapel, Sheep Street	non-conformist chapel
54061	Great Western Railway	railway
54063	Cirencester House	town house (post-medieval)
54064	Barton House	battery
54065	Cricklade Way	battery
54066	Oakley House	town house (post-medieval)
54067	Gloucester Street	battery
54068	Barton Mill	battery
54069	Spitalgate	fieldworks
54070	Ram Inn, Market Place	inn
54071	Museum, Tetbury Road	museum
54072	Cirencester Park	park
54085	Abbey House (2)	town house (post-medieval)
54106	Dollar Street	bridge
54107	Dollar Street	bridge
54127	Querns Hill	culvert
54141	Wilts and Dorset Bank	bank
54150	The Nags Head	public house
54155	26 Gloucester Street	cottage
54156	Thames & Severn Canal	canal
54162	19 Park Street	cottages
54171	Gloucester Street	theatre
54172	Sun Inn	public house
54174	Lewis Lane	waterworks
54175	Bowly's Brewery	brewery
54177	Market Place, Public Pump	public pump
54180	Ashcroft House	urban villa
54181	Chesterton House	urban villa

54182	The Querns	urban villa
54183	Watermoor House	urban villa
54184	Chesterton Museum	museum
54192	Corn Hall	exchange
54193	The Gas House	gasworks
54194	Park Street	war defences
54195	Temperance Hall, Thomas Street	non-conformist chapel
54196	The Fleece Hotel, Dyer Street	hotel
54197	Thomas Street	exchange
54198	Castle Street, Post Office	post office
54199	Bishop Blaize	public house
54200	Three Horseshoes	public house
54201	Bingham Library	library
54203	Unitarian Church, Gosditch Street	non-conformist chapel
54204	Waggon & Horses Inn	public house
54205	Loyal Volunteer	public house
54206	Great Western Inn	public house
54208	Watermoor Station	railway station
54209	Park Lane/Thomas Street	bridge
54210	Cottage Hospital, Sheep St	hospital
54211	Barracks & Cecily Hill	armoury
54212	MSWJ Railway	railway
54213	Bell Hotel	hotel
54214	Town Hall (Parish Church)	town hall
54222	Abbey Grounds	culvert
54223	Watermoor Church	parochial chapel
54224	Watermoor Church Hall	church hall
54225	King's Head Hotel, Market Place	hotel
54226	Gaumont Cinema, London Road	cinema
54227	Police Station, Park Lane	police station
54228	Coles Mill, Lewis Lane	mill
54229	Wesleyan Chapel	non-conformist chapel
54230	Catholic Chapel	non-conformist chapel
54233	Three Compasses Inn	public house
54235	White Lion	public house
54245	Ice House, Abbey Grounds	icehouse
54258	St Lawrence's Almshouses	almshouses
54261	Baptist Chapel, Coxwell Street	non-conformist chapel
54262	Chapel, Park Street	non-conformist chapel
54263	Primitive Methodist Chapel	non-conformist chapel
54264	Presbyterian Chapel	non-conformist chapel
54265	Friends Meeting House	non-conformist chapel
54270	Stocks, Market Place	stocks
54271	Folly, Castle Street	folly
54272	Crown Inn	public house
54273	Swan Inn	hotel
54276	Hodden House, Dollar Street	almshouses
54277	Querns Lane, Almshouses	almshouses
54278	Lewis Lane, Almshouses	almshouses
54279	Almshouses, Gloucester Street	almshouses
54280	Almshouses, Watermoor Road	almshouses
54281	Lloyds Bank	bank
54282	Gloucestershire Banking Co	bank
54283	Savings Bank, Park Lane	bank
54284	Post Office, Black Jack Street	post office
54285	Subscription Library/Reading Room	library
54286	Swimming Baths	swimming baths
54287	Armoury Hospital, Silver Street	hospital
54288	Armoury Hospital, Dollar Street	hospital
54289	Cirencester Workhouse	lock-up
54290	Burial Ground, Watermoor Road	burial ground
54298	Pest House, Watermoor Churchyard	pest house
54302	Royal Oak Inn	public house

54303	Gloucester Street Bridge	bridge
54304	Gooseacre Bridge, Gooseacre Lane	bridge
54305	95 Gloucester Street	smithy
54306	Nelson Inn	public house
54307	Anchor Inn	public house
54308	187 Gloucester Street, at rear	smithy
54309	Duke of York Inn	public house
54310	Gloucester/Dollar/Spitalgate	post box
54311	4-6 Thomas Street, Almshouses	almshouses
54312	Red Lion Inn	public house
54313	St John's Almshouses	almshouses
54315	Kings Arms	public house
54316	Burial Ground, Thomas Street	burial ground
54317	Dolphin Inn	public house
54318	Smithy, Park Street	smithy
54319	Phoenix Public House	public house
54337	Talbot Inn	public house
54338	County Junior School, Lewis Lane	school
54340	Flagstaff	flagstaff
54341	Smithy, Cricklade Street	smithy
54342	Fox Inn	public house
54343	Wheatsheaf Inn	public house
54344	Smithy, Ashcroft Road	smithy
54345	Iron Works, Ashcroft Road	iron works
54346	Smithy, Querns Lane	smithy
54347	Cecily Hill	road
54348	Kings Head Tap	public house
54349	Bear Inn	public house
54350	Memorial Hospital	air-raid shelter
54351	London Road	machine-gun nest
54352	Post Box, Cricklade/Lewis Lane	post box
54353	Cotswold Brewery	brewery
54354	Cotswold Foundry	iron works
54355	Post Box, Dyer Street	post box
54356	Ship Inn	public house
54358	St John's Hospital	passage
54360	Cotswold Avenue	obelisk
54361	Twelve Bells	public house
54362	Cotswold Factory	factory
54363	Watermoor Infants School	school
54364	Smithy, 29 Church Street	smithy
54365	Queens Head	public house
54376	Tetbury Road	machine-gun nest
54380	Cripps Bank	bank
54381	Bowly's Bank	bank
54384	Police Station, Park Lane	court house
54385	South Porch, St John's Church	court house
54386	Fishponds, Cirencester	fishponds
54387	Infectious Diseases Hospital	hospital
54389	The White Hart	public house
54391	Market Hall	market hall
54394	Cricklade Street	mission room
54395	Cricklade Street	mission room
54396	Baptist Chapel, Coxwell Street	non-conformist chapel
54397	The Waterloo	passage
54398	The Flying Dutchman	public house
54399	Swimming Baths Pump	pump
54400	Pumping Station, Lewis Lane	pumping station
54402	Cirencester Park	rifle range
54404	Upper School Victoria Road	school
54405	Powell's School, Gloucester St	school
54406	Powell School, Watermoor	school
54407	British School, Sheep Street	school

54408	Infants School, Thomas Street	school
54409	Sunday School, Cricklade Street	school
54410	Coxwell Street	sewer
54411	Cattle Market	cattle market
54415	Market Place	battery
54417	Corn Hall Buildings	concert hall
54428	Grismonds Tower	icehouse
54429	Old Bull Inn	public house
54430	Great Western Railway	railway yard
54482	Cripps Museum, The Mead	museum
54483	Corinium Museum, Park Street	museum
54484	Police Station, Gloucester St	police station
54485	Mr Webb's School, Dyer Street	school
54486	Mr Webb's School, Coxwell St	school
54487	Watermoor National School	school
54488	School of Art, Dyer Street	school
54489	Girl's High School, The Avenue	school
54490	Mechanics Institute	library
54491	Subscription Library, Dyer St	library
54492	Bingham Hall	concert hall
54493	Bingham Hall	rifle range
54494	Picture House	cinema
54495	The Regal, Lewis Lane	cinema
54496	The Swan	public house
54497	The Black Horse	public house
54498	Phoenix Inn	public house
54499	Hole in the Wall	public house
54500	The Barley Mow	public house
54501	Working Men's Club	men's club
54502	Globe Temperance Hotel	hotel
54503	Temperance Coffee House	coffee house
54504	Cotswold Coffee Tavern	coffee house
54508	Brewery, Cricklade Street	air-raid shelter
54520	St Peter, Roman Catholic Church	non-conformist chapel

Post-Medieval monuments in the environs of the urban sub-form Medium-Sized Market Town (Post-Medieval)

Figure 49.

54061	Great Western Railway	railway
54072	Cirencester Park	park
54129	Royal Agricultural College	quarry
54142	Hare Bushes Quarry	quarry
54147	Royal Agricultural College	college
54148	Cranhams Lane	culvert
54156	Thames & Severn Canal	canal
54178	Pit	quarry
54212	MSWJ Railway	railway
54218	Corner of Stratton Heights	windmill
54232	Dyer St/Grove Lane	toll booth
54234	Tetbury Rd/Stroud Rd	toll booth
54260	Chesterton Cemetery	urban cemetery
54274	Kingshill Quarries	quarry
54301	Chesterton	quarry
54339	East of Love Lane	quarry
54347	Cecily Hill-Park Corner	road
54366	Barton Gravel Pit	quarry
54367	Trinity Road	quarry
54368	Archery House	quarry
54383	Siddington	brickworks
54388	Greyhound Inn, Siddington	inn
54390	Stratton Maltings	maltings
54392	Stratton Mill	watermill

54393	Stratton Mill	watermill
54401	Cirencester Park	reservoir
54403	Baunton	rifle range
54432	Baunton Pumping Station	pumping station
54445	St Mary Magdalene, Baunton	parochial church
54447	Siddington	maltings
54448	Siddington	water-meadows
54449	Village Farm, Preston	farmstead
54450	Church Farm, Preston	farmstead
54453	Dilley's Farm, Baunton	farmstead
54454	Merrillhill Farm, Preston	farmstead
54455	Norcote Farm, Preston	farmstead
54456	St Augustine's Farm, Preston	farmstead
54457	Ermin Farm, Preston	farmstead
54458	Bowling Green Farm	farmstead
54459	Whiteway Farm	farmstead
54460	Cranhams Farm	farmstead
54461	Chesterton Farm	farmstead
54462	Manor Farm, Baunton	farmstead
54463	Church Farm, Siddington	farmstead
54464	Barton Farm, Siddington	farmstead
54465	Plummer's Farm, Siddington	farmstead
54466	Worm's Farm, Siddington	farmstead
54467	Sandy Lane Farm, Siddington	farmstead
54468	Furzen Leaze, Siddington	farmstead
54469	North Furzen Leaze Farm	farmstead
54470	Bowley's Farm, Siddington	farmstead
54471	Dryleaze Farm, Siddington	farmstead
54472	Preston Forty Farm, Preston	farmstead
54473	New Farm, Cirencester	farmstead
54505	Baunton	water-meadows
54506	Preston	water-meadows
54507	Whiteway realignment	road
54509	Preston Place, Preston	vicarage
54510	School, Siddington	school
54511	School, Baunton	school
54512	Preston Mill	watermill
54513	Salutation Gate	tool booth
54514	Siddington	?windmill
54516	Cirencester-Stroud	road
54521	Siddington Field Farm	farmstead
54522	College Farm	farmstead
54523	Siddington Mill	watermill
54524	Cheltenham Road	limekiln
54525	Stratton	quarry
54526	Preston	school
54527	Stratton	school
54528	Ivy Lodge	farmstead
54529	Cirencester-Fairford	road
54530	Cirencester-Gloucester	road
54531	Cirencester-Burford	road
54532	Cirencester-Stow	road
54533	Cirencester-Swindon	road
54534	Cirencester-Tetbury	road
54535	Cirencester-Cheltenham	road
54536	Cirencester-Stroud	road
54537	Cirencester	water-meadows

Undated

54154	Cirencester	trackway
54157	Cirencester	trackways
54244	Kingsmeadow	causeway

APPENDIX C

Research objectives

A good deal is already known about the history and archaeology of Cirencester, but there is still much to find out. Inevitably, the kind of analysis reported here raises as many questions as it solves. These new questions help to set the research agenda for the next phase of studies, focusing attention on gaps in knowledge and prompting interest in previously neglected issues.

The primary role of a set of defined research objectives is to assist in the decision-making process by promoting the deployment of resources towards useful ends and by directing appropriate courses of action when selections have to be made. There is no intention to stifle innovative research or to suggest that the proposals made are in any sense exclusive of other work being undertaken. Chance discoveries and serendipitously prompted inquiries will always have a key role to play in archaeological research as in other lines of scientific investigation. These must be encouraged, particularly from those gifted enough to operate with good effect by developing out from the framework proposed here into spheres presently undreamed of.

A basic set of research objectives for endeavours in and around Cirencester was published in 1990 (Darvill 1990, 9). These were preliminary proposals pending the completion of the Cirencester Urban Assessment Project and have proved useful in focusing interest on important topics during the last 12–18 months. The proposals relating to Cirencester's past which can now be added to the set of objectives follow from reflecting on the results of the CUA Project.

As a major historic town, the archaeological resource of Cirencester also contributes to a broader vision of archaeological and historic studies which extends at least as far as the rest of Britain and the near Continent if not further afield as well. Thus any defined research objectives relevant to what goes on in Cirencester must take account of wider interests and issues. English Heritage have published a national framework for future research strategies (Wainwright 1991) which is derived from extensive consultations with interested parties. Thus in setting out the main headings below, an attempt has been made to translate some of these nationally defined spheres of interest into topics that can be addressed locally.

The list of topics which follow have been arranged under a series of thematic, period, and locational headings. The topics range from the most general to the highly specific, from the internationally relevant to the highly parochial. Some topics could be answered by one timely and well-resourced and well-executed investigation, others will require the careful assembly of data from numerous observations spread over several years. Some are topics that could be addressed without further intervention with the archaeological resource itself, some will only be resolved if and when there are opportunities for large-scale excavations.

(1) Urban process

Cirencester is one of relatively few urban areas in Britain with a large number of successive urban forms. The migration of the focus of settlement between forms provides an interesting phenomenon for explanation as well as a process that has promoted preservation. The following themes and questions may be recognised:

Briton into Roman

* What is the relationship to Bagendon and the nature and extent of later prehistoric settlement in the area?
* What was the origin of the town, was it planted or was there organic growth? Was there, for example, a late Iron Age settlement at the river crossing contemporary with the Bagendon oppidum?
* Are we correct in our interpretation of the extra-mural occupation as a *vicus*? What was its extent and relationship with Bagendon?
* What was the fate of the *vicus* and its inhabitants?
* What was the road pattern at the time of the construction of the first town?
* What was the environment, topography and hydrology of the Middle Churn valley during the early Roman period?

Roman

* When did Roman military occupation commence and finish?
* How did the dark soils near the town walls develop?
* Building the Roman power-base: What happened to the people and monuments of Cirencester in the third century AD?

The medieval periods

* What was life in Cirencester like between the fifth and the eighth centuries?
* What form did urban occupation take?
* Was settlement continuous or were there breaks in occupation?
* What effect did the church have on the development of the town?
* What are the origins of St Cecilia's and St Lawrences's?
* What was the political organisation of the town?
* Why did the later town develop to the north of Lewis Lane?
* How did the town grow?
* What was the role of Cecily Hill?
* When and why did the Gloucester Road suburbs develop?

(2) The elements of urban form

Cirencester is an extensive urban area. Some of its main characteristics and monuments are known, but by no means all. The following questions and issues could be addressed:

Roman Towns

* After the town was established, how long did it take for the principal elements to be established?
* Where are the 'missing' public buildings such as baths and temples?
* Where is the Governor's palace?
* What evidence is there for change within the urban area in the third and fourth centuries?
* What happened to the defences in the third century? What was the sequence of construction and modification?
* The nature, extent, evolution and status of the cemeteries
* How did the aqueduct serve the town?
* Topographic analysis of the town plan

Royal/Ecclesiastical Centre

* Interpretation of the Pre-Conquest church site
* What is the range of structures present?
* Where were the cemeteries?
* Defended places and the status of the settlement
* Role of the Roman road system in determining layout

Medium-Sized Market Town

* Topographical analysis of the town plan
* Where was the castle referred to in documentary sources?
* Property and parish boundaries and ownership patterns
* Markets and fairs in and around Cirencester
* Monastery and town
* Society and space, development of industrial quarters, subdivision of burgage plots
* Street design
* Use of Roman town wall as defence and customs boundary
* Medieval industry
* Changes in water supply
* Demography and disease
* Use of the extra-mural zone
* Changing uses of materials
* Timber buildings in the Cirencester area
* The early use of stone in medieval buildings

Post-Medieval Town

* Transport and communications
* Development of planned Victorian suburbs
* Post-medieval industry
* Public space
* Surveys of building interiors
* Cirencester Park
* Estates and gardens
* Theatre and entertainment
* Non-Conformism
* Charity, philanthropy and education
* Inns
* The Civil War
* The Second World War defences
* Urban overcrowding and infill
* Urban divisions, economic and cultural
* Allotments
* Disease and sanitation

(3) Relationships with the hinterland

The area around Cirencester is relatively free of development at the present time, although the immediate hinterland will experience significant development pressure in the next few years. The following general questions may be posed:

* What was the communication and transport pattern around the town like in Roman and later times? eg development of saltways and drovers' routes, canals, railways
* Where were the Roman towns getting their pottery, stone, tiles and other essential materials from?
* What was the place of Cirencester in local, regional and long-distance trade from Roman to medieval times?
* What was the Roman agricultural base?
* Anglo-Saxon land ownership and administration
* What was the medieval agricultural base? eg role of woodland, common pasture
* Plan and use of the medieval fieldsystems around Cirencester
* Plan and use of the post-medieval fieldsystems around Cirencester
* Farmsteads and agricultural settlements in the hinterland
* Role of early park landscapes
* The changing ecclesiastical needs of the rural community
* What was the settlement pattern around Cirencester? eg village plan analysis

(4) Environment and landscape

The Cirencester region has the potential to allow detailed environmental studies and analysis of the physical evolution and development of the countryside. The peat deposits contained in the valley of the River Churn will be important sources of evidence in this connection.

* Pollen analysis of available peat deposits
* Soil analysis
* Phosphate and heavy metal analysis
* Patterns of exploitation and land-use from archaeological sources
* Historical records of land-use, eg history of enclosure, woodland management

(5) Archaeological materials

The continuing archaeological exploration and investigation of archaeological deposits in Cirencester requires its own fields of research endeavour to enable value-for-money deployment of time and resources. The creation of some of these records and type-series from the material recovered from Cirencester will also assist in the investigation and reporting of other projects in the region.

* Pottery: corpus of local and regional pottery fabrics and forms
* Tiles and building materials: local and regional fabric and material series
* Querns: local and regional
* Building stone and special sources of marble and imports
* Decorative materials like painted plaster etc
* Sources of lead, pewter, copper alloy etc
* Main trading connections represented through imports
* Spatial/functional/status sub-division and variability in the town through studies of the distribution of artefacts

Sites and Monuments Record: The basic record established through the Cirencester Urban Assessment Project is only the starting point for expanding and maintaining a proper record of work and discoveries in the area. It is recognised that the present record is variously deficient in terms of the range of monuments so far identified and the descriptions of identified monuments.

ABBREVIATIONS

ACAO	Association of County Archaeological Officers
Antiq Comm (Camb Antiq Soc)	Antiquarian Communications (Cambridge Antiquarian Society)
Antiq J	Antiquaries Journal
Arch J	Archaeological Journal
Arch NL	Archaeological Newsletter
Arch Oxoniensis	Archaeologia Oxoniensis
BAR	British Archaeological Reports
BGAS	Bristol & Gloucestershire Archaeological Society
BNJ	British Numismatic Journal
Bull Geological Surv GB	Bulletin of the Geological Survey of Great Britain
BULLIAL	Bulletin of the Institute of Archaeology, University of London
CAHS	Cirencester Archaeological & Historical Society Annual Report and Newsletter
CAT	Cotswold Archaeological Trust
CBA GP 13 NL	Council for British Archaeology, Group 13, Newsletter
CBI	Confederation of British Industry
CC GCG	Cheltenham Chronicle & Gloucestershire Graphic
CDC	Cotswold District Council
CEC	Cirencester Excavation Committee
CRAAGS	Committee for Rescue Archaeology in Avon, Gloucestershire and Somerset
CSIR	*Corpus Signorum Imperii Romani*
DoE	Department of the Environment
GC in GCL	Gloucestershire Collection in Gloucester City Library
GCC	Gloucestershire County Council
Gents Mag	Gentleman's Magazine
Gents Mag NS	Gentleman's Magazine New Series
GNQ	Gloucestershire Notes & Queries
Geol Mag	The Geological Magazine
Geol Soc Special Rep	Geological Society Special Reports
GRO	Gloucester Record Office
GSIA	Gloucestershire Society for Industrial Archaeology
Illus London News	Illustrated London News
JBAA	Journal of the British Archaeological Association
JBAA NS	Journal of the British Archaeological Association New Series
J Historical Geography	Journal of Historical Geography
JRS	Journal of Roman Studies
Land Hist	Landscape History
Mem Geol Surv	Memoirs of the Geological Survey
MPP	Monuments Protection Programme
Mus J	Museum Journal
Num Chron	Numismatic Chronicle
Num Circular	Numismatic Circular
OAU	Oxford Archaeological Unit
OJA	Oxford Journal of Archaeology
OUCA	Oxford University Committee for Archaeology
PCNFC	Proceedings of the Cotteswold Naturalists' Field Club
Proc Chem Soc	Proceedings of the Chemical Society
Proc Cotteswold Club	Proceedings of the Cotteswold Club
Proc Geol Assoc	Proceedings of the Geological Association
Proc Geol Soc	Proceedings of the Geological Society
PSA	Proceedings of the Society of Antiquaries
PSA ser. 2	Proceedings of the Society of Antiquaries series 2
Q J Geol Soc	Quarterly Journal of the Geological Society
RAI	Royal Archaeological Institute
RCHME	Royal Commission on the Historical Monuments of England
Rep Brit Assoc	Report of the British Association
RIB	Roman Inscriptions of Britain (see Collingwood and Wright 1965)
Soc Ants Res Rep	Society of Antiquaries Research Report
T Inst British Geographers	Transactions of the Institute of British Geographers
TBAA	Transactions of the British Archaeological Association
TBGAS	Transactions of the Bristol & Gloucestershire Archaeological Association
Trans Woolhope Natur Hist Field Club	Transactions of the Woolhope Naturalists Field Club
WAM	Wiltshire Archaeological Magazine
W & G S	Wilts & Gloucestershire Standard

BIBLIOGRAPHY

ACAO, 1993 *Model briefs and specifications for archaeological assessments and field evaluations*, Bedford
A H C, 1865 Museum of the Royal Agricultural College, *W & G S*, 11th Nov, 6
Alcock, J P, 1966 Some aspects of Celtic religion in Gloucestershire and the Cotswolds, *TBGAS*, **85**, 45–56
Alexander, D, 1980 Cirencester – a rich historic past, *Cotswold Life*, Nov, 38–41
Alexander, D, 1986 Cirencester: a town of grace, history and enterprise, *Cotswold Life*, July, 28–9
Allen, J R (ed), 1899 Important discovery of Roman sculptured and inscribed stones at Cirencester, *Reliquary & Illustrated Archaeologist*, **5**, no 3, 196–201
A N, 1922 Roman remains at Cirencester, *W & G S*, 24th June
Anderson, A S, 1979 A type of moulded imitation samian and its military connections, *Britannia*, **10**, 109–19
Anderson, R, 1932 Street improvements at Cirencester, *W & G S*, 22nd Oct
Anon, 1835–6 Roman monument, *Gents Mag*, **5**, 296
Anon, 1838 Antiquarian researches: Roman remains at Cirencester, *Gents Mag*, **10**, 180
Anon, 1840 Roman antiquities of Cirencester, *Gents Mag*, **13**, 192
Anon, 1842 Review: Bailey's 'History of Cirencester', *Gents Mag*, **18**, 275–8
Anon, 1848 Proceedings of the third annual congress, held at Gloucester, August 1846, *TBAA*
Anon, 1849a Tessellated pavement found at Cirencester, *Gents Mag*, **32**, 357–60
Anon, 1849b [no title], *Illus London News*, 8th Sept
Anon, 1850a Roman art at Cirencester, *Gents Mag*, **34**, 241–7
Anon, 1850b Roman pavement at Cirencester, *Gents Mag*, **33**, 25–6
Anon, 1851a Archaeological Institute [finds in Watermoor], *Gents Mag*, **35**, 410
Anon, 1851b [no title], *W & G S*, 31st May, 3 c2
Anon, 1851c Lecture on the antiquities of ancient Cirencester, *W & G S*, 31 May, 3
Anon, 1852 Archaeological Institute: antiquarian researches, *Gents Mag*, **37**, 73
Anon, 1853 First meeting for 1847 of Cotteswolds Naturalists' Club, *PCNFC*, **1**, 1
Anon, 1854 Intramural burials, *W & G S*, 8th Apr, 2 c1
Anon, 1856a Antiquarian researches, *Gents Mag*, **45**, 400
Anon, 1856b Archaeological Institute, *Gents Mag*, **45**, 402–3
Anon, 1857a Archaeolgical Institute, *Gents Mag NS*, **3**, 71–2
Anon, 1857b Corinium Museum, *W & G S*, 12th Sept, 8 c1
Anon, 1857c Art treasures exhibition, *W & G S*, 16th May, 8 c1
Anon, 1858a The Corinium Museum, *W & G S*, 17th Apr, 8 c1
Anon, 1858b Cirencester County Court, *W & G S*, 18th Sept, 2 c1–5
Anon, 1858c The Corinium Museum, *W & G S*, 11th Sept, 8 c1
Anon, 1860a Cirencester Natural History Society lecture on geology of this area, *W & G S*, 19th May, 8 c2
Anon, 1860b Death of an old inhabitant, *W & G S*, 19th May, 8 c2
Anon, 1860c The Corinium Museum – attendance, *W & G S*, 4th Aug, 8 c2
Anon, 1860d [no title], *Gents Mag NS*, **7**, 594
Anon, 1861 Archaeological Institute, *Gents Mag NS*, **10**, 420
Anon, 1862a [no title], *Gents Mag NS*, **12**, 315
Anon, 1862b Roman remains, *W & G S*, 23rd Aug, 8 c2
Anon, 1863a Antiquarian intelligence, *JBAA*, **19**, 150
Anon, 1863b [no title], *Gents Mag NS*, **15**, 276
Anon, 1865 Roman tessellated pavements at Cirencester, *Illus London News*, 2 Aug
Anon, 1866a The Romans in Corinium, *W & G S*, 30th Jun, 4 c3
Anon, 1866b Remarkable discovery of human skeletons in Earl Bathurst's Park, *W & G S*, 22nd Sept, 4
Anon, 1867a Proceedings of the Association, *JBAA*, **23**, 102, 197, 291
Anon, 1867b Pre-Augustine christianity in Britain, *JBAA*, **23**, 226
Anon, 1868a British Archaeological Assosciation, *W & G S*, 15th Aug, 3–6
Anon, 1868b British Archaeological Association, *W & G S*, 27th June, 4

Anon, 1868c Roman remains found at Cirencester in 1759, *W & G S*, 10th Nov, 3
Anon, 1869a Old Cirencester, *W & G S*, 6th Nov, 6 c1
Anon, 1869b Corinium – Museum of Roman remains, Cirencester, *W & G S*, 2nd Oct, 5
Anon, 1869c 'Old Cirencester', *W & G S*, 6th Nov, 6 c1
Anon, 1869d Proceedings of the Cirencester Congress, 10th-15th August 1868, *JBAA*, **25**, 91–112, 190–214, 283–313, 400–12
Anon, 1869e Proceedings of the Association, *JBAA*, **25**, 67–88, 158–189, 260–282, 382–399
Anon, 1871a Additions to Professor Church's Museum, *W & G S*, 26th Aug, 4
Anon, 1871b The Museum, *W & G S*, 11th Nov, 4
Anon, 1871c The Museum – third guide, *W & G S*, 4th Nov, 4
Anon, 1872 Twentieth General Meeting, *WAM*, **13**, 141–155
Anon, 1873a Recent Roman finds at Cirencester, *W & G S*, 20th Sept, 3–4
Anon, 1873b The Roman pavements at the Corinium Museum, *W & G S*, 12th July, 4
Anon, 1877a Proceedings of the Association, *JBAA*, **33**, 275
Anon, 1877b Bristol & Gloucester Archaeological Society – meeting at Cirencester, *W & G S*, 1st Sept, 2–5
Anon, 1877–8 Transactions at the Annual Meeting, held at Cirencester, on 28th-30th August 1877, *TBGAS*, **2**, 1–26
Anon, 1878 Bristol & Gloucester Archaeological Society, *W & G S*, 21st Sept, 8
Anon, 1880a Archaeological visit to Cirencester, *W & G S*, 5th June, 5
Anon, 1880b Second field meeting, 26th June, *PCNFC*, **7**, 7–9
Anon, 1881–2 First field meeting of Club, 17th May, *PCNFC*, **8**, 65–9
Anon, 1883–4a First field meeting, 22nd May, *PCNFC*, **8**, 137–9
Anon, 1883–4b Transactions at the spring meeting of the Society, held at Cirencester on 8th May 1884, *TBGAS*, **8**, 181–91
Anon, 1884 Bristol & Gloucestershire Archaeological Society, *W & G S*, 10th May, 3–4
Anon, 1887–8 Transactions at the spring meeting held at Cirencester 26th May 1887, *TBGAS*, **12**, 1–5
Anon, 1889 The Corinium Museum, *W & G S*, 4th May, 5 c1
Anon, 1890 Roman pavement, *W & G S*, 11th Jan, 5 c1
Anon, 1891a Interesting 'Find', *W & G S*, 18th April, 5 c3
Anon, 1891b Cirencester Local Board : New Street [Ashcroft Villas], *W & G S*, 1st Aug, 5 c2
Anon, 1892a The Corinium Museum, *W & G S*, 15th Oct, 2
Anon, 1892b Wilts and Glo'stershire Archaeologists at Cirencester, *W & G S*, 27th Aug, 2–3
Anon, 1892c Cirencester Local Board, *W & G S*, 30th Jan
Anon, 1892–3 Proceedings at the annual summer meeting at Cirencester, 23rd-25th August 1892, *TBGAS*, **17**, 1–32
Anon, 1894–5 Second field meeting, 28th June, *PCNFC*, **11**, 235–7
Anon, 1895–7 Transactions at the autumn meeting held at Cirencester, 24th September 1896, *TBGAS*, **20**, 32–7
Anon, 1896 Cirencester Urban District Council, *W & G S*, 27th June, 5 c2
Anon, 1897 The Cirencester Society in London, *GNQ*, **7**, 125–7
Anon, 1903–13 *Durocornovium* (Cirencester), *Ephemeris Epigraphica*, **9**, 517–520
Anon, 1907 Proceedings at the annual summer meeting at Cirencester, 16th-18th July 1907, *TBGAS*, **30**, 23–48
Anon, 1909 Chit-Chat, *W & G S*, 20th Feb, 2
Anon, 1910 *Corinium*, Lecture by Archdeacon Sinclair, picture of Roman Ciceter, *W & G S*, 16th April
Anon, 1913a Corinium Museum, *W & G S*, 22 Feb, 5 c1
Anon, 1913b Discovery of a Roman coffin at The Querns, *W & G S*, 27th Dec, 4 c7
Anon, 1914a Discovery of Roman remains, *W & G S*, 21st Feb
Anon, 1914b Chit-Chat, *W & G S*, 28th Nov, 2 c1
Anon, 1914c Roman remains at Cirencester, *CC GCG*, 9 May
Anon, 1915 Roman remains at Cirencester, *TBGAS*, **38**, 218–9
Anon, 1918 Excursions, 1917, *PCNFC*, **29**, 183–7
Anon, 1919a Proceedings at the autumnal meeting, at Cirencester, on Sept 2–3 1919, *TBGAS*, **41**, 141–62
Anon, 1919b Bristol & Gloucestershire Archaeological Society: meeting at Cirencester, *W & G S*, 6th Sept, 2
Anon, 1920a Roman remains, *W & G S*, 19th June
Anon, 1920b Chit-Chat, *W & G S*, 16th Oct, 2
Anon, 1921a Interesting 'Find', *W & G S*, 12th Nov, 5 c4
Anon, 1921b The Chesterton excavations, *W & G S*, 28th May, 5 c2
Anon, 1921c Roman Britain in 1921 and 1922, *JRS*, **11**, 208–10
Anon, 1922a The Roman Wall, *W & G S*, 4th March
Anon, 1922b Discovery of a Roman well, *W & G S*, 9th June
Anon, 1922c Corinium's City Walls: Excavations at the Poor Law Institution, important discoveries, *W & G S*, 18th March
Anon, 1922d Chit-Chat, *W & G S*, 21st Jan, 2
Anon, 1922e The City Wall, *W & G S*, 25th Feb
Anon, 1922f [no title], *W & G S*, 17th June
Anon, 1922g Corinium Museum, *W & G S*, 7th Oct
Anon, 1922h [no title], *Illus London News*, 22nd July
Anon, 1922i [no title], *Manchester City News*, 25th March

Anon, 1922j [no title], *The Bristol Times & Mirror*, 15th April
Anon, 1922k Roman mosaic pavement near Cirencester, *JBAA NS*, **28**, 134
Anon, 1924a 'Roman Remains at Cirencester': picture of seventy-five years ago, *W & G S*, 8th Nov
Anon, 1924b Chit-Chat, *W & G S*, 19th June
Anon, 1926a Wanderings in Roman Britain: remains in Gloucestershire, Corinium, *W & G S*, 14th Aug
Anon, 1926b Cirencester Bull Ring, *W & G S*, 11th Sept, 2
Anon, 1929 Britain's oldest cross-word puzzle, *W & G S*, 27th Apr, 2
Anon, 1931a Reviews of 'History of Cirencester' by St Clair Baddeley, *W & G S*, 3rd Jan
Anon, 1931b Death of Mrs Wilfred Cripps, *W & G S*, 24th Jan
Anon, 1931c Report of itinerary, 7th July 1931, *TBGAS*, **53**, 27–35
Anon, 1932 The development of Ashcroft – Cirencester firm's enterprise, *W & G S*, 30th April
Anon, 1933 An interesting find – Roman cup dug up in garden, *W & G S*, 13th May
Anon, 1934 Roman Britain in 1933, *JRS*, **24**, 212
Anon, 1935a Earl Bathurst's offer, for the Museum, *W & G S*, 21st Dec
Anon, 1935b Cirencester YMCA, a museum, *W & G S*, 2nd Mar, 4
Anon, 1937 The Public Museum, *W & G S*, 21st Aug
Anon, 1938a Corinium Museum, *W & G S*, 15th Oct
Anon, 1938b New Corinium Museum, opening ceremony today, *W & G S*, 29th Oct
Anon, 1938c Roman Britain in 1937, *JRS*, **28**, 190, 204–5
Anon, 1941a Ancient pavement found, *W & G S*, 1st March
Anon, 1941b Roman Britain in 1940, *JRS*, **31**, 138
Anon, 1948 Roman Britain in 1947, *JRS*, **38**, 93
Anon, 1952 Roman Britain in 1951, *JRS*, **42**, 98, 107
Anon, 1957 Foul play in Roman times! Latest finds at excavation site, *W & G S*, 21st Sept
Anon, 1958 Roman Britain in 1957, *JRS*, **48**, 144–6, 152, 154
Anon, 1959 Roman Britain in 1958, *JRS*, **49**, 127–9
Anon, 1960 Roman Britain in 1959, *JRS*, **50**, 230
Anon, 1961 Roman Britain in 1960, *JRS*, **51**, 186–7, 196
Anon, 1963 Roman Britain in 1962, *JRS*, **52**, 181–2, 198–9
Anon, 1964 Roman Britain in 1963, *JRS*, **54**, 169–171
Anon, 1965a Roman Britain in 1964, *JRS*, **55**, 216, 224
Anon, 1965b Field meetings, 1964, *TBGAS*, **84**, 190–3
Anon, 1968a Editorial, *Antiquity*, **42**, 253
Anon, 1968b Satisfactory progress with Roman 'dig', further exploration on second century mosaic, *W & G S*, 23rd Aug
Anon, 1969a Croome Memorial Lecture, *W & G S*, 14th Feb
Anon, 1969b Editorial, *Antiquity*, **43**, 256–7
Anon, 1969c Roman Britain in 1968, *JRS*, **59**, 225, 243
Anon, 1981 Site review: Preston, Baunton, *Glevensis*, **15**, 42–3
Arkell, W J, 1930 On a boring into Great Oolite at Latton, near Cricklade, Wilts, *PCNFC*, **24**, 181–3
Arkell, W J, 1933 *The Jurassic system in Great Britain*, London
Arkell, W J, 1941 The Upper Oxford Clay at Purton, Wilts, and the zones of the Lower Oxfordian, *Geol Mag*, **78 (3)**, 161–72
Arkell, W J, and Donovan, D T, 1952 The Fuller's Earth of the Cotswolds, and its relation to the Great Oolite, *Q J Geol Soc*, **107**, 227–253
ASC *The Anglo-Saxon chronicle*, ed D Whitelock, D C Douglas and S J Tucker, 1961, London
Astill, G G, 1991 Towns and town hierarchies in Saxon England, *OJA*, **10**, 95–119
Atkinson, D, 1942 *Report on the excavations at Wroxeter, 1923–27*
Atkinson, D, 1957a The Cirencester word-square, *TBGAS*, **76**, 21–34
Atkinson, D, 1957b A fragment of a diploma from Cirencester, *JRS*, **47**, 196–7
Atkinson, D, 1968 Cirencester coin collections, *TBGAS*, **77**, 65–70
Atkyns, Sir Robert, 1712 *The ancient and present state of Glostershire*, London
Aubrey, J, *Monumenta Britannica, or a miscellany of British antiquities by Mr John Aubrey of Easton Piers*, annotated by R Legg, 1980, 2 vols, Dorset
Austin, R, 1911 *Some Gloucesteshire books and their writers*, Gloucester
Austin, R, 1912 Some account of Sir Robert Atkyns the younger and other members of the Atkyns Family, *TBGAS*, **35**, 69–92
Austin, R, 1915 Samuel Rudder, *The Library*, July 1915
Austin, R, 1916 Additions to, and notes on, the 'Descriptive Catalogue of Printed Maps of Glos 1577–1911, by T Chubb', *TBGAS*, **39**, 233–264
Austin, R, 1922 Philip Jones, of Cirencester, *TBGAS*, **44**, 145–153
Austin, R, 1928 *Catalogue of the Gloucestershire Collection*, Gloucester
Austin, R, 1938 New Corinium Museum, Cirencester, *TBGAS*, **60**, 358

Baddeley, W St Clair, 1906 Certain Roman finds at Watercombe near Bisley, *TBGAS*, **29**, 179–80
Baddeley, W St Clair, 1913 *Place Names of Gloucester: a handbook*, Gloucester

Baddeley, W St Clair, 1918a Ancient Cirencester, address: The British-Romano period, *W & G S*, 16th Nov
Baddeley, W St Clair, 1918b Ancient Cirencester [addenda in letter], *W & G S*, 7th Dec, 5
Baddeley, W St Clair, 1918c Ancient Cirencester: the medieval period, *W & G S*, 23rd Nov
Baddeley, W St Clair, 1919a Ancient Cirencester, *PCNFC*, **20**, 85–97
Baddeley, W St Clair, 1919b The making of medieval Cirencester and the abbey of St Mary, *TBGAS*, **41**, 146
Baddeley, W St Clair, 1922a The excavation at Cirencester (*Corinium Dobunorum*) Feb-March 1922, *TBGAS*, **44**, 101–15
Baddeley, W St Clair, 1922b On an inscribed brick-tabula found at Cirencester, *TBGAS*, **44**, 117–120
Baddeley, W St Clair, 1922c Cirencester place-names: Lewis Street, *TBGAS*, **44**, 314–6
Baddeley, W St Clair, 1922d Romano-British mosaic pavements at Cirencester, *Builder*, 9 Jun 1922, 872–4
Baddeley, W St Clair, 1922e Excavation at Cirencester (March 1–25 1922), *W & G S*, 15 Apr
Baddeley, W St Clair, 1922f Romano-British mosaic pavements at Cirencester, *W & G S*, 17th June
Baddeley, W St Clair, 1922g The Roman pavements at Cirencester, *W & G S*, 8th July
Baddeley, W St Clair, 1922h Roman remains at Cirencester, *W & G S*, 22nd July
Baddeley, W St Clair, 1923a A Romano-British altar at Siddington, *TBGAS*, **45**, 291–2
Baddeley, W St Clair, 1923b The Paen at Cirencester, *TBGAS*, **45**, 292–4,
Baddeley, W St Clair, 1924 *A history of Cirencester*, Cirencester
Baddeley, W St Clair, 1925 On certain minor ancient roads to and from *Corinium* (Cirencester), *TBGAS*, **47**, 65–79
Baddeley, W St Clair, 1929 Britain's oldest crossword puzzle – Corinium inscription solved at last, *W & G S*, 20th April
Baddeley, W St Clair, 1930 Notes on portions of a late and secondary Roman road system (cAD 220–390), *TBGAS*, **52**, 151–185
Baddeley, W St Clair, 1931 Details of the Roman capital and some references to Cirencester museum and a number of Roman remains, *TBGAS*, **53**, 33–5
BADLG, 1991 *The British Archaeologists' and Developers' Liaison Group Code of Practice*, (first published 1986), London
Baily's, 1842 *Handbook for Cirencester, containing a history of the town and its antiquities . . . with illustrations*, Cirencester
Baker, N, Dalwood, H, Holt, R, Mundy, C, and Taylor, G, 1992 From Roman to medieval Worcester: development and planning in the Anglo-Saxon city, *Antiquity*, **66**, 65–74
Barber, A, 1989 *Upper Churnside, Cirencester*, CAT Typescript Rep, **9015**, Cirencester
Barber, A, 1990a *15 Sheep Street, Cirencester*, CAT Typescript Rep, **9015**, Cirencester
Barber, A, 1990b *20 Cricklade Street, Cirencester*, CAT Typescript Rep, **9017**, Cirencester
Barber, A, 1990c *11–17 Victoria Road, Cirencester*, CAT Typescript Rep, **9018**, Cirencester
Barber, A, 1990d *7 Corinium Gate, Cirencester*, CAT Typescript Rep, **9023**, Cirencester
Barber, A, 1990e *The Nurseries, 60–62 Watermoor Road, Cirencester*, CAT Typescript Rep, **9034**, Cirencester
Barber, A, 1991a *Siddington Tithe Barn, Glos: archaeological evaluation*, CAT Ltd Typescipt Report, **9157**, Cirencester
Barber, A, 1991b *Love Lane, Cirencester to Siddington, Surface Water Sewer Outfall Scheme*, CAT Typescript Rep, **9160**, Cirencester
Barber, A, 1992 *St Michael's Field, Cirencester, Glos: archaeological excavation*, CAT Typescript Rep, **9298**, Cirencester
Barber, A, and Morton, R, 1990 *Spring mobiles, St Michael's Field, Cirencester*, CAT Typescript Rep, **9015**, Cirencester
Barford, P M, 1988 A plumbata head from Cirencester, *TBGAS*, **106**, 189–200
Barker, J, 1976 William and Rebecca George (Powell) and their town house, now Gloucester House, 60 Dyer Street, in *Studies in the archaeology and history of Cirencester* (ed A D McWhirr), BAR, **30**, 113–125, Oxford
Bassett, S, 1989 Churches in Worcester before and after the conversion of the Anglo-Saxons, *Antiq J*, **69**, 225–56
Bassett, S, 1992 Church and diocese in the West Midlands, in *Pastoral care before the parish* (eds J Blair and R Sharpe), 13–41, Leicester
Bathurst, Earl, 1869 Inaugural address, 10 August 1868, at congress of British Archaeological Association held at Cirencester, *JBAA*, **25**, 21–5
Bede, *Ecclesiastical history of the English people* (eds B Colgrave and R A B Mynors), 1968, Oxford
Beecham, K J, 1887 *History of Cirencester and the Roman city of Corinium*, Cirencester (reprinted 1978, with introduction by David Verey)
Beecham, W K, 1842 *History and antiquities of the town of Cirencester*, Cirencester
Beeby, W T, 1916 Ancient stained glass in the parish church of St John, Cirencester, and its associations, *TBGAS*, **39**, 201–231
Bell, M, 1984 Environmental archaeology in south-west England, in *Environmental archaeology: a regional review* (ed H C M Keeley), DAMHB Occasional Papers, **6**, 43–130, London
Beresford, M W, and Finberg, H P R, 1973 *English medieval boroughs: a hand-list*, Newton Abbot
Berry, C A F, 1949 Centuriation, *TBGAS*, **68**, 14–21
Bertram, Charles, 1809 *Richard of Cirencester: the description of Britain...with the original treatise de situ Britanniae*, London
Biddle, M, 1976 Towns, in *The archaeology of Anglo-Saxon England* (ed D M Wilson), 99–150, London
Biddle, M, 1985 Note on Repton, St Wystan's Church, *Med Arch*, **29**, 168
Biddle, M (ed), 1990 *Object and economy in medieval Winchester*, Winchester Studies **7.ii**, Oxford
Bidwell, P T, 1979 *The legionary bath-house and basilica and forum at Exeter*, Exeter Archaeol Rep, **1**, Exeter
Bigland, R, 1791–1889 *Historical, monumental and genealogical collections relative to the county of Gloucester*, London
Birley, A R, 1981 *The Fasti of Roman Britain*, Oxford
Bishop, G L (ed), 1987 *Wills from Cirencester and district 1541–1548*, Cirencester
Blagg, T F C, 1976 Tools and techniques of the Roman stonemason in Britain, *Britannia*, **7**, 152–172

Blagg, T F C, 1977 Schools of stonemasons in *Roman Britain, in Roman life and art in Britain* (eds J Munby and M Henig), BAR, **41**, 51–73, Oxford

Blagg, T F C, 1980 Roman civil and military architecture in the province of Britain: aspects of patronage, influence and craft organisation, *World Archaeology*, **12**, 27–42

Blagg, T F C, forthcoming *CSIR*

Blair, C (ed), 1988 *Minster and parish churches*: the local church in transition, 950–1200, OUCA Mon **17**, Oxford

Blair, C, and Blair, J, 1991 Copper alloys, in *English medieval industries* (eds J Blair and N Ramsey), 81–107, London

Blair, J, and Sharpe, R (eds), 1992 *Pastoral care before the parish*, Leicester

Bonser, W, 1964 *Romano-British bibliography 55 BC–AD 449*, Oxford

Boon, G C, 1973 Sarapis and Tutela: a Silchester coincidence, *Britannia*, **4**, 107–14

Boon, G C, 1974 *Silchester: the Roman town of Calleva*, Newton Abbot

Boon, G C, 1977 Gold-in-glass beads from the ancient world, *Britannia*, **8**, 193–207

Boon, G C, 1992 Traces of Romano-British Christianity in the West Country, *TBGAS*, **110**, 37–52

Bowly, C, 1889 Local antiquities – letter to the editor, *W & G S*, 2nd Feb, 5 c3

Bowly, C, 1892–3 On a Roman inscribed stone found at Cirencester, *TBGAS*, **17**, 63–7

Branigan, K, 1976 *The Roman villa in south-west England*, Bradford-upon-Avon

Bravender, J, 1850 Farming of Gloucestershire, *J Royal Agr Soc of Eng*, **11**

Bravender, J, 1868a The watershed of the Upper Thames, *PCNFC*, **4**, 240–8

Bravender, J, 1868b The Cirencester amphitheatre, *W & G S*, 5th Sept, 28

Bravender, T B, 1881 *Catalogue of collection of potters' marks, coins, and Roman remains in the Corinium Museum*, Cirencester

Bravender, T B, 1883–4a Recent Roman 'finds' in Cirencester, *TBGAS*, **8**, 309–313

Bravender, T B, 1883–4b List of tokens found at Cirencester, *TBGAS*, **8**, 314–23

Brayley, E W, and Britton, J, 1801–15 *The beauties of England and Wales*, London

Brewer, J N, 1828 *Delineations of Gloucestershire*

Brewer, R J, 1990 Caerwent – *Venta Silurum*: a *civitas capital*, in *Conquest, co-existence and change: recent work in Roman Wales* (eds B Burnham and J Davies), Trivium, **25**, 75–85

Brill, E, 1964 *Portrait of the Cotswolds*, London

Brodie, Rev P B, and Buckman, J, 1845 On the Stonesfield slate of the Cotteswold Hills, *Q J Geol Soc*, **1**, 220–5

Brooks, D A, 1986 Review of the evidence for continuity in British towns in the 5th and 6th centuries, *OJA*, **5**.1, 77–102

Brown, E B, 1909 *Ancient churches around Cirencester, AD 1060–1547*, Cirencester

Brown, E G, 1904 On some Gloucestershire manuscripts now in Hereford Cathedral library, *TBGAS*, **27**, 172–210

Brown, P D C, 1976 Archaeological evidence for the Anglo-Saxon period, in *Studies in the archaeology and history of Cirencester* (ed A D McWhirr), BAR, **30**, 19–45, Oxford

Brown, P D C, and McWhirr, A D, 1966 Cirencester 1965, *Antiq J*, **46**, 240–54

Brown, P D C, and McWhirr, A D, 1967 Cirencester 1966, *Antiq J*, **47**, 185–197

Brown, P D C, McWhirr, A D, and Smith D J, 1969 Cirencester 1967–8: eighth interim report, *Antiq J*, **49**, 222–243

Brown, T, 1865 Depth of water in a well, *W & G S*, 19th Aug, 6 c3

Brown, W, 1889 *Olde Cicester*

Browne, Rev A L, 1935 The Cirencester election of 1695, *TBGAS*, **57**, 269–72

Buckman, J, 1850 Substances employed in forming the tessellae of the Cirencester pavements, *Arch J*, **7**, 347–54

Buckman, J, 1851 Proceedings at the meetings of the Archaeological Institute, *Arch J*, **8**, 187–90, 340

Buckman, J, 1852 On the Cornbrash of the neighbourhood of Cirencester, *PCNFC*, **1**, 262–7

Buckman, J, 1853 Structure and arrangement of tesserae in Roman pavements discovered at Cirencester in August 1849, *PCNFC*, **1**, 47–51

Buckman, J, 1854 On the Cornbrash of Gloucestershire and part of Wiltshire, *Rep Brit Assoc*, **50** & **51**

Buckman, J, 1856a On removal and relaying of Roman tessellated floors (at Cirencester), *Arch J*, **13**, 215–27

Buckman, J, 1856b Antiquities and works of art exhibited, *Arch J*, **13**, 178–9

Buckman, J, 1856c Proceedings at the meetings of the Archaeological Institute, *Arch J*, **13**, 81–2

Buckman, J, 1858 On the oolite rocks of Gloucestershire and North Wilts, *Q J Geol Soc*, **14**, 98–130

Buckman, J, 1860a On some fossil reptilian eggs from the Great Oolite of Cirencester, *Q J Geol Soc*, **16**, 107–10

Buckman, J, 1860b Inundations in antient Corinium, *PCNFC*, **2**, v–vii

Buckman, J, 1866a Roman remains found at Latton, Wilts, *WAM*, **9**, 232–7

Buckman, J, 1866b On the materials of Roman querns, *WAM*, **9**, 291–4

Buckman, J, 1868 On stone roof tiles of Roman date (found at Cirencester), *PCNFC*, **4**, 93–6

Buckman, J, and Newmarch, C H, 1850 *Illustrations of the remains of Roman art in Cirencester, the site of antient Corinium*, Cirencester

Buckman, S S, 1889 On the Cotteswold, Midford, and Yeovil Sands, and the division between Lias and Oolite, *Q J Geol Soc*, **45**, 440–74

Buckman, S S, 1895 The Bajocian of the mid-Cotteswolds, *Q J Geol Soc*, **51**, 388–462

Buckman, S S, 1901 Bajocian and contiguous deposits in the north Cotteswolds: the main hillmass, *Q J Geol Soc*, **57**, 126–55

Buckman, S S, 1903 The Cotteswold hills: a geographical enquiry, *PCNFC*, **14**, 205–242

Builder, 1868 The Roman amphitheatre at Cirencester, *W & G S*, 29th Aug, 6 c1

Burden, J, 1804 *Views of Gloucestershire, no. 1, containing 6 views in the county of Gloucester*, Cheltenham

Burrow, E J, 1919 *The ancient entrenchments and camps of Gloucestershire*, Cheltenham
Burrow, I G C, 1981 *Hillfort and hill-top settlement in Somerset in the first millennium AD*, BAR, **91**, Oxford
Butler, R F, and Jones, L J, 1972 The cross-slabs of Gloucestershire, *TBGAS*, **91**, 150–8

Carus-Wilson, C M, 1959–60 Evidence of industrial growth on some fifteenth-century manors, *Econ Hist Rev*, **12** 2nd ser, 191–4
Carver, M O H, 1987a The nature of urban deposits, in *Urban archaeology in Britain* (eds J Schofield and R Leech), CBA Res Rep, **61**, 9–26, London
Carver, M O H, 1987b *Underneath English towns*, London
Casey, J, 1983 Imperial campaigns and fouth-century defences in Britain, in *Roman urban defences in the west* (eds J Maloney and B Hobley), CBA Res Rep, **51**, 121–4, London
CAT, 1990 *Cirencester and Stratton Bypass, Glos: stage 1, archaeological assessment*, CAT Typescript Rep, **9031**, Cirencester
CAT, 1991 *A419/417, Cirencester and Stratton Bypass: stage 2, archaeological evaluation*, CAT Typescript Rep, **9141**, Cirencester
Cave, R, and Cox, B M, 1975 The Kellaways Beds of the area between Chippenham and Malmesbury, Wilts, *Bull Geological Surv GB*, **51**, 41–55
CBI, 1986 *Code of practice for mineral operators*, London
CBI, 1991 *Archaeological investigation – Code of Practice for Mineral Operators*, (first published 1982), London
CDC, 1984 *Cirencester Local Plan – written statement*, Cirencester
CDC, 1993 *Cotswold District Local Plan: deposit draft – Cirencester, Area 7*, Cirencester
Channon, P J, 1945–7 Geological notes for excursion on July 10th 1946, *PCNFC*, **29**, 60–2
Channon, P J, 1951 A new section at Cowcombe Hill, near Chalford station, Glos, *Proc Geol Assoc*, **62**, 174–6
Cherry, J, 1991 Leather, in *English medieval industries* (eds J Blair and N Ramsey), 295–319, London
Chidlaw, N, and Campbell, M J A, 1988 Sedimentation patterns in the Cornbrash limestone formation of the Cotswold hills, *Proc Geol Soc*, **99**, 27–42
Chubb, T, 1913 Descriptive catalogue of the printed maps of Gloucestershire, 1577–1911, *TBGAS*, **39**
Chudley, R, 1982 *Building: site works, substructure and plant*, London
Church, A H, 1867 *Corinium Museum. A guide to the museum of Roman remains at Cirencester*, (11 editions to 1922), Cirencester
Church, A H, 1873 Recent Roman finds at Cirencester, *WAM*, **14**, 186–92
Church, A H, 1876 Metallic objects of Roman workmanship found at and near Cirencester, *PSA ser. 2*, **6**, 536–40
Church, A H, 1884 Proceedings at meetings of the Royal Archaeological Institute, *Arch J*, **41**, 323–4
Clennell, C H, [no date] Memorials of an ancient Presbyterian meeting house at Cirencester, *Unitarian Historical Society Transactions*, **5**, 262–87
Clews, S, 1983 Cirencester and conflict, *Gloucestershire and Avon Life*, July
Clews, S, 1984 Cirencester: Abbey Grounds renewal scheme, *TBGAS*, **102**, 224–5
Clews, S, 1985 Jefferies Nursery site, Cirencester, *TBGAS*, **103**, 230
Clews, S, 1988 *Cirencester Memorial Hospital: a brief history of the site and buildings*, Cirencester
Clifford, E M, 1933–5 Notes on some Roman villas in Gloucestershire, *PCNFC*, **25**, 237–56
Clifford, E M, 1939 Roman altars in Gloucestershire, *TBGAS*, **60**, 297–317
Clifford, E M, 1942 Working oxen at Cirencester, *TBGAS*, **63**, 168–71
Clifford, E M 1945–7 Second summer meeting, 6 Sept 1946, *PCNFC*, **29**, 76
Clifford, E M, 1946–8 Mosaic floor at Cirencester, *TBGAS*, **67**, 381–395
Clifford, E M, 1948–50 Archaeology, *PCNFC*, **30**, 50
Clifford, E M, 1955a Stamped tiles found in Gloucestershire, *JRS*, **45**, 68–72
Clifford, E M, 1955b Some earthworks in Gloucestershire, *Arch NL*, **5**, no. 8, 154–5
Clifford, E M, 1961 *Bagendon: a Belgic Oppidum*, Cambridge
Clifton-Taylor, A, 1984a *Another six English towns*, London
Clifton-Taylor, A, 1984b Cirencester: the capital of the Cotswolds, *The Listener*, 13th Sept, 10–12
Colgrave, B, and Mynors, B (eds), 1969 *Bede's Ecclesiastical history of the English people*, Oxford
Collingwood, R G, and Richmond, I, 1969 *The archaeology of Roman Britain*, London
Collingwood, R G, and Taylor, M, 1925 Notes on Roman remains in Cirencester, *TBGAS*, **47**, 376
Collingwood, R G, and Wright, R P, 1965, *The Roman inscriptions of Britain, I*, Oxford
Collinson, J, [no date] *Miscellaneous notices relative to Cirencester*
Collinson, J, 1791 *The history and antiquities of the county of Somerset*, 3 vols, Bath
Conzen, M R G, 1968 The use of town plans in the study of urban history, in *The study of urban history* (ed H J Dyos), 113–30, Leicester
Cooke, G A, 1821 *Topographical and statistical description of the county of Gloucestershire, 1804–1811*
Cooke, J H, 1883–4 A Roman road from Corinium to Lydney, *TBGAS*, **8**, 156–8
Cookson, A C, 1914 Roman remains (coffin) at Cirencester, *Great Western Railway Mag*, 26th May, 127
Coombes, B, 1978 Corinium roundabout, *Cotswold Life*, June, 20–1
Cooper, N, 1988 Anglo-Saxon and post-conquest churches in the Cirencester area, in *The Cirencester area*, RAI, 20–4
Cope, J C W, 1980 A correlation of Jurassic rocks in the British Isles: Part 1 Introduction and Lower Jurassic, *Geol Soc Special Rep*, **14**, London
Cope, J C W, 1980 A correlation of Jurassic rocks in the British Isles: Part 2, Middle and Upper Jurassic, *Geol Soc Special Rep*, **15**, London

Countryside Commission, 1990 *Areas of outstanding natural beauty: policy statement* (= CCP 302), Cheltenham
Cox, C, 1964 Milestones of the Stroud district, *TBGAS*, **83**, 119–42
Cox, C, 1967 Turnpike houses of the Stroud district, *TBGAS*, **86**, 118–50
Cox, C, 1991 The Bisley path – an ancient road from *Corinium* to *Glevum, Gloucestershire History*, **5**, 2–5
Cox, J C, 1949 *Gloucestershire: the little guides*, London
Crawford, O G S, 1925 *The long barrows of the Cotswolds*, Gloucester
Cripps, W J, 1877–8 On the ancient church plate at Cirencester, *TBGAS*, **2**, 92–103
Cripps, W J, 1892–3 Recent Roman finds in Cirencester, *TBGAS*, **17**, 12–16
Cripps, W J, 1894 Thirty-ninth general meeting of Wiltshire Archaeological and Natural History Society, August 1893, *WAM*, **27**, 1–10
Cripps, W J, 1898a Roman basilica at Cirencester, lately discovered by W J Cripps, *TBGAS*, **21**, 70–8
Cripps, W J, 1898b Report on the discovery of the Roman basilica of Corinium, *PSA ser 2*, **17**, 201–8
Cripps, W J, 1899 Notes on some of the relics in the Corinium Museum, *TBGAS*, **22**, 68–72
Cripps, W J, 1900 Roman altar and other sculptured stones found at Cirencester, 1899, *PSA ser 2*, **18**, 177–84
Croome, W I, 1953 Gloucestershire churches, *TBGAS*, **72**, 5–22
Croome, W I, 1966 Parish church of St John the Baptist, *Arch J*, **122**, 207–9
Crummy, P, 1990 Metrological analysis, *Current Archaeology*, **11**, 91–3
C T D, 1884 Roman coins found near Cirencester, 1759, *GNQ*, **2**, 94
Cullen, P R, 1970 Cirencester: the restoration of the Roman town wall, 1967–8, *Britannia*, **1**, 227–239

D'Almaine, H G W, 1926 The Roman amphitheatre of Cirencester, *W & G S*, 11th Sept, 6
Dannell, G B, 1977 The samian from Bagendon, in *Roman pottery studies in Britain* (eds J Dore and K Greene), BAR, **30**, 229–34, Oxford
Darby, H C, 1977 *Domesday England*, Cambridge
Darby, H C, Glasscock, R C, Sheail, J, and Veisey, G R, 1979 The changing geographical distribution of wealth in England: 1086–1334–1525, in *J Hist Geog*, **5**.3, 247–62
Darling, M J, 1977 Pottery from early military sites in western Britain, in *Roman pottery studies in Britain* (eds J Dore and K Greene), BAR, **30**, 57–100, Oxford
Darvill, T C, 1978 Perspectives and problems in the study of Gloucestershire in the third and fourth millennia BC, *Glevensis*, **12**, 13–22
Darvill, T C, 1979a A petrological study of LHS and TPF stamped tiles from the Cotswold Region, in *Roman Brick and Tile* (ed A D McWhirr), BAR, **S68**, 309–49, Oxford
Darvill, T C, 1979b The Querns Hospital kitchen garden, Cirencester, *TBGAS*, **97**, 127
Darvill, T C, 1980 Some small groups of stamped Roman ceramic tiles from the Cotswolds, *Glevensis*, **14**, 49–57
Darvill, T C, 1981a Tower Street, Cirencester, *TBGAS*, **99**, 174
Darvill, T C, 1981b Tower Street, Cirencester, *Glevensis*, **15**, 46
Darvill, T C, 1982a *The megalithic tombs of the Cotswold-Severn region*, Highworth
Darvill, T C, 1982b The ARVERI and TPLF stamped Roman ceramic tiles in the Cotswolds and Severn Valley, *TBGAS*, *100*, 47–64
Darvill, T C, 1987a *Prehistoric Gloucestershire*, Gloucester
Darvill, T C, 1987b *Ancient monuments in the countryside: an archaeological management review*, HBMCE Report, **5**, London
Darvill, T C, 1988a *Monument evaluation manual part I: introduction*, London
Darvill, T C, 1988b *Monument evaluation manual part II: single monuments*, London
Darvill, T C, 1988c *Cirencester town centre development: stage 1 archaeological assessment*, Cirencester
Darvill, T C, 1989 *Cirencester urban assessment project: project design*, Cirencester (circulated typescript)
Darvill, T C (ed), 1990 *Cotswold Archaeological Trust Ltd Annual Review 1, 1989–90*, Cirencester
Darvill, T C, 1993 *Valuing Britain's archaeological resource* (= Bournemouth University Inaugural Lecture), Bournemouth
Darvill, T C, and Cox, W L, 1980 Sewer pipeline watching brief, Baunton to North Cerney, *TBGAS*, **98**, 179
Darvill, T C, and Gerrard, C, 1990 Evaluating archaeological sites: the Cotswold Archaeological Trust approach, *CAT Annual Review*, **2**, 10–4
Darvill, T C, and Grinsell, L V, 1989 Gloucestershire barrows 1961–88, *TBGAS*, **107**, 39–105
Darvill, T C, and McWhirr, A D, 1984 Brick and Tile Production in Roman Britain: models of economic organisation, *World Archaeology*, **15**(3), 239–261
Darvill, T C, Saunders, A, and Startin, B, 1987 A question of national importance: approaches to the evaluation of ancient monuments for the Monuments Protection Programme in England, *Antiquity*, **61**, 393–408
Davey, N, 1972 The conservation of Romano-British painted plaster, *Britannia*, **3**, 251–268
Davis, C, 1881–2 The monumental brasses of Gloucestershire, *TBGAS*, **6**, 339–44
Defoe, D, 1724 *A tour through the whole island of Great Britain* (ed P Rogers), 1971
Denning, A, 1972 That opulent town and the Iron Duke, *CAHS*, **14**, 14–5
Denning, A, 1979 The town recaptured, *CAHS*, **21**, 16–19
Devine, M (ed), 1977 *The cartulary of Cirencester abbey*, vol 3, London
DoE, 1983 *Criteria for the selection of Ancient Monuments*, Press Notice 523, London
DoE, 1987 *Historic buildings and conservation areas – policy and procedures* (DoE Circular 8/87), London

DoE, 1989 *Environmental assessment: a guide to the procedures*, London
DoE, 1990 *Archaeology and planning* (= PPG16), London
Doggett, N, 1986 The Anglo-Saxon see and cathedral of Dorchester-on-Thames: the evidence reconsidered, *Oxoniensia*, **51**, 49–61
Douglas, J A, and Arkell, W J, 1928 The stratigraphical distribution of the Cornbrash: 1. The south-western area, *Q J Geol Soc*, **84**, 117–78
Dreghorn, W, 1973 *Geology explained in the Severn Vale and Cotswolds*, Newton Abbot
Durham City/EH, 1992 *Durham City: archaeological conservation and managment project. Summary report*, Dept of Archaeology, University of Durham for City of Durham Council and English Heritage
Dyer, W T, 1872 Flint-flakes from the valley of the Churn at Cirencester, *PCNFC*, **5**, 271–2
Dyke, Rev W, 1870 Antiquities and works of art exhibited, *Arch J*, **27**, 212

Edwards, T, 1961 Cirencester, *Gloucestershire Countryside*, April, 26–29
EH, [no date] *Guide for owners and occupiers of Scheduled Monuments*, London
EH, 1991a *Management of archaeological projects*, London
EH, 1991b *New work in historic churches: an English Heritage statement*, London
EH, 1991c *Exploring our past: strategies for the archaeology of England*, London
EH, 1992a *Managing the urban archaeological resource*, London
EH, 1992b *Development plan policies for archaeology*, London
EH, 1992c *Monument evaluation manual, Part IV: urban areas*, 2 vols, London
Elliott, G F, 1975 Transported algae as indicators of different marine habitats in the English Middle Jurassic, *Palaeontology*, **18**, 351–66
Esmonde Cleary, S, 1987 *Extra-mural areas of Romano-British towns*, BAR, **169**, Oxford
Esmonde Cleary, S, 1989 *The ending of Roman Britain*, London
Etheridge, R, 1895 On the rivers of the Cotteswold Hills, *PCNFC*, **11**, 49–103
Evans, A K B, 1976 The collegiate church at Cirencester: a critical examination of the historical evidence, in *Studies in the archaeology and history of Cirencester* (ed A D McWhirr), BAR, **30**, 46–60, Oxford
Evans, A K B, 1989 Cirencester's early church, *TBGAS*, **107**, 107–122
Evans, A K B, 1991 Cirencester abbey: the first hundred years, *TBGAS*, **109**, 99–116

Florentii Wignorniensis Monarchi Chronicon ex Chronicis (ed B Thorpe), 2 vols, English Hist Soc, 1848–9
Foot, D, 1968 Capital of the Cotswolds, *Gloucestershire Life and Countryside*, Dec, 22–9
Fosbroke, Rev Thomas Dudley, 1807 *Abstracts of records and manuscripts respecting the county of Gloucester, formed into a history . .* , Gloucester
Fox, A M, 1949 A late fourth-century hoard and its container from Corinium, *Antiq J*, **29**, 83–4
Fox, A M, 1951 The date of the Orpheus mosaic from The Barton, Cirencester, *TBGAS*, **70**, 51–53
Frere, S S, 1977 Roman Britain in 1976, *Britannia*, **8**, 411, 413, no 3
Frere, S S, 1983 *Verulamium excavations: volume II*, Society of Antiquaries Res Rep, **41**, London
Frere, S S, 1984a British urban defences in earthwork, *Britannia*, **15**, 63–74
Frere, S S, 1984b Roman Britain in 1983, *Britannia*, **15**, 315
Frere, S S, 1988 Roman Britain in 1987, *Britannia*, **14**, 465, 467, 470
Frere, S S, 1990 Roman Britain in 1989, *Britannia*, **21**, 348, 349
Frere, S S, 1992 Roman Britain in 1991, *Britannia*, **23**, 302–4
Frere, S S, and St Joseph, J K, 1983 *Roman Britain from the air*, Cambridge
Frith, B, 1981 Abel Wantner: an unpublished Gloucestershire historian, *TBGAS*, **99**, 170–2
Frith, B (ed), 1989 *Historical, monumental and genealogical collections relative to the county of Gloucester*
Fulford, M G, 1983 Review of 'Early Roman Occupation at Cirencester' by J S Wacher and A D McWhirr, *Britannia*, **14**, 376–7
Fulford, M G, 1984 *Silchester Defences, 1974–80*, Britannia Mon Ser, **5**, London
Fulford, M G, 1985 Excavations on the sites of the amphitheatre and *forum-basilica* of Silchester, Hampshire: an interim report, *Antiq J*, **65**, 39–81
Fulford, M G, 1989 *The Silchester amphitheatre: excavations of 1979–1985*, Britannia Mon Ser, **10**, London
Fulford, M G, 1992 Iron Age to Roman: a period of radical change in the gravels, in *Developing landscapes of Lowland Britain* (eds M G Fulford and E Nichols), Soc Antiq London Occ Paper, **14**, 23–38, London
Fulford, M G, and Huddleston, K, 1991 *The current state of Romano-British pottery studies*: a review for English Heritage, EH Occ Paper, **1**, London
Fullbrook-Leggatt, L E O, 1936 Saxon Gloucestershire, *TBGAS*, **57**, 110–135
Fuller, E A, 1874 Ancient Cirencester: its streets and hundreds, *WAM*, **14**, 216–28
Fuller, E A, 1877–8 Tenures of land, by the customary tenants, in Cirencester, *TBGAS*, **2**, 285–319
Fuller, E A, 1882 *The parish church of St John Baptist, Cirencester*, Cirencester
Fuller, E A, 1883–4a Hospital of St John, Cirencester, *TBGAS*, **8**, 224–8
Fuller, E A, 1883–4b An account and illustration of an inscribed stone found in the ruins of St John's Hospital, *TBGAS*, **8**, 183–4

Fuller, E A, 1884–5 Cirencester, the manor and the town, *TBGAS*, **9**, 298–344
Fuller, E A, 1886–7 Cirencester free grammar school, *TBGAS*, **11**, 117–129
Fuller, E A, 1890–1 Cirencester castle, *TBGAS*, **15**, 103–19
Fuller, E A, 1892–3a The parish church of St John the Baptist, *TBGAS*, **17**, 34–44
Fuller, E A, 1892–3b Cirencester abbey church, *TBGAS*, **17**, 45–52
Fuller, E A, 1892–3c Cirencester hospitals, *TBGAS*, **17**, 53–8
Fuller, E A, 1892–3d Cirencester grammar school, *TBGAS*, 17, 59–62
Fuller, E A, 1893–4a Cirencester guild merchant, *TBGAS*, **18**, 32–74
Fuller, E A, 1893–4b The register of the chapel of the Blessed Virgin Mary in the parish church of Cirencester, *TBGAS*, **18**, 320–331
Fuller, E A, 1895–6 Cirencester documents, *TBGAS*, **20**, 114–126
Fuller, E A, 1932 Medieval Cirencester, *TBGAS*, **54**, 107–15
Fuller, E A, 1933 Medieval Cirencester, *W & G S*, 8th July
Fursich, F T, and Palmer, T J, 1975 Open crustacean burrows associated with hardgrounds in the Jurassic of the Cotswolds, England, *Proc Geol Assoc*, **86 (2)**, 171–181

Gaffney, C, and Gater, J, 1991 *The use of geophysical techniques in archaeological evaluations*, IFA Technical Paper, **9**, Birmingham
Gardiner, J (ed), 1993 *Wessex Archaeology Annual Review 1992–3*, Salisbury
Garratt-Frost, S, 1992 *The law and burial archaeology*, IFA Technical Paper, **11**, Birmingham
GCC, 1979 *Report of survey: built and historic environment* (= Technical Volume 12), Gloucester
GCC, 1982 *Structure plan for Gloucestershire*, Gloucester
GCC, 1989 *The Upper Thames plan*, Gloucester
GCC, 1992 *Gloucestershire structure plan: first alteration*, Gloucester
Gerrard, C M, 1989a *St Michael's Field, Cirencester: archaeological watching brief*, CAT Typescript Rep, **8907**, Cirencester
Gerrard, C M, 1989b *15 Gosditch Street, Cirencester*, CAT Typescript Rep, **9015**, Cirencester
Gerrard, C M, 1989c *Watermoor development, City Bank Road, Cirencester. Archaeological assessment*, CAT Typescript Rep, **8904**, Cirencester
Gerrard, C M, 1990 *Kingsmeadow public enquiry, Cirencester*, CAT Typescript Rep, **9015**, Cirencester
Gerrard, C M, and Johnson, C, 1989a *32–38 Cricklade Street, Cirencester: architectural survey and archaeological watching brief*, CAT Typescript Rep, **8901**, Cirencester
Gerrard, C M, and Johnson, C, 1989b *Corinium development, Cirencester. Stage 2: archaeological evaluation. Part 1*, CAT Typescript Rep, **8902**, Cirencester
Gerrard, C M, and Walker, G, 1992 Recorded observation at St John the Baptist Church, Cirencester, 1990, *Cotswold Archaeological Trust Annual Review*, **2**, 8–9
Gilmore, J R, 1972 Cirencester Park, *Cotswold Life*, May, 20–1
Glass, H, 1991 Shorncote Quarry excavations, *Glevensis*, **25**, 42–3
Glasscock, R C, 1975 *The Lay Subsidy of 1334*, London
Goodburn, R, 1976 Roman Britain in 1975, *Britannia*, **7**, 352–4
Goodburn, R. 1978 Roman Britain in 1977, *Britannia*, **9**, 455
Goodburn, R, 1979 Roman Britain in 1978, *Britannia*, **10**, 319
Goodier, A, 1984 The formation of boundaries in Anglo-Saxon England, *Med Arch*, **28**, 1–22
Gowing, D, 1983 The population of Samuel Rudder's Gloucestershire, *TBGAS*, **101**, 147–159
Graham, R, 1907 *The abbey of Cirencester and the hospitals of St Lawrence, St John and St Thomas*, Cirencester
Gray, I, 1962a James Dallaway, b1763: a Gloucestershire antiquary and writer, *TBGAS*, **81**, 208–10
Gray, I, 1962b The Lysons Family, *TBGAS*, **81**, 212–3
Gray, I, 1965 Some seventeenth-century token-issuers, *TBGAS*, **84**, 101–9
Gray, I, 1979 A Gloucestershire postscript to the 'Domesday of Inclosures', *TBGAS*, **97**, 75–80
Gray, I, 1981 *Antiquaries of Gloucestershire and Bristol*, Bristol
Green, G W, and Melville, R V, 1956 The stratigraphy of the Stowell Park borehole (1949–1951), *Bull Geological Surv GB*, **11**, 1–61
Green, M, 1982 Wheel-god and ram-headed snake in Roman Gloucestershire, *TBGAS*, **99**, 109–115
Grew, F O, 1980 Roman Britain in 1980, *Britannia*, **12**, 355
Griffiths, N, 1978 A fragment of a Roman cavalry tombstone from Cirencester, *Britannia*, **9**, 396–7
Grundy, G B, 1935–6 Saxon charters and field names of Gloucestershire, *TBGAS*, **57**, 2 vols
Grundy, G B, 1936 The ancient woodland of Gloucestershire, *TBGAS*, **58**, 65–155
Grundy, G B, 1937 The ancient woodland of Gloucestershire: additional notes, *TBGAS*, **59**, 205–9
Gurney, D A, 1985 *Phosphate analysis of soils: a guide for the field archaeologist*, IFA Technical Paper, **3**, Birmingham
Guy, C J, 1986 Archaeological review, Cirencester, *TBGAS*, **104**, 232–3

Hadow, Rev W E, 1877–8 On the monumental brasses at Cirencester, *TBGAS*, **2**, 151–162
Harker, A, 1886 Exposure of the Kellaway's rocks in a recent cutting near Cirencester. Read 1884, *PCNFC*, **8**, 176–87
Harker, A, 1886–7 Third field meeting, *PCNFC*, **9**, 86–7
Harker, A, 1887 Excursion to Cirencester and Minchinhampton, *Proc Geol Assoc*, **10**, 157–63

Harker, A, 1890 On the sections in the Forest Marble and Great Oolite formations, exposed railway . . . Cirencester to Chedworth, *PCNFC*, **10**, 82–93

Harker, A, 1891 On the geology of Cirencester Town: discovery of Oxford clay in deep well-boring at the Water Works, *PCNFC*, **10**, 178–191

Harker, A, 1891–2 Midland and South Western Extension Railway (Cirencester), *PCNFC*, **10**, 219

Harmer, W Scotford, 1901 *Cirencester illustrated: guide to the history, antiquities, educational facilities*, Cirencester

Harmer, W S, 1912 Cirencester: its old streets and houses, *W & G S*, 20th Jan, 41

Harmer, W S, 1924 Cirencester present and past, in *A history of Cirencester* (ed W St Clair Baddeley), 309–28, Cirencester

Hartland, J, 1983–4 The Cirencester-Stroud Road, *CAHS*, **26**, 6–13

Hartland, J, 1984–5 The Cirencester-Lechlade Road, *CAHS*, **27**, 3–10

Hartley, B, 1983 The enclosure of Romano-British towns in the second century AD, in *Rome and her northern provinces* (eds B Hartley and J S Wacher), 84–95, Gloucester

Harvey, J H (ed), 1969 *William of Worcester: the itineraries*, Oxford

Haslam, J (ed), 1984 *Anglo-Saxon towns*, Chichester

Hassall, M, and Tomlin, R S O, 1977 Inscriptions, *Britannia*, **8**, 426–449

Hassall, M, and Tomlin, R S O, 1980 Inscriptions, *Britannia*, **11**, 403–417

Hassall, M, and Tomlin, R S O, 1983 Inscriptions, *Britannia*, **14**, 336–356

Haverfield, F, 1892–5 Roman inscription from Cirencester illustrating fourth century Britain, *Arch Oxoniensis*, 215–26

Haverfield, F, 1893a Romano-British inscriptions, 1892–3, *Arch J*, **50**, 284–5

Haverfield, F, 1893b Three notable inscriptions, *Arch J*, **50**, 308

Haverfield, F, 1895 Notes on *fibulae*, *Arch J*, **62**, 265–9

Haverfield, F, 1899 A Roman charm from Cirencester, *Arch J*, **56**, 319–23

Haverfield, F, 1918–9 An address, references to the Basilica, Roman street plan, the Bathurst Museum and carved stones, *TBGAS*, **41**, 155–7

Haverfield, F, 1920 Roman Cirencester, *Archaeologia*, **49**, 161–209

Haverfield, F, and Jones, H S, 1912 Some representative examples of Romano-British sculpture, *JRS*, **2**, 121–152

Hawkes, S, 1974 Some recent finds of late Roman buckles, *Britannia*, **5**, 386–393

Heighway, C, 1984a Saxon Gloucester, in *Anglo-Saxon towns in southern England* (ed J Haslam), 359–83, Chichester

Heighway, C, 1984b Anglo-Saxon Gloucester to AD 1000, in *Studies in late Anglo-Saxon settlement* (ed M L Faull), 35–53, Oxford

Hemingway, J, 1991 Archaeological review: Watermoor House, *TBGAS*, **109**, 225

Hemsley, R, 1925 Beecham's historical paintings of old Ciceter, *W & G S*, 31st Oct

Henig, M, 1979 A late Roman signet ring from Cirencester, *TBGAS*, **97**, 121–2

Henig, M, 1982 A Roman bronze ring from Cirencester, *TBGAS*, **100**, 253–4

Henig, M, 1985a Two stone figure-carvings from Cirencester, *TBGAS*, **103**, 212–4

Henig, M, 1985b Graeco-Roman art and Romano-British imagination, *JBAA*, **138**, 1–22

Hennessey, B, Hems, L, and Pearce, G, 1990 *Conservation areas in the West Midlands and South-West*, London

Henshaw, C, 1982a Archaeological review: Baunton, east of Ermin Street, *TBGAS*, **100**, 259

Henshaw, C, 1982b Archaeological review: Preston, Witpit Copse, *TBGAS*, **100**, 265

Hereford and Worcester County Archaeological Servic 1993 *The Central Marches Historic Town Survey: pilot study assessment reports*, Worcester

Hewett, C A, 1971 A barn of Plantagenet times, *Country Life*, 30th Dec, 1844

Hewett, C A, 1972 The tithe barn at Siddington, Gloucestershire, *Arch J*, **129**, 145–7

Hibbert, T, and Richardson, L, 1913 The water supply of Cirencester, *PCNFC*, **18**, 175–84

Hicks, Rev F W Potto, 1950 *The story of Cirencester abbey*, Cirencester

Hill, D, 1978 Trends in the development of towns during the reign of Ethelred II, in *Ethelred the Unready* (ed D Hill), BAR, **59**, 213–26, Oxford

Hill, R E, 1971 *The parish church of St John Baptist, Cirencester*, Cirencester

Hillam, J, and Groves, C, 1992 Tree-ring dates from Sheffield University: list 42, *Vernacular Architecture*, **23**, 44–6

Hilton, R H, 1967 *A medieval society*, Cambridge

Hodgson, D, forthcoming, A late Roman courtyard house at South Shields and its parallels, in *Architecture in Roman Britain* (ed P Johnson)

Holbrook, N, forthcoming, Roman bridges in Britain, in *Architecture in Roman Britain* (ed P Johnson)

Holgate, R, 1988 *Neolithic settlement of the Thames basin*, BAR, **194**, Oxford

Hooke, D, 1978 Early Cotswold woodland, *J Historical Geography*, **4.4**, 333–41

Household, H, 1969 *The Thames & Severn canal*, Newton Abbot

Hoyle, J P, 1991 Archaeological review: Victoria Road Infants School, *TBGAS*, **109**, 224, 225

Hull, E, 1855 On the physical geography and Pleistocene phaenomena of the Cotteswold hills, *Q J Geol Soc*, **11**, 477–96

Hurst, H, 1988 Gloucester (*Glevum*), in *Fortress into city: the consolidation of Roman Britain first century AD* (ed G Webster), London

Hussey, C, 1950 Cirencester House, Gloucestershire, the seat of Earl Bathurst, *Country Life*, 16 June, 1796

Hyett, F A, 1895–7a Notes on the first Bristol & Gloucestershire printers, *TBGAS*, **20**, 38–51

Hyett, F A, 1895–7b A catalogue of manuscripts in the British Museum relating to the county of Gloucester . . . Bristol, *TBGAS*, **20**, 161–221

Hyett, F A, and Austin, R, [no date] *Biographical supplement to the bibliographer's manual of Gloucestershire literature*, Gloucester

Hyett, F A, 1895–16 *The bibliographer's manual of Gloucestershire literature, with biographical supplement*, Gloucester
IFA, 1987 *The Institute of Field Archaeologists: Memorandum and Articles of Association*, Birmingham
IFA, 1988 *By-laws of the Institute of Field Archaeologists: code of practice*, Birmingham
IFA, 1990 *By-laws of the Institute of Field Archaeologists: code of approved practice for the regulation of contractual arrangements in field archaeology*, Birmingham
Ings, M, 1992 *Memorial Hospital Grounds, Sheep Street, Cirencester: archaeological watching brief*, CAT Typescript Rep, **9282**, Cirencester
Irvine, J T, 1878–9 Antiquities at Cirencester and Berkeley, memoranda of certain sketches, *TBGAS*, **3**, 256–7
Irving, G V, 1861 On the *iters* of Richard of Cirencester, *JBAA*, **17**, 189–197

Jackson, G P, 1960 The street names of Old Cirencester, *Gloucestershire Countryside*, June 1960, 21
Jackson, R, 1985 Cosmetic sets from late Iron Age and Roman Britain, *Britannia*, **16**, 165–192
Jamieson, A, and Smith, B S, 1968 *Gloucestershire: a local history handbook*, Gloucester
Jane, L C, 1966 *Asser's Life of Alfred*, New York
Jenkins, S C, 1990 *The Midland and South Western Junction Railway*, Oxford
Jennings, R W, 1973 The Cirencester contest and its aftermath, *TBGAS*, **92**, 157–168
Jennings, R W, 1976 The Reverend W F Powell and the restoration of Cirencester parish church, in *Studies in the archaeology and history of Cirencester* (ed A D McWhirr), BAR, **30**, 158–167, Oxford
Jermy, K E, 1990 Probable Roman road from Barnsley Park to Cirencester, *CBA GP 13 NL*, 113, 21
Johns, M, 1980a Cirencester, *Gloucestershire and Avon Life*, Aug, 38–40
Johns, M, 1980b New year, new developments at Cirencester, *Gloucestershire and Avon Life*, Jan, 36–7, 39, 41
Johnson, C, 1990a *Latton Bypass, Wiltshire: assessment*, CAT Typescript Rep, **9030**, Cirencester
Johnson, C, 1990b *Littlecote Park, Berkshire. Archaeological assessment*, CAT Typescript Rep, **9022**, Cirencester
Johnson, C, 1991a *Querns School, Querns Lane, Cirencester*, CAT Typescript Rep, **9149**, Cirencester
Johnson, C, 1991b *Burgess, Querns Road, Cirencester*, CAT Typescript Rep, **9150**, Cirencester
Johnston, D E, 1967 Two mosaicists of the Corinian school, *TBGAS*, **86**, 102–6
Jones, A E, 1983 Protestant dissent in Gloucestershire: a comparison between 1676 and 1735, *TBGAS*, **101**, 131–44
Jones, J B, 1949 *Diurnalia Portulacana: a Romano-British war-time diary for the year 407 AD*, Swindon
Jones, J B, 1952 A Cirencester tile (and its cursive inscription), *Antiquity*, **26**, 88–90

Kähler, H, 1939 *Die Romische Kapitelle des Rheingebiets*, Cologne
Kaye, P, 1971 A town like Cirencester, *Gloucestershire Life*, July, 20–5
Keene, D, 1990 Textile manufacture, in *Object and economy in medieval Winchester, volume i*, (ed M Biddle), Winchester Studies 7.ii, 200–14, Oxford
Kellaway, G A, and Welch, F B A, 1948 *British regional geology: Bristol and Gloucester District*, London
Kenyon, K M, 1948 *Excavations at the Jewry Wall site, Leicester*, Soc Ants Res Rep, 15, Oxford
Kenyon, R F, 1987 The Claudian coinage, in *The coins from excavations in Colchester 1971–79* (ed N Crummy), Colchester Archaeol Rep, **4**, 24–41, Colchester
Kersting, A F, 1951 *Cirencester, a series of illustrations*, London
Keynes, S, 1987 Regenbald the Chancellor, *Anglo-Norman Studies*, **10**, 185–222
King, A, 1978 A comparative survey of bone assemblages from Roman sites in Britain, *BULLIAL*, **15**, 207–232
King, R, 1990a *38 Market Place, Cirencester*, CAT Typescript Rep, **9015**, Cirencester
King, R, 1990b *18 The Avenue, Cirencester*, CAT Typescript Rep, **9015**, Cirencester
King, R, 1990c *Chesterton Playing Fields, Cirencester*, CAT Typescript Rep, **9015**, Cirencester
King, R, 1990d *2 Corinium Gate, Cirencester*, CAT Typescript Rep, **9015**, Cirencester
King, R, 1990e *Watermoor development, City Bank, Cirencester. Stage 2. Archaeological evaluation*, CAT Typescript Rep, **9027**, Cirencester
King, R, 1990f *33 Sheep Street, Cirencester*, CAT Typescript Rep, **9016**, Cirencester
King, R, 1990g *Brewery Car Park, Cirencester. Stage 3 Excavation*, CAT Typescript Rep, **9033**, Cirencester
King, R, 1990h *95 Victoria Road, Cirencester. Archaeological watching brief*, CAT Typescript Rep, **9029**, Cirencester
King, R, 1990i *Old Tetbury Road, Doctors Surgery, Cirencester*, CAT Typescript Rep, **9015**, Cirencester
King, R, 1992 *Burgess Yard, Querns Road, Cirencester: archaeological evaluation*, CAT Typescript Rep, **9276**, Cirencester
Kingsley, N, 1989 *The country houses of Gloucestershire*, vol 1 1500–1660, Cheltenham
Kingsley, N, 1990 Kip's conundrum, *Country Life*, Nov, 60–1
Kingsley, N, 1992 *The country houses of Gloucestershire*, vol 2 1660–1830, Chichester
Kingsley, N W, and Smith, D J H, 1990, *Handlist of the contents of the Gloucestershire Record Office*, Gloucester
Kirby, I, 1968 Gloucester diocesan records, *TBGAS*, **87**, 119–30

Lane, J, and Vaughan, S, 1992 *An evaluation of the impact of PPG16 on archaeology and planning*, London
Latimer, J, 1889–90 Leland in Gloucestershire, *TBGAS*, **14**, 221–284

Leech, R, 1977 *The upper Thames valley in Gloucestershire & Wiltshire: an archaeological survey of the river gravels*, CRAAGS Survey Report, **4**, Bristol
Leech, R, 1981 *Historic towns in Gloucestershire: archaeology and planning*, CRAAGS Survey Report, **3**, Bristol
Leech, R H, and McWhirr, A D, 1982 Excavations at St John's Hospital, Cirencester, 1971 and 1976, *TBGAS*, **100**, 191–209
Leedy, W C, 1980 *Fan vaulting: a study of form, technology and meaning*, London
Leemans, C, 1838 Three sepulchral monuments from Watermoor, *Archaeologia*, **27**, 211–28
Leighton, W, 1946–8 Endowed charity in Bristol and Gloucestershire, *TBGAS*, **67**, 1–20
Leland, J, *The itinerary of John Leland in or about the years 1536–1539* (ed L Toulmin Smith), 1964, London
Levien, E, 1869 On Richard of Cirencester and his writings, *JBAA*, **25**, 120–133
Lewis, M J T, 1966 *Temples in Roman Britain*, Cambridge
Lewis, S, 1835 *Topographical dictionary of England*, London
Liversidge, J, 1962 Cirencester: Romano-British wall painting from the Dyer Court Excavations, 1957, *TBGAS*, **81**, 41–50
Lloyd-Morgan, G, 1983 A note on the diploma in the Corinium Museum, Cirencester, *Britannia*, **14**, 266–7
Long, J A, 1981 Poets' folly, *Country Life*
Lonsdale, W, 1832 Report of a survey of the oolitic formations of Gloucestershire, *Proc Geol Soc*, **1**, 413
Loveridge, G G, 1977 *Watermoor through the ages: reflections on a Cirencester community over 150 years*, Cirencester
Loyn, H, 1961 Boroughs and mints AD 900–1066, in *Anglo-Saxon coins* (ed R H M Dolley), London
Lucy, W C, 1872 The gravels of the Severn, Avon, and Evenlode, and their extension over the Cotteswold Hills, *PCNFC*, **5**, 71–142
Lucy, W C, 1880 On the extension of the Northern Drift and Boulder Clay over the Cotteswold range, *PCNFC*, **7**, 48–61
Lucy, W C, 1888 *The origin of the Cotteswold Club and an epitome of the proceedings from its formation to May 1887*, Gloucester
Lycett, J, 1856 *The Cotteswold hills: handbook introductory to their geology and palaeontology*, London & Stroud
Lyell, A H, 1912 *A bibliographical list, descriptive of Romano-British architectural remains in Great Britain*
Lysons, Rev S, 1860 *Romans in Gloucestershire*
Lysons, Rev S, 1861 *What has Gloucestershire achieved?*
Lysons, S, 1789 An account of some Roman antiquities discovered at Comb End farm, near Cirencester, *Archaeologia*, **9**, 319–322
Lysons, S, 1791–96 *Etchings of views and antiquities in the county of Gloucester hitherto imperfectly or never engraved*
Lysons, S, 1792 Account of Roman antiquities discovered in the county of Gloucester, *Archaeologia*, **10**, 131–6
Lysons, S, 1801–17 *Reliquiae Britannico-Romanae*, London
Lysons, S, 1803–4 *A collection of Gloucestershire antiquities*, London
Lysons, S, 1806 Appendix, *Archaeologia*, **15**, 405–6
Lysons, S, 1817 An account of the remains of several Roman buildings and other Roman antiquities in county of Glos, *Archaeologia*, **18**, 112–125

Mackintosh, M, 1986 The sources of the horseman and fallen enemy motif on the tombstones of the western Roman empire, *JBAA*, **139**, 1–21
Maclean, J, 1892–3 The armory and merchant's marks in the ancient church of Cirencester, *TBGAS*, **17**, 268–321
Maiden, J, 1958 Three Gloucestershire military tombstones, *TBGAS*, **77**, 31–41
Mann, J C, 1961 The administration of Roman Britain, *Antiquity*, **35**, 316–20
Margary, I D, 1967 *Roman roads in Britain*, London
Marshall, A, 1989 Possible Roman/medieval road at Fulford, near Withington, Glos, *TBGAS*, **107**, 210–7
Martin, A T, 1895–6–7 The Cotswolds in the time of the Romans, *TBGAS*, **20**, 255–66
Maxfield, V, 1991 Tiverton Roman fort (Bolham): excavations 1981–6, *Proc Devon Archaeol Soc*, **49**, 25–98
McLees, D, 1988 Cirencester, church of St John the Baptist, in *The Cirencester Area*, RAI, 38–40
McPhail, R I, 1981 Soil and botanical studies of the 'Dark Earth', in *The environment of man: the Iron Age to the Anglo-Saxon period* (eds M Jones, and G Dimbleby), BAR, **87**, 309–28
McWhirr, A D, 1971 Cirencester, *Current Archaeology*, **3** no. 6, 144–152
McWhirr, A D, 1972 Cirencester – 1970, *Glevensis*, **6**, 12–3
McWhirr, A D, 1973 Cirencester 1969–1972: ninth interim report, *Antiq J*, **53**, 191–218
McWhirr, A D, 1974 Cirencester, *Current Archaeology*, **42**, 216–9
McWhirr, A D, 1976a Cirencester (*Corinium*): a *civitas capital* in the west country, in *The Roman West Country* (eds K Branigan and P J Fowler), 81–98, Newton Abbot
McWhirr, A D (ed), 1976b *Studies in the archaeology and history of Cirencester*, BAR, **30**, Oxford
McWhirr, A D, 1978 Cirencester 1973–6: tenth interim report, *Antiq J*, **58**, 61–80
McWhirr, A D, 1981 Cirencester mosaics, *Mosaic*, **4**, 5–7
McWhirr, A D, 1982a *Roman Gloucestershire*, Gloucester
McWhirr, A D, 1982b When the cavalry roamed Cirencester, *Gloucestershire and Avon Life*, April, 39
McWhirr, A D, 1986 *Houses in Roman Cirencester*, Cirencester Excavations, **3**, Cirencester
McWhirr, A D, 1988 Cirencester's contribution to the development of urban archaeology, *Cirencester Miscellany*, CAHS, **1**, 11–16
McWhirr, A D, and Viner, D J, 1978 The production and distribution of tiles in Roman Britain with particular reference to Cirencester, *Britannia*, **9**, 357–77

McWhirr, A D, Viner, L, and Wells, C 1982 *Romano-British cemeteries at Cirencester*, Cirencester Excavations, **2**, Cirencester
Mediocritas, 1873 Ancient Cirencester and its streets and hundreds, *W & G S*, 4th Oct, 5
Miles, D, 1984 Romano-British settlement in the Gloucestershire Thames Valley, in *Archaeology in Gloucestershire* (ed A Saville), 191–211, Cheltenham
Miles, D, and Palmer, S, 1987 Siddington, *Glevensis*, **21**, 48–9
Miller, C, 1990 The model farms of Victorian Gloucestershire, *Gloucestershire History*, **4**, 11–3
Millett, M, 1990 *The romanization of Britain: an essay in archaeological interpretation*, Cambridge
Mills, S, and Reimer, P, 1989 *The mills of Gloucestershire*, Buckingham
Milner, J C, 1981 A medieval road to Cirencester, *Glevensis*, **15**, 9–13
Moberley, G H, 1877–8 Local names near Cirencester, *TBGAS*, **2**, 118–27
Moore, J S (ed), 1982 *Domesday Book: Gloucestershire*, Chichester
Moore, J S, 1989 The Gloucestershire section of Domesday Book: geographical problems of the text, part 3, *TBGAS*, **107**, 123–148
Morgan, T, 1886 *Romano-British mosaic pavements: a list of their discovery and interpretation of their designs*
Murchison, R I, 1832 On the structure of the Cotswold Hills, the country around Cheltenham, *Proc Geol Soc*, **1**, 388
Musty, J, 1973 A preliminary account of the medieval pottery industry at Minety, north Wiltshire, *WAM*, **68**, 79–88

Negus, P E, and Beauvais, L, 1976 The Fairford Coral Bed (English Bathonian), Glos, *Proc Geol Assoc*, **86**, 183–204
Newmarch, C H, 1853 Notes on some Roman buildings at Cirencester, the Roman *Corinium, Antiq Comm (Camb Antiq Soc)*, **1**, 55–8
Norris, H E, 1924 Cirencester British coins – Cunobeline AD 5–41, *W & G S*, 9th Aug
Norris, H E, 1924 A Cirencester Spanish coin, *W & G S*, 10th May

OAU, 1991 *Cirencester Kings Meadow*: archaeological evaluation in advance of Tesco superstore. Preliminary report for project planning, Oxford
Observer, 1867 Railings in the churchyard, *W & G S*, 22nd June, 4
Owens, W H, 1975 In and around Cirencester, *The Lady*, 23rd Oct, 634–5
O'Neil, B H St John, 1952, Cirencester Park Theodosian hoard, *Num Chron*, **6 S 12**, 128–9
O'Neil, B H St John, and Fox, A, 1949 A late fourth-century hoard and its container from Corinium, *Antiq J*, **29**, 83–4
O'Neil, H, 1957 Akeman Street, Quenington, Gloucestershire, *TBGAS*, **76**, 35–43
O'Neil, H, and Grinsell, L, 1960 Gloucestershire barrows, *TBGAS*, **79**, 5–149
Ove Arup, 1991 *York development and archaeological study*, Manchester

Paddock, J M, 1993 *The storming of Cirencester in 1643: an episode in the Civil War*, Corinium Museum, Cirencester
Page, W (ed), 1907 *Victoria history of Gloucestershire*, vol 2, Oxford
Paine, M J, 1969 *Turnpike Trusts of Cirencester*, unpubl thesis
Painter, A C, 1931 Early road planning in the middle Cotswolds, *TBGAS*, **53**, 113–44
Palmer, R, and Cox, C, 1993 *Uses of aerial photography in archaeological evaluations*, IFA Technical Paper, **12**, Birmingham
Palmer, T J, and Fursich, F T, 1974 The ecology of a middle Jurassic hardground and crevice fauna, *Palaeontology*, **17**, 507–24
Parry, C, 1989 Archaeological Review, *TBGAS*, **107**, 257
Parry, C, 1991 Archaeological Review, *TBGAS*, **109**, 235
Parsons, C F, 1976 Ammonite evidence for dating some Inferior Oolite sections in the north Cotswolds, *Proc Geol Assoc*, **87 (1)**, 45–63
Parsons, Richard, [no date] *History of Gloucestershire*, Bodleian Library, MS Rawl. B323
Peacey, A, 1979 *Clay tobacco pipes in Gloucestershire*, CRAAGS Occasional Papers, **4**, Bristol
Pearce, J W E, 1936 Roman site finds from Cirencester, *Num Chron*, **5 S 16**, 261–3
Pearson, D K, 1973 Cirencester, *Cotswold Life*, Dec, 31–8
Perry, R, 1945 The Gloucestershire woollen industry 1100–1690, *TBGAS*, **66**, 49–137
Phillips, E J, 1976 A Roman figured capital in Cirencester, *JBAA*, **129**, 35–41
Pitcher, S, 1925 Ancient stained glass in Gloucestershire Churches, *TBGAS*, **47**, 287–345
Platt, C, 1976 *The English medieval town*, London
Playne, G F, 1877a On the ancient camps of Gloucestershire, *PCNFC*, **6**, 202–46
Playne, G F, 1877b On the recent calcareous deposits of the Cotteswolds, *PCNFC*, **6**, 81–9
Pooley, C, 1860 Brief notes on Cirencester high cross, *PCNFC*, **2**, xii-xiv
Pooley, C, 1868 *Notes on the old crosses of Gloucestershire*
Potter, K R, 1976 *Gesta Stephani*, Oxford
Pounds, N, 1988 Cirencester and the Cotswolds, in *The Cirencester area*, RAI, 7–14
Powell, A, 1910 Detailed description and account of repair of Roman tesselated pavement at The Barton, *TBGAS*, **33**, 69–77
Price, F D, 1938 Gloucester diocese under Bishop Hooper, *TBGAS*, **60**, 51–151
Priestley, W C, 1933 A Roman coffin and other relics unearthed near the Tetbury Road, *W & G S*, 21st Jan, 7 c3–4
Pugh-Smith, J, and Samuels, J, 1993 PPG16: two years on, *Journal of Planning and Environmental Law*, 203–210

Quecester, 1864 The Corinium Museum, *W & G S*, 23rd April, 8 c2
Quesne-Bird, N du, 1971 A mould from Cirencester, *Num Circular*, **79**, 322

Rahtz, P A, 1976 Buildings and rural settlement, in *The archaeology of Anglo-Saxon England* (ed D M Wilson), 49–98, London
Rainey, A, 1973 *Mosaics in Roman Britain*, Newton Abbot
Rambler, 1924 Centenary of finding of Barton pavement, *W & G S*, 10th May
Rambler, 1925 An ancient word-square, *W & G S*, 7th Feb
Rambler, 1926a 'Cirencester' or 'Ciceter', *W & G S*, 11th Sept, 2
Rambler, 1926b Cirencester Bull Ring, *W & G S*, 18th Sept, 2
Ramsay, Sir A C, 1858 *Geology of parts of Wiltshire and Gloucestershire*, London
Rankov, N B, 1982 Roman Britain in 1981, *Britannia*, **13**, 377, 380
Rawes, B, 1977 A check list of castles and other fortified sites of medieval date in Gloucestershire, *Glevensis*, **11**, 39–41
RCHME 1976 *Iron age and Romano-British monuments in the Gloucestershire Cotswolds*, London
RCHME, 1993a *Recording England's past*, London
RCHME, 1993b *Urban archaeology databases: data standards and compilers manual. Part I: compilers manual*, (circulated script report), London
RCHME/EH 1992 *Thesaurus of archaeological site types*, London
Reece, R, 1956 A note on a small excavation at Cirencester, *TBGAS*, **75**, 203–4
Reece, R, 1958 A note on Roman coins found at the Dyer Court excavations, Cirencester, 1957, *BNJ*, **29**, 188
Reece, R, 1962a The abbey of St Mary, Cirencester, *TBGAS*, **81**, 198–203
Reece, R, 1962b The Oakley Cottage Romano-British cemetery, Cirencester, *TBGAS*, **81**, 51–72
Reece, R, 1970a Two 'lost' mosaics at Cirencester, *TBGAS*, **89**, 175–6
Reece, R, 1970b Cirencester Grammar School 1960–61, *TBGAS*, **89**, 11–14
Reece, R, 1972 A short survey of the Roman coins found on fourteen sites in Britain, *Britannia*, **3**, 269–276
Reece, R, 1973 Roman coinage in Britain and the western empire, *Britannia*, **4**, 227–251
Reece, R, 1976a From Corinion to Cirencester – models and misconceptions, in *Studies in the archaeology and history of Cirencester* (ed A D McWhirr), BAR, **30**, 61–79, Oxford
Reece, R, 1976b The Ashcroft site, Cirencester, *TBGAS*, **94**, 92–100
Reece, R, 1980 Town and country: the end of Roman Britain, *World Archaeology*, **12** no. 1, 77–91
Reece, R, 1982 The Roman coins, in *Early Roman Occupation at Cirencester* (eds J S Wacher and A D McWhirr), Cirencester Excavations, **1**, 86–7, Cirencester
Reece, R, 1983 Continuity on the Cotswolds: some problems of ownership, settlement and hedge survey between Roman Britain and the Middle Ages, *Land Hist*, **5**, 11–9
Reece, R, 1988 *My Roman Britain*, Cotswold Studies, **3**, Cirencester
Reece, R, 1990 *Excavations, survey and records around Cirencester*, Cotswold Studies, **2**, Cirencester
Reece, R, 1991a Money in Roman Britain: a review, in *Roman Britain: recent trends* (ed R F J Jones), 29–34, Sheffield
Reece, R, 1991b *Roman coins from 140 sites in Britain*, Cotswold Studies, **4**, Cirencester
Reece, R, and Catling, C, 1975 *Cirencester: the development and buildings of a Cotswold town*, BAR, **12**, Oxford
Rennie, D M, 1957 A section through the Roman defences in Watermoor Recreation Ground, Cirencester, *Antiq J*, **37**, 206–15
Rennie, D M, 1971 Excavations in the Parsonage Field, Watermoor Road, Cirencester, 1958, *TBGAS*, **90**, 64–94
Renow, S, 1985 *Vertical air photography*, IFA Technical Paper, **2**, Birmingham
Richardson, K M, 1962 Excavations in Parsonage Field, Watermoor Road, Cirencester, 1959, *Antiq J*, **42**, 160–182
Richardson, L, 1907–8 Excursion to the mid and south Cotteswolds and to the Tortworth Area, *Proc Geol Assoc*, **20**, 514–529
Richardson, L, 1908 On a new species of pollicipes from the Inferior Oolite of the Cotteswold Hills, *Geol Mag*, Aug 1908, 351–2
Richardson, L, 1910 On the stratigraphic distibution of the Inferior-Oolite vertebrates of the Cotteswold Hills etc, *Geol Mag*, **7**, 272–3
Richardson, L, 1911 On the sections of Forest Marble and Great Oolite...between Cirencester and Chedworth, *Proc Geol Assoc*, **22** pt 2, 95–115
Richardson, L, 1913 A deep boring at Kemble, *PCNFC*, **18**, 185–9
Richardson, L, 1922 A boring at Calcutt, near Cricklade, Wiltshire, *Geol Mag*, **59**, 354–5
Richardson, 1923 Thames Head, *PCNFC*, **21** pt 2, 161–66
Richardson, L, 1924a A boring at Lewis Lane, Cirencester, *PCNFC*, **22**, 53–4
Richardson, L, 1924b Excursion to North Cerney, Calmsden, Winterwell and Ampney Crucis, *PCNFC*, **21** pt 3, 183–5
Richardson, L, 1924c Winterwell, *PCNFC*, **21** pt 3, 219–222
Richardson, L, 1925 Excursion to Cirencester and district, 7–10 June 1924, *Proc Geol Assoc*, **36** (1), 80–99
Richardson, L, 1929 *The country around Moreton in Marsh*, London
Richardson, L, 1930a *Wells and springs of Gloucestershire*, London
Richardson, L, 1930b A boring at Ready Token, near Cirencester, *PCNFC*, **24**, 185–8
Richardson, L, 1933 *The country around Cirencester*, London
Richardson, L, 1936–8 Boreholes' sections: Baunton, near Cirencester, *PCNFC*, **26**, 67–72
Richardson, L, and Sawyer, J, 1907–1909 Excursion to Cirencester, Tues May 12th 1908, *PCNFC*, **16**, 207–212
Richmond, Sir Ian, 1966 Roman Gloucestershire, *Arch J*, **122**, 177–181
Rigby, V, 1977 The Gallo-Belgic pottery from Cirencester, in *Roman pottery studies in Britain and beyond* (eds J N Dore and K Greene), BAR Int Ser, **30**, 37–45, Oxford
Rigby, V, 1988 Gallo-Belgic wares, in 'Excavations at Ditches hillfort, North Cerney, Gloucestershire, 1982–3' (ed S D Trow), *TBGAS*, **106**, 19–85 (see 60–3)

Rivet, A L F, 1966 Summing-up: some historical aspects of the *civitates* of Roman Britain, in *The civitas capitals of Roman Britain* (ed J S Wacher), 101–113, Leicester

Rivet, A L F, 1970 The British section of the Antonine Itinerary, *Britannia*, **1**, 34–82

Rivet, A L F, and Smith, C, 1979 *The place-names of Roman Britain*, London

Robinson, M, 1992 Evironmental archaeology of the river gravels: past achievements and future directions, in *Developing landscapes of Lowland Britain* (eds M G Fulford and E Nichols), Soc Antiq London Occ Paper, **14**, 47–62, London

Rodwell, W and K, 1973 The Roman villa at Rivenhall, Essex: an interim report, *Britannia*, **4**, 115–127

Rolleston, Prof, 1877–8 On the three periods known as the Iron, the Bronze, and the Stone Ages, *TBGAS*, **2**, 128–150

Roper, I M, 1910 Monumental effigies, *TBGAS*, **33**, 96–125

Roper, I M, 1931 *Monumental effigies of Gloucestershire and Bristol*, Gloucester

Ross, C D (ed), 1964 *The cartulary of Cirencester abbey*, vols 1 and 2, London

Rudder, S, 1781 *History and antiquities of Gloucestershire*

Rudder, S, 1779 *A new history of Gloucestershire*

Rudder, S, 1800 *History and antiquities of Cirencester*, 2 edn, Cirencester

Rudge, T, 1803 *The history of the county of Gloucester*, Gloucester

Rudge, T, 1811 *History and antiquities of Gloucestershire*

Russell, J, 1985 The Keynsham Roman villa and its hexagonal *triclinia*, *Bristol and Avon Archaeology*, **4**, 6–12

Russett, V, 1989 Archaeological review: A417/Cirencester bypass survey, *TBGAS*, **107**, 258

Saville, A, 1980 *Archaeological sites in the Avon and Gloucestershire Cotswolds*, CRAAGS Survey Report, **5**, Bristol

Saville, A (ed), 1984 *Archaeology in Gloucestershire*, Cheltenham

Savory, C H, [no date] *History of the abbey and ancient church of St John, Cirencester*

Savory, C H, 1858 *History of the town of Cirencester*, Cirencester

Savory, C H, 1878 *A description of Oakley House and Park, Cirencester*

Sawyer, J, 1896–7 On some ancient roads on the Cotswolds, *TBGAS*, **20**, 247–54

Sawyer, P, 1968 *Anglo-Saxon charters. An annotated list and bibliography*, London

Scaife, R, 1991 Trinity Mill, Bagendon. Pollen analysis, in *A419/417 Cirencester and Stratton Bypass. Stage 2: archaeological evaluation* (ed CAT 1991), CAT Typescript Rep, **9141**

Schofield, J, 1987 Recent approaches in urban archaeology, in *Urban archaeology in Britain* (eds J Schofield and R Leech), CBA Res Rep, **61**, London

Schofield, J, and Palliser, D, 1981 *Recent archaeological research in English towns*, London

Sewell, E C, 1907 Short note on the basilica, *TBGAS*, **30**, 37

Sewell, E C, 1922a Roman remains at Cirencester, *W & G S*, 1st July

Sewell, E C, 1922b Roman remains at Cirencester, *W & G S*, 15th July

Sewell, E C, 1924–6 Discovery of a Romano-British interment at Stratton, near Cirencester, *TBGAS*, **22**, 299–301

Sewell, E C, 1926a Cirencester or Ciceter, *W & G S*, 18th Sept, 2

Sewell, E C, 1926b Corinium Museum, letters to the editor, *W & G S*, 21st Aug

Sewell, E C, 1927 Discovery of a Romano-British interment at Stratton, near Cirencester, *W & G S*, 26th March

Sewell, E C, 1929 Romano-British mosaic pavement at Cirencester, *W & G S*, 5th Oct

Sewell, E C, 1930 Roman mosaic pavements at Corinium, *Proc Cotteswold Club*, **24**, 97–101

Sewell, E C, 1933 The Corinium Museum, Cirencester, and its curators, *TBGAS*, **55**, 317–21

Sewell, E C, 1934 The Corinium Museum at Cirencester, and its curators, *W & G S*, 30th June

Sewell, E C, 1935 The Roman palindrome found at Cirencester, *TBGAS*, **57**, 152–7

Sewell, E C, and Powell, A H, 1910 The Roman pavement at The Barton, Cirencester, *TBGAS*, **33**, 67–77

Shaw, M 1989 Northampton, *Current Archaeology*, **91**, 241–4

Sheail, J, 1972 The distribution of taxable population and wealth in England during the early sixteenth century, *Trans Inst Brit Geog*, **55**, 111–26

Shirley, E P, 1867 *Some account of English deer parks*, London

Simpson, J J, 1931 The wool trade and the woolmen of Gloucestershire, *TBGAS*, **53**, 65–97

Sims-Williams, P, 1983 The settlement of England in Bede and the Chronicle, *ASE*, **12**, 1–41

Sinclair, J S, 1931 *Parish church of St John the Baptist at Cirencester*, Cirencester

Skinner, Rev John, 1824 Continuation of journal from Cheltenham to Birdlip and Cirencester, November 10th 1824, *British Museum* Add MS 33679

Slater, T R, 1976a The town and its region in the Anglo-Saxon and medieval periods, in *Studies in the archaeology and history of Cirencester* (ed A D McWhirr), BAR, **30**, 81–108, Oxford

Slater, T R, 1976b Estate ownership and nineteenth-century suburban development, in *Studies in the archaeology and history of Cirencester* (ed A D McWhirr), BAR, **30**, 145–57, Oxford

Slater, T R, 1976c The Cirencester Improved Dwellings Company, 1880–1914, in *Studies in the archaeology and history of Cirencester* (ed A D McWhirr), BAR, **30**, 171–97, Oxford

Slater, T R, 1977 Landscape parks and the form of small towns in Great Britain, *T Inst British Geographers*, **2.2**, 314–331

Slater, T R, 1978 Family, society and the ornamental villa on the fringes of English country towns, *J Historical Geography*, **4.2**, 129–144

Smart, G, and Anderson, M, 1990 *Planning and management of areas*, (= CCP 295), Cheltenham
Smith, A H, 1964–5 *The place-names of Gloucestershire*, Cambridge
Smith, C R, 1852 Remarks on recent researches at Cirencester, *JBAA*, **7**, 64–6
Smith, D, 1976 Medieval timber building: a surviving fragment, in *Studies in the archaeology and history of Cirencester* (ed A D McWhirr), BAR, **30**, 109–112, Oxford
Smith, D J, 1974 Roman mosaics in Britain before the fourth century, in *Actes du IIeme colloque la mosaique antique, Vienne (Isere), 1971*
Smith, I, 1972 Ring ditches in eastern and central Gloucestershire, in *Archaeology and the landscape* (ed P J Fowler), 157–167, London
Smith, J, 1608 *Men and armour in Gloucestershire in 1608*, 2 edn, 1980, Gloucester
Smith, W 'Strata', 1815 *Geological map of England and Wales*
Smith, W 'Strata', 1819 *Geological map of Gloucestershire*
Sommer, S, 1984 *The military vici of Roman Britain*, BAR, **129**, Oxford
Steane, J, 1985 *The archaeology of medieval England and Wales*, London
Startin, B, 1988 The Monuments Protection Programme, *Conservation Bulletin*, **6**, 1–2
Startin, B, 1991 Protecting the archaeology of our historic towns, *Conservation Bulletin*, **13**, 14–15
Stenton, F M, 1971 *Anglo-Saxon England*, Oxford
Strong, D, 1971 The Corinthian capitals, in *Excavations at Fishbourne* (ed B Cunliffe), vol 2, 11–15
Stukeley, W, 1721 Drawings in a journey with Mr Roger Gale 1721, *Bodleian Library* MS Top gen.d.13
Stukeley, W, 1776 *Itinerarium curiosum*, 2nd ed, London, (first edition 1724)
Sullivan, P, 1924 Scratch dials in Gloucestershire, *TBGAS*, **46**, 169–186
Swan, V G, 1975 Oare reconsidered and the origins of Savernake ware in Wiltshire, *Britannia*, **6**, 37–61

Tann, J, 1965 Some problems of water-power – a study of mill siting in Gloucestershire, *TBGAS*, **84**, 53–77
Tate, W E, 1943 Gloucestershire enclosure acts and awards, *TBGAS*, **64**, 1–70
Taunton, J H, 1868 Remarks on the watershed of the Cotteswolds, in connexion with the water supply to the metropolis, *PCNFC*, **4**, 249–54
Taunton, J H, 1872 Sapperton tunnel on the Thames & Severn canal, *PCNFC*, **5**, 255–270
Taunton, J H, 1886 Baunton mill Boring, *PCNFC*, **9**, 60
Taunton, J H, 1887 Some notes on the hydrology of the Cotteswolds and the district around Swindon, *PCNFC*, **9**, 52–69
Taylor, C C, 1983 *Village and farmstead*, London
Taylor, C S, 1889 *An analysis of the Domesday survey of Gloucestershire*, BGAS, Bristol
Taylor, C S, 1890–1 Early christianity in Gloucestershire, *TBGAS*, **15**, 120–38
Taylor, C S, 1891–2 Gloucestershire in the eighth century, *TBGAS*, **16**, 208–230
Taylor, C S, 1892–3 The Danes in Gloucestershire, *TBGAS*, **17**, 68–95
Taylor, C S, 1895–7 Cotswold in Saxon times, *TBGAS*, **20**, 267–306
Taylor, C S, 1917 The Norman settlement in Gloucestershire, *TBGAS*, **40**, 57–88
Taylor, H M, and Taylor, J, 1965–78 *Anglo-Saxon architecture*, Cambridge
Taylor, J N, 1970 A Cirencester treasure trove, *TBGAS*, **89**, 177
Taylor, M V, and Collingwood, R G, 1921 Roman Britain in 1921 and 1922, *JRS*, **11**, 208, 239
Thompson, W, and Sewell, E D, 1914 Excursion to Cirencester, *PCNFC*, **18**, 212–7
Thornton, A, 1967 *The mosaic pavements of Corinium, the Roman Cirencester*, Cirencester
Thorpe, B (ed), 1848–9 *Florentii Wignorniensis Monarchi Chronicon ex Chronicis*, 2 vols, English Hist Soc
Todd, M, 1977 'Famosa Pestis' and Britannia in the fifth century, *Britannia*, **8**, 319–325
Tomkins, R, 1987 *Street names of Cirencester*, Cirencester
Tomlinson, M J, 1986 *Foundation design and construction*, 5th ed, London
Torrens, H S, 1982 The geology of Cirencester and district, in *Early Roman occupation at Cirencester* (eds J S Wacher and A D McWhirr), Cirencester Excavations, **I**, 72–8, Cirencester
Toulmin Smith, L (ed), 1964 *The itinerary of John Leland in or about the years 1536–1539*, London
Townsend, G F, 1869 Incidents at Cirencester during the Civil War, 1642–1646, *JBAA*, **25**, 149–57
Toynbee, J M C, 1964a *Art in Roman Britain*
Toynbee, J M C, 1964b *Art in Britain under the Romans*, Oxford
Toynbee, J M C, 1976 Roman sculpture in Gloucestershire, in *Essays in Bristol and Gloucestershire history* (eds P McGrath and J Cannon), BGAS, 62–100, Bristol
Trow, S, 1990 By the northern shore of the ocean. Some observations on the acculturation process at the edge of the Roman world, in *The early Roman empire in the west* (eds T Blagg and M Millett), 103–18
Tucker, C, 1849 Collections illustrative of Roman occupation in Britain, no. 1 Corinium, *Arch J*, **6**, 321–34

Upton, C, 1909 On the occurrence of Chara-Nucules in the Forest Marble of Tarlton, near Kemble, Glos, *PCNFC*, **16** pt 3, 237–9
Urban, Mr, 1835–6 Roman sepulchral stone found at Cirencester, *Gents Mag*, **4**, 302
Urban, Mr, 1837 Roman sepulchral monuments found near Cirencester, *Gents Mag*, **7**, 586–8

Verey, D, 1970 *Buildings of England: Gloucestershire, vol I, the Cotswolds*, London
Verey, D, 1973a Two Victorian architects' work in Gloucestershire, *TBGAS*, **92**, 5–11

Verey, D, 1973b Architect of great assurance: Samuel Whitfield Daukes, *Country Life*, 6th Dec, 1914–5

Verey, D, 1976 The architect and architecture of Watermoor House, in *Studies in the archaeology and history of Cirencester* (ed A D McWhirr), BAR, **30**, 168–70, Oxford

Vernon, T, 1985 The past is your compass, *Gloucestershire and Avon Life*, Mar, 40–41

Viner, D J, 1969 Cirencester Excavation Committee 1969, *Glevensis*, **4**, 15–6

Viner, D J, 1973a Cirencester: 1971–2, *Glevensis*, **7**, 15–8

Viner, D J, 1973b An iron signet ring from Cirencester, *TBGAS*, **92**, 208–9

Viner, D J, 1973c *Guide to the surviving monuments of Corinium: the Roman Cirencester*, Cirencester

Viner, D J, 1976a *Cirencester as it was*, Nelson

Viner, D J, 1976b The Corinium Museum at Cirencester: redevelopment and conservation, *Mus J*, Jun 1976, 5–6

Viner, D J, 1976c The Thames and Severn Canal in Cirencester, in *Studies in the archaeology and history of Cirencester* (ed A D McWhirr), BAR, **30**, 126–44, Oxford

Viner, D J, 1979 Excavations in Cirencester – twenty years on, *Glevensis*, **13**, 35–8

Viner, D J, 1980a The Cirencester word-square, *Glevensis*, **14**, 59–60

Viner, D J, 1980b *The Corinium trail: a guide to Roman Cirencester*, Cirencester

Viner, D J, 1982 Cirencester, two quarter-staters of EISU, *TBGAS*, **100**, 260

Viner, D J, 1984 Tetbury Brewery and Cirencester Maltings, *GSIA*, 34–6

Viner, D J, 1985 The turnpike house, *Period Home*, Aug 5–12

Viner, D J, 1988 *Cirencester town station: an outline history*, Cirencester

Viner, D J, 1991 Lock-ups at Cirencester and Bisley, *TBGAS*, **109**, 207–17

Wacher, J S, 1961 Cirencester, 1960: first interim report, *Antiq J*, **41**, 63–71

Wacher, J S, 1962 Cirencester, 1961: second interim report, *Antiq J*, **42**, 1–14

Wacher, J S, 1963 Cirencester 1962: third interim report, *Antiq J*, **43**, 15–26

Wacher, J S, 1964a Cirencester 1963: fourth interim report, *Antiq J*, **44**, 9–18

Wacher, J S, 1964b A survey of Romano-British town defences of the early and middle second century, *Antiq J*, **119**, 103–13

Wacher, J S, 1965 Cirencester 1964: fifth interim report, *Antiq J*, **45**, 97–110

Wacher, J S, 1966 Earthwork defences of the second century, in *The Civitas Capitals of Roman Britain* (ed J S Wacher), 60–9, Leicester

Wacher, J S, 1972 *Corinium*

Wacher, J S, 1974 Villae in urbibus? *Britannia*, **5**, 282–4

Wacher, J S, 1975 *Towns of Roman Britain*, London

Wacher, J S, 1978 *Roman Britain*, London

Wacher, J S, 1981 *Cirencester Roman amphitheatre*, London

Wacher, J S, and McWhirr, A D, 1982 *Early Roman occupation at Cirencester*, Cirencester Excavations, **1**, Cirencester

Wainwright, G J, 1991 *Exploring our past: strategies for the archaeology of England*, London

Walcott, M E C, 1878 Abbeys of Winchcombe, Hayles, Cirencester, and Hales Owen, *JBAA*, 333–47

Walker, G T, 1989a *Abbey Grounds, Cirencester*, CAT Typescript Rep, **9015**, Cirencester

Walker, G T, 1989b *20 Cricklade Street, Cirencester. Archaeological assessment and evaluation*, CAT Typescript Rep, **8908**, Cirencester

Walker, G T, 1990 *Roman Town Wall, Abbey Grounds, Cirencester*, CAT Typescript Rep, **9020**, Cirencester

Walker, G T, and Barber, A, 1989 *Corinium Development, Cirencester. Stage 2: archaeological evaluation. Supplementary report*, CAT Typescript Rep, **8903**, Cirencester

Walker, G T, 1993 *A419/417 Cirencester and Stratton Bypass, Gloucestershire. Archaeological appraisal of objectors route R5*, CAT Typescript Rep, **93106**, Cirencester

Walker, G T, and Gerrard, C M, 1990 *Parish Church, Cirencester*, CAT Typescript Rep, **9015**, Cirencester

Walls, R, 1986 Langley's mill, Cirencester, *CAHS*, **28**, 4–17

Walters, R C S, 1928 *Ancient wells, springs and holy wells of Gloucestershire*, Bristol

Walthew, C V, 1975 The town house and the villa house in Roman Britain, *Britannia*, **6**, 189–205

Wantner, Abel, [no date] History of county of Gloucester, *Bodleian Library* MSS Top.Glouc.c.2–3

Ward, J, 1892 Notes on archaeology in provinical musuems. 14 – the Corinium Museum, Cirencester, *Antiquary*, **26**, 149–53

Watkin, W T, 1880 Recent Roman discoveries at Maryport, Beckfoot and Cirencester, *Arch J*, **37**, 320–22

Watkin, W T, 1886 Roman inscriptions discovered in Britain in 1885, *Arch J*, **43**, 286

Webster, G, 1959 Cirencester: Dyer Court Excavations, 1957, *TBGAS*, **78**, 44–85

Webster, G, 1960 The Roman military advance under Ostorius Scapula, *Arch J*, **115**, 49–98

Webster, G, 1970 The military situation in Britain between AD 43 and 71, *Britannia*, **1**, 179–97

Webster, G, 1988 A copper-alloy terret from Tower Street, Cirencester, *TBGAS*, **106**, 203–4

Weigall, A, 1926 *Wanderings in Roman Britain*

Wells, C, 1973 A palaeopathological rarity in a skeleton of Roman date, *Medical History*, **17**, 339

Welsford, J, 1987a *Cirencester: a history and guide*, Gloucester

Welsford, J, 1987b *Cirencester in old photographs*, Gloucester

Welsford, J, and Grace, P, 1990 *Cirencester in the 1930s and 40s*, Nelson

Wethered, E, 1891 The Inferior Oolite of the Cotteswold hills, with special reference to its microscopical structure, *Q J Geol Soc*, **47**, 550–70

Whaite, H C, 1929 *St Christopher in English medieval wall painting*, London
Whatley, E, 1894–5 On the discovery of skeletons at The Barton, Cirencester, and other Roman finds of 1896, *TBGAS*, **19**, 394–398
Whatley, E, 1895–6 Recent Roman finds at The Barton – skeletons, coins, pottery etc, *TBGAS*, **20**, 5
Wheeler, L, 1992 *Cirencester amphitheatre: the excavations 1962, 1963 and 1966*, Unpublished MA in Post-Excavation Skills, University of Leicester
Whimster, R, 1989 *The emerging past: air photography and the buried landscape*, RCHME, London
Whitelock, D, Douglas, D C, and Tucker, S J (eds), 1961 *The Anglo-Saxon chronicle: a revised translation*, London
Wild, J P, 1970 Button-and-loop fasteners in the Roman Empire, *Britannia*, **1**, 137–55
Wilkinson, D J, 1982 Archaeological review: Town Court (Brewery), *TBGAS*, **100**, 260–1
Wilkinson, D J, 1984a Archaeological investigations in St Michael's Field 1983, *CAHS*, **26**, 23–5
Wilkinson, D J, 1984b Cirencester: St Michael's Field, Querns Hospital, *TBGAS*, **102**, 224
Wilkinson, D J, 1986 Archaeological review: Cirencester, *TBGAS*, **104**, 233
Wilkinson, D J, 1988a Archaeological observations at Tower Street, Cirencester, *TBGAS*, **106**, 201–3
Wilkinson, D J, 1988b Cirencester: site report, *Britannia*, **19**, 465–7, no. 6
Wilkinson, D J, 1988c The Roman quarry at The Querns, Cirencester, *TBGAS*, **106**, 204–7
Wilkinson, D J, and McWhirr, A D, forthcoming *Cirencester: Saxon church and medieval abbey*, Cirencester Excavations
Williams, A, 1879 *Lays and legends of Gloucestershire*
Williams, J H, Shaw, M, and Denham, V, 1985 *Middle Saxon palaces at Northampton*, Northampton Development Corporation Arch Mon, **4**, Northampton
Williams, T W, 1908 Gloucestershire medieval libraries, *TBGAS*, **31**, 78–195
Willmore, H H, 1939 Stone coffins, Gloucestershire, *TBGAS*, **61**, 135–171
Wills, J, 1989 Archaeological review: Cirencester, Victoria Road School, *TBGAS*, **107**, 254
Wills, J, 1990 Archaeological review, *TBGAS*, **108**, 194–5
Wilmott, A, 1980 Kenchester (*Magnis*): a reconsideration, *Trans Woolhope Natur Hist Field Club*, **43.2**, 116–33
Wilson, D R, 1970 Roman Britain in 1969, *Britannia*, **1**, 293
Wilson, D R, 1971 Roman Britain in 1970, *Britannia*, **2**, 275
Wilson, D R, 1972 Roman Britain in 1971, *Britannia*, **3**, 339
Wilson, D R, 1973 Roman Britain in 1972, *Britannia*, **4**, 307, 309
Wilson, D R, 1974 Roman Britain in 1973, *Britannia*, **5**, 448
Wilson, D R, 1975 Roman Britain in 1974, *Britannia*, **6**, 271, 273
Witchell, E, 1877 On the angular gravel of the Cotteswolds, *PCNFC*, **6**, 146–153
Witchell, E, 1886a On the pisolite and the basement beds of the Inferior Oolite of the Cotteswolds, *PCNFC*, **8**, 35–49
Witchell, E, 1886b On the basement beds of the Inferior Oolite of Gloucestershire, *Q J Geol Soc*, **42**, 264–71
Witts, G B, 1883 *Archaeological handbook of the county of Gloucester*, Cheltenham
Woodward, H B, 1894 The Jurassic rocks of Britain, the Lower Oolitic Rocks of England (Yorkshire excepted), *Mem Geol Surv*, **4**, 509
Woodward, H B, 1895 The Jurassic Rocks of Britain, the Middle and Upper Oolitic Rocks of England (Yorkshire excepted), *Mem Geol Surv*, **5**, 36
Woodward, S P, 1853 Geology of the district explored by the Cotteswold Club, and . . . clay subsoil of the College Farm, *PCNFC*, **1**, 2–8
Worcestre, W de, *Itineraries* (ed J H Harvey), 1969, Cambridge
Worssam, B C, 1984 Constitution of northern drift at a Cotswold site, *Proc Geol Assoc*, **98**, 269–70
Wright, R P, 1964 Roman Britain in 1963: inscriptions, *JRS*, **54**, 177, 180
Wright, R P, 1967 Roman Britain in 1966: inscriptions, *JRS*, **57**, 203, 208
Wright, R P, 1968 Roman Britain in 1967: inscriptions, *JRS*, **58**, 206, 210, 213
Wright, R P, and Hassall, M W C, 1971 Inscriptions, *Britannia*, **2**, 289–304
Wright, R P, and Hassall, M W C, 1972 Inscriptions, *Britannia*, **3**, 352–67
Wright, R P, and Hassall, M W C, 1973 Inscriptions, *Britannia*, **4**, 324–337
Wright, R P, and Hassall, M W C, 1974 Inscriptions, *Britannia*, **5**, 461–470
Wright, R P, Hassall, M W C, and Tomlin, R S O, 1976 Inscriptions, *Britannia*, **7**, 378–92
Wright, T 1863 On some Roman antiquities recently found at Cirencester, the Roman *Corinium*, *JBAA*, **19**, 100–5

Yorke, B, 1990 *Kings and kingdoms in early Anglo-Saxon England*, London

Zeepvat, R J, 1979 Observations in Dyer Street and Market Place, Cirencester in 1849, 1878 and 1974/5, *TBGAS*, **97**, 65–73

CARTOGRAPHIC REFERENCES

Cartographic references consulted during the course of the Project are listed chronologically within the parishes of Baunton, Cirencester (with Stratton), Preston and Siddington.

General

Ordnance Survey, 1875 25″ map.
Ordnance Survey, 1875 1:500 map.
Ordnance Survey, 1921 25″ map.
Geological Survey of Great Britain (England and Wales), sheet 252 Swindon (solid and drift), sheet 235 Cirencester (drift).

Baunton

No *Inclosure Map*.
Tithe Map, 1849, whole parish, surveyed by John Bravender; apportionment (1,310a). GRO GDR/T1/19.
A survey of the manor of Baunton in the county of Glos, the estate of Thomas Master Esq. 1768, surveyed by Giles Coates. GRO D674b P10.
A plan of the manors . . . belonging to Thomas Master Esq. 1774. See Cirencester and Stratton.
Estate and parish map of Baunton, Preston, Stratton and Cirencester. *c*1775. GRO D1388.
Baunton Field Gardens. 1849. GRO D674b P12.
Plan of the parish of Baunton in the county of Gloucester. 1849. GRO D674b P11.
Abbey Estate, parishes of Baunton, Preston, Stratton and Cirencester. 1858. GRO D674b P5.

Cirencester (including Stratton)

No *Inclosure Map*, but see below, and Preston.
Tithe Map for Cirencester and Preston (including Wiggold Farm, now in Ampney Crucis). 1838, surveyed by Richard Hall. GRO GDR/T1/55 G5.
Maps surveyed, parish of Stratton, in preparation for inclosure and draft inclosure maps. *c*1771. GRO D674b P37–40.
Part of Stratton parish west of Gloucester–Cirencester road, surveyed in preparation for inclosure. *c*1771. GRO D674b P37, P38, P40.
Part of Cirencester parish and north-west area of town showing town walls, buildings, inclosed fields. *c*1771, surveyed by Ric. Richardson. GRO D674b P14.
Plan of the Manors . . . belonging to Thomas Master Esq, parishes of Stratton, Baunton, Preston, Cirencester. 1774, surveyed by Ric. Richardson. GRO D674b P44.
Survey of Chesterton tything in the parish of Cirencester in county of Gloucester. 1777, surveyed by B.F. Lewis. GRO D2525.
Plan of borough town of Cirencester showing property of T.B. Howell Esq. 1795. GRO D2525.
Plan of borough town of Cirencester. 1795. GRO Pc.594(L), photocopy 235(s); original owned by Bingham Library, Cirencester.
Powell chantry estates in the parish of Cirencester. 1799. GRO P86/CH1/78.
Lands adjoining river Churn and canal in parish of Cirencester. *c*1800. GRO D674b P20.
Plan of the tything of Chesterton in the parish of Cirencester in the county of Gloucester. 1807, surveyed by Hall & Son. GRO D2525.
Small area of Cranham Farm, south of town. *c*1810, surveyed by Hall & Son. GRO D1388.
A sketch of the allotment of land in the North Meadow to the Trustees of Powell's Charity, Cirencester. *c*1813. GRO D1441.
Plan of the Barton Farm etc in parish of Cirencester . . . belonging to Rt Hon Henry Earl Bathurst. *c*1820. GRO D2525.
Whole of town centre of Cirencester. 1835. GRO photoc 236(S).
Plan of town showing buildings, wards, road, rivers, woodland. 1835, surveyed by John Wood. GRO D674b P48 (photoc 948(N)).
Plan of the Eight Acres and Townsend Ground let out in small lots for field gardens. 1835. GRO D674b/E39.
Map of the Borough of Cirencester 1837. 1837, surveyed by J Dewhurst of London. GRO D2525.

Land exchange between Stratton and North Cerney. 1840. GRO D2525.
Plan of land at Cirencester belonging to Mr Lloyd arranged in lots. 1840, surveyed by A & C Paul of Cheltenham. GRO D1388.
Chesterton farm house and buildings. 1841. GRO D674b P24.
Land adjoining London and Burford Roads, owned by Miss Master. 1847. GRO D674b P15.
Map of property belonging to Trustees of late Joseph Cripps, Esq. 1847. 1847, surveyed by Bravender & Trinder. GRO D2525 box 29.
Bowling Green Farm. 1848. GRO D674b P16.
The New Mills and surrounding fields, water and woodland. 1848. GRO D674b P34.
Part of the Abbey estate (includes Stratton and Baunton). 1849. GRO D674b P42.
Cirencester Park around Cecily Hill, Timber Office. *c*1850. GRO D2525.
Part of Broad Ride, Cirencester Park, Swiss Cottage, Cricket Ground. Mid 19th century. GRO D2525 box 29.
Section of the Broad Ride, Cirencester parish. Mid 19th century. GRO D2525.
Map of Hailey Wood and places adjacent [Cirencester, Sapperton, Rodmarton, Coates]. 1856. GRO D2525.
Farm lands in parishes of Cirencester, Stratton & Daglingworth, property etc of Rt Hon Earl Bathurst. 1857, surveyed by Charles Matthews. GRO D2525.
Plan and terrier of Chesterton farm in parishes of Cirencester & Siddington, property of Rt Hon Earl Bathurst. 1857, surveyed by Charles Matthews. GRO D2525.
Cirencester, Stratton, Daglingworth, Glos: Exchange. 1859. GRO D2525.
Allotment gardens in Sheep St, Castle St, Sheep St Lane, Cirencester. *c*1860. GRO D2525.
Coates and Cirencester, county of Gloucester, Exchange. 1862. GRO D2525.
Copy of plan on deed of Conveyance Earl Bathurst to Cirencester Burial Board [land at Chesterton]. 1869. GRO D2525.
St Lawrence's Hospital Charity. *c*1880. GRO D2525.
Parish of Cirencester, ground plan of the Market House. *c*1880. GRO D2525.
Abbey estate, plan of building land, between R. Churn and Victoria Road. 1899–1910. GRO D1388.
Unpublished: plan of town annotated with notes showing discoveries made by F W Taylor. 1911. Formerly in Cripps Museum, now in Corinium Museum, Cirencester.

Preston

Inclosure map for Preston and Stratton. 1770. GRO D674b/P2, D674b/P38 and P40.
Tithe Map see Cirencester and Preston 1838.
Part of manor of Preston for the Right Worpp. Thomas Master Esq. 1687, surveyed by Oliver Langton of Purton. GRO D674b/P1.
Part of Preston parish, mainly N of Cirencester-Fairford road, showing inclosed fields, owners. *c*1770. GRO D674b P31.
A Plan of the parish of Preston. 1770, surveyed by Rich Richardson Jn. GRO D674b P2.
Parish of Preston showing strips in east, naming some occupiers. 18th century. GRO D674b P29.
Plan of part of Preston around village naming owners of small areas of land. 1842. GRO D674b P33.
Plan of proposed railway in South Cerney & Preston [not carried out]. 1846. GRO D182/VI/4.
Plan – farm occupied by Mr Herbert, including farm bldgs, woodland. 1861. GRO D674b P35.
Plan of glebe land and Mr Cripps' freehold land in Preston parish. 1862. GRO D674b P36.

Siddington

Inclosure Map for Siddington, 557 acres. 1779, Bathurst Frederick Lewis of Cirencester. GRO Q/RI 127.
Siddington tithe map – exchange of glebe only. 1845. GRO GDR/T1/162.
A Plan of Siddington Quarry Field. 1772. GRO D2525 Box 29.
The Manor and Parishes of Siddingtons in the county of Glos. *c*1778. GRO D2525.
Plan of Glebe lands in the parish of Siddington in the county of Glos. 1806, surveyed by Hall & Son. GRO D2525.
Plan of the consolidated parishes of Siddington in the county of Glos. *c*1845. GRO D2525.
Plan showing the Cottages and Gardens at Siddington. 1850. GRO D2525.
Shows whole of parish of Siddington. *c*1870. GRO D2525 box 29.

INDEX

Compiled by Susanne Atkin

AS = Anglo-Saxon; BA = Bronze Age; IA = Iron Age; med = medieval; post-med = post-medieval; RB = Romano-British.

A page number followed by (2) indicates that there are two references to the subject on the page.

Page numbers in *italic* indicate illustrations.

Abbey Grounds 22, 30, 52, 59, 77, 94, 110, 113, 122, 139, 140, 141, 152, *168*, 169; Roman defences (town wall etc) *58*, 65, 67, 70, 77, 140, 161, 165, 169, street metalling 59; pre-Conquest church 93, 107, 169
Abbey House 18, 109, 119, *120*, 126, 169
Abbey Mill 104, 107
Abbey Nurseries 77
Abbey Road Garages, RB site 81
Abbey of St Mary (Augustinian) 17, 18, 30, 93, 98, 99, *100*, 103, 105, 107–11, 114, 117, 118, 141, 165, 167; Abbey Church 17, 107, 110, 140; courtyard house 65, 167; precinct 45, 106, 107, 108, 114, 139, 140, 141, 169; pre-Conquest church 93, 107, 110, 140, 169
accumulated deposits 9, 10–11, 12, 45, 76–8, 93–4, 113–14, 134, 138, 167, 169–70
Admiral's Walk 22, 39, 57, *58*, 78
aerial photography 9, 25, 29, 35, 49, 56, 158, 159
agriculture *31*, 86, 118, 135–7
Akeman Street 52, 53, *80*
Alfred's Hall *see* Woodhouse, The
Almery Gate 108
Almery Grange 107
almshouses *100*, 113, *120*, 123, 128, 137, 167
amphitheatre 17, 18, 58, 62, 78, 79, *80*, 81, *82*, 84, 86, 104, 140, 144, 149, 152, 165, 167; early med fortifications 87–8
Ancient Monuments and Archaeological Areas Act 1979 9, 24, 149, 152, 166
Archaeological Assessment 156, 157, 158, 159, 160
Archaeological Resource Management 147–73 *passim*
Archebalds, med manor house *100*, 105, 118
Areas of Outstanding Natural Beauty (AONB) 33, *151*, 152
Armoury, Cecily Hill *120*, *131*, 132
Ashcroft 25, 72, 128, 169
Ashcroft Gardens 139, 141
Ashcroft House *120*, 124
Ashcroft Road 59, 60, 77, 123, 130, 139; Mycalex site 22, 56, *58*, 63, 87, 107
Aubrey, William, antiquarian 17
Avenue, The *58*, 59, 63, 123, 124, 167, *182*
Ayshecroft 106

Bagendon 5, 22, 55, 56, 86; Mesolithic site 47; IA 49; *oppidum* 77; parish 97, 136
banks (buildings) *120*, 123, 131
barns 136; Siddington Tithe Barn 115, 117, *117*, 118, 137, 149, 152, 167
barrows: prehistoric, bowl 48, long 47, *50*, 118, 149, 167, round 48, *50*, 56, 167; Roman *80*, 82–3, 86, 167, *and see* Grismond's Tower; Tar Barrow(s)
Barton Farm 97, *100*; early med/AS cemetery 87, 88, *88*, 90, 95, *96*, 97
Barton Field 106
Barton Grange 107–8
Barton House 123, 131
Barton Lane *see* St Lawrence's Hospital
Barton Mill (Chester Mill), watermill 30, 97, *100*, 104, 131
Barton, The: Roman/RB period 18, *80*, 85, 86, 88; gravel extraction 30, 137, 144; cemetery *see* Barton Farm
basilica 7, 20, 22, 25, 43, 45, *58*, 61–2, *61*, 72, 73, 75, 78, 86, 140, 165, 167, *183*
Bath Gate 67, 70, 78, *80*, 81, 165; building outside 53, 84, 85; Roman cemetery 22, 39, *58*, 79, 81, 85; street metalling 60, 81
Bath Road 134
Bathurst family 124; Earls 20, 21, 63, 124, 128
Baunton 4, *5*, 25, 26, 36, 44, 134; designation 33; Exhibition Barn 48, 52; land classification *31*, *32*; parish 95, 152, *and see* Witpit Copse; peat deposits 33; Prior's Court 115; St Mary Magdalene, chapelry/church 92, *116*, 117, *133*, 134; *Thwyselede Weye* 115; prehistoric period *50*, 144; med 115; post-med 132, *133*, 134, 135, 136
Baunton Downs, RB settlement *80*, 81, 86
Beeches, The 22; prehistoric adze 48, *50*; Roman *23*, 72, 85; wells 30
Beeches Nursery Field *50*, 56
Beeches Road, Roman house complex 39, *58*, 65, 74, 76(2), 85, 86, 87, 167, *168*, 169
Bingham Hall, King Street 64, *120*, 129, 132, 134
Bingham Hall Gardens, Roman remains 59, 64, *64*, 72, 73, *73*, 74
black earth (dark earth) 76, 87, 91–2, 93, 94, 105
Black Jack Street 91, 99, *100*, 103, 107, 123
bones, faunal 86, 105
botanical remains 105
Bottehall/Boot Hall *100*, 102, 118
Bowling Green *80*, 81, 84, 137, 144, *168*, 169
Bowling Green Farm *133*
Brain(e)'s Mill (watermill) *100*, 104
breweries *120*, 130
Brewery car-park 56, *58*, 60, 77, 113, 138, 139, 141, 161, *168*, 169–70
brickworks 30, *133*, 137
bridges: Roman 78–9, *80*; med 98–9, 106, 118, Clement's Bridge or Groomstoole 98, 99, *100*, *102*, 103, Gildenbrigge (later Bailiff's Bridge) 98, *100*, New Bridge 99, *100*, St John's Bridge 98–9, *100*, Swyne Bridge 98, *100*, 103; post-med *120*
Bronze Age 48–9
bronze working 104
buildings: Listed Buildings 33, *150*, *151*, 152; standing buildings 36, 105, 113, 138, 165; *and see under periods*
Bullring 18, 79
Burial Grounds *120*, 152–3

Butcher(s) Row 99, *100*, 103
Butter Row 103

canals 18, 45, 119, *120*, *133*, 134, 135, 137
castle 17, 45, 98, *100*, 106–7, 114, 139
Castle ditches 113
Castle Street 91, 99, *100*, 105, 107, 119, *120*, 130, 131, 141; Nos 45–49 105
cattle market *120*, 130–1; coffins 79
Cecily Hill 66, 91, 94, 98, *100*, 123, *131*, 132, 134, 139; mill site 101, 104
Cecily Street 99, *100*
cellars 25, 77
cemeteries: Neolithic/early BA 49; Roman/RB 18, 22, 25, 39, 47, *58*, 79, *80*, 81–4, *82*, 85, 86, 144, 149, 167; early med/AS 87, 88, *88*, *89*, 90, 95, *96*, 97; post-med 45, 128, *133*; *see also* barrows
Cerney, South, charter 95
Cerney, North *5*; North Plantation 52
chapelries 95, *116*, 117
Cheltenham Road 132
Chester Lodge 169, *and see forum*
Chester Mews, ditch 53
Chester Street *58*, 59, 72, 124, 141
Chesterton 128, 130, *133*;
Chesterton Farm, settlement 149
Chesterton House *100*, 105, *120*, 124, 129
Chesterton Lane, quarries 30
Chesterton woods 118(2), 144
churches and chapels 17, 144
Roman cemetery churches 84, 93;
early med: pre-Conquest (AS) *89*, 90, 91, 92–3, *92*, 94, 95(2), *96*, 97(2), 107, 110, 111, 140, 169; St Cecilia's chapel 17, 84, *89*, 93, *100*, 107, 111, 114; St Lawrence's chapel *89*, 93, *100*;
med 98, *100*, 106, 111, 113, 115, 117, 118, Norman 111; Abbey Church 17, 107, 110, 140; St Cecilia's church *100*, 111, 118, 140; St John the Baptist (parish church) 17, 18, 98, *100*, 102, 105, 110, 111, 113, 114, 118, 126, 129, 139, 140, 167, crypt 103, Roman street metalling 59; St Lawrence's church *100*, 111, 118, 140;
post-med 120, 126–8, *133*, Holy Trinity 126–7, non-conformist chapels *120*, 122, 127–8
Church Street 59, 123, 124, 130
Churchyard Cross 99, *100*, 149
Churn, River 29, 67, 71, 113; crossing of 49, 52, 55, 78–9, *80*; Inner Churn 30, 103; mills 97, 137; pre-/early Roman course 30, 52, 70; valley of 30, 33, 77
cinemas 129
Cirencester Excavation Committee (CEC) 3, 7, 17, 22, 23, 39, 66, 79, 140, 172
Cirencester House 124
Cirencester Park 18, 33, 45, 79, 85, 86, 111, 117, 119, *120*, 124, 126, 129, 132, *133*, 134, 135, 136, 137, 141, 144, 153
City Bank (Watermoor) 22, 30, 52, 65, 77, *168*, 169
Civil War 131–2
Clark's Lane site *80*, 85
cloth industry 98, 99, 103–4, 130
coal 30
coins 39; Dobunnic 49; Roman 53, 64, 65, 71, 74, 76, 81, 82, 86, hoard 71; med 105
Conservation Areas 33, 152
Corinium Gate 76, *168*, 169; No.7 76
Corinium Museum 21, 22, 24, 165, 173
Corin Street (now The Avenue) 124
Corn Hall 130
Cotswold Archaeological Trust (CAT) 4, 23, 39, 140, 165, 172, 173
Cotswold Area of Outstanding Natural Beauty (AONB) 33, *151*, 152
Cotswold Community, IA settlement 51
Cotswold District Council 4, 24, 170
Cotswold Mill 59
Cotteswold Naturalists' Field Club 18, 20
County Planning Policy 155–6
Court Hill 115
court house 129; of Knights Hospitallers 99, 101
Coxwell Street 99, *100*, 103, 104, 141; post-med buildings 119, *120*, 123, 127, 130
Cranhams Lane 132
Cricklade Road, burials 83
Cricklade Street 77, 91, 99, *100*, 103, 105(2), 123, 130(2), 132, 134, 140, 141; Nos 32–38 124, *125*, *126*
Cripps, Wilfred and Helena 20–1, 22, 25, 34, 38, 61, 66, 72
crosses, standing 99, *100*, 103, 106, 114, 140
Crowthorne, hundred of 115
Crundel, *Crundles* 84, 118

Daglingworth Brook 135
deer park *116*, 117, 118, 167
defences: Roman *see under* Roman period; med period 98, 107
de Pirie(s) town house *100*, 105, 118
Dobunni 49, 55, 57, 77
documentary sources 36, 37, 39, 40, 77, 94, 113-14, 130, 140, 159
Dollar Street *58*, 98, 99, *100*, 105(2), 108, 119, 123; bridge 99(2), *120*; Hodden House 123, 128; Nos 6 & 8 119
Domesday Book 88, 91, 93, 94, 95, 97, 105, 113, 115, 118, 140
ducking stool 101, 103
Dyer Court 22, 87
Dyer Court House 59, 63, 76
Dyer Street 141; Roman period *58*, 167, mosaics 18, *19*, 20, 63, 78, 129, street metalling 59; early med 91; med 99, *100*, 101, 103, 105, street name 99, 103–4; post-med 119, 123, 127, 129, *133*

early medieval period 44, *46*, 87–97, 139, 169, 188; buildings 91–2, 93
English Heritage 4, 24, 147, 149, 152, 153, 155, 158, 165, 166, 170, 172, 173; Monuments Protection Programme (MPP) 3, 8, 9, 11–12, 149
Environmental Assessment 154–5
Ermin Street 51, 52, *54*, 60, 62, 63, 72, *80*, 83, 114

Field Evaluation 156, 157, 158, 161
Firs, The *see* Victoria Road
flints and flintworking, prehistoric 47, 48, *50*
footwear manufacture, Roman 84, 85
ford (Walfrid Marescal's) 99, *100*, 103
fort (Roman), Leaholme 22, 49, 52, 53, *54*, 55, *55*, 56, 57, 67, 140, 169
Forum car-park 45, 77, 138, 139, 141, 161, *168*, 169
forum (Chester Lodge) 56, 57, *58*, 61, 62, 74, 77, 86, 87, 93, 140, 167
Fosse, use of name (*Le Fosse*) 99
Fosse Way 52–3, 54, 68, *80*, 81, 83, 84, 95, 114
fulling mills 18, 104
Furzen Leaze Farm, Siddington 118, *133*

gallows 48, 103, 115
Gaol, med *100*, 103
Gas Works *120*, 129
gates and gateways 45, 98; *see* Bath Gate; Gloucester gate; Roman period; Silchester gate; *Verulamium* gate
Gaumont Cinema *58*, 60, 61, 78, 141, *168*, 169
geology 26, *28*, 29
Gildenbridge, watermill 97, *100*
Gloucester 57, 65, 74, 92, 93, 94, 106; Kingsholm 53, 55
Gloucester gate *58*, 67–8, 81, 83, 167
Gloucester Road 134, 139
Gloucestershire County Council 170, 172
Gloucester Street 34, 81, 91, 94, 98, 99, 101, 104, 105, 122, 123, 127, 129(3), 130(2), 132, 139
Gosditch Street 59, 98, 99, *100*, 103, 104, 119, 127, 131
Grammar School (Field) 22, 59, 63, 73
granges *100*, 107–8
Gregory's Nursery 18, 73
Grismond's Tower (barrow) 17, 43, *80*, 83, 86, 167; as Grismund's (Grismond's) Mount 17, 48, 94, 95; Gurmond's Mount 18; post-med icehouse *120*
Grove Lane *133*
Guardianship monument 24, 33, 152
Gunstool(e) (Daglingworth) Brook 98, 101, 103, 104, 113
Gurmund, and the legend of the sparrows 94

Hare Bushes 30, 48, 52, 126, *133*, 137
High Cross 99, *100*, *102*, 103, 140
horn trade 130
Hospital Gate *see* Spitalgate

hospitals 45, 113, 129, 134, *and see* St John's Hospital; St Lawrence's Hospital
hydrology 30

icehouses *120*, 137
Inchthorpe 91, 99
inns and taverns (public houses) 18; Bell Ale House 18; Church Tavern *100*, 103; Dakker Gate Inn *100*, 103; The Fleece 119, *120*, 130; Swan 103, *120*; med 103, 106; post-med *120*, 122, 129–30
Iron Age 33, 49, 51, 56, 86

Kemble 95, 135
Kenchester 57
Kingshill 49, 86(2), *133*, 137, 144
Kingshill Lane 52, 53, *80*
Kingsmead 83, 88
Kingsmeadow 52, 70, *80*, 83, 167
King Street, Roman walling 72

Langley Mill *100*, 104, 118, 167, 169
Latton 33
Leaholme 22, 87, *and see* fort
Leaholme Court 139, 141
Leaholme Gardens 59, *and see macellum*
leather trade 104, 130
Leauses 73, 105–6
Leauses Grounds, Roman temple 25
Le Beche(s) (The Beeches) *100*, 105, 106, 118
Le Fosse (later Lewis Lane) 99
Le Lewes (the Leauses) 105–6
Letherwell (spring) 103
Lewis Ground 18
Lewis Lane 18, 29, 30, 71, 76, 77, 91, 92, 98, *100*, 119, 123, 128, 129, 130, 140; street name 99
limekilns 132, 137
Lock's Timber Yard, mosaic 22, *58*
lock-up *100*, *120*, 129, 161
London Road 76, 77, 123, 128, 134; Orchard House 59, 105
London Road Cross 99, *100*
Lynches, The, trackway 114

macellum 58, 60, 62, 71, 75, 78, 86
maltings 132, 137
Market House 130
market place 62, 77, 91, 94, 98, *100*, 103(2), 105, 106, 119, 129, 130, 131, 134, 137, 141, 161, 167
Master family 124, 126
medieval period 40, 43, 44, 45, *46*, 86, 98–118, 139, 140, 144, 167, 169, 188–90; artefacts 104; buildings 102–3, 105–6
Mesolithic 47
mills *100*, 118, 130, *133*, 137; *see* Abbey Mill; Barton Mill; Braine's Mill; fulling mills; Langley Mill; New Mill; St Mary's Mill; watermills; windmills
Minety 115
moated sites 115
Monmouth House *100*, *102*, 105, 118
moot site 115, 118
More's Place *100*, 106, 118
mosaics *21*, 63, 64, 72, 77, 78, 85, 140; Four Seasons (Dyer St) 20, 63, 129; Hunting Dogs (Dyer St) *19*, 20, 63, 129; Lock's Timber Yard 22, *58*; 'Marine scene' (60 Dyer St) 18, 20, 63; Orpheus pavement (The Barton) 18, 20, 63, 85
museums 24, 129; Bathurst Museum (Tetbury Road) 20, *21*, 24, 63, *120*, 129; Chesterton House *120*, 129; Cripps' Museum 20, 24, 120; *see also* Corinium Museum
Mycalex factory site *see* Ashcroft Road

National Planning Legislation 153–4
Nelthorpe family 25
Neolithic period 47–8, 118
New Cross 103
New Farm 100, 106, 118
New Mill *100*, 104, 169
New Mills 130
New Road 124, 129
Norcote Farm, Preston: chapelry *116*, 117; med settlement 115, *116*, 135, 144; post-med *132*
Norman Arch *see* Spitalgate

Oakley Cottage 22, 81
Oakley House 124
Oakley Villas 30
Oakley Wood 26, 99, 135
Orchard House, London Road 59, 105

palaeoenvironment 33
Palaeolithic sites 47
parish boundaries 95
parishes 4, *5*, 10, 25, 36, 43–4, *and see* Baunton; Preston; Siddington; Stratton
Park Lane 99, *100*, 103, 129, 131, 141; as Lawditch Lane 107
Parks and Gardens 33, *150*, *151*, 153
Park Street 91, 107, 111, 122, 123, 127, 130; No.10 107; *see also* castle
Parsonage Field 22, 59, 63, 76
Partridge Way 104
Paternoster School 138, 141, *168*, 169
Perry Moor 115
Phoenix Way, RB road 81
Pig Cross 99, *100*, 103, 140
pillow mounds 118
place-names 36, 37, 95
Planning Policy Guidance (PPG16) 149, 153, 154, 156, 158, 159, 160, 170, 172
Police Station 22, *120*, 129, 140; Roman period 59, 63, 76, 77(2), 78
pollen 97
post-medieval period *29*, 30, 40, 44, 105(2), 113, 119–37, 138, 139, 140, 141, 169, 190–4
prehistoric period 44, 47–51, *50*, 56, 144, 185–6
preservation 161
Preston 4, *5*, 26, 36, 44, 144, 152; All Saints church 95, *96*, 115, 117; designation 33; land classification and use *31*, *32*; place-name 95; mesolithic site 47; Neolithic 48; BA complex 48, *50*; RB settlement 81; med 115; post-med *133*, 134, 136, 137; *see also* Norcote Farm
Price's Row, Watermoor 53, *58*, 59
public health *see* sanitation 20
public houses *see* inns and taverns
Purley Avenue 59, 61
Purley Road 59, 72, 107

quarries and quarrying *29*, 30, 40, 57, 60, *80*, 81, 84, *84*, 85, *133*, 137, 144
Queen Street, Redlands 59
Querns Hill 59, 123
Querns Hospital Kitchen Garden 81, 84, *84*
Querns Lane 76, 77, 98, *100*, 119, 123, 130, 138, 139, 141, *168*, 169; Roman, building 76, 169; street names 99
Querns Lane House 59
Querns Road 60, 65, 70, 76
Querns, The *82*; Neolithic and BA barrows, long 47, 48, *50*, round 48; RB cemetery 18(2), 25, 79, *80*, 81, 84, 167, stone quarries 30, 57, *80*, 84; med 118; post-med *120*, urban villa *120*, 124; *see also* amphitheatre

rabbit warren 118
railways 20, 45, 119, *120*, 132, *133*, 134, 135, 137
Regal Cinema 59
Regenbald, clerk 93
religious buildings: med 106, 107–11, 115, 117; post-med 126–9; *see also* Abbey of St Mary; churches and chapels
ridge and furrow 118
ring ditches 48–9, *50*
roads and trackways: prehistoric *50*; Roman/RB 17, 47, 51–3, 56, *58*, 81, 114, 139; med 114, 140; post-med 134– 5; trackways 56, 86; *see also* Akeman Street; Ermin Street; Fosse Way; Whiteway
Roman period (and Romano-British) 38, 43, 44, 45, *46*, 47, 51, 56, 57–86, 91–2, 105, 139, 140, 149, 186–8; architectural fragments 72–4, *73*; bath-house 72; cemeteries and burials 18, 22, 25, 47, *58*, 79, *80*, 81–4, 86, 144, 149, 167; cemetery churches 84, 93; defences 17, 18, 45, *58*,

65–71, 76, 77, 78, 85–6, 98, 107, 140, 152, 161, 165, 167, 169; domestic housing *58*, 63–5, 76, 77, 78, 85, 86, 87, 139, 167, 169; gates and gateways 45, 67–8, 70, 98; industry 84–5; *insula* 63, 71, 75, 78; public baths 71; public buildings 57, 60, 61–2, 72–3, 75, 76, 78, 84; quarries *84*; settlements 33, 49, *80*, 81, 85–6; shops *58*, 62–3, 78; streets 60–1, 94; temple 25, 71, 72, 75; tessellated pavements 20, *58*, 63, 71, 72, 77, 78; theatre *58*, 62; vicus 56, 57, 140; *and see* amphitheatre; *basilica*; fort; *forum*; *macellum*; mosaics; tombstones
Royal Agricultural College 20, 30, *80*, 81, *133*, 134, 137
rural areas 141, *143*, 144, *151*; Roman 78–86; early med 95, 97; med 43–4, 98, 114–15, *116*, 117–18; post-med 134–7

St Augustine's Farm 144
St John's Hospital, Spitalgate *100*, 111, 113, 118, 128, 140, 149, 152, 167
St John's Meade 106
St John's Meadow 137
St Lawrence's Hospital (med) 17, 91, *100*, 111, 113, 167; chapel *89*, 93; used as Almshouses *100*, 113, *120*, 128, 167
St Mary's (or New) Mill *100*, 104
St Michael's Field 59, 138, 139, 140, 141, *168*, 169
St Michael's Park 60
St Peter's Road 59, 60, 128, 138, 139, 141
St Thomas's Hospital (Weavers' Hall), Thomas Street *100*, 105, 111, *112*, 113, 114, 118, 128, 141, 167
sanitation and public health 20, 103, 124
Scheduled Monument Consent 35, 149, 159, 160
Scheduled Monuments 9, 24, 33, 48, 149, *150*, *151*, 153, 158, 159, 167, 170, 172
School Lane 77
schools *100*, 103, 106, *120*, 129, *133*, 134
settlements: Neolithic and Early BA 48, *50*; IA 33, 49; Roman/RB 33, 49, *80*, 81, 85–6, 144; early med 88, *89*, *96*; med 115, 144
Seven Hundreds 95
Shambles, The 99, 103, 131
Sheep Dip *80*
Sheep Street 59, 67, 70, 99, *100*, 127; No.33 60, 61, 65
Shepherds Piece 137
Shoe Lane 99, *100*, 103
Shorncote quarry 49
Siddington 4, *5*, 25, 26, 36, 44, 144; boundary 95; churches 25; designation 33; Frazier's Folly 115; land classification and use *31*, *32*; place-name 95; Tithe Barn 115, 117, *117*, 118, 137, 149, 152, 167; BA ring ditches 48–9, *50*; IA 49; RB settlement 144; med 44, 115; post-med 44, 132, *133*, 134, 135, 136, 137; *see also* Furzen Leaze Farm
Siddington House 115, 144
Siddington Langley manor 115
Siddington, Lower, pre-Conquest churches 95, *96*
Siddington St Mary 134; church 115, *116*, 134; manor 115; mills 97; *Wondenewell* 115
Siddington St Peter 134; church 115, *116*; coal 30; mills 97; moated mansion house site 115; *Sherston Brugge* 115
Siddington, Upper 95, *96*, 115, *116*
Silchester gate 52, *58*, 67
Silver Street 99, 101, 107
Sites and Monuments Record (SMR) 3, 7, 24, 25, 34, 153, 158, 172, 173
Somerford Keynes, Spratsgate Lane, IA site 49, 51
Somerford Road, Chesterton 85
Spitalgate 99, *100*, 108, 109, *110*, 132; as Hospital Gate 18; as Norman Arch 25, 108; *see also* St John's Hospital
springs 30, 72, 103
Spyringate Grange 107
Stepstairs (Steep Stairs), tombstones 18, 83
Stepstairs Lane 124, 141
stocks 129
Stratton 4, 26, 115, 134, 135, 136, 137; boundary 95; brickworks 30, *133*; land classification an use *31*, *32*; mills 97; pre-Conquest church 95, *96*; quarry *29*, 30; St Peter's Church 115; topography *27*; watermill 118
Stratton Field, BA 48, *50*
Stratton Heights, windmill 137
Stratton Mill *133*; Roman burial 84
street systems: Roman/RB 60–1, 77, 78, 94; early med (AS) 91, 98; med 98– 9, *100*, 102, 106, 114
Stukeley, William, *frontispiece* 17, 18, 25, 71, 79, *110*
suburbs: med period 45; post-med 45, 124
sunken featured building, AS 88

tanning trade 104, 130
Tar Barrow(s) 17, 48, 53, *80*, 82–3, 86, 115, 126, 144, 149, 167
Telephone Exchange 59
Tetbury 106
Tetbury Road 79, 130, *see also* museums
theatres: Roman *58*, 62; post-med *120*, 129
Thomas Street 99, *100*, 105, *120*, 123, 127–8, 141; *see also* St Thomas's Hospital
tollhouses *133*, 135, *136*
tombstones 18, 22, 25, 79, 83, *83*, 84, 111; of Julia Casta 18, 79
Torre Castle *see* Tar Barrow(s)
Tower Street 59, 77, 111, 124, 139, 140, 141, 165, 167, *168*, 169
town hall *120*, 129
town wall *see* Roman period, defences
Trewsbury, IA occupation 56
Trinity Church Gates 59
Trinity Mill 97, 136
Trinity Road *133*; see also Union Workhouse

Union Workhouse 20, 22, 66, *66*, 111, *120*, 129; Workhouse Garden 66

Verulamium Gate 22, 52, 53, *58*, 60, 66, 67, *68*, *69*, 70, 71, 81, 82; bridge 78; cemetery outside 82
Victoria Road 22, 124, 141; Roman 59, 63(2); The Firs 39, *58*; 72, 73; *see also* Lock's Timber Yard
vicus see Roman period
Vikings 90, 92
villas, Roman *80*, 85, 86

waterlogged deposits 77, 94, 139, 169
Waterloo car-park 65, 77, 138
water-meadows *133*, 136, 137
watermills *96*, 97, *100*, 104, 118, *133*, 137
Watermoor 25, 52, 76, 105, 113, 124, 129, 135, 138, 139, 140, *168*, 169; Roman period 18, 59, 65, 66, 67, 84, 167; *see also* City Bank
Watermoor Common 124
Watermoor Hospital Garden 67, 70–1
Watermoor House *120*, 124, 167, 169
Watermoor Road 59, 124, 128, 139; Church of the Holy Trinity *120*, 126–7, 141; Health Centre site 56; Nos 60–62 60; The Sands 67, 69, 70; *see also* Price's Row
Watermoor School 59
water supply 30; Roman 72; med 103; post–med 129
Weaver's Hall *see* St Thomas's Hospital
Wellhill Plantation, barrow 48, *50*, 144, 149, 167
wells 30, 62, 129
Welsh Way 114
West Market Place 59, 99, *100*, 103, 137, 167
West Way 104
Whiteway 49, 52, *54*, 55, 81, 86, 108, *133*, 135; or Wiggoldway 114
Wiggold, chapelry 117
William of Worcester 17, 43, 107, 109
windmill *133*, 137
Witpit Copse: Roman finds 86; med (?)farmstead site 115
Woodhouse, The (Alfred's Hall) 124, *128*
woodland *31*, *32*, 33, 118, 126
woollen industry 33, 98, 99 130
Workhouse *see* Union Workhouse
Workhouse Lane 66
Worm's Farm *80*, *133*